SPANISH-AMERICAN LITERATURE

SPANISH-AMERICAN LITERATURE

A History

VOLUME ONE

by Enrique Anderson-Imbert
HARVARD UNIVERSITY

second edition (1969)
revised and updated
by Elaine Malley

first edition (1963)
translated from the Spanish
by John V. Falconieri

Wayne State University Press
Detroit / Michigan 1969

CONTENTS

VOLUME ONE

VOLUME TWO

Prolog / *p. 441*

Translator's Foreword / *p. 448*

PART THREE: CONTEMPORARY PERIOD

XII. 1910-1925

Authors born between 1885 and 1900 / *p. 453*

Historical framework: Social Revolution in Mexico and the effects of World War I.
Cultural tendencies: Modernist artifice set aside in favor of a simpler expression of American reality. Experimentation in new "isms."

guay: Ballesteros / (xii) Argentina: Ricardo Güiraldes /
2. Essay / Alfonso Reyes / Pedro Henríquez Ureña / Martínez Estrada / C. THEATER / From Mexico to Argentina
/ Ramos, Herrera, Eichelbaum

XIII. 1925-1940

Authors born between 1900 and 1915 / p. 565

*Historical framework: The outbreak of World War II. The
Depression. Greater participation by the masses in government leadership.*
*Cultural tendencies: Vanguardist literature. Pure poetry and
surrealism.*

Introduction / A. MAINLY POETRY / Pure Poetry
and Surrealism / (i) Mexico: Pellicer, Villaurrutia, Go-
rostiza / (ii) Central America: Cardoza y Aragón, Coronel
Urtecho / (iii) Antilles: Florit, Guillén, Ballagas, Cabral,
Palés Matos / (iv) Venezuela: Queremel, Gerbasi / (v)
Colombia: Pardo García, Maya, Carranza, Rojas, Aurelio
Arturo / (vi) Ecuador: Carrera Andrade, Gonzalo Escu-
dero / (vii) Peru: Adán, Westphalen / (viii) Bolivia / (ix)
Chile: Pablo Neruda / (x) Paraguay / (xi) Uruguay: Sara
de Ibáñez / (xii) Argentina: Molinari, González Lanuza,
Bernárdez / B. MAINLY PROSE / 1. Novel and Short
Story / (a) Narrators More Subjective than Objective /
(b) Narrators More Objective than Subjective / (i) Mexico:
Agustín Yáñez / (ii) Central America: Miguel Ángel
Asturias, Salarrué, Carlos Luis Fallas / (iii) Antilles: Alejo
Carpentier, Novás Calvo, Dulce María Loynaz, Laguerre,
Bosch / (iv) Venezuela: Uslar Pietri, Díaz Sánchez / (v)
Colombia: Osorio Lizarazo / Caballero Calderón / (vi)
Ecuador: José de la Cuadra / (vii) Peru: Ciro Alegría, José
María Arguedas / (viii) Bolivia / (ix) Chile: Bombal,
Brunet / (x) Paraguay: Casaccia / (xi) Uruguay: Onetti,
Amorim / (xii) Argentina: Jorge Luis Borges, Eduardo
Mallea, Roberto Arlt / 2. Essay: Picón-Salas, Germán Ar-
ciniegas / C. THEATER / (i) Mexico: Usigli / (ii) Cen-
tral America / (iii) Antilles / (iv) Venezuela / (v) Colom-
bia / (vi) Peru / (vii) Bolivia / (viii) Chile / (ix)
Uruguay / (x) Argentina: Nalé Roxlo

XIV. 1940-1955

Authors born between 1915 and 1930 / p. 688

*Historical framework: World War II ends. The "cold war."
Evolution toward planned economies.*

Cultural tendencies: Surrealism. Existentialism. Neo-naturalism.

GENERAL CHARACTERIZATION / A. MAINLY POETRY / INTRODUCTION / (i) Mexico: Octavio Paz, Alí Chumacero / (ii) Central America: Cardona Peña / (iii) Antilles: Cintio Vitier / (iv) Venezuela: Ida Gramcko / (v) Colombia: Cote Lamus / (vi) Ecuador: Alejandro Carrión / (vii) Peru / (viii) Bolivia / (ix) Chile: Arenas, Parra, Arteche / (x) Paraguay: Elvio Romero / (xi) Uruguay: Idea Vilariño, Sarandy Cabrera / (xii) Argentina: Etchebarne, Devoto, Wilcock, Girri / B. MAINLY PROSE / 1. NOVEL AND SHORT STORY / (i) Mexico: Arreola, Rulfo, Fuentes / (ii) Central America: Monterroso, Joaquín Beleño, Ramón H. Jurado / (iii) Antilles: Virgilio Piñera, René Marqués / (iv) Venezuela / (v) Colombia: García Márquez / (vi) Ecuador: Adalberto Ortiz / (vii) Peru: Zavaleta, Ribeyro / (viii) Bolivia: Botelho Gosálvez / (ix) Chile: Fernando Alegría, José Donoso / (x) Paraguay: Roa Bastos / (xi) Uruguay: Martínez Moreno, Benedetti / (xii) Argentina: Murena, Cortázar, Denevi / 2. ESSAY / From Mexico to Argentina / C. THEATER / (i) Mexico: Magaña, Garro / (ii) Central America / (iii) Antilles / (iv) Venezuela / (v) Colombia / (vi) Peru: Salazar Bondy / (vii) Chile: Heiremans / (viii) Paraguay / (ix) Uruguay: Antonio Larreta / (x) Argentina: Del Carlo, Dragún

XV. 1955-1966

Authors born since 1930 / p. 746

Historical framework: The First Communist Regime in Hispanic America.
Cultural tendencies: Awareness of the literary profession. Change in values.

GENERAL CHARACTERIZATION / A. MAINLY POETRY (i) Mexico: Montes de Oca / (ii) Central America: Chávez Velasco / (iii) Antilles: Fernández Retamar / (iv) Venezuela: Calzadilla / (v) Colombia: Arango / (vi) Ecuador / (vii) Peru / (viii) Bolivia / (ix) Chile: Efraín Barquero, Jorge Teillier / (x) Paraguay / (xi) Uruguay: Ibargoyen Islas, Washington Benavides / (xii) Argentina: María Elena Walsh / B. MAINLY PROSE / 1. NOVEL AND SHORT STORY / (i) Mexico: Mojarro / (ii) Central America / (iii) Antilles: Marcio Veloz Maggiolo / (iv) Venezuela: Salvador Garmendia / (v) Colombia / (vi) Ecuador / (vii) Peru: Vargas Llosa, Congrains Martín, Castro Arenas, Oviedo / (viii) Chile / (ix)

PROLOG

Of the many dangers an historian of literature risks, two are quite serious: that of specializing in the study of isolated great books, and that of specializing in the study of the circumstances under which those books were written. If the historian elects the first, he produces a collection of unconnected critical essays, that is, a history of literature containing very little history. If he chooses the second, the result will be a series of external references to the process of civilization, that is, a history of literature containing very little literature. Is it possible to achieve a history of literature that fulfills both the true historical and the true literary function? At least, it is possible to attempt one. It would be a history that gave meaning to the expressive moments of certain men who, through the passing of the centuries, set themselves to write. Instead of isolating the literature produced, on one hand, and the circumstances under which it was produced, on the other, this history would integrate the two within the concrete existence of the writers. Each writer asserts those esthetic values that he has formed while contemplating the possibilities of his historical environment, and these are the values that should constitute the real subject matter of any history of literature.

This is all well and good, as theory. But if we were mindful only of esthetic expression, to what thin line would this history which we are about to offer reduce itself? The effective contributions of Spanish-American literature to international literature are minimal. Yet we Spanish-Americans have done a great deal if one were to consider the many obstacles with which our literary creation has had to contend and is still contending. The Inca Garcilaso, Sor Juana Inés de la Cruz, Andrés Bello, Domingo Sarmiento, Juan Montalvo, Ricardo Palma, José Martí, Rubén Darío, José Enrique Rodó, Alfonso Reyes, Jorge Luis Borges, Pablo Neruda, and a dozen more, are figures who would do honor to any literature. But, in general, we are afflicted by improvisation, disorder, fragmentation, and impurity. Necessarily, many unaccomplished writers will have to be included here.

We cannot prevent a certain amount of farrago from slipping into this history. But to be sure, what does interest us here is the reality which has been transmuted into literature. Although we witness, respectfully and patiently, a long procession of writers and try to understand their contribution, the fact is that we anxiously look for the few who have expressed esthetic values. Our subject is Literature, that is to say, those writings that can be assigned to the category of beauty.

Of course, in the first chapters we had to admit many men of action or thought who wrote chronicles and treatises without any artistic intentions; yet, even in these cases, it was the literary portion of their writings that we valued. But as we approach our own times we must be more demanding in discriminating between what is and what is not literature. Once we reach our own age, we are only interested in those writers who cultivate poetry, prose poems, the short story, the novel, and the theater. We only consider essayists insofar as they are men of letters. Had this been an extended history of culture instead of a compressed history of literature, we would also have included critics, philosophers, historians and patrons of art; or even had sociology been our aim, we would have included information about journals, literary gatherings, prizes, and the like. But this book does not aspire to include all. We are fully aware that in Spanish America there are often extraordinary personalities in literary life who study and promote literature, but who do not produce it. Furthermore, at times the men who most influence literary groups are precisely the ones who write neither poetry, nor novels, nor dramas. It may be lamentable, but it is obvious that they do not belong to a history of poetry, novels, and dramas.

The literature of the Americas we are going to study is the one which was written in Spanish. We do not ignore the importance of the masses of Indians; however, in a history of the expressive uses of the Spanish language in America, it behooves us to listen only to those who expressed themselves in Spanish. For this same reason we will not refer to the writers who were born in Spanish-America, but who wrote in Latin (like Rafael Landívar), in French (like Jules Supervielle), or in English (like W. H. Hudson). Nor will we consider those authors who, although they wrote in Spanish, did not write of American experiences (like Ventura de la Vega.) On the other hand, we will include in our history those foreigners who lived among us and used our language (like Paul Groussac).

It is well known that history is a continuous process. We will, therefore, introduce writers in the order in which they came into the world and entered into literary life. But, although history is an indivisible succession of events, we could not represent it without certain conventions which we call periods. In order to be useful, this breaking up of history into periods should adjust itself to historical facts and respect the complexity of each epoch. Thus, a system of periods must be consistent with the principle which it adopts, but it does not need to be regular. On the contrary, excessive regularity would indicate that the historian, through his great desire to embellish his vision, is allowing himself to be carried along by symmetries and metaphors. There are periods of long stability. There are short, rapid periods. In the fear of falsifying literary development through the use of subjective figures, we have chosen an inoffensive criterion: an historical-political classification in three parts, "The Colony," "One Hundred Years of the Republic," and the "Contemporary Period." But within these broad divisions we have shaded in certain generations, attempting to make the external framework of political coincide with esthetic tendencies. The dates heading each chapter indicate the years during which these generations came into being and produced: *"Gestación"* and *"Gestión,"* as Ortega y Gasset put it. In order that the outline might be more useful, we have also indicated the approximate birthdates of the authors. But, when historical sense demands, we shall alter the outline and situate a borderline author on whatever side best suits our purposes.

That we should be arranging the materials of this history into periods does not mean that we are neglecting other regulative criteria: those of nationality, genre, schools, and themes. What we have done is to subordinate these criteria to chronology. In other words, our method is systematic when it groups fundamental literary phenomena chronologically, and asystematic with regard to everything else. It is more difficult this way, but there is less falsification of history.

To have grouped the authors by country would have been to break the cultural unity of Spanish America into nineteen illusory national literatures. To have had recourse to the rhetorical categories of genres would have obliged us to have dismantled the work of any writer who cultivated various types of literature and to have distributed the pieces throughout several chapters under the headings of "poetry," "narrative," "essay," and "theater," not to mention the difficulty involved in classifying the subgenres. To have insisted on schools and "isms" would have caused us to fall into the vice of giving substance to mere ideal concepts, thus, giving more attention to collective styles than to individual ones. To have made our history revolve around certain themes would have been superficial: what counts, after all, is the treatment of the theme, not the theme itself. In spite of what has been said, the reader will find, especially in the last chapters, an arrangement according to nationality (from north to south), in genres (from verse to prose and, within prose, fiction, essay, and theater) and in schools (from the more imaginative to the more realist).

We must remind the reader who opens the book here and there, with the intention not of reading it, but of consulting it, that what he has before him is a history and not an inventory of names. In other words, its value lies in the total interpretation of a continuous process; a series of names, even a series of sentences, only makes sense if it is reached after first reading many pages back. Trusting in the fluidity with which the themes are formed and developed we have boldly incorporated into the text those lists that other historians prudently hide in separate notes. To read just the lists would be tantamount to ignoring the esthetic category to which the names belong. One might ask, why not delete those ugly pieces of census? But they are not pieces of census, they are clouds, constellations, woods, highlands, and dales in an historical landscape. The great quantity of names brings

out the fact that, because there is so little communication among
the Spanish-American countries, literary values are fixed in local
markets: to omit these names would hurt national pride. Now
that we have touched on the matter of national honor, the reader
must remember that in a history, constructed in one unit as this
one is, the number of pages devoted to any particular writer is no
measure of his importance. There are writers of really great
stature who can be dealt with in brief critiques. On the other hand,
other writers of less value require a more extensive treatment if
they illustrate a movement, a genre, a theme, or a cultural reality.
One final point: there are precocious writers and there are writers
who are tardy in maturing. In establishing their place within a
period, what we take into consideration is not the chronological
sequence of their books but the years that shaped the authors, the
historical climate they breathed during their formative period.

An historian of literature cannot read every book (an entire
life would not be enough) but neither can he limit himself to
commenting only on those books that he has read (if he did this,
he would not set down an objective historical process but his
autobiography as a reader). In order to offer a complete panorama of what has been written during the past four hundred
years in a continent that is now divided into nineteen republics, the
historian is obliged to utilize the data and judgments of others.
There are several ways of conducting this huge informative enterprise. One way, the most serious from a scholarly point of view,
but the least practical from the point of view of a manual, is to
interrupt the exposition at every step with bibliographical references, footnotes, citations within the text, appendices, and careful
acknowledgement of the works of hundreds of colleagues which
are used and reworked. Another way, the one we have risked, is
to appoint oneself the Editing Secretary of an imaginary Stock
Company of Spanish-Americanists and to invert into a fluid
history all that is known among all of us. In this case the historian
constructs an optical apparatus, with lenses and mirrors, through
which he looks out on the range of letters; and he consolidates
his own observations and those of other observers in a book with
"form"—a form having unity, continuity, smoothness, and round-

ness. Composite art. In this way, pages based on a direct knowledge of texts are intermingled and occasionally integrated with
others that indirectly summarize scattered studies. The bibliography is only a guide for the reader; it is not a listing of the
sources that we have used. These sources are innumerable. We
read constantly, and every time we found something that was
compatible with the plan of the book, we unhesitatingly incorporated it. There was the searching through overall histories, partial
monographs, journal articles, and book reviews. We even went
further by writing to critics in different places and using their replies in the systematic construction of this vast synthesis. As
we traveled through the countries of Spanish America, we approached literary groups and, pen in hand, took notes which later
were utilized. Thus, in some cases, this *History* may be able to
give the first fruits of ongoing research that is still unpublished.
That is to say that we conceived this *History* as a living and vora-
cious body: the peril lies in our having created a Frankenstein!
Our desire has been to render a public service: to bring together
dispersed material, to classify the medley of data, to illuminate
with a single light the dark corners of a Spanish America in-
wardly shattered and badly misunderstood, and to present the
reader with a *Summa*. Although many have contributed to this
History, it advances in a single, uninterrupted line. It is a collective yet uniform work. In our desire for verbal economy we have
not had room even to cite the most authoritative specialists. We
hereby declare our debt to their investigations. We have worked,
therefore, in part as architect and in part as bricklayer. In the
entire *History* there is not a single citation, not even when the
criticism follows other historians closely. Nor do we cite our own
scholarly contributions published elsewhere. In those contributions we rigorously analyzed textual styles; but in this *History*
we occasionally recast what we have not before analyzed directly.
Yet, let us not exaggerate. This *History* is personal in conception,
in arrangement, and in a good deal of its commentary. As each
new edition appears, we make corrections in it. If we find that, out
of immediate urgency, we hastily mended a hole with a piece that
did not match, we replace it later upon more accurate, more lei-

surely and more solid examination. Our *History* is in a provisional stage; some day it will reach a definitive stage. The more its material enters directly into our possession, the more personal it becomes. As we write with an open horizon we see it grow with our growing knowledge.

E. A. I.

TRANSLATOR'S FOREWORD

This *History* is the most comprehensive compilation of studies of the literature of Hispanic America ever written. It is vast not only for the number of pages but also for the breadth of its topics, for the depth of its chronology, for the scope of its geography, and for the magnitude of its philosophic, historical, and cultural framework in which it is neatly ensconced; it is intense for the compactness of its organization and of its prose: all the chaff has been threshed out. The compact prose reflects perfectly the manner in which the author has compressed almost six centuries of literature into such few pages. What is more stunning is that withal it remains a history of *literature,* achieved without sacrificing non-literary data. The key to this accomplishment lies in the richness of the author's language as he dissects literary forms, literally; that is, with the very instruments of the creative artist. The *History* is replete with unexpected vocabulary, turns of syntax, plays on words and ideas, tropes, metaphors which, instead of obfuscating, illuminate the creative process of so many of the writers.

It has been our intention to mirror this prose style in every respect, but all translation-mirrors have their imperfections, and images sometimes yield untrue refractions. (May there not be any distortions!) We tried to trade expression for expression, figure of speech for figure of speech, and if the trading were not possible in one place, we tried to make up the deficiency elsewhere; yet, we may not have been able to liquidate all our indebtedness to the original. If the rhythm of the English prose is not the accustomed or traditional one it is because the original is likewise an unusual and non-traditional Spanish. We hope the readers will become attuned to the new beats.

This is the translation of the greatly augmented third edition of Professor Enrique Anderson Imbert's *Historia de la literatura hispanoamericana* published by the Fondo de Cultura Económica of Mexico City. Since this edition Professor Anderson has added some authors and data pertaining to them, as well as slight modifications of the text. In this respect, the translation has taken one step beyond the original.

Enrique Anderson Imbert, a native of Argentina, is the most outstanding authority in this field, and a teacher revered and admired by many students. Professor Anderson's literary tools, alluded to above, come to him naturally: he is a very respected author in Spanish-American letters, forming part of the very history he writes.

The introduction of this *History* to Anglo-America is propitious at this time because interest in Hispanic-American art and literature is increasing. With the passage of time the artistic and literary production of Hispanic America multiplies at an incredible rate. We need only cast a glance at the table of contents of this *History* to note that the first half encompasses the years 1492 to 1910, while the second half covers the last 50 years or so. The acceleration is patent; the character of the literature, from what once may have been imitative and lagging, now takes on greater variety, newness and autonomy.

As a great number of the works have not been put into English, it was deemed proper to include the original titles with the translated titles. If a title reoccurs after it has been translated, the English title is repeated and not the original. Only Hispanic-American titles are translated; others, including Spanish, are left in their original tongue. Titles of short stories or of poems are translated, but the original is omitted, especially when the full title of the collection is given. Orthodox American English spelling was used throughout the work. In those cases where "ink-saving" orthography appears (e.g. *prolog* rather than *prologue*) it is solely due to the dictates and policies of the Wayne State University Press.

I wish to record here my appreciation and indebtedness to Professor Claude C. Hulet, of the University of Southern California, for having read the greater portion of the translation and to Professor James R. Stamm, of Michigan State University, for having read sections of the work. Their observations, suggestions, and criticisms were well received and of great value. To Professor Harold Murphy of Marshall University go my thanks for his courteous and patient aid in reading the manuscript. Grateful acknowledgment is made to Mrs. Patricia Davis of the Wayne State University Press for her efforts in preparing the text and index for printing. To Professor Anderson Imbert I extend my eternal and humble gratitude for his faith in me, for his patience with me, and for the guiding hand which led me through so many reefs and pitfalls. And finally I wish to thank Mrs. Diana N. Falconieri for the material aid and spiritual comfort that can only be repaid in the heavens.

J. V. F.

PART ONE
The Colony

I. 1492-1556

Authors born between 1451 and 1530

Historical framework: Discovery, exploration, conquest, and colonization under the Catholic Monarchs and Charles V.

Cultural tendencies: First Renaissance. From the obsolescent genres of medieval aspect (chronicles, missionary theater) to the importation of ideas (Erasmianism) and forms (Italianate poetry).

Introduction

Spanish literature of this period is generally considered a first renaissance and is characterized by its importation of forms and ideas, especially from Italy. The conquistadors and the missionaries brought the literature of Spain to the New World. They brought it in their ships and in their heads. Even writers came. And as these Spaniards began to write in America, they naturally relied upon the literary trends dominant in Spain. Although there were a few isolated Erasmians, in general this early phase of the colonization reflects, at first glance, medieval features. This first glance is an optical illusion like that of the recession of the sun in Ecuador.

The books which were being circulated and printed were, in the main, ecclesiastical and didactic, to be sure. But, putting aside those written in Latin and in the indigenous tongues (only that literature produced in the Spanish language interests us here), there remain two genres, the chronicle and the theater, which, although medieval in appearance, acquire creative power upon contact with the new American reality.

27

The Chronicles

To reiterate, the men who came to the New World were driven by the spiritual force of the Renaissance, but they were still guided by a medieval vision. They came from Spain, where the Renaissance never gave up its medieval legacy; they came from the people, normally slow in accepting change; and even those who came from the educated classes were neither contemplative nor creators of beauty, but men of action. The last sight of their homeland must have been the Gothic cathedrals. In fact, on reading their chronicles, we seem to be reading contemporaries of the Gothic era rather than contemporaries of the Renaissance. Their chronicles penetrate reality without defining it, without enclosing it, in the same manner that Gothic churches pierce the sky with aery structures in which sculpture and stained glass triumph. Chronicles without architecture—fluid, complex, free, formless, like a conversation—wherein realistic anecdotes range on one side and Christian symbolism on the other. These chronicles lack the composition, the unity, the congruence, the artistic and intellectual loftiness of the Renaissance creations. In spite of their apparent medievalism, the chroniclers gave to their pages a new kind of vitality and unconventional emotion, perhaps because they wrote spontaneously and almost without training about actual experience, or because, no matter how sophisticated they were, they allowed the marvels of the New World to penetrate and exalt them.

The first chronicler was, naturally, CHRISTOPHER COLUMBUS (1451–1506). The letter which tells of his first voyage was printed in 1493. In a Spanish prose learned in Portugal, the Genovese Columbus set about to describe clumsily what he had seen. But he barely saw America—he believed himself to be sailing toward Asia; moreover, he was blinded by greed for gold. He must have been disappointed with his own discovery— wretched islands inhabited by naked beings. And although he made an effort to appear enthusiastic—thus complying with his own need for publicity—he was unable to appreciate either the American landscape or the American himself. Upon reading

Columbus' narrative, the Europeans confirmed old utopian dreams and were able to give substance to two of the great themes of the Renaissance: natural man, happy and virtuous; and nature, luxuriant and paradisiacal. Basically, the most vivid passages in Columbus' chronicle gave no direct insight into America, but rather a reflection, like clouds on a quiet lake, of traditional literary figures. Columbus moved with Renaissance man's desire for discovery, but his mind was still tempered in the medieval forge. Although he was not a man of letters, he had read enough of real and imaginary voyages, of myths, ballads and folk tales so that they had slipped into his spirit, coloring and transfiguring the reality of the New World: vegetation became a garden landscape; the birds of the Antilles, Provençal nightingales; even the natives were poetized into noble figures or into prodigious monsters. The promise of earthly paradise or of the land of the Amazons forever trembled on the horizon. The constant comparisons with Europe also clouded his perception of the singular aspects of the New World; his words began to classify the new objects into European categories. He did not describe for the sheer love of describing as some conquistadors did later. He was taking inventory—an inventory of riches (future rather than present). But Columbus observed details, for example, one about the dog "that does not bark." And even today, on reading his words, we feel every now and then the esthetic pleasure that a witness of faraway and awesome places always communicates to us. Because we respond imaginatively to Columbus, his unadorned remarks on the naked beauty of the Indian, the gentleness of his laughter and gestures, the soft warm air of the green isles, the minuscule life of the cricket and the grass, appear to take on literary style.

His observations on the appearance and customs of the natives are more numerous, meticulous, and discerning than those on the natural setting of the islands. This interest in the human element rather than in the panoramic was typical of an entire tradition of travel chronicles, ranging from the real adventures of Marco Polo to the fantastic ones of Amadis de Gaula. Columbus, feeling himself more an adventurer than a man of science—after all, it had been the men of science who rejected his computations—wrote to satisfy his European readers' curiosity about adventures among unknown peoples, not to supply information for cosmographers, mathematicians, navigators, and naturalists. Only on his third voyage did he note down the position of the stars, but even in this instance his inspiration was more poetic than scientific: "I was filled with great admiration" for the North Star, he says. He adds that the differences in measurements in the newly discovered sky convinced him that the earth was not spherical as he had believed, but possessed the form of a woman's breast, with the nipple high up near the sky, and for this reason "ships could rise on a gentle incline, there to enjoy a more gentle climate." On this lovely nipple of land with the curves of a woman, Columbus situated Paradise, a fountain of "precious things" crowned with an even greater "diversity of stars."

Columbus' Men / Those who accompanied Columbus also left accounts. The Sevillian physician, DIEGO ÁLVAREZ CHANCA, was the first to describe the flora of the New World, although, like others, he preferred to speak of human marvels rather than the marvels of nature. FRIAR RAIMUNDO PANE was the first European, so far as is known, to speak an American tongue; he was the first teacher of Indians. He initiated American ethnography. His notes on the religious and artistic culture of the Indians on the island of Hispaniola are first-hand accounts. He heard the songs through which the Indians transmitted their cosmogony and their history ("by which they were ruled as the Moors are by their writings")—songs which were accompanied by musical instruments which Pane also described. HERNANDO COLÓN (1488–1539), who accompanied his father on his fourth voyage, was one of those bookish Renaissance men attached to everything European. Incited by the need to defend his family's prerogatives, he wrote *The Life of Admiral Christopher Columbus* (*Vida del Almirante Don Cristóbal Colón*), of which there is a Spanish version.

As can be seen, the most notable feature in the writings of this entire first group of travelers is the attention given to the inhabitants rather than to the land itself. (An exception is the *Compendium of Geography* [*Suma de geografía*, 1519] written by the explorer Martín Fernández de Enciso, which was one of the first scientific systematizations that embraced the New World.) The same can be said of the letters of Amerigo Vespucci which are not included in this history, for they were not written in Spanish. However, it was because of them that some mapmakers from Lorraine baptized the New World as the world of Amerigo: America.

Controversy over the Indians / As we have already said, it was by virtue of the first reports on the discovery of America that the Utopian dreams of a paradisiacal landscape and of a noble savage were reaffirmed. But also at an early date there were a few chroniclers who on occasion denigrated the American landscape and who declared its inhabitants to be inferior men without souls, basing their claims on Aristotelian notions of the natural inequality that exists among men. In the eighteenth century de Pauw will use such testimonials upon which to base his theories of a degenerate America.

The Indian, then, had his detractors and panegyrists. The controversy went from words to deeds. If, as Columbus himself says, the Indians believed that the white men had come down from heaven, they were soon to be disenchanted. The Spaniards charged with such violence and candor that the conquest quickly took on a human, all-too-human, quality. The transplanting of European culture, the servitude of the Indian, intermarriage, and the shaping of an original society had begun. The conquest was a military undertaking and at the same time an effort to make Christian precepts prevail. Since the Church had given the Spanish Crown the power to direct ecclesiastical affairs as well as affairs of state in the New World, political thinking was inspired by theological thinking; and, as a consequence, abstract ideas affected the behavior of the most remote lives. Theologians and jurists had counseled the Catholic monarchs to proclaim the freedom of the natives; but they had also advised the assignment of Indians to different *repartimientos*, where they would be forced to work. (Under the system of *repartimientos* a group of Indians was assigned to a Spanish employer or landowner.)

The Dominican fathers, who had arrived on the island of Hispaniola (today the Dominican Republic and Haiti) in 1510, protested against the *repartimientos*. Thus a few short years after the founding of the first colony in America, there originated one of the most profound moral lessons in history: men of a conquering nation bringing under discussion the righteousness of conquest itself. If it was not literature that changed the outlook of the Spaniard toward the life of the Indian, it was the artistic use of language in the sacred oratories of Friar Antonio Montesinos and others. The Dominicans denied absolution to any Spaniard who reaped benefits from the *repartimientos*. Complaints and threats finally resulted in King Fernando's convening a body of learned and conscientious men in 1512. As a result, the *repartimientos* were not abolished, but they were regulated in such a way as to allow free labor in theory and forced labor in practice to coexist.

These theological and juridical opinions were based on the medieval philosophy concerning the nature of monarchical power, the delimitations between spiritual and temporal matters, and the relation between Christianity and the infidels. This philosophy, insofar as it applied to America, meant the following: the Indians are free and rational individuals. When they defend themselves unaware of the evangelizing intentions of the Spaniards, they are within their rights and cannot be deprived of their property nor enslaved; but, of course, they are not in any way entitled to political power. If, after the Indians have been taught the truths of the Church-State of Spain (that the power of the world resides in the Pope and that he gave the Indian lands to the Spanish king), they insist on resisting the preachings of the Catholic faith, then the wars are just and the Indians may be invaded, despoiled, and subjugated. They were free so long as they conformed to the Church. If they did not, the Spaniards would change from "peace-makers" to "conquerors."

This Christian imperialism had its repercussions in certain practices during the occupation of the New World. One was the custom, initiated in 1513, of "requirements." Each captain was obliged to explain briefly the Christian concept of the world to the Indians so that they might know what to abide by; then they were required to deliberate and recognize the overlordship of the Church, and (because of the papal donation of the lands to Spain) also of the king. If they did this, they were received with love; if not, they were warred upon. The captains complied with these formulas, serving them up in a platter of official language. But naturally, the Indians could not understand any of it. This was neither farce nor foolishness, but a curious example of the desire to weld abstract ideas to deeds. These ideas were stirred up by the controversies concerning the freedom of the Indians that had been enkindled by the Dominicans of Hispaniola: FRIAR PEDRO DE CÓRDOBA (1482–1521), who wrote a manual *Christian Doctrine for the Instruction of Indians* (*Doctrina cristiana para instruc-ción de los indios*, Mexico, 1544); FRIAR ANTONIO MONTESINOS; and others.

Father Las Casas / These friars defended the Indian from military rapacity and enlisted in their crusade the most intractable chronicler of America, BARTOLOMÉ DE LAS CASAS (1474–1566). In his long and turbulent life, this tumultuous Andalusian defended the principle that only the peaceful conversion of the Indians was legitimate. Those who had despoiled and subdued them had to return all properties if they wanted to save their own souls. Either the Spaniards must return to Spain, leaving things as they had found them, or they had to conquer by dint of holy water and scapularies, and with the Indians' permission. While he defended this principle, he penned a whole gallery of portraits and scenes which are among the most interesting of the age. He wasn't a writer, but a writing paladin. His prose flowed like a wide, slow, and unending river, rock-studded, difficult to navigate, and open to a thousand digressions; yet, the reader occasionally discerns an evocative phrase skimming on the surface. The fire of his indignation when he tells of the iniquities of the Spaniards, the intellectual keenness of his irony when he removes the hypocritical Christian mask from the face of avarice, the aggressive polemics against other chroniclers and doctrinaires, and the sagacity with which he associates the physical and psychological in his biographical sketches, reveal a writer in Las Casas. He was morally superior to his fellow countrymen in America, but he was not so lofty that he could not enjoy their gossiping. There he was, watching and hearing humanity agitated by passions of ambition, power, faith, rebellion, adventure, glory, and knowledge. And he understood these men well, even when their actions were impelled by non-spiritual motives. He poked and stirred up their consciences (hence, the psychological quality of many of his pages) and there is a malicious mockery in the way he exposed their selfishness. As he sketched them, he would reduce their heroic stature. For example, he showed Cortés as timid, "withdrawn and humble" before Velazquez's servants, and later Cortés is shown laughing cynically, recalling his depredations as "the pagan pirate." Or if he depicted his subjects as being heroic, he also projected their rabid quality, as he did in the admirable picture of the slight, quick, and fearless Alonso de Ojeda who was so short that in order to shield himself completely all he had to do was to kneel behind his buckler. Ojeda had never seen his own blood until, wounded by an arrow, he ordered the torn muscle to be cauterized with white-hot searing irons. He threatened the hesitating doctor with the gallows; then he wrapped himself in vinegar-saturated bedsheets and without a complaint awaited the return of his health in order to resume running Indians through with his sword.

To demonstrate the terrible impact that the Spaniards produced, even while mortally wounded, he describes the scene in which Pedro de Ledesma, his brains exposed, his body broken and bloody, was putting Indians to flight while lying on his back yelling: " 'If I get up!'—with this threat alone they [the Indians] would bolt and flee in terror, and it was no wonder, for he was a fierce man, large in body and with a deep voice." Las Casas was also sensitive to the physical beauty of these men, as in the scene in which the youth Grijalva is bedecked by one of the chieftains with leaves of gold. He remarked: "It was worth a great deal to see how beautiful Grijalva became."

A great verbal portrait-painter was Las Casas—depicting the voice, the figure, the countenance, how well this or that man played the guitar, the headaches that prevent studying, the way a horse was made to gambol, the way one laughed, or gazed, or held his head, and so on. His indignation prompted sermons which were not his best writings. But it also prompted episodical adventures in which the Spaniards had the role of villains and the Indians "that of people of the Golden Age lauded for so long by poets and historians"; here indeed we can enjoy the fruits of his literature. His *History of the Indies* (*Historia de las Indias*) was begun in 1527 and included the period up to shortly before his death. His *Brief Account of the Destruction of the Indies* (*Brevísima relación de la destrucción de las Indias*) was published in 1552. It has more historic exactness than his opponents have claimed. In this respect he was superior to Oviedo, to Pedro Mártir, to Gómara, and to Herrera. But Las Casas possesses merit not because he may have been the first to proclaim those ideas which aroused his passions, but because he defended them with valor, enkindling them with love, setting forth problems in a new and vast reality. In a history governed by Providence, he considered himself a man of destiny. The Indians, his protégés, were descendants of the lost tribes of Israel. These peoples were those who would embrace the Church if, as Las Casas prophesied, the destruction of the Indies were punished one day by the destruction of Spain.

Colonial Expansion and the Chronicles / Although Las Casas moved from place to place, he centered his activities in Santo Domingo because this was the cultural center of the New World. It was there that the first convents and schools were established; it was there the first pedagogical books were written; and there the colonial expansion was initiated.

Certainly endowed with an extraordinarily virile temperament were these men who emerged from ordinary people to make their way through uncharted mountains, rivers, jungles, deserts and seas, to raise everywhere the pillars upon which the Spanish Empire was to be built. They explored the Antilles, they discovered the Pacific Ocean and the Río de la Plata, they took possession of Mexico and Peru, they trod from Florida to the Mississippi, they fought the Arauco Indians of Chile, they founded cities in Nueva Granada, they colonized Argentina and Paraguay, and they explored the Amazon River. Out of these expeditions came chroniclers—soldiers and missionaries—aware of the importance of their deeds, who wrote what they saw, and the pleasure with which they wrote enhanced their unpolished prose. They have left not only documents which made the sixteenth century known to history, but also confidences in which their souls were revealed to literature. It was America that awakened in the majority of them the desire to write, and they did so in a language that was fairly uniform though hasty, turbulent, and murky.

The protests of humility and incompetence of these chroniclers

is not always attributable to the false modesty that Ernst Robert
Curtius found prevalent throughout antiquity and the Latin
middle ages. They are often a sincere admission of their poverty
of expression. Occasionally these men would brag about writing
the way they spoke, to distinguish themselves from Europeans,
who took great pains in the arrangement of their words to describe a new world they had never seen.

Conquest and Learning: Oviedo / GONZALO FERNÁNDEZ DE
OVIEDO (1478–1557) lived in the Indies, as an official representative of the Crown rather than as a conquistador, from 1514 to
1556, interrupting his American residence with six visits to
Spain and sojourns at court. His field of observation was small
(the Caribbean, principally the islands of Haiti, or Hispaniola,
and Cuba, and the continent from Darien to Nicaragua), but in
those years this was the center of action. As soon as he arrived he
began to set down what he saw and heard in papers that accumulated until they resulted in the *General and Natural History of the
Indies* (*Historia general y natural de las Indias*), covering the
years from 1492 to 1549, the last date recorded. It is more chronicle than history, since it deals with current actuality not yet finished but still in the making. In 1526, while in Spain, he published
his *Summary of the Natural History of the Indies* (*Sumario de la
natural historia de las Indias*), which he had just presented to
Charles V to give him an account of the nature of his overseas
possessions. It was actually a summary of the more ambitious
History he was writing. It was not, however, an abridgment of his
History. On the contrary, pages from the *Summary* eventually
passed into the *History*. The *Summary* covers what Oviedo had
seen and heard up to 1525; in the *History*, which he continued to
write until 1549, he displays much greater knowledge, at times
correcting what he had said in the *Summary*. But the fact that he
wrote the *Summary* from memory, far from where his papers
were, endowed it with a charming unity, in spite of its miscellaneous content. Oviedo was, above all, a naturalist, capable of
transmuting nature into poetry. In the *Summary*, describing the
natural wonders of the Antilles, he is in his element. It was with

some reluctance that later, forced by his ambition to write an all-encompassing history, he was to turn from his description of nature to tales of human conflicts. Meanwhile, in the *Summary*, he dwells with pleasure on animals, fruits, rivers and indigenous rites, a whole world of sensations and excitement recollected in autobiographical anecdotes. We do not maintain that the *Summary* is more valuable than the *History*. Because of its brevity and conciseness, a wealth of observation is sacrificed in the *Summary* that is displayed only in the profuse *History*. But the *Summary* brings out more clearly that Oviedo's first inclination was to express his delight in the natural wonders that opened out to his senses. While others in Europe were rediscovering the value of ancient cultures, Oviedo was discovering in America the value of novel experiences in a completely new environment. He preferred a historiography founded on direct observation as opposed to the humanist historiography of his times.

In dedicating the *Summary* to Charles V he said that, like his model, Pliny, he would give personal testimony to what he heard and saw. "Do not look, Your Majesty, at anything except the newness of what I am trying to express." That "newness" was not just American geography, but also the philosophic meaning that Oviedo gave, for the first time, to the discovery. He described the non-European elements, the uniqueness "of the secrets and things that nature produces" in the newly explored lands. A man of the Renaissance, but of the Spanish Renaissance, Catholic, and preserver of medieval traditions, Oviedo gave a tranquil vision of the universal order—God, nature, man are part of an intelligible system. We know God by studying nature; then nature invites us to a superior spiritual life for which God has endowed us appropriately. And because the nature of the New World was unknown, to contemplate it was to complete our knowledge of God.

The *Summary* was expanded into the *General and Natural History of the Indies* (*Historia general y natural de las Indias*, 1526–1549) with an interpretation which, departing from the new American reality, arrived at the justification of the imperial policies of Charles V. God had elected the Spaniards to implant a universal Catholic monarchy. Oviedo's point of view was, then,

that of an imperialist. He maintained that the feats of the Spaniards
were superior to any known to history or literature. This did not
keep him from dipping his pen in the fires of hell to depict the
depravities of the conquistadors, for example those of Pedrarias,
Hernando de Soto, Francisco Pizarro. His attack on the Spaniards
was no gentler than that of Las Casas. The difference lies in that
Las Casas' concern was for the minority, he was more consistent
in his denunciations, more Christian in his attitude toward the
Indian. Oviedo represented the point of view of the establishment,
he frequently contradicted himself, and he despised the Indian.
Oviedo saw, of course, the rapacity of the conquistadors, but to
him it seemed accidental. On the other hand, the defects that he
saw in the Indians seemed to him inherent. It was the defects of
their savageness which, depriving them of their understanding of
the true religion, deformed their souls. Yes, Oviedo admitted that
the Indians had souls; what they lacked was rational sufficiency.
The ugliness of soul was converted into ugliness of body. Spiritual
inferiority, of historic origin, was converted into material inferiority, of ethnographic origin. Christianity, with its moral perfections, would give light to the spirit and, in turn, the spirit would
give light to the countenance. Meanwhile, the Indians must pay
for their idolatry.

In his moments of greatest impatience, Oviedo believed that
the Indians were shades of Satan that had to be exterminated.
They were men, not beasts, but so vicious, vile, cowardly, degenerate, superstitious, ungrateful, deceitful, lazy, and stupid that
they had to be treated like beasts. They were to blame for their
own destruction because they were incapable of forming part of
the Catholic empire of Charles V. When Las Casas accused
Oviedo of speaking about things he had not seen, he was referring
to the latter's deprecation of the Indian. The fact is that the real
Indian could not be seen in the sixteenth century—he was either
the abstraction of the good man or the evil man. And for Oviedo
he was the evil man whom God had punished by the hand of the
conquistador. He was not enthused, then, with what he saw; yet,
upon describing an *areyto* (dance with recitative) that he saw in
Hispaniola in 1515, he remembered that this indigenous custom

of commenting on historical facts and of preserving traditions was similar to the old Spanish ballads. His head was full of them, and he mentioned a few.

Just as it was possible for him to be an imperialist and at the same time condemn Spanish abuses, so it was possible for him to be anti-Indian and still create an American ethnography. In the customs of the Indians, however barbarous, he found traces similar to those known in European history. It was sentiment more than prejudice that kept him from understanding the native customs. He saw things through European eyes and was determined, furthermore, to belittle the Indians. In the beautiful Anacaona, first American poetess of record—although her lyrics, intoned by the Indians in the *areytos*, are lost—Oviedo saw beauty, indeed, but also moral dissolution. He had a taste for literature as can be seen from the first book he put together (more as a translator than as an author), *Claribalte* (1519), a book of chivalry and adventure. Later, perhaps because of the influence of Erasmus, he became ashamed of this useless fiction and severely condemned all novelistic genres. By now his life was oriented by an imperious ethical sense which made him value the truth of history and not the beauties of fantasy. The heart of his great body of writings, then, was history. He was a self-taught man who tried to please whoever employed him (this is the reason for his thesis that the Indies belonged to the early Spanish kings—even before Columbus), but he did all he could to gather documentation, and in this sense, he was a conscientious historian. He relates something he has heard; when he hears a new account, he annexes it without altering the former one; sometimes he compiles several versions of the same event; he does not verify the discrepancies, but honestly identifies his informant. "I could not be everywhere," he said —and he was right, for while he was writing the conquistadors were spreading through Rio de la Plata, Peru, Nueva Granada, Mexico, and other places which he wanted to incorporate into his history, even though he did not know them. However, instead of setting for himself a single criterion of authenticity, he amassed fragments of the truth, aware all the time that "some men are endowed with a greater understanding than others." His history is a chronicle, and his chronicle is at times an intimate diary. He also used written sources and cited them faithfully. Nevertheless, his early fondness for the novels of chivalry and for the wonders of the imagination slips into his historical works without his realizing it. They abound with medieval divination, alchemy, magic, bestiaries. Wonderful monsters of literary tradition reappear on the American landscape; knights-errant reappear masked as conquistadors. And is not there an after-taste of chivalric literature in his enjoyment of ancestral lineages and coats of arms described in his treatises on nobility, though he says that his models were the *Portraits and Generations* (*Generaciones y semblanzas*) of Fernán Pérez de Guzmán and *Illustrious Men* (*Claros varones*) of Fernando del Pulgar? We are referring to Oviedo's *Fifty Stanzas on Spanish Nobility* (*Quincuagenas de la nobleza de España*) and *Fifty Stanzas on Illustrious Men or Battles* (*Quincuagenas de varones ilustres o Batallas y quincuagenas*). The latter is in the form of a dialog between Sereno, who interrogates, and the Mayor (or rather Oviedo, mayor of Santo Domingo, in Hispaniola), who answers.

Novels of chivalry, classic myths, poetic and heroic forms of literature operate in Oviedo's work, negatively but with a positive energy. In deprecating these fictions Oviedo brings out the real wonders of a variegated vegetation and of truly dauntless men.

Conquistadors in Mexico / Not all the chroniclers had something all their own to say. From the viewpoint of literary history only a few of the testimonials concern us, for example, those of two really distinctive men, Hernán Cortés and Bernal Díaz del Castillo, who were associated in the same enterprise.

HERNÁN CORTÉS (1485–1547) dispatched five letters to Charles V between the years 1519 and 1526. The first one has been lost and is replaced by another also addressed to Charles V by the City Council of Veracruz. These letters of Hernán Cortés are the important ones. There are others, as well as documents, which express his love for the conquered lands, one example of which is his will: "I order that if I should die in this kingdom of Spain . . . my bones [be taken] to the New Spain." In his *Letters*

Cortés speaks unemotionally, and one can only guess the sudden animation in his face when he relates, not so much what he does, but what he sees in his walks about the city and the marketplace. He was the first soldier to discover the greatness of an indigenous civilization. Soldier indeed he was, and his goal was conquest; but even while he was overpowering everything through persuasion, intrigue, politics, falsehood, and brutality, he knew how to appreciate the value of the social organization of the Aztecs. It is not because of literary lassitude that Cortés confessed his inability to communicate to the king the wonders that he saw; it was really the feeling that Mexican reality was greater than the mental framework that he had brought from Spain. He felt that the very language he spoke was a wide-meshed net that could not pull up all the new things he saw. "Since I cannot name them I shall not express them." In describing a temple he says: "there is no human tongue that can express its grandeur and uniqueness."

Cortés perceived the ideal forms of an indigenous culture. However, after contemplating them, he destroyed them. He had, like all of his companions, a soul shaped by the hierarchical notions of Church and Empire. Obedience to Church and Empire gave his soul a swordlike hardness with which to cut the knots that his admiration had tied earlier. The first sign of disrespect on the part of the Indians would occasion a "we Spaniards" and "those Indians" attitude that reduced the moral radiance of his letters though not the value of his evocative prose. He was an audacious man who demanded the vassalage of all the Indians and their immediate conversion to Catholicism. He decreed and threatened. If they acquiesced, there would be peace; if not, he would torture, he would assassinate, he would scorch, he would massacre. He advanced dauntlessly, friendly to the submissive, terrible to the rebellious. As he relates, he does not obstruct the image of the Indians by interposing his own massive personality. Quite the contrary. If we sympathize with the Indians, as we make our way through the chronicle, it is partly due to Cortés sympathetic treatment. He shows them frightened, confused. At times they resort to diplomacy or to conspiracy; at times they are scandalized or contemptuous, determined in every way to rid themselves of those

Spaniards who, with their horses, their gunpowder, their armor, do not retreat before anything. And when the Indians finally rise up in arms, Cortés puts words in their mouths that justify their warring upon the Spaniards. Cortés was not sincere in the aims he proposed in his *Letters* to the Emperor, and if there is anything lacking in them, it is frankness. But if he did not reveal the Indians' true temper of mind, it was not because of insincerity, but because he was unable to conceive of it.

Having demolished the indigenous culture, Cortés began to set up the Colony. In his fourth letter he points out the defects of the Spanish colonization—the unworthy friar and the rapacious *encomendero*. (*Encomendero* was the recipient of an *encomienda*, an assignment by Royal decree of lands to be exploited, not unlike a feudal state.) The restrained tone of his *Letters* was not so much a reflection of his temperament as it was of his ability. He was an irascible leader whose temple veins used to swell, Bernal tells us, during his frequent disputes. But, like most leaders he knew how to control himself and domineer with coldly contained words. And this is how he shows himself to us in his *Letters*—cool, with the coolness of one who puts up a front. He was a Caesar, more like Borgia than Julius. "He was somewhat of a poet, who knew Latin very well and conversed with good rhetoric," reports Bernal.

BERNAL DÍAZ DEL CASTILLO (1492?–1584) who was one of Cortés' soldiers, recognized the courage, the effectiveness, and the dignity of Cortés; but he added to the idea of Hero (so dear to the Renaissance biographers of Cortés) his own idea of the importance of masses (the body of the Spanish army, the populace). He does not belittle Cortés; he humanizes him. He surrounds him with people, he has him move and speak with everyday gestures, and in this fashion another history of the conquest of New Spain emerges, not the true one but a more colorful one. *The True History of the Conquest of New Spain* (*Verdadera historia de la conquista de la Nueva España*) is one of the most impassioned chronicles ever written in Spanish, and perhaps the one most passionately discussed. Say what one will, reading Bernal is a pleasure. The reader is taken by the contrast between the extraordinary value of the narration and the simplicity of materials with which it is woven. Bernal was not trained to write, nor was he a soldier who had great deeds to recount. He was an obscure person who never distinguished himself in anything, but he was so ambitious that thanks to these defects—not being a writer and not being a hero—he succeeded in producing a genial work. Bernal, a man from the masses, democratizes historiography and during his prolonged old age he writes about what no one knows better than he. "And I say again that I, I and I, and many times I say, that I am the oldest [of the conquistadors], and I have served His Majesty as a good and dutiful soldier." The force with which the "I" pounds down throughout the *True History* produces a new sound to which we must attune our ears in order to be able to enjoy it; because it is not the heroic I, but rather the slightly discontented, resentful, covetous, vainglorious, vituperative I of an intelligent plebeian who says everything in a cataract of minutely detailed recollections. Bernal does not adorn, does not pick and choose, does not organize, does not dissemble. And because he lacked a feeling for literary form he gave us the most informative and complete of the Mexican chronicles. The literary form that he does, indeed, handle well is the narrative. He relives the past minute by minute, confusing the essential with the accidental, as in a lively conversation. With one jerk he pulls us from our seats, placing us in the sixteenth century, and we see what the Spanish people were like during their first days in the Americas. He even records the slightest phenomena of New World phonetics. Although Bernal was a Castilian, there is evidence that he mixed the consonants *c* and *s* as the Andalusians do. The first linguistic sediments in America were from Andalusian pronunciation (sixty-seven per cent of the Spanish population was from Andalusia by 1509; seventy per cent by 1519), and Bernal learned to *sesear*, that is, to pronounce *c* before *e* and *i* as *s*, in America. On the other hand, his vocabulary comes from the language he heard in Spain: it has been estimated that, out of the 4,300 words he uses, less than 100 are of American origin. He speaks with the breath of an entire social group. A chronicler of the masses, his "I" becomes "we." Bernal remembers the heroic romances of literature, so he knows it would be easier to simplify his account with individual actions

adorned rhetorically in the manner of the epics, but what he desires to relate is the efforts of the masses and therefore he chooses
that difficult road, suspecting that he cannot accomplish his end
with brilliance. He was aware of the strength of his chronicle and
would even call himself coyly "an unlettered idiot." We maintain
that he was being mock-modest because he knew how to reinforce
his story with timely references to proverbs, romances, novels
about chivalry, and epic poems. The possibility that he might even
have made use of *La Celestina* has been pointed out. In his final
chapter Bernal refers to a conversation in which two discharged
soldiers reproach him for speaking so much about himself. And
who else should say it if not he? "Should it be babbled by the birds
that were flying over the fields while we were in battle, or by the
clouds that passed overhead? Should it not be the prerogative of
the very officers and soldiers who were in the thick of it to say it?"
"It is not my intent to praise myself in this, for it is the simple
truth; and these are not old accounts of many years gone by, of
Roman history or of imaginative tales of poets . . ."

Las Casas is the chronicler who defends the Indian from the
rapacity of the Spaniard, and Bernal is the chronicler of rapacity
itself. And precisely for this reason we can see how Las Casas
exaggerated his accusations, and how unjust are those who, mis-
using his *Brief Account of the Destruction of the Indies*, consolidated the black legend against Spain. Because in Bernal not
everything was due to greed—there were also the idealistic drives
of glory, Christianity, loyalty to king, concept of empire—something chivalric, in short. In fact, he is the only chronicler who ven-
tures to cite novels of chivalry, which, as is well known, constituted
the favorite reading from the end of the fifteenth century to the
middle of the sixteenth. Those tales of knights-errant who sallied
forth into enchanted lands excited the imagination of the conquistadors at a time when every printed book was taken to be the
truth and moved their spirits to heroic undertakings in which they
hoped to find treasures, wonders, and glorious adventures. The
influence of these novels is subtly reflected, but the chroniclers did
not cite them, partly because the moralists and humanists of the
sixteenth century railed against them (the point was reached

where they were were prohibited), and it would not have been proper, in "service reports," to support one's own chronicle with such despised material. Bernal Díaz, on the other hand, in describing his first impressions of the Aztec capital cannot help bringing forth his *Amadís*. "From the moment that we saw all those towns and villages in the water, and other great cities on land, and that road, so level and straight, leading to Mexico, we were all amazed and remarked that those towers, temples and lakes resembled the enchanted places described in the *Amadís*, because of the great towers of *cués* they had under water. Some of our soldiers even said that what they saw was a vision experienced between sleeping and waking. It is not to be wondered that I set it all down in this manner, for there is much to ponder over here." Indeed, these men had read the *Amadís*. From one of the *Amadís* sequels came the place name of California—the name of the island of black Amazons in the *Exploits of Esplandián* (*Sergas de Esplandián*). They had also read *Palmerín*, and from the second offspring of the *Palmerín* series came the place name of Patagonia —in the *Primaleón*, Patagón was the name given to a monster with a human trunk and a canine face. The ethnographic observations and geographic legends of the travelers excited the imagination of novelists; and the adventures that the novelists related excited the imagination of the travelers. Offshoots of these first Mexican chronicles would be those of Hernando Alvarado Tezozómoc (*ca.* 1520–*ca.* 1600) and Diego Muñoz Camargo (*ca.* 1526–*ca.* 1600).

Missionaries in Mexico / The conquest and colonization of Ibero-America are too complex to be judged rashly—they were neither the black legend of monsters nor the white legend of saints. It was a violent collision of civilizations, and if the Spaniard could not respect the culture of the Indian, at least he made an effort to understand it. No other people did so. Spain, especially through the work of its friars, demonstrated a new kind of intellectual curiosity. The friars wanted to Christianize the Indians; that is, they wanted them to stop being Indians. But in order to attain this profound change in the personality of the peoples of the New World, the friars had to become part of that personality. Consequently, before they could Christianize they became Indianized themselves. They began by learning the indigenous languages in order to catechize better. They constructed grammars and dictionaries; they wrote in the native language. The Crown required the teaching of Castilian. By 1550 it had been repeated over and over again that it was necessary "that those people learn our Castilian tongue and that they accept our good breeding and customs." However, there were times when the friars dedicated themselves more resolutely to the learning of indigenous languages than to the teaching of Castilian. What was the reason for this? Were they afraid that along with the Castilian the Indians would adopt the blasphemies, heresies, deviational tendencies, sorceries, and new ideas that were perturbing the religious conscience of sixteenth-century Spain? Did they believe that ignorance of the Castilian language would be a holding dike to allow time to catechize the uncorrupted minds with purity? Did they wish to become indispensable? If they, and only they, were able to communicate with the Indians, they would possess an advantage over all other Spaniards. Were they learning indigenous languages in order to better implant Spanish? What *is* certain is that the friars had slipped into the inner recesses of the indigenous soul; and there, before building Christian faith, they admired the spirit of non-European cultures. The indigenous past—customs, traditions—appeared before European eyes, not so much because friars had moved to the New World, but because they had moved into the souls of the inhabitants of the New World.

FRIAR ANDRÉS DE OLMOS (1500–1571), for example, put into Castilian "Preachments of the Elders" (*"Pláticas de los ancianos"*) recalled by the oldest of the Indians in Mexico. With these dissertations the Indians educated their youth. A disciple of his was FRIAR BERNARDINO DE SAHAGÚN (1500–1590) who defended the existence of rhetorical art among the Indians and who transcribed their discourses (comparing them to those of classical European culture) and their hymns to the gods. As a Christian of zealous faith, Sahagún believed that Satan hid himself in the religious chants of the Mexican Indians so that he might better plot his evils; however, Sahagún made an effort to study in Nahuatl to understand the Indians better and to educate them so that they themselves could record their traditions in Castilian script. In his *General History of the Things of New Spain*

(*Historia general de las cosas de Nueva España*)—written in the Mexican language and later rewritten by himself in Castilian—this Franciscan missionary collected ethnographic and folkloric information in an objective manner, that is, respectful of the objects studied. This affection for the Indians induced FRIAR TORIBIO DE BENAVENTE (d. 1569) to change his name to MOTOLINÍA, "the poor one." His attitude is symbolic: "This is the first word that I know in this language, and so that I may not forget it, from this point it shall be my name." In his *History of the Indians of New Spain* (*Historia de los indios de Nueva España*) he opposed Las Casas. Motolinía thought that faith should be implanted quickly "by force if necessary," while Las Casas insisted that the conversion of the Indians should be preceded by preparing them through adequate instruction. Motolinía does not excuse the conquistadors, but he places their cruelty on a relative basis comparing it with that of the Spaniards in Spain. Other religious chroniclers were: Diego de Landa (1524–1579), Jerónimo de Mendieta (1525–1604), Alonso de Fuenmayor (d. 1554), Friar Domingo de Betanzos (d. 1538), and Friar Martín Ignacio de Loyola (*ca.* 1548–1598), whose *Itinerary of the New World* (*Itinerario del Nuevo Mundo*) was revised by Juan González de Mendoza (1545–1618).

The Defenseless Spaniard: Cabeza de Vaca / Of the contact between Europeans and Indians, the only extant impressions are those of the Europeans; nevertheless, the Indians were discovering the white man at the same time that they were being discovered by him. How did they look upon the white man? We do not know. The Spaniards took it upon themselves to collect some of the things the Indians thought. They (the Indians) could not believe that the Spaniards were mortal and drowned one in an attempt to prove it (Juan de Castellanos); or they thought they were too cruel to be human, but must be the offspring of the sea (Girolamo Benzoni); the horrified Indians refrained from having children, or they practiced collective suicide. (On one occasion, Las Casas relates, some Indians were going to commit suicide, but did not do so because the Spanish overlord threatened to hang himself from another tree, and they feared that he would continue to torture them in the next life.) Generally the white man appeared disfigured by the complicated apparatus of civilization. But in the case of ALVAR NÚÑEZ CABEZA DE VACA (1490?–1559?) we see European man and American man, for the first time face to face in their naked state. And we can imagine how the Indians looked upon this fellow creature, an exhausted and defenseless Spaniard. The "relation" of his wanderings has come to us in three versions.

In modern editions it is known under the title *Shipwrecks* (*Nau-fragios*). The *Shipwrecks* scarcely is of interest to the historian (although it has much for the ethnologist in view of the strange information it yields on the customs of the Indians), but that is where its merit lies. Its interest does not depend, as in other chronicles, on heroic deeds, or on conquests, or on the background of opulent indigenous civilizations, but rests purely and exclusively in its narrative quality. Cabeza de Vaca left Spain in 1527. He suffered so many shipwrecks that his vessels were finally scattered with the cry, "every man for himself." He arrived on land with a handful of Spaniards. Hunger, struggles with the Indians, hardships, disease. Little by little they began dying off. Finally four remained: he, Dorantes, Castillo, and the Negro Estebanico. Captured by the Indians, maltreated by some, idolized by others, Cabeza de Vaca covered a great distance on foot (from the Gulf of Mexico to the Gulf of California). Nine years of captivity converted him, in physical appearance at least, into another Indian. He could only be proud of one thing—being a man. He walked about naked as the day he was born, eating what the Indians ate, living and speaking like them, different only in his Christian faith. When in 1536 he stumbled upon some Spaniards on horseback, he relates "they were greatly disturbed upon seeing me so strangely dressed and in the company of Indians. They kept looking at me for some length of time, so astonished, that they neither spoke to me nor managed to ask me anything."

Cabeza de Vaca knows how to tell a story. He centers his stories around the "I," and without losing sight of his reader (he is one chronicler who writes for his reader) he evokes his adventures in a style which is rapid, rich in detail, impressive, and conversational yet dignified. It is one chronicle that can be reread with pleasure. While reading, one visualizes constantly—such is the strength of his description. There is not a single obscure page in this adventure story with a happy ending.

He returned to Spain, famous. In 1540 he went back as governor general of the provinces of Rio de la Plata. The *Commentaries* must have been written by his secretary, Pero Hernández, under his direction.

Chronicles of the Conquest of Peru / The conquest of the Aztec empire and its adjacent territories was now complete and the conquistadors looked for another Mexico. The Garden of Eden, El Dorado, the City of the Caesars, the realm of the Amazons, in short, everything that they did not find in the campaigns of the north, now they feverishly sought in the south. Sea explorations had already touched the outer edges of South America (Vespucci, Magellan, Solís, Cabot), but it was after 1530 that land explorations opened the mysterious interior to the geographic vision of the epoch. Francisco Pizarro discovered in Peru, as Cortés had done in Mexico, a stupendous civilization—the Incas. And there appeared new riches of the conquered lands and new chronicles by the conquerors. It is possible that Spain might not have understood until then the value of its own imperial undertaking. But the great riches that the conquest of Peru produced and chronicles that were revealing the growing expanse of territorial possessions must have opened the eyes of Charles V. Perhaps he began to suspect that America was something more than an obstacle on the road to the Orient. Had not Francisco López de Gómara just told Charles V, upon dedicating to him his *General History of the Indies*, that "the greatest thing next to the creation of the world, omitting the incarnation and death of Him who created it, is the discovery of the Indies; and for this reason, they call it The New World"? We will mention several chroniclers, pointing out that those who contributed most to the formation of a picture of the history of the Incas were Cieza de León, Agustín de Zárate, and Sarmiento de Gamboa.

PEDRO CIEZA DE LEÓN (b. between 1520 and 1522 and d. in 1560) left one of the most extensive and objective chronicles on the conquest of Peru, the internecine struggles of the Spaniards, the Inca civilization, and its geographic setting. "Many times," says Cieza, "when the other soldiers rested, I busied myself writing." But this soldier who writes his own recollections is following a plan, that of a vast history. The *First Part of the Chronicle of Peru (Parte primera de la Crónica del Perú)* was published in 1553. The second part or *The Dominion of the Incas (Del señorío de los Incas)* was published only in 1880. The third part began to be published in 1946, and the fourth seems to have been lost. Cieza looks down upon the Indians from above as savages capable of cruelty and of the "impious sin of sodomy."

From a literary point of view one of the best chroniclers was AGUSTÍN DE ZÁRATE (d. after 1560). He witnessed the rebellion of Gonzalo Pizarro. His *History of the Discovery and Conquest of Peru* (*Historia del descubrimiento y conquista del Perú*) is meritorious for its commentaries written in "awkward and badly assorted words," according to the author, but in reality very profuse in movement, method, and even style. In judging the overlords of Cuzco his tone is condemnatory. He left us a historical monument, beautiful for its clarity and elegance, even though his work elaborates on the materials of other chroniclers.

PEDRO SARMIENTO DE GAMBOA (1530–1592), who considered the Incas tyrannical usurpers, was the favorite of Viceroy Toledo, the uprooter of the Inca line. Gamboa's *History of the Incas* (*Historia de los Incas*) gives us vivid pictures of the terror and infamies perpetrated by the natives.

JUAN POLO DE ONDEGARDO (d. 1575) and JUAN DE MATIENZO (d. 1570) also collaborated with Viceroy Toledo. De Matienzo, who was magistrate in Charcas (La Plata, then Chiquisaca, today Sucre), added *Government of Peru* (*Gobierno del Perú*) to the legal literature that attempted to prove the just title of the king to the new lands.

FRANCISCO LÓPEZ DE XEREZ (1504–1539), secretary to Francisco Pizarro under whose charge he wrote the *True Account of the Conquest of Peru and the Province of Cuzco* (*Verdadera relación de la conquista del Perú y provincia de Cuzco*, 1534), with painstaking care pondered the deeds of the conquistadors up to the death of Atahualpa. The anonymous manuscript of the first narrative poem of *The Account of the Conquest and Discovery of Marquis Francisco Pizarro in Search of the Provinces Which We Now Call the New Spain* (*Relación de la conquista y descubrimiento que hizo el marqués don Francisco Pizarro en demanda de las provincias y reinos que agora llamamos Nueva Castilla*) has been attributed to Xerez. It is an epopee of America consisting of 283 epic octaves written probably in 1537, closer in style to that of Juan de Mena than to the Renaissance models. Other chroniclers were JUAN DE BETANZOS (1510–1576) who heard the Indians' recollections of the Inca legends and artlessly collected his versions in *Summa and Account of the Incas* (*Suma y narración de los Incas*), and two clerics of the same name, CRISTÓBAL DE MOLINA ("the Chilean" [1494–

1580?] who was witness to the expedition of Almagro; "the *Cuzqueño*" [from Cuzco] who has transmitted to us a luxurious account of "Fables and Rites of the Incas" ["*Fábulas y ritos de los Incas*"]). The Indians were generally looked upon "as if they were dumb beasts and even worse than donkeys." This attitude was protested in 1550 in Lima by DOMINGO DE SANTO TOMAS, author of the first *Grammar or Art of the Common Language of Peru* (*Gramática o arte de la lengua general del Perú*) in which he strove to demonstrate the beauty and subtlety of the native language. PEDRO DE VALDIVIA (1500–1553) whose *Letters* (*Cartas*) describe beautifully the founding of Serena in Chile.

Among the first chroniclers of Peru, ALONSO HENRÍQUEZ DE GUZMÁN (1500 and d. after 1544) is noteworthy, if not for his literary value (although he did write verse and knew the poetry and theater of his times), for his originality. Traces of picaresque literature have been noticed in his autobiography. Nevertheless, his unscrupulous attraction to adventure is not that of a rogue. Unlike the rogue, he does believe in a respectable social order; the trouble is that he does not occupy in that social order the position that he would like. Even so, he was somewhat roguish, especially in the first part of the *Life and Customs of Don Alonso Henríquez de Guzmán, Destitute Nobleman* (*Vida o Libro de la vida y costumbres de Don Alonso Henríquez de Guzmán, caballero noble desbaratado*).

In our use of the words "picaresque"and "rogue" (a literary figure in Spanish Renaissance literature) we would like to make it clear that in these chronicles written by men of the people we are more concerned with their reflection of a social *situation* than with the form of literature they represent. During the Renaissance period of Charles V the medieval Christian mind acquired an aggressive individualism that denounced false social hierarchies and proclaimed the equality of men, a bitter egalitarianism that exalted the value of effort (not necessarily heroic effort—merely the biological effort to survive and not perish of hunger). *Lazarillo de Tormes* and other texts prove that there was a new attitude of rebellion and nonconformity. All of this is reflected in the chronicles of those who went to America, even though not always in a literary fashion.

Chroniclers of New Granada / Together with the rogue-conquistadors were the knight-errant-conquistadors. We know that the novels of chivalry were slowly losing their fascination and that Cervantes, in that superb exercise of literary criticism—*Don Quixote*—reduced them to the ridiculous. Something of the Don Quijote, with his bewildering fluctuation between reality and fantasy, could be seen in a number of conquistadors who were capable of cruelty and self-denial because in those mirrors of reality and fantasy the light of morality was absurdly refracted.

And one of the conquistadors sounds to us like the real Don Quijote—GONZALO JIMÉNEZ DE QUESADA (1499–1579). He was a humanist who wore his Latin learning well, but almost everything he wrote has been lost. There are good reasons for attributing to him the *Compendium of the Conquest of New Granada* (*Epítome de la conquista del Nuevo de Granada*) which is extant. Rodríguez Freyle reproaches him for "not writing the events of his times, although he was a learned man." His contemporaries were wont to cite him and profit by his writings and his oratory. His sphere of action and observation was the "new realm of Granada." Tangential to his sphere was *The Antijovio*, a refutation of the Italian historian Paolo Jovio. He had a taste for poetry and even wrote some. He was a protagonist in the controversy (still alive in America even though in Spain it had already died out) between pure Spanish verse and Italianate verse. The short meters of the old ballads and lays were arriving without interruption; and for serious poetry, there were the strophes made famous by Juan de Mena. The oldest anonymous poem on the conquest of Peru was written around 1548 in couplets of *arte mayor*. Gonzalo Jiménez de Quesada and other poet-soldiers had their ears trained to the octosyllable. When they heard for the first time the Italianate hendecasyllables they did not know how to enjoy them. "The verses left such a bad sound in their ears / that they judged them to be prose / with superfluous rhymes," Juan de Castellanos was to say about Lorenzo Martín, the captain who heartened his starving soldiers with his pleasantries, torrents of couplets and improvised quatrains. And referring to Jiménez de Quesada, he would add, "And he contended with me many times / that the old Castilian meters were / those fitting and proper for having been brought forth / from the bosom of that language / and that the hendecasyllables were alien newcomers, adopted / from a different and foreign mother."

The fever for discovery was so high that three expeditions, Jiménez de Quesada's, Belalcázar's, and Federmann's, suddenly ran across each other in the valley where Bogotá rises today. The legend of El Dorado had attributed fantastic riches to this region. It was said that a chieftain, surrounded with treasures greater than those of Mexico and Peru, had the habit of bathing in the nude with his body covered with gold dust. There were other legends: the fountain of youth, the silver mountain range, the land of cin-

namon. The last legend attracted Orellana in his exploration of
the Amazon.

The Amazons / No sooner had the followers of Orellana become
disillusioned with the cinnamon legend than they became captivated by the legend of certain women who lived apart from men—
the Amazons. The chronicler of Orellana's voyage was FRIAR
GASPAR DE CARVAJAL (1504–1584). His *Account of the Recent
Discovery of the Famous Great River of the Amazons* (*Relación
del nuevo descubrimiento del famoso río Grande de las Amazonas*) relates without embellishments, without emphasis of expression, his impressions of 1541–42. The esteem in which these
writings were held depended on the real, direct, and faithful experience that he transmits, and not on his style. As Gonzalo de
Oviedo observed, Friar Carvajal "should be believed if only for
those two arrow wounds, one of which tore out or crushed his
eye." The stamp of validity for this literature rests on the fact that
the author was there, looking upon the reality being described,
pierced by the arrow of this same reality. Carvajal wanted to see
everything. He left us observations on the character of the Indians
in war and in peace, on their musical instruments and dances, on
their weapons and dugout canoes. In spite of his lack of resources,
in spite of his wounded eye, he does appreciate the gayety of the
islands that the brigantines were beginning to leave behind. He is
a realist-observer; yet the myth of the Amazons so obsessed him
that he believed that the women who fought alongside their husbands were Amazons, and he describes them as captains from the
"good land and dominion of the Amazons." Other traces of fantasy give his chronicle the quality of poetry, as in the case of the
rare bird who was perched on an oak by the shore, and "began to
screech at great speed flee, flee, flee . . ." Then there are the
Christian miracles, such as God's intervening to save him, which
also add brushstrokes of highlights to the adventures of this one-
eyed, spirited and pious friar on the great river labyrinth until he
emerges into the Atlantic "from the mouths of the dragon."

In the Region of the Río de la Plata / Juan Díaz de Solís discovered the
Río de la Plata in the early part of 1516. Other navigators—Magellan,
Elcano—proved that this was not the end of the southern land and that if

they wanted to find a route to the east and Cathay, the islands of spice, they would have to go much farther down. But there were those who preferred to remain there, attracted by legends like those of the Mountains of Gold and the White King, which promised easy treasure. The first Spanish settlements on the Río de la Plata—Asunción and Buenos Aires—were, therefore, attempts to discover roads to fantastic riches. Only as the legend disintegrated would definitive colonization begin. In those plains and hills, poor in metals, they found aborigines of rudimentary culture spread out over a large territory in various linguistic groups. Asunción was the center of a colony that, in an attempt to occupy regions populated by Indians, found itself isolated on the plain, its back to the sea, and for several years it depopulated the city of Buenos Aires. Don Pedro de Mendoza had founded Buenos Aires in 1536 on the shores of the Río de la Plata. Eventually the chronicler of this expedition was to be the German, ULRICH SCHMIDL, but as he did not write in Spanish he does not belong to our literary history. Instead, it was the soldier and friar LUIS DE MIRANDA (1500?), who accompanied Pedro de Mendoza, who inaugurated literature in the region of the Río de la Plata. In a crude and fragmentary "romance" of one hundred and fifty octosyllabic verses, with a broken verse at the end of each strophe, he later described the native siege, the destruction of the city and the hunger—hunger such that "they also ate the flesh of men." Confronted with this picture of horror, he wrote about it, with no poetic spirit but with certain ingenuity, representing the Argentine land allegorically as a treacherous woman who kills her six Spanish husbands, one after another. Only God, he says, could give such a widow a "wise, strong and daring" husband. This husband was to be in 1580 Juan de Garay. But until then the first permanent colony in the south of the continent was Asunción in Paraguay. Luis de Miranda went there; Cabeza de Vaca arrived there in 1540 with his secretary Pero Hernández; and there the three were victims of the same political disturbance.

PERO HERNÁNDEZ (*ca.* 1513?) wrote his *Commentaries* (1554) in which he narrates the unfortunate lot of Alvar Núñez Cabeza de Vaca in Asunción from 1540 to 1545. It is the first Spanish book on the conquest of the Río Plata region. He who approaches the struggles between Spaniards in sixteenth-century Asunción with historical sympathy can move through the pages of the *Commentaries* with ease, because its defects are not too disturbing. It stands in defense of Cabeza de Vaca and in opposition to Irala. His factious nature, on one hand, denounces impetuous Spanish customs, and on the other, reveals a basic pity for the ill-treated mass of Indians. That is what makes the accusations dramatic. Since accusatory literature is made with gestures ("he did that," "I did this"), the prose, which otherwise would ramble on sluggishly, moves in impulsive strides. Cabeza de Vaca helped Hernández edit the first chapters. In one of these chapters, where reference is made to Cabeza de Vaca's second crossing from Spain to the New World, we have the pleasant episode about the cricket: a soldier, upon leaving Cadiz, brought a cricket on board the vessel so that he could hear it sing during the voyage; to the great annoyance of its owner, the cricket would not sing; suddenly, it began to sing because it sensed the proximity of land; from that moment "every night the cricket would give us his music." Hernández is pleasant. His descriptions are colorful and he knows how to tell a story.

In Paraguay's Asunción we will also find a Spanish woman, Doña Isabel de Guevara, who had arrived at the Río de la Plata with the expedition of Pedro de Mendoza. Her letter of 1556, addressed to the governing princess Doña Juana, is the first literary document that protests the unjust neglect of women. Isabel had been one of the co-founders of Buenos Aires; twenty years later she describes the hunger, calamities, burdensome tasks, and even the war efforts carried out shoulder to shoulder with the men: "The men became so enervated that the poor women were laden with all of the work, like washing clothes, curing the men, preparing what little food they had, cleaning them, acting as sentinels, stoking the fires, manning the crossbows whenever the Indians carried on an attack, even taking care of the ships, helping those men to stand by their posts who were still able to, shouting and fighting on the battlefield, taking command and putting order in the ranks of the soldiers, because since women are able to subsist on less food, we had not fallen into such a weakened state as the men."

Let us here close our review of the chronicles. They are so numerous (we have only mentioned a few) that already in those years an attempt to list them was made by ALONSO DE ZORITA (1512–1566?), *Catalog of the Authors Who Have Written Histories of the Indies* (*Catálogo de los autores que han escrito historias de Indias*).

Renaissance Literature

If the chronicles and the missionary theater maintained medieval traits, there were other activities that accentuated Renaissance elements. Even when these activities were not literary they were at least inspired by books, like the Utopia attempted by Vasco de Quiroga (1470–1565) in Mexico, a reflection of Thomas More's *Utopia*. Erasmianism, which affected the thinking of a few men in the New World, was to a certain degree Utopian.

P. Carlos de Aragón who arrived in America in 1512 delivered sermons which, according to Las Casas, showed that "he did not esteem the doctrine of St. Thomas." Even more anti-scholastic was FRIAR JUAN DE ZUMÁRRAGA (arrived in America in 1527; d. 1548), first bishop and first archbishop of New Spain, who had printed in Mexico a *Brief Doctrine* (*Doctrina breve*, 1544) with passages from Erasmus scarcely retouched, and a *Christian Doctrine* (*Doctrina cristiana*, 1545 or 1546) with echoes from Juan de Valdés. He believed in the rationality of the Indians and in the salvation of their souls at a time when many other Spaniards—following Aristotle—considered them slaves by nature; and his school for Indians of both sexes, his use of the press to put books in their hands and his other contributions to Mexican culture were inspired by this generous thought.

Also an Erasmian was LÁZARO BEJARANO (Spain; b. beginning of the sixteenth century; lived at least until 1574). In Seville he had written poetry between 1531 and 1534. He belonged to a circle of poets, intimates of Gutierre de Cetina. About 1541 he lived in the city of Santo Domingo in Hispaniola where he wrote satires against priests, politicians, and private persons. In 1558 he was accused before the Inquisition of mocking scholastic theology and of exalting Erasmus. Lost is his *Apologetic Dialog* (*Diálogo apologético*) in which he defended the dignity of the aboriginal population of America, not as a priest (from whom charity is expected) but as an administrator and master of Indians. Juan Méndez Nieto (1531–*ca.* 1617), a doctor with an inclination for literature, relates that because of an anonymous satire by Lázaro Bejarano, "they arrested all the poets" so that they might apprehend the author. The fact is there were many poets. No matter how little education they had, it was considered sufficient for trying one's hand at writing. It was a collective impulse. Names of writers are preserved even if almost all of what they wrote is lost. Lázaro Bejarano, who had already written poetry in Gutierre de Cetina's circle, as we have said, must have been the first to bring to America, in 1535, verses in the Italian manner. Before this time verses in octosyllables, hexameters, and in *arte mayor* were composed. Juan de Castellanos, of whom we shall speak immediately, blames the inability to crush Enriquillo's rebellion (1519–1533) in Santo Domingo on the softness of the muses. And he was generous in saying that many of the peots of Santo Domingo, like FRANCISCO DE LIENDO (1527–1584), for example, could "well polish this that I polish / and be laughing at my verses; / would that I had them to lend support / in this work that I here compose."

JUAN DE CASTELLANOS (1522–1607) arrived in America still a youth, and in America he became a humanist and a writer. From America he knew about Garcilaso's work and, imbued with the spirit of the Renaissance, in his discussions with Jiménez de Quesada on Castilian versification he sided wth the new meters derived from the Italian school. His not-at-all-elegiac *Elegies of Illustrious Men of the Indies* (*Elegías de varones ilustres de Indias*, 1589) constitute one of the longest poems written in the world; and, of course, the longest in the Spanish language. He started off with Columbus (consequently, his verses are the first dedicated to Colombus). Castellanos was rich in experience. He wrote with a sure memory in his old age about all he had lived through from Puerto Rico to Colombia, giving us the different highlights of his life as an acolyte, a pearl fisherman, a soldier, an adventurer, an enjoyer of Indian women, and a parish priest. If one were to read these verses like one who listens to the rain, it might occur to him that if all the rhetorical scaffolding were taken down an enlivened and variegated narrative mass of innumerable episodes would appear.

The reader may also notice in Castellanos a love for the American land, a Creole's and realist's attitude that merits our sympathy. He considered himself an American Spaniard, different from and superior to the newly arrived Spaniards, of whom he made fun. Among those chroniclers who first used indigenous words, he was one of those who took most pleasure in doing so. *Bohíos*, "Indian huts," *macanas*, "clubs," *jagüeyes*, "cisterns" are imprinted with all their color and descriptive strength in evocative passages. His syntax is clumsy; his tone of voice, like that used in everyday conversation, is fluid and natural; his view of the conquest is clear in its heroic as well as in its daily aspects. He was sincere, passionate, and facetious. A good example of his irony (even having some elements of mock-heroic stylization and of parodying the eclogue) is the passage that refers to the Spanish peasants brought over by Las Casas to colonize the coast of Cumaná. These were peasants armed like knights, with red crosses on their breastplates, accompanied by their shepherdesses (after all, there was the question of "populating"), unfit to fight and, in effect, ultimately destroyed by the Indians. (Castellanos respected Las Casas, but he repeated the legend of the "knights in brown" caricatured by Oviedo.)

Castellanos knew that his language was shabby; he used to say "a simple language of truth and exactness," but he trusted that the things of America are so noteworthy that "by themselves they elevate the style." He was not a poet, but his verses are stirring when they tell a story, especially if it is about something painful or tragic. He embroiders his *Elegies* with differently colored threads taken from literature, history, and classical mythology. He had read Vergil, Ovid, Horace, Seneca, Terence. And, during a time when curiosity for things exclusively Greek was exceptional, he reveals having read Xenophon and others in the original. He did not re-create the classics as Garcilaso did; rather than assimilating, the plots of his chronicles were interwoven with the texts. From the Spanish literature he made use of Juan de Mena, Gar-

cilaso, Ercilla, and perhaps *El Cartujano*. The chronicles of
Oviedo and of López de Gómara were among his sources for the
historical part of the poem. He wanted to keep to the facts, but
because he believed in the supernatural, an imaginative and ro-
mancing light occasionally crept into his paintings. Because of
his realist's attitude, he used the word *novela*, "romance," dispar-
agingly; for example, it seemed to him that all that talk about
Amazon Indians was "light-headed romance." But, after rejecting
all the deception, he reserved the right to embellish his tales with
comparisons taken from literary tradition: Indians like nymphs
and naiads "such as those that appear in poems," so beautiful that
"Jupiter would desire to be their husband"; Indian women, for
their part, looking upon the Spaniards as "lascivious and lusty
fauns"; monsters in the form of hermaphroditic giants or of two-
headed dwarfs a foot high; bewitchments out of books of chivalry;
there is, in a word, a flux and reflux of real life and literary life.
Among his best descriptions are the ones about the earthquakes
of Cubagua, of the Island of Margarita in the Lake of Maracaibo.

While some Spaniards (Núñez Cabeza de Vaca, for example)
went around nude like Indians, others carried on a refined cultural life. Mexico already had a university, and one of its profes-
sorial chairs was held by FRANCISCO CERVANTES DE SALAZAR (b.
before 1515; d. after 1575). He arrived in Mexico in 1551 with
a humanistic culture already demonstrated in his Latin works. He
continued writing in Latin. His various dialogs, in the manner of
Vives, described the university, its streets, buildings, and the en-
virons of Mexico City; made rapid comparisons of the same things
in Spain; and contained quick philosophical reflections, notes on
the education of the mestizo, and a certain relativism in compre-
hending the native culture. Already there were mestizos who
knew Latin, and even some who were teaching it. For his *Chronicle of New Spain* (*Crónica de la Nueva España*), which he wrote
in Spanish, he profited from the *Letters* of Cortés (whom he knew
personally) and from many other written sources (Motolinía,
Herrera, etc.). He was a man of vitality. Archbishop Moya de
Contreras, in a report of 1575 to the King, described him thus:
"He likes to talk and is susceptible to flattery, [he is] frivolous,

fickle, and dishonest, and so convinced that he is going to be Bishop that some people have already made fun of him. After twelve years of being a prebendary [a clergyman] he has not shown traces of ecclesiastical spirit and is unreliable." What matters, however, is that Cervantes de Salazar knew how to see with his own eyes the conquistadors, the things of America, and the grandeur of the city of Mexico. Before he arrived in Mexico, he flattered Hernán Cortés by attributing to him, in an epistle of 1546, a noble but imaginary Italian genealogy. Furthermore, he invented the legend of Cortés' burning his ships in order to compare him with the Greco-Roman heroes. But, after having arrived in Mexico, his words on Cortés, in his *Chronicle*, were objective.

Other Spanish writers, such as Gutierre de Cetina, arrived in Mexico. His contributions to America are insignificant—he barely alluded twice to the new lands. If, as they say, he wrote a theatrical piece in Mexico, it has been lost; and if he left any trace, it was the importation of the Italianate hendecasyllable. Perhaps it was Gutierre de Cetina, a guest in Mexico, who lullabied the Mexican FRANCISCO DE TERRAZAS (1525?–1600?) with Italian melodies. Terrazas wrote good sonnets "in the Italian style," an amatory epistle in tercets, and an unfinished poem on the *New World and Conquest* (*Nuevo Mundo y conquista*), which is too mild for its epic theme. This is an epic poem that opens the Cortés cycle on the conquest of Mexico.

Fantasy and the New World

Fantasies, born and developed for centuries, were transplanted to the New World—paradise, the fountain of youth, the seven enchanted cities, the eleven thousand virgins, giants, pigmies, dragons, children with hoary hair, men with tails, bearded women, headless monsters with eyes in their stomachs or in their chests, monkeys that go about playing the cornet. It is natural that this combination of man, beast, and myth would sharpen the preoccupation over the problem of how the New World had become populated, who the people were, whence they had come, and what were the abilities of these people whom the Spaniards found enveloped in the light of fantastic cosmogonies and zoological systems. We see, side by side, the speculations made by the medieval mind and also by the Renaissance mentality, an attitude we would call scientific today. Disengaged from the traditions that weighed upon them while in Spain, some Spaniards felt an awakening of intellectual curiosity for the strange reality that surrounded them. This is the conflict between the theological and the scientific which will become more marked with the passage of time, as we shall see in the succeeding chapters.

Theater

We have said that there were two kinds of artistic activities which, upon initial contact with the new American reality, acquired creative power although retaining an archaic, medieval appearance—the chronicle and the theater. We have examined the chronicle. On the theater there are only indirect references. The first, a representation of the end of the world in the Nahuatl language (1533), was in Mexico. The conquistadors celebrated their holidays in their own way with mystery plays, preludes, interludes, mummeries, etc.

It is recorded that during these years religious plays were composed by Friar Andrés de Olmos, Friar Juan de Torquemada, Luis de Fuensalida and others. Micael de Carvajal (1490?) visited Santo Domingo in 1534: it is possible that by then he was writing *Tragedy of Josephine* (*Tragedia josefina,* 1535), a religious play remarkable in the theater before Lope de Vega. In his miracle play *The Court of Death* (*Auto de las Cortes de la Muerte,* 1557)—whose ending was written by Luis Hurtado de Toledo—Carvajal presented some Indians who complain of the abuses inflicted by the Spaniards. Many pieces originated in Spain.

To have catechized the Indians so spectacularly, the missionary theater must have been quite original. With the aim of propagating the Christian faith, the missionaries adapted to the theatrical forms of the Middle Ages the incipient dramatic art of the Indians—floral fiestas or *mitotes,* ritual ceremonies, songfests, dances, pantomimes, and comical improvisations that aped the movements of animals or deformed humans, etc. The Church lent theological meaning to those spectacles which at times were prepared in the native languages. The Spanish chronicles abound in allusions to this theater from 1535 onward; Motolinía has left us a gracious description of the mystery play about the fall of Adam and Eve presented by the Indians in their own language (Tlaxcala, 1538). The combination of nature and scenery is impressive. At times the participants are so many that the stage collapses. The spectacle ordinarily ends with the baptism of great masses of Indians. The *Conquest of Jerusalem* (*Conquista de Jerusalém*) celebrated on the feast of Corpus Christi in Tlaxcala dates from 1539; it is an open-air representation of the wars between the Moors and the Christians.

The needs of this type of representation influenced the architecture of the "open chapels," a kind of open-air theater capable of accommodating an immense audience. These spectacles were so well attended that the crowds overflowed the churchyard and moved into the streets. They were scenes of sacred history or of sacred allegories, interspersed with comic moments and even military parades.

The Inca regions all had their fiestas of this type. In Lima from 1546 and in Potosí from 1555, theatrical pieces were presented, some in Quechua, some in Castilian. The Inca Garcilaso describes several. In 1550 under the direction of the chief magistrates and the military, plays were presented in Guayaquil as rehearsals for the battles against Indians and pirates; and they utilized scenes from the *Cid*, the *Amadís* and the *Exploits of Esplandián* (*Sergas de Esplandián*).

Hence, the intermingling of Indian and Spanish elements produced an original dramatic type. Partly because the missionaries were not playwrights or men of letters, but above all because they resorted to theatrical forms that were more ancient and had less artistic merit than those being performed at that time in Spain (to stress more effectively the catechetical and pedagogic effect of these forms), the fact is that the colonial theater was born from an effort at adaptation and not from a creative effort. In spite of this, the dramatic form that resulted was highly original. It will seem a retrogression to medieval performances if we only fix our attention on the progress of the Renaissance theater in Spain; but, on the other hand, if we focus on the new American reality, we will understand that this dramatic type was innovational and open to many possibilities. The participation of masses of people in open-air scenes, for example, could have evolved toward theatrical forms not dependent on the Church. The audience was not just audience; it participated in the performances with sham battles and dances. Unfortunately the missionary theater languished and disappeared in the second half of the sixteenth century. The Church itself drowned the theater, in cleansing it of its initial secularity. (An example of this purging is the one imposed by the Third Mexican Council in 1585.)

Political grudges sometimes appeared on the stage in the form of farces in which the authorities were made sport of. These were even presented in Rio de la Plata, where the cleric, JUAN GABRIEL DE LEZCANO, appears to have composed one between 1544 and 1552.

II. 1556-1598

Authors born between 1530 and 1570

Historical framework: Colonization under Philip II. Spanish imperial power is broken and the momentum of the conquest begins to lose its vitality. Social institutions, meanwhile, are consolidated.

Cultural tendencies: Second Renaissance and Counter Reformation. Chronicles tend toward verse forms. Traditional and Italianate poetry. European-patterned theater. First writers born in America.

Introduction

Spain closes in upon itself, incorporates poetic forms it once imported, and seeks national formulas—the second renaissance and counter reformation are upon her. In the colonies the writers live by borrowing. This is natural. And the borrowings are profuse; much more than has been believed because, despite the publicized prohibitions of kings and inquisitors, all sorts of fiction—Latin, Italian, and Spanish poetry; pastoral, picaresque, and sentimental novels; books of chivalry; plays; Erasmian writings; histories, legends, allegories, didactic pleasantries—circulated throughout America in amazing abundance. One must not expect this literature, derived from the mother country, to engender a colonial literature of equal vigor. The circumstances were quite different. In Spain, literature was the manifestation of a numerous populace, unified, steeped in tradition, fond of long-winded and sustained dialog, sure of itself, vital and powerful; in the colonies, literature was practiced by a limited number of cultured nuclei mustered about small institutions, human islands amidst illiterate masses, dilettantes feeling incapable of persistent efforts in literary apprenticeship, timidly imitative, devoid of the legal, commercial, and technical apparatus of the book-printing trade, discouraged by material difficulties. The colonies, then, kept pace with the mother country, but always a step behind.

In the preceding chapter the writers we studied were almost all Spaniards. There were those who came to the new land already possessing literary training, and others in whom the vocation for writing developed after their arrival in America, but they all had Spanish souls attuned to European cultural forms. In this chapter we shall see how the descendants of the Spaniards start writing. These are "children of the earth," Creoles like Terrazas or mestizos like the Inca Garcilaso, who are to transform colonial society. Mestizos' souls, enriched by the double vision of two historic worlds, begin to reveal a new society, unknown in Europe—a society in an occidental frame but with vigorous indigenous traditions. Some write in their native tongues and therefore escape beyond the boundaries of this history. There are, among those who write in Spanish, overtones of love of their own native traditions, and also of protest against alien prejudices. Nevertheless, the literary penchant of mestizos and Indians sprang from the example set by Europeans, because the indigenous population did not have a literature of its own.

Chroniclers

However remiss Spain had been in appreciating earlier the value of the conquest of America, and the chroniclers had written on their own initiative, now the king looked with favor upon the history of New World affairs (in 1596 Philip II appointed Antonio de Herrera y Tordesillas "Chief Chronicler of the Indies," who responded in 1601 by publishing the first part of the *Decades* and in 1615 the second).

A new group of conquistadors and missionaries produced a new group of chronicles. Some chroniclers repeated things already recorded or, at best, added recent happenings to what was already known; others described for the first time regions recently conquered. Some chronicles are composed in a poor style, useful only to the historian; others are composed in a more elevated style. More often than not there was artistic awareness, or better still, literary awareness; indeed, some chronicles, such as those of the Inca Garcilaso, in prose, and those of Alonso de Ercilla, in verse, form part of the best literature of the period.

Because these chronicles sprang up along the travel routes of the New World, we shall conduct our examination by following the same routes: Mexico, Peru, Río de la Plata, Chile. But first let us deal separately with Father JOSÉ DE ACOSTA (1539–1616) who, because of location and character, cannot be classified with the rest of the chroniclers. "I must let myself be guided by the thread of reason, even though it may be a thin one, until it completely disappears from before my eyes," he used to say. It is gratifying to find, in a Jesuit of the counter reformation, so much curiosity for the causes of creation, and above all, so much independent judgment vis-à-vis the authorities. He holds Aristotle lightly, and he is even ready to dispute the Bible, which he does, in his desire to understand the problems of the new American environment. In 1590, at the end of the century of discovery, his *Natural and Moral History of the Indies* (*Historia natural y moral de las Indias*) is published. As the title indicates, the history deals with the "natural" aspects of the Indies (the first four volumes) as well as the "moral" aspects (the rest of the volumes). In the first section he studies what we would call today the physical and natural sciences, and in the second section he studies problems of culture: religion, history, politics, education, etc. These two perspectives, natural and moral, comprise his vision of a world, which, for Acosta, of Jewish origin, but a Catholic and an Aristotelian, was organized into one hierarchic whole. It is not the historical element of his *History* that is most valuable. Acosta dealt with sources, and whoever searches for historical materials can gather them from these sources. What *is* interesting in Acosta's *History* is his anti-historical attitude. Meditating over what he has seen, Acosta no longer is amazed at man's diversity in the New World. The Indian was not so different from the European. In both one could see the spiritual light of universal man and even customs preserved from a distant common cradle. Furthermore, he adds:

"It is well-known that even in Spain and Italy there are groups of men, who except for their gestures and shapes, have little in common with man."

The year following the appearance of Acosta's *Natural History*, another description of nature appeared in Mexico: JUAN DE CÁRDENAS' *Problems and Marvelous Secrets of the Indies (Problemas y secretos maravillosos de las Indias,* 1591). It is interesting that Cárdenas, an Andalusian, already sees differences between the Spaniards born in the Indies and the Spaniards of Spain, the former appearing to him to be more refined, discreet, and polished.

The Spaniard born in the Indies is already called a "Creole." The geographer, Juan López de Velasco, gave him this name somewhere between 1571 and 1574. "Those who are born of Spaniards, who are called Creoles and are everywhere known and recognized as Spaniards, are already known to be different in color and size. . . . And it is not only the physical qualities that change. The qualities of the spirit follow those of the body, and as it undergoes change, so do they." Hernando de Montalvo wrote from Asunción in 1579 that "Creoles and Mestizos have very little respect for the authorities . . . little respect for their parents and superiors."

During this period no great original chronicles were written in Mexico. The one by FRIAR JUAN DE TORQUEMADA (*ca.* 1563–1624) *Indian Monarchy* (*Monarquía indiana,* 1615) is a second-hand work. "Certainly if I were to put down all the things I have found written in ancient notebooks—beyond what I have seen verified—it would resemble books of chivalry which do not pretend to be anything but mountains of lies." If only the things he put down in his chronicle were as readable as a book of chivalry! A few mountains of lies, with their touch of fantasy, can assuage the dullness of a chronicle. Torquemada's is dull, and interesting only for the documents it includes—he copied Friar Jerónimo de Mendieta's *Ecclesiastical History of the Indies (Historia eclesiástica indiana)* at that time still unpublished. On the other hand, the *History of the Indies of New Spain (Historia de las Indias de Nueva España)* by FRIAR DIEGO DURÁN (b. before 1538–1588), written on the basis of Náhuatl documents and first-hand data, is delightful.

Of the Mexican chroniclers born during these years the most notable is JUAN SUÁREZ DE PERALTA (b. between 1537 and 1545; d. after 1590). One can discern in him the softness of the young man of means who enjoys his inherited advantages. This Creole, who used to say of himself that he possessed only "a little grammar, but a great inclination for reading histories and associating with learned persons," was one of the first to write in Mexico. His *Treatise on Horsemanship (Tratado de la caballería de jineta y brida,* 1580) was the first book published by an Hispanic-American author on a secular subject. He followed with a

Book on Veterinary Art (*Libro de alveitería*) still unpublished.
Toward 1589 he wrote *Treatise on the Discovery of the Indies*
(*Tratado del descubrimiento de las Indias*) which is one of the
best pictures of Creole life in sixteenth-century New Spain. Of the
forty-four chapters, the first seventeen refer to the "origin and beginnings of the Indies and Indians" and to the conquest of Mexico.
His concept of the indigenous past, which is not original since he
is following Sahagún, Durán, Motolinía and others, is interesting
as an indication of what the first Creoles believed to be their own
historical background. The remaining twenty-seven chapters deal
with the years in which his family established itself in Mexico.
His father, who was a brother-in-law of Hernán Cortés, had been
a conquistador. Suárez' style becomes visual and vivid as he relates what he saw and what he lived through. For example, the
series of episodes that end with the execution of Avila are not
wanting in novelistic vigor. After the arrival of Martín Cortés,
Hernán's son, the gentlemen landowners squandered their estates
on feasts, games, extravagances, bullfights, hunting parties, ban-
quets, parades, etc. Philip II decided to put an end to so much
festivity by depriving the landowners of their economic privileges:
the *encomiendas*. It is the gaiety of the years of the viceroyalty
that Suárez de Peralta evokes with nostalgia. He delighted in telling anecdotes and liked to spice them with irony. It is easy to see
how a conquistador's son differs in spirit from a conquistador;
even more, how the spirit of the Creole is different from that of
the Spaniard. There is, here and there, a glimmer of sympathy for
the "Lutheran corsairs" of England. He speaks to us with pity
and even with sympathy for several soldiers, somewhat intoxi-
cated, who said jokingly that the people should kill all the Spanish
authorities and "rise up with the land." They were hanged, he
says, "guiltless." Suárez de Peralta is proud that there has not
been nor can there be until the day of judgment "another land like
Mexico." Since this was his fatherland, he wanted to keep it
forever in a festive mood.

The chronicler of Colombia and Venezuela was FRIAR PEDRO DE AGUADO
(d. after 1589), whose literarily colorless *History of Saint Martha and the
New Kingdom of Granada* (*Historia de Santa Marta y Nuevo Reino de*

Granada) relates "things that I have seen and touched with my hands."
All the more reason some of the things he relates should be exciting, as for
example that the Indians of New Granada, believing that the Spaniards were
cannibals invading the land in search of food, fought desperately. His
scenes of the tyranny of Aguirre in Margarita are hair-raising.

For Peru we could add new names to the list given in the preceding
chapter, both Spaniards and Creoles. Of interest is the *History of Peru*
(*Historia del Perú*) by DIEGO FERNÁNDEZ of Palencia, Spain, an unpolished
soldier, who arrived in Peru after the conquest. The details of events he
witnessed are well-worded in the second part, but in the first part he copied
previous reports. MIGUEL CABELLO BALBOA (Spain, 1530–1608) is delightful
in his descriptions of Inca lore, in *Southern Miscellany* (Miscelanea
Austral). He had a literary education. FRIAR REGINALDO DE LIZÁRRAGA
(Peru, *ca.* 1539–1609) in *Description and Population of the Indies* (*Descripción y población de las Indias*) gives an account of what he saw in his
travels through Peru, Tucumán, Río de la Plata, and Chile. It is a type of
traveler's guide, full of advice and practical information, but written with
perception, detail, simplicity and variety. His point of view is that of the
Spaniard—as he speaks of Creoles, Mestizos, and Indians his scorn increases
in degree. But Lizárraga, the son of a conquistador, feels the difference between the "old conquistadors" who founded a new nobility by dint of sacrifices and the "settlers who came after the land was cleared," who benefited
from the efforts of others and took possession of what did not belong to
them. He complains that the descendants of the old conquistadors are
spurned and replaced by newcomers who "don't even know how to blow
their noses, nor have they once in their lives reached for their swords." His
book represents the post-conquest society with the wounds of the civil war
not yet healed. FRIAR MARTÍN DE MURUA (d. 1616) left a *History of the
Origin and Genealogy of the Inca Kings of Peru* (*Historia del origen y
genealogía real de los Reyes Incas del Perú*). The Indian and mestizo
chroniclers, on their part, give us another interpretation of things. We do
not include PEDRO GUTIÉRREZ DE SANTA CLARA, a mestizo and the bastard
son of a conquistador, because he was born in Mexico (1521–1603) and in
his *History of the Civil Wars of Peru* (*Historia de las guerras civiles del
Perú*) he pretended to be an "eye witness." His sources were documentary,
but he disguised them to lend authority to his vast fund of fresh anecdotes.
He illustrated a history written by someone else. His descriptions, which are
good, are peppered with proverbs and ballads. No, we do not include him.
However, we *do* include FATHER BLAS VALERA (Peru, *ca.* 1538–1598) and
FELIPE GUAMÁN POMA DE AYALA (Peru, 1526?–d. after 1613). The latter,
in *The First New Chronicle and Good Government* (*El primer Nueva
Crónica y Buen Gobierno*), recounts the greatness of the Inca period and
the sufferings of the Indians during the colonization. He is a pessimist. According to him, fate buffets the Peruvians, and there is no help for this sad
state of affairs, nothing can be done about it! He is well informed and
scrutinizes conquerors and conquered from within. He does not conceal his
resentment toward the Church. Because he transcribed Quechua poems that
were sung or recited, he performed a service that neither Valera nor the
Inca Garcilaso achieved.

The Inca Garcilaso de la Vega / The most gifted of the mestizo writers is the INCA GARCILASO DE LA VEGA (Peru, 1539–1616). He descended from Inca and Castilian nobility (his mother was an Indian princess; his father a Spanish captain), and moreover, on his father's side, from a family illustrious in the history of letters. The fusion of these diverse racial and cultural worlds in his person was the point of departure in his career as a writer. At twenty-one years of age he went to Spain; he was destined not to return. A bastard, a mestizo, uprooted, on the fringes of society, the Inca Garcilaso made his way to the top of the European society of his time. He did it by uniting the diverse racial worlds of his background in his awareness of himself as a writer. He purified his mixed blood by resorting to writer's ink. He insisted on being known as a mestizo: "because it is a name that was given to us by our fathers, and because of what it means, I proclaim myself to be one wholeheartedly, and I feel honored to be one." He did not feel any racial handicap. Even though he was writing in Spain, in those years the physical traits that distinguished Mestizos and Spaniards neither added to nor detracted from their value as persons. He enjoyed privileges as the son of a commander, he immersed himself intimately in the life of Spain, and he was able to live without having to do manual work. The tone of humility in the introductions to his works was one that was customary among contemporary writers, and he knew it. He says, "In their prologs . . . I have noticed that . . . authors make apologies." His disillusions were those of any Spaniard who sought recompense in vain or who felt frustrated in his aspirations to military glory. He was not a mestizo who was uneasy about his Indian coloring, living with resentment and writing with bitterness. The fact is that as an Inca he was writing for both Indians and Spaniards "because I have been endowed by both nations." He was proud to be the descendant of a Spanish chieftain of the conquest of Seville, on his father's side (*The Genealogy of Garci Pérez de Vargas*) (*La Genealogía de Garci Pérez de Vargas*) and to be a noble American Indian, on his mother's side. But he decided to call himself "Inca" because this exotic name evoked the image of "the natural man," more innocent, more moral—in Renaissance eyes—than

European man, and because by so doing he put himself beyond the reach of hostile questions on "purity of blood" that maligned Spanish converts, whether Jewish or Moorish.

In 1590 he published a new translation of the *Dialoghi d'amore* by the Neoplatonist, Leon Hebreo, which he undertook for the delight of feeling penetrated by the Renaissance spirit of order and harmony. He decided to put into writing what he had heard from a friend of his, a veteran of the Hernando de Soto expedition to Florida (1539–1542). The result was: *Florida* (*La Florida del Inca*, 1605). He could not help coloring the accounts of his friend because his own literary tastes intervened, and one can discern influences of everything he had read. He had read Greek, Latin, and Renaissance historians, and with these examples in mind, he proposed to save heroic deeds from oblivion, to teach the truth, to enthuse readers with his artistic resources, and finally, to convert history into "a teacher of life" whose concrete program was conquest and Christianization. God was making use of Spain to conquer and Christianize. Consequently, Spanish imperialism was considered providential in origin, and the crown of Spain had a religious motive for extending its jurisdiction into the lands of Florida. The Inca, who had read the "portraits" written by his relative Pérez de Guzmán, imagined the psychological traits of his characters. He adorned the action, in classic fashion, with imaginary speeches. In fact, a good deal of imagination enters into his history. Since Aristotle, it had been repeated that poetry surpassed history because it recorded not only how things had happened but also how they should have happened. The Inca also believed in the dignity of fantasy. Of course, fictional events must approach truth and shy away from falsehood. And since the humanist of the Renaissance considered novels of chivalry false, the Inca, who had read them with pleasure in his youth, came later to consider them hateful.

The only legitimate stand was to believe in novels having an historical basis or in histories that incorporated novelistic elements. Yet, in his *Florida*, influences from the epic poems of Ariosto, Boiardo, and Ercilla appear, as well as episodes similar to those in Byzantine and Italian novels and in books of chivalry;

hence, his pages take on the brilliance of imagined adventure, with shipwrecks, long-lost people, sudden encounters, singular combats, the exploits of one hero against a prodigious host, Indians cut in two with one blow of a sword, imitations from classical antiquity, strange cities, exotic landscapes, sumptuous feasts, storms and misfortunes, descriptions of treasures, queens, palaces, arsenals and scenes which, in a false feudal framework, introduce Indians as "noble savages," eloquent in their feelings of honor. The written sources—chronicles, histories, poems—and the oral source of the friend who had participated in the expedition, gave him the facts; then he would embellish them. "I wrote the history of Florida, which indeed is florid, not in my own dry style but in the flower of Spanish prose," he said. While he was "tidying up" his *Florida* he was writing the *Royal Commentaries* (*Comentarios reales*), his most outstanding work. The first part was published in 1609; the second, finished four years later, was destined to be published after his death under the title *General History of Peru* (*Historia general del Perú*, 1617).

We have already said that in the chroniclers of the Indies what is of interest is the value of their personal perspectives, not the objective value of their historical reconstruction. However, in dealing with a chronicler of the standing of the Inca Garcilaso, we should be aware of the problem of his historical accuracy, even if only to dispense with it and, with a free mind, to study his imagination and his style. The Inca has been the target of three different critical fusillades, though the bullets join in flight and strike the bull's-eye. Those who disbelieve in the possibility of a great non-European civilization declare that the *Royal Commentaries* are "fairy tales," "a Utopian novel," not an historical text. Other historiographers of hypercritical heuristics and hermeneutics tear apart the mass of facts in the Inca's work with an analytical but uncomprehending attitude. A third group, in defense of the Spanish conquest and colonization, decides to discredit what they consider, erroneously, the Inca's Indian outlook.

In apposition to these disparagers, recent investigations are wont to corroborate Garcilaso in the order of events of the Inca conquests and in his geographic and historical exactness. Many of the legendary elements he uses were pointed out critically by the Inca himself: "and if some of the above-mentioned matters and others to be recorded seem fabulous, I bethought it proper that I not fail to write them down, so as not to remove the foundation upon which the Indians base the best and most grandiose events they relate concerning their empire." Be that as it may, one must not forget that Garcilaso was a reader of works of historical content and familiar with many kinds of historiography, from the scrupulously erudite to that embellished by humanism, including novelized historiography. His methods were advanced. He based his work on what he himself had seen and on traditions that had been passed on to him verbally. To complete these findings he exacted written reports from his fellow writers. He studied manuscripts and compared the observations of other chroniclers. He entitled his work *Commentaries* (*Comentarios*) because it was his intention to explain and correct the texts of Spanish historians. It is true that when he cites sources (which he does frequently) he does so to enhance his own version, which, in spite of his reference to sources, has great narrative ingenuity. But his notes are very painstaking and truthful. He took advantage of all available data, and he even made the science of linguistics an auxilliary to history—something new in those days.

The Inca was hurt that the Spaniards misunderstood the Indian culture because of their ignorance of the Quechua language. This idea that a language is a way of thinking and that only he who can speak it may delve into the country's "customs, rites and ceremonies" led him to write a cultural history: he is able to do it— he says—because he has learned Quechua from his "mother's breast." Even more, he proposed that Quechua should be taught part of a bilingual education. As a matter of fact, he never doubted in order to maintain the unity of the Indians. But this must be a the virtues of the Castilian language, which he enriched with his own prose precisely because he wanted it to thrive in the New World. Garcilaso yielded to the Utopian aspirations of his time without belittling his own direct knowledge of the real Peru. Some Spanish humanists: communal property, the indoctrination given of his notions about the ideal Inca regime he held in common with to barbarians, the benevolent paternalism of prince philosophers. Furthermore, Garcilaso was convinced of the fundamental one-ness of mankind. In spite of differences in race, climate, and era, psychologically all men were alike in his opinion. That was the reason the minds of the Indians of Peru had been inspired by myths similar to those of Europeans. "The Inca kings and their *amautas,* who were their philosophers, refract in a natural reful-gence the image of the true God and Our Lord." All religions are uniform in the light of this "natural refulgence." The cosmogonies of the Indians are related to those of the pagans and the Christians. And the Inca holds an interest for us because of parallel legends— that of the Deluge, for example.

The theme of the just war and evangelization, theoretical axis of his work, runs through the entire literary apparatus of those years. Garcilaso considered the conquest and colonization beneficial. History is a gift of providence. The Incas, in civilizing the crude people they had encountered, had prepared them for a higher civilization which the Spaniards were to bring centuries later. It was the same thing the Romans had done—they prepared the barbarians for the advent of Christianity. In other words, "Cuzco was another Rome in its own realm." There is beauty in the story of how the Sun sent his son, Manco Capac, down to earth from the sky to teach men to be rational instead of animals. Garcilaso's was the Christian concept of the moral dignity of man in harmony with God and the world. In his serenity there was something of the stoics whom he also read. He had need of stoicism undoubtedly, to overcome his sadness. He had suffered because of the civil wars in Peru; he had traveled the road from opulence to poverty, from high esteem to scorn. Perhaps he felt a certain indigenous fatalism. But his sadness (which rises like a tide to inundate many pages of the second part of his *Commentaries*) had much to do with his conception of history. He saw something tragic in history. But his disillusionment was not negative; he knew how to discover the enchantment of adverse destinies. The fact that he compares the end of the Incas to that of a "tragedy" (second part, Book VIII, Chapter XIX) indicates not only his concept of historic fatalism but also his artistic sensibility. He considered it a tragedy like that of Seneca, the Cordovan, whom Garcilaso read in Cordoba while writing his *Commentaries*.

In chapter XV of Book I of the first part he tells how he used to hear about Inca cosmogony from his mother, relatives, and elders. This passage is famous for its emotional evocation and for the vivacity of its prose in which not only does one hear the dialog, but one sees the gestures of those who speak.

The Inca takes pleasure in telling a story. Instead of giving us quick summaries, he enjoys dawdling in the successive scenes of his story. His syntactical equilibrium corresponds to the equilibrium of a thought process which clearly proceeds with symmetry and ordered constructions. In the swing of the pendulum from simple to complicated language, the style of the Inca swings to the simple side. His style is not one that was in vogue during the years in which he wrote, but was modeled on prose forms of the middle of the sixteenth century.

Furthermore, he followed the example of stylistic simplicity set by the chroniclers he had read: Cieza de León, Acosta, Gómara, Zárate, and Blas Valera. His completely natural syntax is without loose or ill-articulated components. He says: "My maternal language, which is that of the Incas; . . . my alien language, which is Castilian." Yet it was Castilian more than the language of his Indian mother that was his tongue. What an admirable prose! How polished and painstaking! What order and what care in the logical and clear presentation of his memoirs. He measured his work like an architect. And he felt the pleasure of dominating a rich cultural landscape from the vantage point of the mestizo who looks out from two historical planes—the Indian and the European. The artistic importance of his *Commentaries* is enhanced because it draws attention to this privileged personal perspective. He acts with art upon the reader. So that a particular chapter "not be too short" he includes the story of Serrano (chapter VIII) which is so similar to that of Robinson Crusoe.

There were other episodes similar to situations dealt with in masterpieces of Spanish literature; the story of the Inca Llora Sangre and Prince Viracocha calls to mind Calderon's *La vida es sueño*. And the story of Don Rodrigo Nuño and the galley-slaves of Peru brings memories of Cervantes' *Don Quixote*. Inca Garcilaso's image of the Spaniard he addresses and his need to make the New World intelligible explain his constant shifting between Indian and European categories.

Prosperous Lands and Poor Lands / Prosperity was not a condition equally shared in every colony. There was a rapid flowering in Mexico and Peru, and by the beginning of the seventeenth century these colonies offer a fairly rich cultural background, as we have seen. In other parts there was a decline, as in Santo Domingo; in others, as in Paraguay and the Río de la Plata, life was arduous. From this latter region a chronicler emerges somewhat belatedly who depicts the coarseness of life in those early times, the mestizo, RUIZ DÍAZ DE GUZMÁN (Paraguay, 1554?–1629). Unfortunately he did not leave us the chronicle of his own days as a conquistador. The work known as *Argentina in Manuscript* (*La Argentina manuscrita*) and finished by 1612 has come to us incomplete in several manuscripts (none of which is the original) with textual variants. Its contents concern the discovery and conquest of Río Plata provinces and are interrupted precisely in the years that the author intermingles with the men whose history he had written. He collects legends because he believes in them; and because he does believe, he tends to stamp a certain fabulous quality even on very real episodes. Is the episode of the woman Maldonada and the lioness, for example, a legend told as reality or reality told as a legend? This is a theme, reminiscent of Androcles and the Lion, whose first Castilian version comes from *The Book of Exemplary Tales* (*El libro de los ejemplos*) by Sánchez de Vercial written at the beginning of the fifteenth century. Another episode, the one about Lucia Miranda, the captive, was to have great vogue in the literature of the Río Plata. The Spaniards would take women from the Indians. The Indians did the same occasionally with Spanish women. This went on well up into the nineteenth century, and these scandals entered into poetry, theater, and the novel (Lavardén, Echeverría, Ascasubi, Hernández, Mansilla, Zorrilla de San Martín, etc.). Ruiz Díaz de Guzmán tells about pygmies, Amazons, miraculous interventions by saints, such as the one about Lucia Miranda. His sources are hearsay and his prose reflects the conversational style. Although a mestizo, his viewpoint is always that of the European side of his family.

Epic Literature

Ercilla / Some chronicles became literature. And there was literature that had value as chronicle, for example, that of ALONSO DE ERCILLA Y ZÚÑIGA (1534–1594). The bloodiest episodes in Peru were not between Spaniard and Indian, but between Spaniard and Spaniard. A group of men who descended from Peru to Chile clashed with the warrior tribes of the Araucanians; whence emerged the first epic poem of America, Ercilla's *La Araucana*. During the Renaissance there were epics that imitated the classics (Pierre de Ronsard), novelistic epics that recounted deeds of medieval knights (Ariosto, Boiardo, Balbuena), religious Christian epics (Milton), and epics on contemporary heroic events (Camoens, Ercilla).

Ercilla, one of Philip II's courtiers, already possessed a good literary education when he arrived in America at the age of twenty-one. "I have passed many climes, I have moved under many constellations," he says. And what he saw and imagined in Chile he glorified in the octaves of his epic poem *La Araucana*. It is a chronicle, no doubt, but quite different from all those mentioned up to now, since what is of most value in it is its esthetic nature. In *Apollo's Laurel* (*Laurel de Apolo*) Lope de Vega pegged him well: "Don Alonso de Ercilla bears such wealth of the Indies in his genius / that he comes all the way from Chile / to enrich the muse of Castile." In other words, the point is that the Indies are part of the genius of Ercilla, not that Ercilla is part of the reality of the Indies. The Indies have their source in Ercilla, not Ercilla in the Indies. They are his own phenomena, springing from his writer's mind and imagination.

La Araucana emerged in the evolution of the epic genre as a specimen of rare plumage. It was the first work in which the author appears as an actor in the epic he describes; it was the first work that lent epic dignity to events still in process; it was the first work that immortalized with an epic the founding of a modern nation; it was the first work of real poetic quality that centered around America; it was also the first work in which the author, caught in the midst of a conflict between ideals of truth and ideals of poetry, laments the poverty of the Indian theme and the monotony of the warrior theme, revealing at the same time the intimate process of his artistic creation. It may be that *La Araucana* will not soar as high as *Orlando Furioso, Jerusalem Liberated,* and *The Lusiades,* but it did fly high on its own wings. In the flutter of epics that filled Hispanic skies—Lope de Vega's *Jerusalem Conquered (Jerusalém conquistada),* Valbuena's *Bernardo,* Hojeda's *Cristiada*—*La Araucana* fluttered magnificently. Ercilla arrived from Spain with a mind already formed by Renaissance literature, by theology, and by juridical discussions on the conquest of the New World. While he fought, he wrote. But his poetry was not dictated by what transpired. Proof of this lies in the fact that the twenty-two cantos relating events he had lived through are no better than the fifteen that refer to happenings prior to his arrival. The poetry flowed from his Renaissance Spanish soul—reader of Vergil, Lucano, and Ariosto, soldier of the Catholic kingdom of Philip II, and enemy of the Indian (not because of greed, but because the Indian was an enemy of his faith). Yet he turned America into poetry with extraordinary descriptive precision in his narration of epic episodes, in his character sketches, in nearly one hundred comparisons exaggerated in the traditional epic style (but much more monotonous because of the predominance of zoological images. Comparisons with mythological themes are less abundant). There are a few metaphors that are surprising because they stem from new perceptions. What Ercilla did not describe was the Chilean landscape.

More memorable than the combats in Lope's *Jerusalem* or Valbuena's *Bernardo* are those of Lautaro, Tucapel, and Rengo. Ercilla relates them clearly and at length. He even gives character to his Indians (the generous Lautaro, the savages Tucapel and Rengo, the heroic Galvarino, the courageous Caupolicán). As Homer admired Hector, Tasso Saladin, and Boiardo Agricane, so Ercilla admires his enemies. This is a literary trait, a Spanish trait; nevertheless, the Chileans are free to consider *La Araucana* a national poem. When Ercilla tired of the New World he would escape into love scenes, prophecies, supernatural apparitions, lyrical dreams, embellished mythological stories, imaginary voyages. This weakens the unity of epic construction on the one hand, but on the other, it converts *La Araucana* into one of the most complex poems of Golden Age literature. Following Lucan's example, Ercilla gave the most immediate events epic proportions, and the scenes of wizardry and marvels do not break the line of historical truthfulness because, after all, they formed part of the folklore and literature of the sixteenth century. "A true history" it is; except that Ercilla was a poet and a reader of all that the Spaniards read in his day, not only the authors already mentioned, but dozens more (the Italians from Dante to Sannazzaro, the Spaniards from Juan de Mena to Garcilaso de la Vega) and his poetry has all the grace of the Renaissance. The three parts of *La Araucana* appeared successively in 1569, 1578, and 1589; and for the first time Spain felt that America had a literature.

La Araucana's Sequels / There were continuations, imitations, and emulations, and *La Araucana* became part of the body of the great literature of all times. The influence of the poem, especially in America, was deep and long-lasting, and not confined to epic poetry. In the field of epic poems having New World themes, there sprouted *Arauco Tamed* (*El arauco domado*, 1596) by the Chilean PEDRO DE OÑA; *Purén Untamed* (*Purén indómito*) by HERNANDO ALVAREZ DE TOLEDO (b. 1550); *Elegies of Illustrious Men of the Indies* (*Elegías de varones ilustres de Indias*) by JUAN DE CASTELLANOS; *Antarctic Wars* (*Armas antárticas*, written between 1608 and 1615) by JUAN DE MIRAMONTES Y ZUÁZOLA, a soldier who took part in the struggle against the pirate Cavendish and sang about America with the dash and imagination of a poet trained in the finest techniques of the epic of the golden century. *Wars of Chile* (*Guerras de Chile*, 1610) attributed to JUAN DE MENDOZA MONTEAGUDO; and those poems inspired by the conquest of New Spain: *The New World and Its Conquest* (*Nuevo mundo y conquista*, ca. 1580) by FRANCISCO DE TERRAZAS; *Intrepid Cortés* (*Cortés valeroso*, 1588) and *Mexicana* (1594) by GABRIEL LOBO LASSO DE LA VEGA; *History of the New Mexico* (*Historia de la nueva Mexico*, 1610) by GASPAR PÉREZ DE VILLAGRA; *Pilgrim of the Indies* (*Peregrino indiano*, 1599) by ANTONIO DE SAAVEDRA GUZMÁN (b. before 1570). This *Pilgrim of the Indies* is a kind of rhymed diary of the military operations of Hernán Cortés, from the time he left for Cuba until the conquest of Mexico. Sometimes the epic tone is sweetened by the rhetoric of love.

When we think of *La Araucana* all the other poems seem mediocre (with the exception of Oña's). With *La Araucana* at the top of the epic ladder, we place on a very low rung the *Argentina* (1602) by MARTÍN DEL BARCO

CENTENERA (1544–1605). He follows models of medieval didactic poetry
more than Ercilla does, and hence there is an archaic air even in his versification, which is irregular. Without a breath of poetry he versifies his recollections of adversities and failures suffered in the region of the Río de la
Plata. He is a realist in certain episodes, but his attitude is not critical. He
prefers truculent exaggeration, accentuated violence. What remained alive
of his mediocre poem was its name, *Argentina*, an imitation of names like
Araucana, Aeneid, Iliad. He did not invent it, but his insistence on the poetic
adjective "argentine" and its noun form "the Argentine" as a name of the
river and country was the origin of the modern name of the Republic. As
easily as these poems submit to "true history," they escape into the novelistic, the fantastic, and even the allegoric, following the manner of Boiardo
and Ariosto.

The State of Literature

Those who advanced literature in America knew very well that
their voices were being lost in its echoless deserts. Some Spaniards
who never came here generously praised the intellectual life of the
Indies. It was a kind of courtesy, a building of credit for the future,
a desire to improve matters. Francisco Sánchez in *Quod nihil
scitur* (1581) said: "How much ignorance prevailed up to now
in the Indies! Now little by little they are becoming more religious,
more keen, more cultured than ourselves." And years later Cervantes in *Voyage of Parnassus* (*Viaje del Parnaso*, 1614) and
Lope in *Apollo's Laurel* (1630) will also make generous references to Hispanic-American writers. But, could the Spaniards
imagine what was happening in the minds of their colleagues in
the colonies? Could they measure the determination that the colonial writers needed in order to overcome so much discourage-
ment? Their solitude, their timidity in taking the initiative, the
lack of stimulus, the material obstacles in printing and marketing
books, made them look humbly upon the great literary production
of Spain. When Nebrija wrote his *Grammar* he believed that the
Castilian language had reached its fullest development. These
were the years of the *Celestina* and of the discovery of America.
But the Spaniards who came to America and their children, either
Creoles or mestizos, realized that in Spain literature continued to
develop. In 1492 the speech of the expelled Spanish Jews remained static in its pre-classical mold, but the speech of the Spaniards who came to America that very year continued its historic

life. Hispanic-America did not remain a pre-classical linguistic
province because the conquest and colonization were realized
in the epoch of Garcilaso and Fray Luis, of Cervantes, Lope, and
Quevedo. From 1520 to 1600 Hispanic-American society became
established. Yet the steady flow of Spanish population (which
was to continue in the seventeenth and eighteenth centuries)
continuously displayed the horizon of literary glories of Spain.
There was undoubtedly some Creole resentment against the Spaniard. A satiric sonnet of the last half of the sixteenth century cited
by Baltasar Dorantes de Carranza in *Brief Report of New Spain*
(*Sumaria relación de las cosas de la Nueva España*, 1604) protested against the new arrival who "comes from Spain over the
briny sea / to our Mexican homeland / an unsponsored boor
/ wanting in health and deficient in money," and who "afterwards
despises the place where he acquired esteem, good taste and property."

However, in spite of this resentment, the colonial writers found
Spain's literature seductive. For this reason, alongside the ballads,
folk songs, and carols, a pretentious literature emerged: Latin
verses and dialogs (like those of Francisco Cervantes de Salazar);
Italianate and Petrarchan sonnets in the manner of Garcilaso and
Gutierre de Cetina (like those of Francisco de Terrazas, already famous in 1577); epic poems (like those of Ercilla and his descendants); and a kind of fifteenth-century verse in the manner of
Jorge Manrique (like those of Pedro de Trejo, who practiced all
genres and styles and even innovated meters and strophes). There
were so many poetry competitions that González de Eslava says in
one of his *Colloquies:* "There are more poets than manure." Indeed not even Vergil could have extracted one verse of gold from
that manure—"*de estercore Ennii.*" The gold was in Spain, and
prosists and versifiers, feeling literarily poor, were dazzled by
the distant glitter. An anonymous Latinist, upon dedicating his
version of *Brief Meditations* (*Meditatiunculae*) to Cortés' second
wife, said to her: "I willingly did what I could in the translation of
this book; if my vernacular is not as polished as that weaved by
some Castilian rhetoricians, one should not marvel; after so many
years of roaming about these barbaric nations and lands, where

one deals more in the language of the Indians than in Spanish, and where one who is not a barbarian among barbarians is considered a barbarian, it is not surprising that I should forget the elegance of the Castilian tongue." When they could, they went to Spain and there they would write and publish their works.

The manuscript *Flower of Sundry Poetry* (*Flores de varia Poesía*) compiled in Mexico, is dated 1577. It is anonymous, although it is believed that Juan de la Cueva was one of its compilers or that it was he who took it to Spain. Here is a mixture of verse written by peninsular Spaniards, by Spaniards living in America, and even by Creoles (Terrazas, Carlos de Sámano, Martín Cortés, Juan de la Cueva, Gutierre de Cetina, Juan Luis de Ribera, González de Eslava, etc.). There were writers then, by the carload, albeit they were insignificant. Rosas de Oquendo, in his *"Sonnet to Lima"* (*"Soneto a Lima"*), satirizes "Poets by the thousands, of scanty wit." We have already said that to write was an irresistible collective yearning. Not only did writers write, but they wrote about writers. Juan de Castellanos, about whom we have already spoken, left a gallery of illustrious men of the pen. A very incomplete list of Peruvian writers may be found in DIEGO DE AGUILAR Y CÓRDOBA's *The Marañón River* (*El Marañón*, 1538) and in the anonymous *Discourse in Praise of Poesy* (*Discurso en loor de la poesía*). EUGENIO DE SALAZAR Y ALARCÓN (1530?–1608?), a poet from Madrid, who wrote in verse about a "description of the lake of Mexico" (*"descripción de la laguna de México"*), telling how Neptune, to come to know this country, dug a subterranean path and burst out in the center of the valley, forming this lake, collected data on the intellectual life of Santo Domingo in his *Miscellany of Poetry* (*Silva de poesía*). Thanks to him there are preserved five sonnets and some blank verse by the earliest known poetess of the New World—the religious LEONOR DE OVANDO (d. after 1609), who possessed this intense vision of the "divine Spouse of my soul": "who suffered only to give me life; / And I know that for me alone he would suffer / And that he would redeem only me / if in this world he created me alone."

In a history of church oratory FRIAR ALONSO DE CABRERA (*ca.* 1549–1606) would have to stand out. Because of the artistic force of his words he also belongs to the history of literature. As a preacher his attitude was original, and the prose of his sermons is equally original. Instead of stringing out his sentences, as was customary in his age, he wrote brief, simple phrases, constructing them with clarity and enriching them with anecdotes of popular customs.

Satire

The times were just right for satire. It was carried on many lips, especially those of MATEO ROSAS DE OQUENDO (Seville?, 1559?; he probably came to America in 1585; in 1621 he was still living in Lima). A tireless traveler—from Argentina to Mexico—he belittled everything he saw. In his long "Satire of Things that Occur in Peru in 1598" (*"Sátira a las cosas que pasan en el Perú, año de 1598"*) he described a small segment of colonial society; his most violent verses were against women of doubtful morals and impostors. He despised the poor who, upon arriving in America, gave themselves airs of nobility while in reality they were the offspring of ordinary laborers. His having indulged in the very vices that he ridicules gives his autobiographical passages a picaresque tone not lacking in overtones of "baroque naturalism." He also wrote satires during his Mexican period. In his "A Gallant's Satire to a Creole Lady who Praised Mexico to Him" (*"Sátira que hizo un galán a una dama criolla que le alababa mucho a México"*) he gives vent to his ever-growing Spanish resentment against Creole life. Nevertheless, one can notice that after living many years in the colonies, his animosity against the Creole and his initial European arrogance slackened. In Mexico he managed to express some enthusiasm. With the passing years it seems the New World endeared itself to him.

Theater

As they conquered or founded cities, the Spaniards transplanted European cultural organization. The Spaniards carried their institutions to all the conquered lands, and everywhere chroniclers and even writers emerged. But the capitals of the first two viceroyalties, Mexico and Lima, were the centers of a more alert, complete, and continuous civilization. They even possessed a theater. As Agustín de Rojas observed in *Pleasant Journey* (*Viaje entretenido*, 1603) Juan del Encina began to write plays "during the days that Columbus discovered the great wealth of the Indies and the New World." In reality Juan del Encina was not "the father of the Spanish drama"; rather, with the presentation of the double eclogue during the Christmas of 1492, he became its secularizer. And the theater came to America.

We have already said that the first missionary theater was disappearing in the second half of the sixteenth century. The expurgation of its profane elements made by the Church, the change in customs, the growth of the cities, university and humanistic tastes, all contributed to opening the way for a European-patterned theater. The Latinist tradition of the Church colleges—allegorical dialogs on sacred themes, plays and tragedies in Latin or partly in Latin represented by the collegers in cloisters—was brought to Mexico and Lima by the Jesuits. Little has remained of this scholastic theater, an example being the inferior five-act tragedy, *Triumph of the Saints* (*Triunfo de los santos*, Mexico, 1578), attributed to Father Juan Sánchez Baquero and Father Vincencio Lanucci. The theme of Diocletian's persecution of the Church and the triumph under Constantine is versified in the Renaissance and Italianate manner, but it has little value. In addition to the missionary and scholastic theater, there was another type available to Spaniards and Creoles. The latter attended ecclesiastical ceremonies, processions, entertainments, receptions for viceroys, pageantries, dances, and liturgical pieces—skits, interludes, preludes, mysteries, and even plays and tragedies with Biblical or allegorical themes—presented on stages that were becoming more and more secular. This theater suffered from the competition of the Renaissance Spanish theater, not only because of the repertory but also from the presence of theatrical companies from Spain. In 1565 publishing houses in Spain began producing collections of plays that were quickly sent to America, and it is possible that the Spanish play enacted in 1568 in Guayaquil was taken from one of these volumes. In 1599 the first Lope de Vega play was presented in Lima. Local plays were also written. The little that has been saved of this Creole theater is a prose interlude by CRISTÓBAL DE LLERENA (Santo Domingo, 1540—dead by 1627) presented in Santo Domingo in 1588. This satire of the public administration earned Llerena's expulsion from the island.

We are more familiar with the activities in Mexico of HERNÁN GONZÁLEZ DE ESLAVA (1534–1601), author of sixteen colloquies, eight preludes, four interludes, and some miscellaneous poetry. It is a pity that his earthy pieces have been lost, because the one extant, the *Interlude between Two Ruffians* (*Entremés entre dos rufianes*), which is more short story than theater—in the form of two successive soliloquies connected by a few gestures —reveals a certain humor. He was a good versifier, at times excellent, ingenious, facile, but stifled by the many compromises with viceroyal and ecclesiastical authorities. The blame was not exclusively his. All who wrote for the festivals of the Corpus Christi and for the court feasts had to submit to an established set of theological and political rules. Furthermore, the Inquisition read all plays prior to their performance. González de Eslava condescended and, consequently, his colloquies move in a void, like the movement of a loom on which nothing is woven. He tended toward realism (that is why it is lamentable that his non-ecclesiastical pieces have been lost), but he translated his vision of reality in allegories having no dramatic force. It was a sort of journalism in which the outstanding events of colonial life were reported in empty and pretentious language. The viceroy orders the construction of seven forts as a defense against the attacks of the Chichimeca Indians? González de Eslava writes a colloquy converting the forts into the seven sacraments and the voyage of merchants from Mexico to Zacatecas into the voyage from earth to heaven. A textile factory for woolens is established? He has Penance spinning the wool of the Divine Lamb in the mill-church. At times, as in the *Colloquy of the Count of Coruña* (*Coloquio del Conde de la Coruña*, composed in 1580 upon the viceroy's arrival to Mexico), the allegorization is insincere, art-less, and without austerity. The Count's entrance into Mexico symbolizes the entrance of God into the Soul. God equals King, and Count Coruña equals Christ because (and notice to what levels this pseudoreligious palace descends!) Count signifies companion which is what Christ is, and Coruña is made up of *"Cor,"* heart, and *"uña,"* claw, which pulls us away from sin. Because of its Hispanic-American linguistic medium and its observations on history and customs, this theater is of more interest to philologists than to theater-lovers. Even its clear and well-constructed verses tell us little. In the *Colloquy of the Four Doctors of the Church* (*Coloquio de los cuatro doctores de la Iglesia*), for example, the following lessons in Church doctrine are given to two shepherds: The Eucharist, the virginity of Mary, Christ's redemption of man, and the reason for the irredeemable fallen angels, together with the usual inquisitorial threats of burning, torturing, knifing and persecuting whoever does not believe to the last word the lessons of the four theologians. From a theatrical point of view it is a pure conceptual game. The verses play in the void with nothing new to say and without being able to say anything new.

González de Eslava was a Mexican by naturalization. The first Mexican by birth in theater history was JUAN PÉREZ RAMÍREZ (1545?), author of the allegorical play in verse form, *Spiritual Marriage between the Shepherd Peter and the Mexican Church* (*Desposorio espiritual entre el Pastor Pedro y la Iglesia Mexicana*, 1574). It has been said that the Spaniard, Juan de la Cueva, who lived in Mexico (1574–77), learned a few things from this Ramírez before returning to Spain to open the way that led to the theater of Lope de Vega. We need not concern ourselves with Juan de la Cueva here. The only thing in his work that we can classify as American is a view of the Mexican landscape in his epistles.

The Jesuits of Asunción in Paraguay held spectacular theatricals, especially in the Corpus Christi procession, in which they merged Indian rites and ecclesiastical themes with allegorical dances, pantomimes in costume, scenes of St. Michael fighting with a dragon or Christians fighting Moors or angels fighting demons. They also composed mystery plays and colloquies. The oldest record is about a play dated 1596 composed by the Jesuit, ALONSO DE BARZANA (1528–1598), an expert in Indian languages. Sometimes plays were composed combining the Spanish, Latin and Guarani languages.

III. 1598-1701

Authors born between 1570 and 1675

Historical framework: The colonies under the decadence of the last Hapsburgs: Philip III, Philip IV, and Charles II. Loss of American possessions.

Cultural tendencies: From the Renaissance to the Baroque. Literary plenitude.

Introduction

Despite political and economic decadence, Spanish literature was extraordinarily enriched by a new vigor. In the first years of the seventeenth century, with the work of the geniuses, Cervantes and Lope de Vega, the apogee of the Renaissance is reached. Both authors' lives begin in a period of splendor, but in their last years they experience the Spanish decadence. The national crisis is revealed in what is called the Baroque style which, if not new, is now consolidated and dominant.

Born during the last years of the Council of Trent or shortly thereafter, these baroque authors found themselves in possession of a great literature that had run its course, and at the same time they were facing a void, since Spain had turned its back on the ebullient and vital culture of the rest of Europe. There was bitterness, anguish, resentment, disillusionment, fear, pessimism, and at the same time national pride; there was resignation to being out of step with the life and thought of the world, yet a desire to attract the world's attention and wonder by the use of language of great affectation. The equilibrium of the soul was broken, and literary endeavor grotesquely cultivated the ugliness of things (as in Mateo Alemán) or gave itself over to forms that were obscure for the uninitiated, difficult even for the cultured few. Although Góngora enjoyed the benefits of classical erudition, he rejected classical clarity and wished to complicate his language so that, like Latin, it might be "worthy of persons capable of understanding it," that it might be a cultist art for the elite who take pleasure in the ingenious speculative effort and guesswork involved in solving intricate stylistic difficulties. Quevedo, although in another direction, took on with the same expenditure of ingeniousness a style called "conceptist," in which logic takes delight in its own agility rather than in its movement to a conclusion. In Gracián, philosophy was also an activity in a linguistic sphere beyond the reach of the masses, where subtleness is more valuable for being subtle than for being true.

Alongside the great prosists—to whom we should add Saavedra Fajardo—the seventeenth century gave us the great poetic theater. Lope has already been mentioned. We may add Tirso, Mira de Amescua, Alarcón, and finally Calderón de la Barca, the last great figure of the "golden age." After the death of Calderón in 1680, only a few scarce embers remain kindled, more ash than fire.

The Baroque Comes to America / In this period the colonies, as always, received all that Spain gave them. Immediately after being published, the *Quixote* and the *Guzmán de Alfarache* embarked for America. The plays of Lope also arrived. And on occasion the writers themselves came. Cervantes was not allowed to come, but among the most famous men who did come were Gutierre de Cetina, Juan de la Cueva, Mateo Alemán, Tirso de Molina. Luis Belmonte Bermudez was to write his twenty-five plays only after his return to Spain. Francisco de Lugo y Dávila, Governor of Chiapas in the Vicerealm of New Spain, published his *Theatre of the People* (*Teatro popular*) in Madrid in Spain in 1622, "moral novels" after the style of Cervantes. These were only visitors and their influence was very vague. Mateo Alemán, who wrote "Incidents in the Life of Fray García Guerra, Archbishop of Mexico" ("Sucesos de Fray García Guerra, Arzobispo de México," 1613) and a treatise on orthography to which he seems to have given more importance than to his *Guzmán de Alfarache*. Even the vice-roys devoted themselves to poetry, as in Peru did Juan de Men-doza y Luna, Marquis of Montesclaros (1571–1628) and the Prince of Esquilache (1581–1658).

Catalogs, libraries, and bookstores yield a surprising quantity of poetry, fiction, theater, and history. In the private library of a single obscure Mexican there were, in 1620, Latin authors (Ver-gil, Cicero); Italian (Boccaccio, Aretino, Boza Candioto, Sanna-zaro, Ariosto, Tasso); Portuguese (Camoens); and, naturally, Spanish (Ercilla, *La Celestina*, López de Enciso, Antonio de Guevara, Lorenzo Palmireno, and poetic anthologies like López de Ubeda's *Garden of Divine Flowers* (*Vergel de Flores Divinas*, 1582), and Pedro Espinosa's *Flower of Illustrious Poets of Spain* (*Flores de poetas ilustres de España*, 1605). Another Mexican, Pérez de Soto, born in 1608, who was brought out of obscurity by an inquisitorial trial, had in his library 1,663 volumes in vari-ous languages, one-fifth of which was in *belles lettres*—two dozen pastoral, chivalric, and picaresque novels, collections of short stories (for example, those of *Conde Lucanor*), writings of Eras-mus, *La Celestina*, epic and lyrical poetry by Greek, Roman, Renaissance, and baroque (Góngora, of course) writers. A list of books being sold by a Mexican shop in 1683 is equally informa-tive: among the 276 titles are *El Lazarillo* and works by Góngora, Lope, Calderón, Rojas Zorrilla, Cervantes, Quevedo, Pedro Mexía, Pérez de Montalbán, and Gonzalo de Céspedes.

Literature was also forming part of the gay open-air fiestas. In a "game of rings" (*juego de sortijas*) celebrated in Peru in 1607 (in the manner described by Luis Gálvez de Montalvo in *The Shepherd of Fílida—El Pastor de Fílida*) several horsemen cos-tumed as Don Quixote and other knights-errant marched out in review. In 1621 in Mexico, in a "*mascarada*," or street proces-sion on foot or on horseback, where persons parade, symbolizing figures from mythology, history, and theology, there were famous knights-errant from novels, like Amadís, Palmerín, Don Quixote, as well as Sancho, Dulcinea, and other personages.

In general, the colonies were even more conservative than the metropolis. Europe had become divided by the Reformation and the Counter Reformation, and Spain was the center of orthodoxy. Great changes were occurring, especially in the countries of the north; in the course of a few decades constellations of non-Hispanic minds were to revolutionize the image of the world with a philosophy based on the free exercise of reason and on the experimental study of nature. Meanwhile Spain, wedded to scholasticism, eyes glued to revelation and authority, would continue to live in the illusion of a stable world; and to keep the colonies static as well, Spain reinforced its intransigence there. Although the colonies were very far from Europe and only a handful of Spaniards and Creoles could read or write, lost as they were in immense expanses of land or surrounded by masses of Indians, there were some who broke out of the encirclement and became familiar with contemporary ideas of Descartes and others. These Creoles, like Sigüenza y Góngora and Sor Juana, who were stirred up by the new science, were exceptions to the scholastic verbalism that dominated the seminaries and the universities. The feudal society in which they lived obligated the Creoles to hide their resentment and adulate the ruling-class Spaniards with ceremonies, verses, triumphal arches, lavish shows, and literary competitions of "conceptist" skill. We find progressive and retrogressive movements; conflicts between the beliefs of the Middle Ages and new facts; insecurity, fear, daring, and timidity; illusion and deceit; impulse to action and a withdrawing into the soul; a lust for life and an obsession with death; dryness of style and astonishing florescence of ornamentation, all moving to and fro in the lands of America. To orient himself to these modes of life, today's historian must place road signs at the two extremities of this period: Renaissance and baroque.

Plan

It is significant that this century is so cleanly cut by two literary geniuses, both born in America: the Renaissance prose writer, Inca Garcilaso de la Vega and the baroque poetess, Sor Juana Inés de la Cruz. We studied the former, because of his age, in the previous chapter; although, considering the dates of his writing, he would fit well here. Sor Juana marks the end of the century, if not of this chapter.

How can the subject matter of this chapter be organized? By styles, from Renaissance to baroque? By birthdates of the authors? By nations, from Mexico to Argentina? By a scale of excellence from Alarcón and Sor Juana? By prose and verse forms? None of these criteria would manage to unravel the disorder of so much uneven and scattered literary activity. Even groupings by genres, which is what we will attempt, will be unsatisfactory, because there were writers who cultivated more than one, and there were cases of hybrid genres.

A. MAINLY POETRY

Some of the chroniclers already reviewed used to interpolate verses in their chronicles or would scribble them in the margin. Ripples of poetry in a sea of prose. The theater also may be considered poetry since it was written in verse. This section, then, cannot be rigidly considered as the only storehouse of poetry. Yet, we shall see the great poets of this period. However, in order to see them in their proper perspective, we shall have to mention many versifiers who left little poetic deposit. And since these poets are also prosists, how can we avoid speaking of prose again? The literary historian tries to divide the waters, but they insist on joining again.

BERNARDO DE BALBUENA (Spain–Mexico, 1561 or 1562–1627) lived during exactly the same years as Góngora; and like Góngora, he felt the necessity of inventing an affected, ornamental, and aristocratic form of expression. But, although he Gongorized at times (in 1604 he said: "in what part of the world have poets been known as worthy of veneration as the poignant don Luis de Góngora?") Balbuena's baroque style was independent; at least it ran unbridled, now this way, now that, along a course filled with a wide variety of styles, which at the end of the sixteenth and the beginning of the seventeenth century opened out on a field of

Spanish letters where virtuosos of the language displayed their talents. For here is the discovery of the baroque writers: language is a sovereign body that can writhe, leap, become immobile in an enigmatic gesture, suddenly open its arms and give forth metaphors, then draw itself in to assume obscure conceptual attitudes, always replete with adornment, always proud of not being commonplace language. The very first octave Balbuena offered a lady as a description of the city of Mexico were the eight seeds from which the chapters of *Grandeur of Mexico* (*Grandeza mexicana*, 1604) grew. Each verse would serve as a heading to a chapter. In this way, the *Grandeur of Mexico* emerged as though in a nursery, not with large forest trees, but rather with delicate garden plants. Balbuena wishes to please—in the first place, the lady to whom he dedicates the poem, and also the powerful persons in Mexico. He has been living as a humble village priest for many years; in this moment of his life, perhaps unhappy about his own obscurity, he begins to praise the city in which he would like to occupy a better position. Descriptions of Mexico already existed in the current prose of the chroniclers, in the incidental verses of minor poets, and in the Latin dialogs of Cervantes de Salazar. Now Balbuena gives us a description in the baroque manner, "ciphered," he says, that is, constructed intelligently in one small poetic unity. He had the epic gift, as proven by the *Bernardo* (1624), a baroque variation on a theme by Ariosto, but in the *Grandeur of Mexico* he avoids the epic of the conquest. It is more garden than forest, but a garden with tall plants or, rather, a greenhouse garden that seems immense because we see it through the magnifying glasses of baroque style (an erudite garden, too, because at intervals its plants come from Vergil and others). We are not given the poetry of the minuscule, of the humble, of the simple, but rather a view of court luxury, of the "grandeur of Mexico," which was only the exterior aspect of the Mexican reality. The structure of that "grandeur" is clear: there are not as many turns of expression, conceits or images as we find in Góngora and in Quevedo; but although his imagination does not twist the axes of reality, he covers them with embellishments. His inventive style is found in these embellishments; at times it is so

energetic that the embellishment acquires a complete and autonomous beauty, ceases to be an embellishment functioning for an
underlying phrase, and becomes pure poetry in and out of itself,
sheer opulence of elegant language, delight in description and
daring in fantasy. Clarity of construction is a Renaissance trait.
Balbuena writes his epistle in hendecasyllabic tercets with quatrains at the end of each part, following the Italian tradition of
poems of chivalry, this clarity of construction making the value of
those isolated moments of artistic invention more visible. In his
esthetic ideals he followed the Italians more than the Spaniards.
His pastoral novel, *The Golden Age in the Forest of Eriphyle*
(*Siglo de Oro en las selvas de Erífile*), written in Mexico around
1585–90, but published in Spain in 1608, skips over the Spanish
Dianas and Galateas to dive happily into the Italian source:
Sannazaro's *Arcadia*. In Balbuena's eyes the pastoral world is
already an empty one. Its myths and symbols have lost their content, their intellectual force. On the other hand, they remain as
artistic forms. He imitated Sannazaro precisely because he saw
him from a great distance, in an esthetic perspective. As in Sannazaro, his descriptive elements prevail over the narrative. The
shepherds, after singing their joys and sorrows, with all their
thoughts devoted to the absent shepherdesses, withdraw incon-
spicuously to one side. While the action calms down, the landscapes come into view dressed with all the luxuriance of a
baroque-colored fantasy. It is classical literary tradition that
moves Balbuena, but his vitality lies in the filigree. He is attracted
by the unreal, the contrived, the artful. He described the city of
Mexico, but within a dream and guided magically by a nymph.
Hills, plains, woods, caves, and rivers all belong to an ideal geography. It is a fugue in which verse pursues prose and the supernatural the natural. The language of metaphors, mythological
allusions, allegories, dreams, and incredible dialogs ends up by
evading reality, leaving in its wake barely a trace of art.

Gongorism in Mexico / Góngora's influence in Mexico was earlier, better, and greater than anywhere else in Hispanic-America.
It is possible that manuscript copies of *Polifemo* and the *Soledades*

may have circulated in Mexico before they were published in Spain. Be that as it may, Góngora entered Mexico around 1600, in the shipments of *Romanceros* and *Flower of Illustrious Poets* (*Flores de poetas ilustres*). We have already seen how in Balbuena there were manifestations of Gongorism, although they were tenuous, since his cultism was personal and independent. As the seventeenth century wears on, the Mexican Gongorists multiply: Miguel de Guevara, Salazar y Torres, Arias de Villalobos, Francisco de Castro, Ramírez de Vargas, De la Llana, and hundreds more. We have already mentioned the much anthologized and imitated "Song at the Sight of a Disillusion" by Matías de Bocanegra. Of the work of LUIS DE SANDOVAL Y ZAPATA (fl. 1645) only vestiges remain, but among these fragments are splendid poetic flowers like the sonnet "Winged Eternity of the Wind" (*"Alada eternidad del viento"*). In him, more than in anyone else, lovely fantasy and rigorous geometry combine in resourceful forms. The recent re-evaluation of Góngora has wrought changes in the judgment on numerous Hispanic-American Gongorists. Undoubtedly most of them amused themselves by constructing formal complicated works, but one could not expect to find a beautiful surprise at the end of each of their poetic labyrinths as one could in Góngora. The poets wanted to display ingenuity in their concepts and culture in their images. They abhorred a vacuum and they tried to fill the hollowness of their times (in which energies were in tension but repressed) with baroque deceptions. Once minds became excited by the interplay of pure forms, they could no longer stop, and at times did not even attempt poetry. Instead they constructed rebuses, riddles, conundrums, and feats of letter combinations; reversible poems to be read up and down, and down and up; the same letters arranged in different words; disconnected letters which acquired meaning through their sounds; systematic display of all the letters of the alphabet; puns and other plays on words; compositions in which every word begins with the same letter; *centos* composed of unrelated fragments; echoes and double echoes; compositions, which, losing neither meaning nor rhyme, could be read three ways, in their totality and, also, split into two independent series;

quatrains glossed, verse by verse, with four successive ten-line stanzas; acrostics further complicated by the use of glosses, and so on. However, in this literature of misguided effort there are also polished verses in which the human, social, and historic landscape of Mexico is reflected; verses by themselves are literary landscapes against which greater figures, like Sor Juana, will stand out. Furthermore, it was not only Góngora who was venerated as a "prince of lyricists." Poets also read Garcilaso, the Argensolas, Lope de Vega, Fray Luis de León, San Juan de la Cruz, Herrera, Calderón, and Quevedo. In fact, it was Góngora who sang loudest in the midst of a multitude of poets. And it was poetry that raised its voice in the baroque era. There were surprising cases of variety and innovation in metrics and strophes, as in the Mexican Juan de la Anunciación. The Hispanic-Americans imitated or composed *centos* for the numerous poetry contests that were celebrated on religious or civil holidays. Some contests demanded an emulation of Góngora. In general, these contests document the fact that there were groups of poets who read one another; they wrote for one another and so became their own public. This is the activity of humanists and erudites who pride themselves on belonging to an aristocracy where one gains admittance only through the use of certain intricate passwords. The genre is what least matters—it can be a simple carol or a full-blown epic poem. The only thing that matters is that the symbols be pushed to their extreme. It is curious that out of this highly erudite poetry, there should emerge indigenous and even Afro-Spanish expressions. However, in baroque literature popular elements are not spontaneous, but contrived. Negroes are referred to as "jet with a soul." The poetry competitions were the noisiest, most colorful and exciting events in the literary life of the New World. Hundreds of poets participated in them, all anxious for public recognition. (Bernardo de Balbuena remembered with pride that in 1585 he had triumphed over three hundred rivals.) The city dressed itself in all solemnity for the occasion, and there were sumptuous processions along the specially decorated streets. All the arts collaborated in the festivities. Those poets who received awards had the satisfaction of earning the plaudits of the crowd as they read their compositions aloud, and, in addition, had the hope of gaining the plaudits of posterity, because it was the custom to publish the best poems and an account of the competition in a deluxe volume.

The Parthenic Triumph (*Triunfo parténico*) by CARLOS DE SIGÜENZA Y GÓNGORA (Mexico, 1645–1700) is a description and collection of the competitions of 1682 and 1683. Sigüenza y Góngora would be more outstanding in a list of illustrious personalities in the colonies than in a history of literature. He was an illustrious personality because, in spite of being an obedient Catholic, his intellectual curiosity set him apart from scholasticism and opened his eyes to the advantages of reason and experiment. His *Astronomical and Philosophical Terms* (*Libra astronómica y filosófica*) is important in the history of ideas in Mexico in this sense: it implies a will to investigate new truths instead of leaning on the erudition of authorized truths. He wrote, then, on unliterary themes like archeology and history, mathematics and applied sciences, astronomy, geography, ethnography. And when he wrote verses, he gave us the dregs of the baroque. He was a relative of Luis de Góngora y Argote, and perhaps because of this distant relation some critics have wanted to study whether the Mexican Góngora also withdrew from Gongorism. There is no question about it. What he withdrew from was poetry. As we read him we are so depressed that when, in the middle of all the verbiage, a few words of poetic transparency arise, it seems that finally we will witness the miracle of an oasis. Nevertheless, it turns out to be a mirage. In these poetic odds and ends—the language ground up by the cultist and conceptist machine—we can find a good verse, at times a revealing word, but rarely a stanza, and never a poem that is really worthwhile. In *Indian Spring* (*Primavera indiana*, 1662), his first book, there is more poetic achievement than in those that follow (if the strophes xxx, xxxi, xxxiv, xlvi, lviii, lx, lxiv, lxvi and lxxviii could be considered good expressions). As a historian he wrote longer-lasting pages, and perhaps in a history of literature his place is that of chronicler of minor events. The prose of these chronicles was conversational, unlike the empty and gnarled prose with which he larded his little poetical works; and his narrative art at times becomes so effective (in "Letter to Admiral Andrés de Pez," for example) that one reads with pleasure. These pages on the mutiny of the Indians in June of 1692 are most interesting. One sees, hears, and smells everything, such is the force of the details. His storytelling gifts are best noticed in the *Misfortunes That Alonso Ramírez Suffered at the Hands of English Pirates (Infortunios que Alonso Ramírez padeció en poder de ingleses piratas*, 1690), which has the vivid movement of a novel. By writing about the adventures of others in the first person, the author gained the freedom to dramatize scenes objectively selected. It is not a novel, but a travel book, written with the purpose of recording real episodes and giving information about natural and human geography. Alonso Ramírez was one of those long-suffering, vital, virile Creoles in whom lived the spirit of the Spanish conquistadors. But he was now living in other times. Ramírez was born in Puerto Rico in 1662 and, without realizing it, was sunk in the political decadence of Spain. Exactly one century after the defeat of the Spanish Armada he was captured by the English "heretical pirates"; underwent terrible humiliations—the least of which was to hear the English call the Spaniards "cowards and chickens." Once he gained his liberty, a little over two years later, he and his men sailed in terror because they felt that all the seas were full of Englishmen. Spain had lost its enterprising vigor, and in America the Creole suffered from the impairment of his political honor. Sigüenza y Góngora speaks of the heresies of France and England; while Spain, having withdrawn more and more from the creative centers of Europe, now bases its pride on its Catholicity. Because of the cultural decline of the Spanish-speaking peoples, it is very surprising to see the rising strength of Sor Juana. Among the writings of Sigüenza y Góngora that have been lost is a "Funeral Eulogy of the Celebrated Mexican Poetess Sor Juana Inés de la Cruz" (*"Elogio fúnebre de la célebre poetisa mexicana Sor Juana Inés de la Cruz"*). They had been friends, and in one of her sonnets the little nun calls him "sweet, sonorous Mexican swan." It seems incredible that Sor Juana should really admire Don Carlos' poetry—she was so far above it.

Sor Juana Inés de la Cruz / The most harmonious, gracious, and modulated voice of the Baroque period in Hispanic-America was that of SOR JUANA INÉS DE LA CRUZ (Mexico, 1648–1695). It is difficult to evaluate it, in part because the baroque style is difficult to evaluate, but mainly because the fascinating life of the little Mexican nun predisposes us to judge sympathetically anything she wrote. The entire Mexican court was convinced of her genius, and the Church was also, so much so that it became alarmed at her fame. In 1650 the Portuguese Jesuit Antonio de Vieyra had delivered a sermon disputing what St. Augustine and St. Thomas held was Christ's greatest expression of love at the end of His life. Forty years later Sor Juana commented on it in a letter, "Crisis of a Sermon," which the bishop of Puebla decided to publish with the title *Athenagoric Letter* (*Carta athenogórica*, 1690), that is, "letter worthy of the wisdom of Athena." The bishop preceded it with a missive to Sor Juana, which bore the pseudonym *"Filotea de la Cruz."* In it the bishop advised Sor Juana to select subjects more carefully, to read the Gospel more, and to employ her talents on religious matters. Sor Juana wrote her *Reply to Sor Filotea de la Cruz* (*Respuesta a Sor Filotea de la Cruz*, 1691), one of the most admirable autobiographical essays in the Spanish language. Here she tells of her early desire for learning, her insatiable intellectual curiosity, the disadvantages of being a woman, her efforts to free herself of the impertinences, prejudices, incomprehension, and stupidities with which people trammel their betters. The prose is splendid: fine, flexible, philosophical, and above all, of an extraordinary efficacy in the defense of her spiritual calling. Her beliefs are orthodox. There is no doubt. But she has almost a rationalist's vigor and many of her protestations of humility have an ironic ring, sometimes hidden, other times not. After asking herself, "Am I perchance more than a poor nun, the most insignificant creature of the universe, and the least worthy of your attention?", she adds that recognizing this "is not affected modesty." Indeed it is.

Sor Juana knows she is right and expounds her case with agile dialectics. She is admonished to apply her industry to the sacred books and not to the secular. But, replies Sor Juana, "My not having written much on sacred subjects has not been out of distaste for them, nor out of lack of application, but because of excessive fear and reverence for those Sacred Scriptures, for whose understanding I recognize myself as incapable and for whose handling I am so unworthy . . ." She prefers verses and plays, "because a heresy against art is not punished by the Holy Office, but with laughter by the discreet and with censure by the critics." What authority does she hold for sacred matters? "Let's leave these to those who can understand them, for I want no truck with the Holy Office." "What is true, and what I shall not deny (first, because it is known to everyone; and then, although it operates against me, because God has given me the grace of desiring the greatest love of truth), is that since the first ray of reason struck me, the inclination to letters has been so vehement and powerful that neither the reprimands of others (of which I have had many) nor my own reflections (of which I have made not a few) have sufficed to dissuade me from following this natural impulse that God placed in me: He knows why and wherefore." There are those who believe—she says—that knowledge is superfluous and even damaging in woman. In view of "the total denial of a matrimonial life" her only recourse was to become a nun—this was "the most decent course I could elect by way of securing the salvation I desired." Therefore, "all of the little impertinences of my nature: the desire to live alone, the desire not to have compulsory obligations that would interfere with the liberty of my studies, or the noise of people that might break the reposed silence of my books, had to yield and be repressed." She wanted to flee from herself—"but, wretched me! I brought myself with me [to the convent] and I brought in this addiction to study, my greatest enemy, that I cannot determine whether the Heavens gave me as a natural gift or as a punishment, for to extinguish or hinder it by the duties that Religion demands, would make me explode like gunpowder . . ." "I returned (not really, for I never ceased), I persisted, I say, at the studious task . . . of reading, and rereading, of studying and restudying, with no other teacher than the books themselves." She complains of "the great labor not only because of the lack of a teacher but of classmates with whom to confer and to apply what was studied, having for a teacher only a mute book and for a classmate an insensitive inkwell, and instead of explanation and exercise, many disturbances, not only for religious obli-

gations . . . but of those chores inherent in community life . . . I
cannot express with what envy I hear others say that knowledge
has cost them no anxiety. Happy they! As for myself, not knowledge (which I still do not possess), but the desire for knowledge
has cost me so much . . . My poor studies have navigated (or better said, have foundered) against the currents." She suffered persecutions, ill will, and hatred from those who believe that ignorance is saintly and abhor the loftiness of the spirit. What! Isn't an
angel more than a man because it understands more? Is it not in
his understanding that man is superior to the brute? "They have
come to request that study be prohibited to me. One time they
succeeded with a very saintly and very guileless mother superior
who believed that study was something reserved for the Holy
Office, and she ordered me not to study: I obeyed (for about three
months while her authority prevailed) insofar as not taking up a
book, but insofar as not studying in absolute I could not oblige,
for although I did not study in books, I studied in all the things
that God created, His universal machinery serving me as literature and as books." Should a woman be ashamed perhaps of such
inclinations? She follows with examples of illustrious women who
are cited so often in human as well as divine letters. Sor Juana
mentions them in a long list, and she smiles with irony at the notion that women are considered inept while men, "just by virtue
of being so, considered themselves sages." She proposes education
for women administered by women. Concerning her criticism of
Father Vieyra—in her *Athenagoric Letter*—is she not as free as
he? "As I was free to disagree with Vieyra so is any person free to
disagree with my opinion." The *Athenagoric Letter* and the *Reply
to Sor Filotea* are the two greatest prose works of Sor Juana, which
are followed in importance by *Incarnation Exercises* (*Ejercicios
de la Encarnación*) and *Offerings of the Rosary* (*Ofrecimientos
del Rosario*).

To fully appreciate the intellectual liberty of Sor Juana Inés,
one must place her in the ecclesiastical milieu of her times. The
Catholic society mirrors the total society with its submissive and
rebel elements. Sor Juana's behavior was not a worldly rebellion
—we have already said that she was an orthodox Catholic, fearful

of heresies and scandals. But, within the bosom of the Church, she
had the impulse to liberty, perhaps stimulated by the restlessness
of the seventeenth century, an intellectual restlessness of which
Descartes' *Discourse on Method* had been one of the sources. (In
addition to this restlessness, she was tormented by an inner anxiety
that we cannot explain although it is apparent in her work—she
never found innermost peace, and her final asceticism in renouncing learning definitively to dedicate herself to pious deeds, was perhaps less religious than is believed.) Her flight from the world
and from her condition as a woman, her intellectual narcissism,
her manner of treating amorous themes, seem to contain a certain
mark of neurosis. It is as if Sor Juana, deep in her subcon-
scious, felt a conflict between her feminine nature and the
yearning for masculine authority, or between being cared for by
the Church and being neglected by the best minds of the century,
with whom it was impossible for her to come into contact (as she
says in her sonnet: "I pursue with love one who ungratefully
leaves me / and flee ungratefully from one who lovingly pursues
me").

The autobiography of her deep thirst for knowledge that Sor
Juana offers in her *Reply* already had a poetic counterpart in *First
Dream* (*Primero sueño*), a *silva* (that is, an irregular metrical
form) of extreme baroque style after the manner of Góngora's
Solitudes, where Sor Juana relates the flight of her soul toward
learning. The *Reply* and the *Dream* throw light upon each other.
Through the *Reply* we become aware of certain aspects of the
the genesis of the *Dream*. "For I have never written anything (in
verse) through my own desire," she says, "but rather on the be-
seeching and behest of others; so that I remember having written
nought for my pleasure except a little paper they call the *Dream*."
And on a prior occasion, "not even my dreams were free from this
continuous movement of my imagination; rather it is wont to
operate in them with more freedom and less difficulty, imparting
greater clarity and serenity to the daily affairs that they preserve;
disputing matters, making verses, of which I could make a long
catalog, and of arguments and subtleties that I have arrived at in
a state of sleep better than awake." The *Dream*—a *silva* of almost

a thousand verses—is constructed with systematic thought: the soul, by virtue of nocturnal dreams, climbs to the heights in order to reach, in a single moment of rapture, the vision of all things created and, having failed, returns now with more humility to undertake the methodic and conceptual understanding of the simple to the complex, not without doubts, contradictions, scruples, and fears, until Sor Juana awakens and opens her eyes to a world enlightened by the rays of a new day. The desire for knowledge has failed; we are not capable of knowing either the universe or a particular object. But the failure (and in verses 781–826 Sor Juana's thinking becomes so ambiguous that her ambiguity seems to be deliberate) is like that of Phaeton, the valiant and unfortunate god who wanted to drive the chariot of the sun, created fires, and was punished. Sor Juana is in sympathy with the adventure of knowledge, a knowledge that is willing to venture everything, without fear of failure. If the punishment that this venture incurs is not made public, is it because she does not want anyone else to follow that destructive example? Or is it because she wants only a few to hazard it? The sincerity with which Sor Juana lived her life charges her verses with energy. She Gongorizes, but her Gongorisms are superficial. It happens to be the style of the period: such formulas as "if not B, A," "this, then," verses with contrasts and correlations, neologisms, Latinisms, syntactical dislocations, tropes and metaphors, mythological allusions, and cultisms from all literature, chromatic ornaments, musical effects, difficult charades, and deliberate obscurities. However, occasional beauties scintillate with originality in this period style. Even more—in a certain sense *First Dream* is the poem that best represents not only Sor Juana, but her entire epoch. There were many baroque poems, but in *First Dream* there is a sincere identification between a personal life and a collective style. The deceptive strategems of the baroque served as a hiding place for Sor Juana. Feeling the absence of love, she renounced the world—"rouged deceit"—and in solitude she withdrew into the innermost reaches of her being; there, her intelligence became her consolation and her joy. But she had to silence her intelligence, for it would have seemed impertinent and even heretical in a woman. The hermetic quality of the baroque came to her aid. The *Dream*, through its theme and through its cultist style, was an autobiography with a secret cipher. The world is unreal: what is real is one's inner life. Through dreams she absents herself from the world, and she awakens contemplating the truth which is her intellectual activity as a solitary person. The rest of her poetry was circumstantial. If we separate the mishmash of pure versification—with allegories, commemorations and court gossipings—there remains a nucleus of great poetry in the form of sonnets, ballads, *décimas* (ten octosyllabic verses), and quatrains. In some of her carols she captures nimbly and playfully the popular soul of Mexico. The poetry reflects her life in the country, in the city, and in the convent. Nevertheless, her personal experiences cannot be distinguished from her literary experiences.

At times she speaks not of what she has lived but of what she has learned in the lives of others. Therefore, her themes are not to be taken as her own. Hers is a poetry rich in intelligence—intelligence of life, but always intelligence. If she loved, or was loved, we know not, but in her excellent lyric poetry the amatory ones are enchanting. More than that, her lyric verse, especially the amorous type, is what really made her famous. In the ballad "I bring a care with me" she evokes the love of adolescence, a love that is human, insane, extreme. With masterliness—and femininity —Sor Juana examines the love theme: separation, jealousy, neglect, rancor, abandonment, death. Of course the reader must be very careful not to confuse love with mere rhetoric. The quatrains directed to the viceroy's wife (Amarilís, Filis, and Lisi in the verses) are protestations of affection very common in courtly poetry. From medieval Provence to Renaissance Italy, and thence to baroque Spain, the dithyrambic convention of singing to the noble and the powerful continued. The merits of the eulogized lord and the love offered by the poet were celebrated in hyperbolic fashion. The neoplatonic theories had just reinformed the convention that gave no more significance to the quatrains of Sor Juana, a woman, to another woman of the court, than to the sonnets of Shakespeare, a man, to another man of the court.

She was not only mistress of this chord, but of all those she struck: religious and secular, hermetical and popular, in conceits, emotions and customs. Since Garcilaso, hers has been the school of great Spanish poetry; and she emulated the baroque poets of the seventeenth century, closer to the concepts than to the cultists. She threw unexpected light on a style that in Spain was receding into the dusk. Eagerness for intellectual knowledge sharpened her mind, and in that state of mental sharpness, the little nun renovated with joy and enthusiasm the vitality of poetic inventiveness. What was a withering in others in her was a blooming. To play with her intelligence was a thrilling adventure. To feel intelligent was disquieting. The movement of concepts—in highly varied correlations—was like the fluttering of the wings of a bird escaping from its cage. As soon as an event in her life offered itself to her verse, it was immediately amplified by a complicated reasoning. This reasoning was as vital as the event that occasioned it, so that the baroque interplay did not disturb the lyrical ascent. (Remember, for example, the sonnets "Divine rose that in gentle culture," "Stay, shadow of my elusive good.") The best she wrote was in the baroque style (to the above we add the sonnets: "This that thou seest, rouged deceit," "Diuturnal infirmity of hope," "Green enravishment of human life," "Inés, when they scold thee for being roguish," "This evening, my beloved, when I spake to thee," "That Fabian may not love me, on being loved," "He who leaves me, ungrateful one, I seek as lover," "Silvio, I abhor thee and yet condemn," "Love begins because of disquietude"; the *redondillas:* "Foolish men who accuse," "This amorous torment"; the ballads: "Let us feign that I am happy," "If to give ye the good years," "There it goes, although it ought not to," "When, divine deities"; the *ovillejo:* "Painting the beauty of Lisarda").

Her theater, sacred and profane, was baroque and swung in Calderón's orbit. In addition to eighteen preludes, *"loas,"* two farces, *"sainetes,"* and one *"sarao"* or afterpiece, she wrote three mystery plays, *"autos":* the most admirable, *Divine Narcissus (El Divino Narciso,* 1698), and then *The Martyr of the Sacrament (El Mártir del sacramento)* and *Joseph's Scepter (El cetro de José).* Because of its value as a spectacle, its lyrical songs, the rigor of its intellectual construction, the intertwining of Biblical and Greco-Latin themes, the originality in the handling of poetic ideas and intuitions, and the vigorous parallelism of Indian and Christian rites, *Divine Narcissus* is one of the better mysteries in all Castilian literature. Sor Juana was acquainted with and profited by Calderón's play *Echo and Narcissus*. However, she surpassed it with an allegory with which she ambitiously intended, not necessarily to educate the Indians—in spite of the Indian personages in the *loa*, which was joined to the *auto*—but to please the cultured Spaniards of Madrid. Using the reports of the chroniclers for her base—especially those of Juan de Torquemada—she presented in the *loa* the Aztec rite in which Huitzilopochtli, God of Seeds, is eaten in a kind of host kneaded with flour and blood, showing the Devil's astuteness in deception by imitating Christian communion. For the purpose of demonstrating to "Occident" and "America" —two personages that symbolize the indigenous pre-Cortés culture—that the God of the Catholics and the Eucharist are true, "Religion" presents for them a mystery play, the *auto* of *Divine Narcissus*. Reworking Ovid's version of the Narcissus myth, Sor Juana puts on the stage a Christ-Narcissus, who looks like a spring of water and there sees reflected human nature. Since the latter was created in the image and likeness of God, Christ "seeing His image in the man, fell in love with Himself," dies for love and leaves the host, white flower of the Eucharist, as a remembrance and as an admonishment. Of her two plays, *The Obligations of a Home* (*Los empeños de una casa*, 1683), a cloak-and-sword comedy, and *Love Is a Labyrinth* (*Amor es más laberinto*, 1689), a mythological-courtly play, whose second act was written by Juan de Guevara, the first play is the better. The play *The Obligations of a Home* (Calderón had written one entitled *The Obligations of a Chance Occurrence—Los empeños de un acaso*) is very entertaining. It develops from deception to deception, from misunderstanding to misunderstanding, with scenes in the darkness or semi-darkness, concealments, disguises, cloaked figures. The action, of a few hours' duration, takes place in Toledo, and its twists and turns are so vertiginous that it takes flight. Even the characters suffer from vertigo. They do not know whether they dream or are awake; they do not understand what is happening around them and are unaware that they have been thrown into the midst of some stage trickery. One of them invokes the Mexican rogue, Martín Garatuza: "inspire some scheme for me that seems of Calderón's design." Calderón, in fact, is the master who taught Sor Juana how to enmesh human destinies. Nevertheless, like a kaleidoscope, this baroque interplay of mirrors and illusions has its geometry.

One can imagine Sor Juana smiling mockingly at the foolishness of men and women who believe it possible to impose love. Don Pedro loves Doña Leonor, but Doña Leonor loves Don Carlos. Don Juan loves Doña Ana, but Doña Ana loves Don Carlos. At the end, the only happy couple are the sincere lovers—the good Don Carlos and the discreet and beautiful Doña Leonor, in whom Sor Juana seems to have portrayed herself. In spite of the affectation and conventionality of the dramatic situations, the dialog goes on revealing a keen understanding of the secrets of the heart and the motives for human conduct. In the *sainete* interposed between the second and third acts, someone, speaking of plays, affirms "those of Spain are always better," and that no one in Mexico would dare boo "a play by Calderón, Moreto or Rojas." It may be for this reason that *The Obligations of a Home*, aspiring to the greatest prestige, places its action in Spain (there is, however, one Mexican character, the *gracioso* or comic servant, Castaño). Now that this *sainete* has been mentioned, we can say that it has one exceptional value—while the interlocutors wait for the third act of *The Obligations of a Home*, they poke fun at the first two acts; it is a case of internal duplication: Sor Juana converts into theatrical spectacle the ordinary conversation which goes on during the intermission of a performance and creates in this way an interpenetration, quite modern, of public and stage, of critics and actors. This procedure, which breaks through the frontier between fiction and reality, is used surprisingly in the third act when Castaño, disguised as a woman, suddenly directs himself to the audience and consults the women on intimate items of apparel. Sor Juana synthesized all the currents valued and practiced in the first half of the century: traditional, Renaissance, and baroque; popular, cultured and low-bred; here a stanza after the fashion of

San Juan de la Cruz, there a *silva* after Góngora, or a *décima* after Calderón, or a ballad after Lope, or a folk song after Quevedo. She had us hear the voice of the Negro in her poetry. The Negro theme already existed in the literature of Hispanic-America. Negroes arrived in 1502, in the fleet of Nicolás de Ovando, and they appear in the chronicles. The poets of the Renaissance (Castellanos, Ercilla) presented them as inferior people. But Sor Juana, with the open curiosity of the baroque, poetizes the Negro and uses him to give color and rhythm to her poetry. Later on the Negro will interbreed into the population of America and will participate in our literature until he will succeed in reaching a splendid expression in the twentieth century.

Other Baroque Poets in South America / Within the space available, we will dwell only on a few other baroque poets. JACINTO DE EVIA (Ecuador, b. 1620) published in Spain a *Bouquet of Sundry Poetical Flowers Gathered and Cultivated in the Early Springtime of His Life* (*Ramillete de varias flores poéticas recogidas y cultivadas en los primeros abriles de sus años*, 1676), in which were collected compositions from his own garden and from those of his contemporaries, among them the Colombian poet Hernando Domínguez Camargo ("To a waterfall through which the Chillo brook plunges down," written in the form of a colt metaphor) and the Ecuadorian Father Antonio de Bastidas ("To the same brook, in the form of a bull metaphor"). Both poems were inspired by the description of a brook "in the form of a serpent metaphor" which was in the second of Góngora's *Solitary Musings*.

There were all types of verses: lyrical, sacred, heroic, panegyric, epigrammatic. At times Evia submerged himself in baroque obscurity and at time emerged above the clear surface. HERNANDO DOMÍNGUEZ DE CAMARGO (Colombia, 1606–1659), the first poet of this country chronologically as well as in the quality of his poetry, has historical value.

He did not squander the precious materials left him by Góngora. Without impairment they are there for us to see: hyperbaton, alliteration, mythological allusions, Greek constructions. There are direct images of the real America—he would say, "my America," "my clime," "my cradle"—but even there, flora and fauna harden into ornaments. The language of the culture, containing zodiacs, Pomonas, is superimposed on his speech as an Hispanic-American poet. His metaphysics are also baroque. In describing a beautiful woman he tells us that her lips are "a short stream of carmine in which candid swans hide." The corpse of a suicide hanging from a tree is a "tragic comet of life, fatally vibrating in the dusky air." The bee that sucks in white flowers is "a burnished sponge that drinks pearls." "The soul is a fish that cannot swim except in the deep rivers of the veins." The ballad "To a waterfall through which the Chillo brook plunges down," which, as we said, was included in Evia's *Bouquet*, moves like water and like a colt, both of which the author has joined in a forceful image; and it continues to appear in anthologies. He not only inherited Góngora, he fused the material in a crucible, gave it new forms and stamped them with his own die.

Domínguez Camargo's poems that appear in Jacinto de Evia's *Bouquet* are clearer, easier, and indeed more anthological than his unfinished *Heroic Poem of Saint Ignatius of Loyola* (1666). This poem, however, was his most full-blown work, where the syntax, the vocabulary, the metaphors, and the learned references of baroque style press around the biography of the saint of his devotion. (He was a Jesuit, but later abandoned the order and became a secular priest.) The theme of sainthood is not treated ascetically. On the contrary, the poet escapes to the sumptuous and vivacious realm of pure form and there begins his decorations. The baroque handled religious symbols esthetically. The poems about St. Ignatius' life primarily are meant to defend Spanish Catholicism against the heresies that were spreading throughout the rest of the world. It has already been noted that the military epic was succeeded by the religious epic; and the biographies of St. Ignatius (by Rivadeneyra and by Nieremberg) inspired heroic poems. To awaken the piety of the masses, Jesuitism resorted to anecdotes, ornamentation, hyperbole, convoluted images, pompous symbols. It was with this baroque rhetoric that the hagiographic poems appeared in America.

The first, by the Andalusian LUIS DE BELMONTE Y BERMÚDEZ (b. before 1587 and d. in 1630?), was published in Mexico in 1609. Then, the already-mentioned *Ignatius of Cantabria* (1639) by Pedro de Oña, and the *Heroic Poem to Saint Ignatius of Loyola* by Domínguez Camargo. Even after the Ignatian theme had lost its initial vigor, we find in the eighteenth century another *Heroic Poem to Saint Ignatius of Loyola* by Father Aguirre. We continue the list of baroque poets. FRANCISCO ALVAREZ DE VELASCO Y ZOR-RILLA (Colombia, 1647–d. after 1703) admired Quevedo (in the same way Domínguez Camargo admired Góngora), but he intended to concern himself "more with the simplicity rather than the elegance of style." He revealed himself a poet in his "Elegies to the Virgin" at the opening of his *Sacred, Moral and Laudatory Rhythmics* (*Rítmica sacra, moral y laudatoria*, 1703?). LUIS DE TEJEDA (Argentina, 1604–1680) left rough drafts of manuscripts, also late copies of doubtful fidelity. Out of all his production he left some successful verses. They are not sufficient to give him weight, but he was the first worthwhile poet to appear in what today is Argentina. Almost all of what we have left pertains to his later life when he withdrew to the Dominican cloisters, repentant of his stormy conduct, to weave auto-biographical verses ("Ballad of His Life"), sacred verses, and, of less importance, explicative prose. Tejeda conceived, without finishing it, a plan for *Lyrical Crowns* (this is the title of a modern edition) in the form of a rosary: the prayers are distributed on three crowns, and on each crown appear the autobiographical and the sacred. On this structure he arranged his compositions which were of every type then cultivated. His style is generally baroque in vocabulary, syntax, and interplay of conceits. He had learned this stylistic affectation in Spanish books. Góngora was among his many readings, and his language was occasionally Gongorized on the surface. The introducer of Baroque style in Peru seems to have been Friar JUAN DE AYLLÓN (Peru, 1604), author of a euphuistic and soporific *Poem to the Canonization of the Twenty Three Martyrs of Japan* (*Poema a la canonización de los veintitrés mártires del Japón*, 1630). Góngora, Quevedo, and Calderón are present in LUIS ANTONIO DE OVIEDO HERRERA, Count of La Granja (1636–1717), Spaniard by birth, Peruvian by virtue of his work, author of the poetic composition *Life of Saint Rose of Lima* (*Vida de Santa Rosa de Lima*, 1711) and of the *Sacred Poem of the Passion of Christ* (*Poema sacro de la pasión de Cristo*), in addition to ballads, sonnets and plays. Another voice of religious literature is that of JUAN DE PERALTA (Peru, 1663–1747), whose *Three Journeys in Heaven* (*Tres jornadas del cielo*) is also inspired by the Bible, more by the Psalms than by the Song of Songs.

The one we must dwell on in Peru is JUAN DE ESPINOSA MEDRANO (b. after 1632–d. 1688). This mestizo used to be called *"El Lunarejo"* because of the *lunares* or moles on his face. He wrote at least the *Mystery Play of the Prodigal Son* in Quechua. Other Quechua pieces have been attributed to him; it has even been presumed (without foundation) that it was he who wrote

Ollantay, the drama with Spanish structure and Quechua language and whose origin is still in dispute. In Spanish he composed the Biblical drama, *To Love One's Own Death* (*Amar su propria muerte*), with plots *à la* Lope and verses *à la* Calderón. His sermons were noteworthy. He was at his best when writing cultist prose. He had studied at the University of Cuzco, and his discourses, collected in *The Ninth Wonder* (*La novena maravilla*, 1695) reveal a terse and elegant wisdom. He was a Góngora enthusiast, and his greatest glory rests in his *Apologetics in Defense of Don Luis de Góngora* (*Apologético en favor de don Luis de Góngora*, 1662). When "*El Lunarejo*" was born, not only had Góngora been dead ten years, but also important critical battles had been waged in Spain between Gongorists and non-Gongorists. But literary life was not as intense in the colonies, and the movement of literary tastes was much slower. "*El Lunarejo*" complained in his dedication to the *Apologetics* of being in the periphery of things in the province, "far from the heart of the monarchy, receiving little cheer from the very warmth that gives life to literature and courage to genius."

Góngora was not in need of defenders in America—even those who reproved his poetical language imitated him, like Oña. For this reason the *Apologetics* is of value as an American reply to the rejections of Góngora in Spain. A copy of the anti-Góngora commentaries by the Portuguese Manuel de Faria e Souza came into the hands of Espinosa Medrano. "It seems that I am late in starting this task," says the latter, "but we Creoles live very far away; furthermore, when Manuel de Faria pronounced his censure Góngora was dead, and I not yet born." There is, then, no new contribution to the debate. On the other hand, there is in this belated baroque poetics an understanding of the stylistic value of Góngora that is much more subtle, alert, appropriate, prudent, and brilliant than in the earlier Spanish apologias. "No one ever spoke ill of Don Luis de Góngora except those who envied him or did not understand him; if he is to blame for this incomprehension, then blind men have cause to quarrel with the sun." What Espinosa Medrano is assessing in Góngora is the latter's verbal inventiveness, the energy with which he gives old literary treatment a new and surprising slant of beauty, his expansion of the Spanish language in order to insert the fresh tendencies of Latin. It is the lyrical brilliance, the lucid logic, the aristocratic bearing, that make him exclaim: "Long live the very learned and flowery Góngora, may he live long in spite of all the envies."

Satire

The fish net of literary history, however closely woven it may be, cannot hold all the schools of ballads and popular, festive, satiric, improvised, and burlesque poems which are so small that they escape through the mesh. It is sufficient to mention the most important of the satirists of this epoch, JUAN DEL VALLE CAVIEDES (1652?–1697?). An Andalusian by birth, he arrived at the mountain plains of Peru as a child, later moved to Lima, dissipated his life between gambling and women, fell into the hands of doctors; and against his doctors he wrote quatrains, ten-verse stanzas and ballads in which not only each epigram but also every adjective has a terrible aggressive power of its own. He attacked them for their ignorance, vices, and false prestige. The verses of his *Parnassus' Tooth* (*Diente del Parnaso*)—an allusion to his biting style: "chunks from my bite," he used to say—were not published during his lifetime, nor immediately after his death, but they were well known. He wrote dramatic exercises constructed allegorically: *Interlude of Mayor-Love* (*Entremés del Amor Alcalde*), *Dance of Doctor-Love* (*Baile del Amor Médico*), and *Dance of Gambler-Love* (*Baile del Amor Tahur*). This comic vein, with Quevedo-like witticisms, continued for some time; but in his later years, he acquired a mature, reflective attitude, and he wrote sonnets and other compositions with religious emotion and in a tone of repentance and melancholy. He had not been a futile imitator of the Spanish baroque writers. He was acquainted with them and knew the writers from whom the baroque writers had profited; but he possessed intellectual independence, individual inspiration, and a concise and gleeful style. In his *Letter* to Sor Juana he was proud that his only university had been his own spirit and that he had studied men more than books. His good sense, not in conformity with the superstitions of his time, is impressive. His poetry, satiric as well as religious and lyrical, is the freshest in colonial Peru. He will undoubtedly occupy a more distinguished place in literary histories (including ours) when his works are better edited. Still unverifiable is the authenticity of some of the compositions attributed to him, especially by members of the academy of the Marquis of Castell-dos-Rius at the beginning of the eighteenth century. "The poet of the levee," as he was called, has also been harmed by the excessive attention given to his satirical poems, of rough and ugly humor. After all, the most immature of these constitutes but a minute part of his total output, love poems, religious poems, and satirical poems (against doctors and other professionals, and also against women).

Heroic and Religious Epics / While still bishop of Puerto Rico, Bernardo de Balbuena had to flee, in 1625, before the incursions of Dutch pirates. Another bishop, Friar Juan de la Cabezas Altamirano, suffered more: he was kidnapped in 1604 by the French buccaneer, Gilbert Giron. And this episode is the theme of the first Cuban poem, *Mirror of Patience* (*Espejo de paciencia*, 1608) by SILVESTRE DE BALBOA (b. between 1564 and 1574; d. between 1634 and 1644). It is surprising that this poem, in two cantos having 145 epic octaves that flow clearly, simply, and with narrative force, should sprout suddenly in the midst of the cultural desert that was Cuba. It is a rhymed chronicle—perhaps Balboa was writing beneath the shade of the Ercilla tree—but this is no account of the struggles of Spaniard against Indian, or of Spaniards against Spaniards, but of Spaniards against "Lutheran" pirates, as Balboa calls them. In his prolog to the reader, Balboa confesses his imitation of Horace; and in the poem, reminiscences of Ariosto and Tasso are recognized, perhaps not directly, but through Italianate Spanish poets like Luis Barahona de Soto, who himself had imitated the *Orlando Furioso* in his *The Tears of Angelica* (*Las lágrimas de Angélica*). The influence that is missed is that of Góngora. There is no baroque in *Mirror of Patience*. On the contrary, the stupefaction before the heresy of the French, the admiration for the patience with which the bishop suffers all, and the final heroic vengeance are conveyed in plain hendecasyllabic lines, sententious but without conceits, with mythological adornments but without cultist forms, almost always prosaic, although with an occasional poetic sparkle, especially in the narrative. All this equilibrium—although keeping the logical axis too much in view—makes Balboa a minor poet outside the literary frame that dominated in his time. In view of the fact that it was the novelist and poet, José Antonio Echeverría, who left us in his own handwriting the two extant versions of *Mirror of Patience* (with insignificant variants), it was believed at one time that the entire poem, and even the existence of Balboa himself, could have been a hoax. It is possible that Echeverría, while copying, may have modified and modernized the missing original. What is certain is that the *Mirror of Patience* is a work apart, singular even for its Creole, Cuban, and national feeling. "O happy island of Cuba!" it says. It is a "little Creole Negro" who will deceive the pirate into putting into land; it is an Indian who becomes the only victim of the French in the final battle; it is a Negro—"O, Creole savior, honorable Negro"—who thrusts the lance into the chest of Gilbert Giron and kills him. And when the bishop returns to Cuba, a freed man, the mythological gods come out laden with flowers and fruit of the American landscape to receive him. In this way indigenous words enter into the Horatian literary phraseology. The religious theme intertwines with the heroic: in the first canto, the suffering of the bishop; in the second, the vengeance against the heretic. But what dominates this second part is the color of blood. This interlacing of themes of Christian humility and bellicose fury is very significant. Balboa lies between two traditions. Epic poetry had acquired such prestige in Spain that poets emerged intent on singing not only about the deeds of the conquistadors, but also those of the saints. In addition, it placed alongside the epics of princes, the epic of Christ. Poems on the passion and death of the religious hero already begin to appear by the fifteenth century. But it was after the Council of Trent that the epical-religious genre was filled with the squalls of the Counter Reformation. Furthermore, Tasso changed the meaning of heroic verse. Balboa restricted himself to a comparison of the bishop with Christ.

During these very years, another poet, DIEGO DE HOJEDA (1571–1615) in a monastery in Lima, wrote a vast poem on Christ himself. In Hojeda's *Christiada* there is but one theme: "I sing to the Son of God, Human and Dead." His doctrinal sources were the writings of the Church Fathers, the Gospel, Castilian sermons, religious treatises, lives of saints, the ideas of St. Augustine, St. Thomas Aquinas, and even Suárez; but literature came to the aid of his pen: Homer, Vergil, Dante, Girolamo Vida, Tasso, Du Bartas, Hernández Blasco, Ariosto, Boiardo, and the Spanish poets from the end of the sixteenth century and the baroque poets of the beginning of the seventeenth. Despite its baroque digressions, the work—divided into twelve books—follows a much more rigorous plan than other epics. Nevertheless, it is not this plan, nor the eloquence of the preachings, nor much less the theocratic rapture, that saves the *Christiada* for today's reader. Naturally, in a poem of such length having such a universal theme and dedicated to such a diverse public, we will find many modes, many styles, many reminiscences from different cultural sources. It is like a museum where everyone can admire what he pleases—the Biblical phrase, the sacred oratory, the Renaissance tenderness. But there are, here and there, indications of an ornate, colored, metaphoric style, with a taste for contrasts, enumerations and overrefined detail; and perhaps it is these baroque dynamics that strike our fancy. Hojeda amplifies passages from the Gospel, loading them with adornments. He takes episodes from the classical period and modifies them by using them allegorically: thus Aeneas' and Achilles' shields are converted into the complicated vestments of Christ. Theology itself is poetized with post-Renaissance language, as in the beautiful oration personified in Book II. Even his love for Christ is personal, concrete, rich in imagination and in sensory experiences. This intense love gave many of his octaves a lyrical and luxuriant brilliance. In the scene where Christ washes the feet of his disciples, the beauty of his hands is transferred to the light, to the water, to the flowers, in a joyous tremor. And when he describes the handsomeness of his unclothed body, the way in which he is whipped and jeered, Hojeda's love inspires one of the most poetic moments in all the literature of this cycle. His friend in Lima, Diego Mexía de Fernangil, dedicated 200 sonnets to the life of Christ. And, regarding Mexican literature, Corchero y Carreño's *The Vindication of Christ* (*Desagravios de Cristo*), the anonymous *Passion Poem* (*Poema de la Pasión*), and the *Eighth Wonder* (*Octava maravilla*) by Francisco de Castro should be cited here.

That the epic was now no longer up to its previous mettle is apparent in the *Arauca Tamed* (*Arauco domado*) of PEDRO DE OÑA (Chile, 1570–1643?). This Creole, born amidst the landscape and Indians that Ercilla had taken as the subject of his poem, also decided to imitate Ercilla, but he deviated from that reality even more than his model did. Oña was born almost the same year in which the first part of *La Araucana* appeared; he was eight when the second part appeared, and nineteen when the third was published. By the time *Arauco Tamed* was published in 1596—the first book in verse by an Hispanic-American author —a lot of literature had flowed beneath the bridges of the *Araucana*, and Oña, although inspired by Ercilla, was not planning to compete with him. "Who would dare to sing of Arauco / after the superbly rich *Araucana*?"

Oña turned to the epic, but discouraged by the conviction that that art form was "so refined and so perfectly developed," that, to continue after Ercilla, "would not be perfection but corruption." He related, therefore, the same heroic material (above all, that which Ercilla had given from Canto XIII of the second part on), but forcing his style in the less heroic sections. The Ercilla elements of the *Arauco Tamed* do not have the value of the voluptuous, mellow, and picturesque passages that Oña esteemed as true poetry. His battles, his portraits of Spanish soldiers or Indian warriors, his chronicle, his rhetorical technique of having past events enter into his poem (Oña's "prophecies" follow those that Ercilla puts in the mouths of Belona and Fitón), show him up as inferior to Ercilla. On the other hand, Oña brought to the Araucanian epic a new spirit, lax in determination, baroque in language. There were also embellishments and idealizations in Ercilla, but the procedure becomes more dense in Oña (after all the most outstanding example of baroque poetics, Góngora, is this: an intensification of recognized artifices). Even the octave is modified in his poem—*ABBAABCC* instead of *ABABABCC*— making it more gracious and light, "with more softness," as the poet himself said. The tone of his voice is more lyrical; at least it is more personal. The perception of things, especially their hues, indicates that Oña's eyes are attentive to the miniature images that form in his consciousness. It was a reflexive attitude in the search of images as well as concept that led him to a type of description which is at once intellectual and visual: "The green surface of the earth / seemed white, with white bones, / and the spilled blood reddened / the clear streams of the sierra." Oña had one poetic advantage over Ercilla: his thought did not center on the great abstractions of theology, but by illustrating his thinking with minute observations of daily life, he achieved that force of expression that the discovery of new objects gives. Oña is richer in metaphors than Ercilla, not only because he has more of them, but also because they are newer and more surprising. In addition to the classical images—with animals, plants, and minerals—Oña invents metaphors in which one of the meanings points to commonplace things. He is so observant of objects that, although inanimate, they become animate; although immovable, they move, all in an explosion of impulses. The pennants that stream in the wind try to break loose from their staffs and fly off in the air; the light struggles with the branches of the trees; the water approaches with joy to receive the naked body of Fresia. They were not always American objects, and for this he has been most reproached. But, after all, no poet is obliged to document the reality of his country with typical descriptions. Oña shied away from truthful representation because that was the impulse of the baroque imagination: mythology, a wealth of exotic names, bookish idyls, aristocratic movements. Oña's epic, like the body of a gymnast, relaxes certain muscles and flexes others; the flexed ones are those already described by Ovid's elegant bucolic art. It is a musculature in motion, nevertheless, because of the violent contrasts. Toward the end of his life Oña compressed the baroque language that was spread throughout the *Arauco Tamed* and gave us another historical poem, *El vasauro* (1635) which, indeed, is interwoven almost strophe by strophe with all the conceptist and cultist threads of the epoch, especially of Góngora's. *El vasauro* related, without unity, the deeds of the Catholic monarchs and of the ancestors of the Viceroy of Peru from 1465 to 1492. (The *"vasauro"* is the *áureo vaso* or golden vessel that the monarchs presented to Andrés de Cabrera.) Ercilla still has his influence on Oña, as does the whole Italian and Spanish Renaissance. But, it must be repeated, Góngora still dominates even the poets who most resist him; and although Oña spoke ill of Góngora, he uses Gongoresque metaphors, syntax, and cultisms in *El vasauro* as well as in *Ignatius of Cantabria* (1639).

B. MAINLY PROSE

1. Novelistic Sketches

Narrative began in the New World as it had begun in the Old: with historiography. Herodotus was the father of history and of the story. Our chroniclers also had this double paternity. To accentuate the likeness, let us remember that Herodotus, the first anthropologist who described contacts between the cultural patterns of different peoples, is also the antecedent of our chroniclers, who describe contacts between Spaniards and natives. But we shall not find a pure narrative literature during these years.

The royal decrees that from 1531 prohibited the circulation of novels were not totally obeyed. The few and poorly equipped presses of the New World, kept under the constant vigil of the authorities, of course, had to abide by the law; and, in fact, in the colonies no novels were published (or, as they were then called, "feigned stories," "books of romance that deal with profane and fabulous matters"). The printing in Mexico of Bramón's *The Goldfinches of the Virgin* is explained by the religious nature of the book, as shall be seen immediately. On the other hand, however, those decrees that restricted the circulation of novels printed in Spain were not complied with. They circulated, obviously. Once they reached the colonies there were attempts to destroy them, but it was not known whether the Church mandates order-

ing the burning of "vain books . . . that are entitled *Dianas*, by
any author whatsoever, and . . . the *Celestina*, and the books of
chivalry" (First Synod in Santiago, Argentina in 1597) were
carried out. To write a novel was a long undertaking, planned for
a particular public, and one must imagine what went through the
minds of the Hispanic-American writers. Besides the legal ones,
other physical and psychological impediments must have discouraged possible colonial novelists. The manuscript had to be
sent to the authorities in Spain for the printing permit with the
risk that it might be lost, not to mention the years of waiting involved. Even though the permit might be granted, the Spanish
monopoly of printers was another barrier. In America the presses
were devoted to the clergy. Furthermore, the cost of printing
was prohibitive. Nor could one count on a reader market in
America. Perhaps there was inertia in the construction of organic
works. Whatever might have been the case, the fact is there were
no novels written in the New World. But why should this cause
amazement, if in the Old World the novel still did not have proper
esteem? The novel was to acquire standing only in the nineteenth
century under the bourgeois political regimes. From the modern
point of view of the "large public," the insignificance of the novel
in the seventeenth century seems lamentable; but it is only natural
that no one should feel at that time "obliged" to write novels as
they were to write poetry, theater, or didactic prose and sacred
orations. It was Cervantes who created, with his *Don Quixote*, the
modern novel, but this type of novel was better understood outside of Spain. The moral exigencies that falsified reality and the
cultivation of an overwrought prose which lends itself little to
narration and dialog, were responsible for Spain's not profiting
from the lesson inherent in Cervantes and in the picaresque novels.
The novel declines rapidly. From the middle of the seventeenth
century we can scarcely find one that is really a novel. The novels
of chivalry and the pastoral novels, so popular in the earlier
period, became extinct in the seventeenth century. Now the taste
for fantasy found satisfaction not in the novel but in the theater.
There was, then, no novel in the colonies. We can only speak of
novelistic qualities in the chronicle and colonial histories.

In Mexico the first novels were pastoral. The genre had been initiated in Spain with the *Diana* (1559?) of Jorge Montemayor. In a short time a whole family of similar novels appeared which were immediately passed on to America and there imitated. The first Mexican pastoral novel was *The Golden Age in the Jungles of Erifile* (*Siglo de Oro en las selvas de Erífile*) by Bernardo de Balbuena. We have already studied it. The second was a pastoral novel dealing with the Divine, *The Goldfinches of the Immaculate Virgin* (*Los sirgueros de la Virgen sin original pecado*, 1620) by FRANCISCO BRAMÓN (Mexico, d. after 1654). Within this genre Bramón builds his own road, albeit a short and narrow one. The similarities to his models are external: braiding prose and verse, the stylization of nature by means of an aristocratic selection of exquisite objects, embellishing metaphors, allusions to classical myths, sentimental effusion, lyrical imagination, and dialogs between shepherds who are simply fur-clad embodiments of Platonic ideas. But with these pastoral trappings Bramón is to construct another class of narration. His goal is religious— to defend the purity of the Virgin Mary. All the action—parleys, promenades, processions, dances, songs, masses, games, incision of Marian symbols on tree barks, theological discourses, architecture of arches, musical orchestrations, bullfights, and theatrical presentations—is an apologia of the mystery of the immaculate conception of Mary. (The goldfinches, because they are singing birds, symbolize the shepherds who sing to the Virgin.) The central narrative thread links the immediate reality, especially space and time. Geography, nature, and ethnography are clearly situated: "in these Mexican gardens," "the Cathedral of Mexico," a "youth who represents the Realm of Mexico surrounded by Indians," American plants, indigenous instruments, and Aztec dances. History is also well-delineated—it alludes to King Philip III and contemporary events. Allusions to a non-pastoral reality, such as religious, university, and artistic activities of the city, give *The Goldfinches* an air of the autobiographical novel. There is a curious metamorphosis of a genre—the pastoral novel becomes sacro-pastoral and pastoral-academic. *The Goldfinches* is the history of how the poet Francisco Bramón (who under the name of Anfriso becomes a shepherd only to rest from a competitive examination he has just undergone at the University of Mexico) conceives, writes, and represents the "Mystery of the Triumph of the Virgin and Mexican Couplets in Her Praise" (*"Auto del triunfo de la Virgen y Gozo mexicano"*) to return at once to the university where he will triumph academically "with the green laurel of the Faculty of Canons." Two undulating lines, fiction and reality, crisscross here and there, with fiction readily reducing itself to reality or reality rising to the level of fiction. The protagonist is real and unreal, and the "mystery" he writes is also real and unreal; in this way the work in which they appear is simultaneously art and life. Genres within genres, real-author within protagonist-author, the reader feels himself a spectator in a literary workshop. As in Velázquez' baroque painting, "Las Meninas," the desire for immortality makes Bramón paint himself within the painting in the very act of painting. Yet, despite this interesting form of the interior duplication of the novel—a real author slips into his own fiction and there we see him in the process of writing a theatrical piece—*The Goldfinches of the Virgin* is a tiresome work, written in an inflated, pompous, and unbearable manneristic prose. Another Mexican work with novelistic elements is that of Sigüenza y Góngora, *The Misfortunes of Alonso Ramirez*, already described in our study of this author.

BISHOP JUAN DE PALAFOX Y MENDOZA (Spain–Mexico, 1600–1659) wrote verses, religious works, even a treatise on spelling. Because of their narrative interest, we shall speak of only two of his works. In *On the Nature of the Indians* (*De la naturaleza del indio*), in order to praise the virtues and merits of those "most useful and most faithful vassals of the Indies," he had recourse to anecdotes which not only are worthwhile as pleasant stories, but also allow us to hear the intelligent and cultured reflections of some of the Indians. *The Christmas Shepherd* (*El pastor de Nochebuena*, 1644), tending toward baroque tastes, is the allegory of a devout shepherd who, accompanied by angels, recounts his travels and adventures through the regions of good and evil populated by personifications of vices and virtues. Hundreds of figures, drawn from fantasy and theology, move about in tiresome artistic harness—descriptions, dialogs, subtleties, mystic language. The background and ideas are traditional. Symbols and parables surge from sacred literature, although the influence of profane literature is also noticeable.

JUAN RODRÍGUEZ FREILE (Colombia, 1566–1640?), a Creole from Bogotá and son of a conquistador, composed the chronicle of the "conquest and discovery of the new realm of Granada" up to the year 1636, the last in which he wrote. The book was known by the title *The Ram* (*El Carnero*); no one knows why. Was "Ram" the name given to manuscript folios? In example nineteen of the *Book of Cats* (*Libro de los gatos*, 1400–1420) a wolf takes on the habit of a monk but instead of saying "Our Father" he says "ram"; consequently, many monks, instead of learning the rules of their order, preoccupy themselves with the "ram," that is, the meals, wine, and mundane vices. Is this the meaning of the title of the chronicle under study? Or does the title refer metaphorically, in view of the many lives and honors interred in it, to the common graves called "*carneros,*" in which hospitals and churches buried the dead? The *Carnero* is in effect a graveyard of war notices, changes in government, customs, psychological portraits, adventures, scandals, crimes, historical data, and legends. Rodríguez Freile attempted to be accurate, and he described evil in order to moralize upon it. But, fortunately, he was imaginative. "If it is true that painters and poets have the same kind of power, then the chroniclers should be included among them," he used to say. What he writes is not false like "those who write books of chivalry." But his own work, which he calls "orphan damsel," he will adorn with "borrowed clothes and jewels," and with "the most graceful flowers." These adornments in the composition of *The Ram* are the most pleasant: anecdotes, jokes, digressions, reflections, allusions to literary works, sermons, rascally tales, adventures, love affairs and adulteries, crimes and vengeance, intrigues, ambushes, and witchcraft. Thus, in this scandalous chronicle the risqué and bustling life of Bogotá passes before us as on a stage. In his narrative he used dialog, the theme of honor and the dramatic devices of the theatre of his time, which he had seen during his stay in Spain.

His unpolished yet appealing style bristles at times, thanks to baroque technique, with a great use of secret doors, intercepted letters, handkerchief messages, disguises, escapes, and duels. He possessed a sense of humor, a narrative dynamism, and the ability to create a lively dialog. He had read picaresque literature. He had also read—and one can discern it—the Greco-Latin writers and Fray Luis de Granada. He was writing at the age of seventy and was still obsessed with the beauty of women, whom he describes untiringly, although he tells us that their beauty is the temptation of the devil: "Oh beauty, cause of so many evils! Oh women! I don't wish to speak bad of them, nor of men; but I must say that men and women are the worst vermin God created." *The Ram*, a most original book, gives us, in bold and unadorned prose, passages of novelistic value. In spite of his moralizing mind, Rodríguez Freile enjoys the scandals and improprieties that he pursues in the currents of his narrative art. The narrative tradition that he is following is that of the novels and the chronicles. He utilizes authors like Pero Mexía, Antonio de Guevara, and especially Fernando de Rojas, whose *Celestina* he cites from memory. In turn, *The Ram* became a literary source of customs and history for nineteenth-century writers. In a certain sense Rodríguez Freile was the first short-story writer in the colony. The background of *The Ram* is historical, but it is embroidered with more than twenty stories (almost half the book) about robberies, murders, sorcery, love affairs, and curious episodes.

DIEGO DÁVALOS Y FIGUEROA is the author of *The Austral Miscellany* (*Miscelánea Austral*, Lima, 1602), a curious work in which there is an admixture of fact and fiction, heroic deeds and spiritual evocations. His neat language is filled with numerous citations and translations of Renaissance authors. The plot revolves around the author, who, fleeing from an unfortunate love affair, ends up in America where the marvels of the New World overwhelm and dazzle him.

CATALINA DE ERAUSO (Spain, 1592?–1650?) wrote, it seems, about her travels and adventures through Peru and other parts, always disguised as a man and living like a man. Copies of "reports" of 1625 and of 1646, whose originals are attributed to her, are preserved. These brief, simple reports written in the third person are similar to those submitted by conquistadors and soldiers to the king in order to win recognition for their services. The scandalous theme of the man-woman invited all kinds of fantasies, among them the legend of the nun Alférez, already treated by playwrights in the seventeenth century (e.g., Pérez de Montalbán). In 1829 Joaquín María de Ferrer published a picaresque *History of the Nun Alférez* which, according to him, was an authentic autobiography; if this were the case (and we believe not) the colony would have its novelette.

FRANCISCO NÚÑEZ DE PINEDA Y BASCUÑÁN (Chile, 1607–1682) in *My Happy Captivity or the Reason for the Protracted Wars in Chile* (*El cautiverio feliz o razón de las guerras dilatadas de Chile*) tells us of his own experiences as a prisoner of the *Araucanians*. Between this experience of 1629 (his captivity lasted seven months) and the moment of relating it (his manuscript was dated 1673), he felt the desire to create literature, to present his father don Álvaro as a great conquistador, to achieve merit by bringing out his own virtues as captain and good Christian, to serve the Church, to denounce the outrages of bad Christian Spaniards in the Indies. His criticism of the conquest, evangelization and colonization of Chile is the most vigorous one of this epoch and perhaps explains why it remained unpublished until the nineteenth century.

His recollections are almost novelistic. In fact, this was the first chronicle in which an essentially novelistic element appears—the building up of suspense in the action. The chieftain Maulicán took in Pineda from the field of battle, wounded. It was a great honor to have in captivity no less than the son of the feared don Álvaro. Maulicán attempts to convince the other chieftains to spare the life of the prisoner to whom he promises freedom. Will Maulicán succeed in saving Pineda from the bloodthirsty Indians lurking around? Will he keep his promise to free him? The Indians grant the custody of the illustrious captive to Maulicán. Furthermore, must Maulicán return his captive? If he does, Pineda will be executed. Maulicán, the protector of Pineda, takes him on a trip to Repocura. Intrigues. Skirmishes. In every town, dancing and feasting, drunken brawls, adventures. They arrive at Repocura, and Maulicán refuses to relinquish his captive to the other chieftains. He hides him, takes him from one place to another. Finally, Pineda returns to the arms of his father—Maulicán kept his word! Pineda's psychological observations are also worthwhile, novelistically speaking. And even the doctrines he wishes to promulgate —the truth of Christianity, the goodness of the Indians when they are evangelized properly by the Christians, the damage caused by the bad Spaniards—are expressed novelistically: in the form of dialogs, the Indians denounce in eloquent discourses the cruelty of Spanish men and women as "the reason for the protracted wars in Chile." Pineda, educated by the Jesuits, has read humanistic and religious literature. He has also read picaresque, chivalric, and pastoral novels. And it is not always possible to distinguish between the literary embellishments of real-life scenes and pure episodic invention.

Literature, then, embroiders on fact. At any rate, the impulses which advance the narration do not always come from actual recollections, but sometimes from motives especially calculated for their bookish effects. Furthermore, in writing his memoirs Pineda is so punctilious in pointing out good and evil, the just and unjust, virtue and sin, that he illustrates his table of values with fictional episodes. For example, his surprising scruples vis-à-vis women. From the outset of the conquest, the Spaniard fell upon the nude and semi-nude women of America. Columbus, on his very first voyage, tells us how he had to intervene. And the chronicles reveal, more or less freely, the sexual frenzy of the Spaniards. Núñez Pineda is the one Spaniard who shuns Indian women. Several of them pursue him. They are single and gay and virginity means nothing to them. They want to give themselves to him. Even the beautiful and nubile daughter of Maulicán tempts him. And the chieftains themselves wish that he would give pleasure to the enraptured Indian maidens. But Pineda hides, sneaks away, prays to be liberated from the temptation of the flesh. It is not that he is insensitive to beauty. On one occasion he saw the mestizo daughter of Chief Quilalebo bathing among other Indian girls. "She stood out among the other girls for her

whiteness, her discretion, and her beauty. . . . Even though I
wanted to take my eyes off that sexual sight, I could not." "Let
us contemplate for a moment the most difficult temptation put
before me by the spirit of evil on this occasion: a nude woman,
white and clean, with great, black eyes, long eyelashes, eyebrows
in the shape of a bow from which they shot Cupid's arrows, her
hair so long and so thick that it could serve as a coverlet, fell down
her body to her legs, and other particulars that were sufficient at
that moment to carry away my senses and my spirit." If Pineda
did not yield to the Indian girls who offered themselves to him, his
attitude was highly exceptional among Spaniards. He probably
did yield, and with pleasure, but by the time he was writing his
chronicles he was carrying out important military functions and
naturally did not want to tell the truth. In fact, he had to suppress
it because all of Lima knew—from the daughter of Maulicán
herself—about the attentions and temptations he had been subjected to. Between 1633 and 1635 the premiere of an anonymous
play was performed that "represented these loves very poetically."
He had no recourse, therefore, but to lie. Pineda tends to choke
the narrative with religious, moral, and political reflections; but
fortunately for the hedonist reader, the narration recovers its fire
and gives us the quick rising flame of descriptions that are among
the best in Hispanic-American chronicles. Remember, for example, the return of the captive, safe and sound, to the arms of
his old father. His ethnographic descriptions are interesting.

He describes realistically the customs, feasts, food, sexual practices, superstitions, rites. He cultivates good habits, bathes every
day, eats roast with his *chicha* (a strong fermented drink). During his captivity he exhibits modesty, understanding, sympathy.
In one passage he describes a Spanish woman, captured by the
Araucanos and adapting herself well to their life, giving documentary evidence of the creation of a mestizo breed—a typical
phenomenon in Chile and even in the Argentine pampas. For it
was the Indians who procreated what has been called "the mestizo
in reverse." The war of the Indians in the southern part of
America was so fierce and prolonged that a great number of
Spanish women fell into their power and became mothers of

mestizos who continued to fight against the Spaniards. In his landscapes—stormy landscapes, with clouds of squally winds and
torrential rains—efforts to use ornamental, aristocratic expres-
ions appear: "we arrived as night drew its curtains," "the splendors of dawn began to dispel the confused mists of the night,"
"daybreak arrived with signs that the pregnant clouds again would
discharge their icy offspring." Baroque, surely, but not too much
so. He was familiar with the obscure and difficult style of concep-
tists, and he even tells us that it was practiced by the Indians:
"because also among the barbarians there are learned preachers
who set a value on not being understood by anyone." In general,
Pineda was a plain writer. The verses he interpolated amidst his
prose were translations or paraphrases from the classics and also
inventions of his own. He preferred the quiet, simple ballads of
sober but sincere tones.

Friar JUAN DE BARRENECHEA Y ALBIS (Chile, d. 1707) wrote
the *Restoration of the Empire* (*Restauración de la Imperial*,
1693), a history containing a novelistic embryo.

2. Chronicles, Treatises and Didactic Books

The first chronicles of the conquest were like a series of intaglios
from which we made a bas-relief of the New World recently discovered. They were not literature, but we were able to read them
with the attitude of the reader of literature. In the seventeenth
century the struggles, conquests, and the founding of cities continue—and the chronicles keep coming. But these chronicles, unlike those of the early conquistadors, are not amazed at the
newness of things, for they were written by the children or grandchildren, or by those who had come to tread on land already
cleared. Nevertheless, a new narrative theme appears in the seventeenth century—the struggles with the Dutch and English corsairs.
One may wonder whether the chronicles of the seventeenth century in general are less interesting than those of the two previous
periods. If we lost interest, perhaps it is because we no longer see
the chronicles outlined against the background of nature and
ethnography, but against the brilliance of a literature which is
being cultivated now as a luxury. A comparison between the

chronicles and the purely literary works of the same period dims the luster of the chronicles, to the point that we can barely see the great transition from Renaissance to baroque. Since chronicles appear together with religious and didactic treatises (at times the same author indulges in all these activities; at times all these activities appear in a single volume), it does not matter if the subgenres are mixed. The writings of clergymen, jurists, travelers, frizzed with baroque curlicues, are wont to cross over the threshold of literature.

Having been written in Náhuatl, the chronicle of FERNANDO DE ALVA IXTLILXÓCHITL (1568–1648) does not enter into this history; nevertheless, it is a valuable work, not only for its historical data, based on pictographs and information gathered directly from old Indians, but above all for its literary substance: legends, poetic songs, and elegiac poems.

Four chroniclers of real merit stand out. Bishop CASPAR DE VILLARROEL (Ecuador, 1587?–1665) is a pleasant chronicler to read. He initiated his studies in Quito, was ordained in Lima, went to Spain (for about ten years he traveled between Lisbon, Madrid, and Seville), returned to America, first as a bishop in Santiago de Chile and then in Arequipa. "To write has been a continuous temptation for me ever since a tender age," he said. And he added, with a candid smile: "I composed several booklets judging that each would be another step to the top." At the same time he also ascended toward literary recognition, thanks to his anecdotal and gossipy prose. His attitude was that of the conversationalist; and, in the handling of sacred literature (and also profane), he always found the occasion to tell a story, if not from life, at least lively: parables, events, recollections. When he narrates bookish episodes, he animates them with humor and applies them to contemporary situations. Of his prolific work we mention *Comments and Discourses on Lent* (*Comentarios y Discursos sobre la Cuaresma*), *Sacred and Ecclesiastical Moral Histories* (*Historias sagradas y eclesiásticas morales*), and, above all, *Pacific-Ecclesiastical Government or Union of Two Powers, Pontifical and Royal* (*Gobierno, eclesiástico-pacífico o Unión de los dos cuchillos pontificio y regio*, 1656–1657). The latter title refers to the canonical and pontifical rights. In the Indies the ecclesiastical authorities vie with the civil and military authorities, and Villarroel wishes to reconcile both powers by using his knowledge of human vanities, his talent for getting along with people, and his friendly and sometimes ironic intelligence. He admired Spain but defended the Creoles against the incomprehension, ignorance, impertinence, and injustice of the Spaniards in the viceregal court, and he even demanded that the government of the colonies be vested in those born there.

The Jesuit ALONSO DE OVALLE (Chile, 1601–1651) wrote a *Historic Account of the Dominion of Chile* (*Histórica relación del reino de Chile,* 1646) in a prose excellent for its sensitivity to the beauties of the landscape. His greatest merit lies in the lingering descriptions of natural scenery. Besides describing the countryside, he also described the city and some Chilean customs. His inventory of beautiful sights smacks of touristic advertising; he wants to attract missionaries from Europe, so he tells them that everything resembles Europe, except that in Chile there are no bedbugs. His pages, then, are addressed to Europeans, and in his eulogy of Chile, he follows European models, like the eulogy of Spain composed by Isadore of Seville. However, he does install Chile, and the Andes, in the realm of literature. He describes passages where rocks take on marvelous colors, the rivers reflect unsuspected images, and the sea loses itself in the infinite. His prose is not baroque; on the contrary, it is almost colloquial in its slowness, repetitions, and long periods. But it assumes a poetic tint and imaginative dash whenever he is enthused. The contrast between his good passages and the rest of his prose indicates that Ovalle did not lack talent, but rather time or the desire to be artistic. He is a naturalist with imagination. In the chapter about the mountain range, for example, he becomes ecstatic and his fantasy adds impressions of light. He imagines that he is on the top of an Andean peak. From there, he tells us that, while the air is blue and serene over his head, he sees the rain falling from the clouds at his feet upon the people below. Or he tells us that "the rainbow that we see from the land crossing the sky is seen from these heights extended along the earth as a footstool at our feet, while those who are on the ground see it above their heads. . . ." The first part, descriptive and historic, is superior to the second which deals with the Society of Jesus.

Bishop LUCAS FERNÁNDEZ DE PIEDRAHITA (Colombia, 1624–1688), like the Inca Garcilaso and Alva Ixtlilxóchitl, had in his veins royal indigenous blood. Though not as novelistic as the Peruvian nor as objective as the Mexican, Piedrahita, nevertheless, is one of the important chroniclers of America; and, like these two, he exalted the pre-Hispanic cultures, especially that of the Chibchas. He documented his work as best he could, searching archives in Spain, corresponding with other historians, and reading carefully the chronicles of others. He put Juan de Castellanos in prose and utilized the manuscripts (later lost) of Jiménez de Quesada; and he not only gave us descriptions of indigenous customs and historical events but he also interpreted them philosophically and morally. His own value, he used to say, consisted "of putting in less ancient language" what others had written about the conquest. Pure modesty. His *General History of the Conquest of the New Realm of Granada* (*Historia general de las conquistas del Nuevo Reino de Granada*, 1688), although uneven, is well written; and, at his best he manages to be elegant. Because of his preacher's attitude he tended to have sententious and oratorical moments.

Friar PEDRO SIMÓN (Spain, 1574–*ca.* 1630) arrived in America in 1604 and left some *Historical Notes* (*Noticias historiales*) on the realm of New Granada that harbored so many imaginary things they struck the fantasy of his readers. He speaks of Indians who drag their ears along the ground, who sleep under water, and who feed themselves by smelling fruit since they have "no ordinary way of expelling excrement from their bodies." He was, nevertheless, a slow, lengthy, and tedious writer, although he could describe in detail the excesses of the tyrant, Lope de Aguirre. FRIAR BERNABÉ COBO (Spain, 1582–1657) ranged over the Antilles, Venezuela, Peru, and Mexico and in his *History of the New World* (*Historia del Nuevo Mundo*, 1636) he described the natural and especially the botanical geography of these areas more than the history. In order to counteract the false and exaggerated notions that were being propagated throughout Europe, he corrected them in accordance with the phenomena he saw. Friar ANTONIO DE LA CALANCHA (Bolivia, 1584–1654) was a chronicler of the order of St. Augustine. In his *Moralized Chronicle* (*Crónica moralizada*, 1638) he described the skies and the lands of Peru and Bolivia with an abundance of detail on colonial life. DIEGO DE LEÓN PINELO (*ca.* 1590), author of *Paradise in the New*

World (*El Paraíso en el Nuevo Mundo*); PERO MEXÍA DE OVANDO, author of *The Woman from Ovando* (*La Ovandina*, 1621); DIEGO DE ROSALES (1603–1677), who is more of a realist than Ovalle, wrote *General History of the Realm of Chile* (*Historia general del reino de Chile*); FRANCISCO DE AVILA (Peru, 1573–1647), in combating the idolatry of the natives through his writings, incidentally preserved some beautiful legends; Friar AGUSTÍN DE VETANCOURT (Mexico, 1620–1700?). Father MANUEL RODRÍGUEZ (Colombia, 1638–1684) wrote *The Amazon and the Marañón Rivers* (*El Marañón y Amazonas*) in a prose of relative literary merit, clear but capable of dramatic effects and of rhetorical gleanings, as in the description of the eruption of the Pichincha. Friar DIEGO DE CÓRDOVA SALINAS, after the *Life of Saint Francis Solano* (*Vide de S. Francisco Solano,* Lima, 1630), published a well-written *Franciscan Chronicle of the Provinces of Peru* (*Crónica Franciscana de las Provincias del Perú,* 1651), replete with details on almost half a century of religious life in Peru and other parts, together with a description of viceroyal Lima (shaken at the moment by earthquakes and piratical assaults) and observations on geography and ethnography. Father ALONSO DE ZAMORA (Colombia, 1645–1717)—another mestizo— was the chronicler of his own religious order. Inferior to Piedrahita in style, he was nevertheless a good observer of nature, although he did lack the imagination of a landscapist. JOSÉ DE BUENDÍA (1644–1727) is the author of *The Star of Lima Converted into a Sun on Its Three Crowns* (*La estrella de Lima convertida en Sol sobre sus tres coronas,* 1680). Father FRANCISCO DE FIGUEROA (Colombia, fl. middle seventeenth century) authored *Account of the Missions of the Company of Jesus in the Land of Maynas* (*Relación de las misiones de la Compañía de Jesús en el país de los Maynas*), with details on Indians and customs. Friar FRANCISCO VÁZQUEZ (Guatemala, 1647–1713), ORTIZ Y MORALES (Colombia, b. 1658). Friar PEDRO TOBAR Y BUENDÍA (Colombia, 1648–1713) was chronicler of the miracles of the local Virgin. JOSÉ ORTIZ Y MORALES (Colombia, 1658) has shown us colonial society in his *Curious and Doctrinal Observations* (*Observaciones curiosas y doctrinales,* 1713). Father FRANCISCO XIMÉNEZ (Spain-Guatemala, 1666–1729) was a historian. Father JUAN ANTONIO OVIEDO (Colombia-Mexico, 1670–1757) was one of the precursors of the great Jesuit humanists. FRANCISCO ANTONIO FUENTES Y GUZMÁN (Guatemala, fl. 1689) was author of *Historical Precepts* (*Preceptos historiales*). JUAN BAUTISTA DE TORO (Colombia, d. in 1734) authored *The Religious Layman* (*El secular religioso,* 1721), wherein one observes the Creole spirit versus Spanish arrogance. ANTONIO RUIZ DE MONTOYA (Peru, 1583–1652), *Spiritual Conquest Made by the Society of Jesus in the provinces of Paraguay, Parana, Uruguay and Tape* (*Conquista espiritual hecha por los religiosos de la Compañía de Jesús en las provincias del Paraguáy, Paraná, Uruguay y Tape,* 1639). FRANCISCO ZARQUE (1601–1691), *Distinguished Missionaries of the Society of Jesus in the province of Paraguay* (*Insignes misioneros de la Compañía de Jesús en la provincia del Paraguáy,* 1687).

In this section we have mentioned writers distinguished principally for their prose. We shall end by a reference to a form of prose that achieved great loftiness and feeling, written by a woman we have already spoken of —Sor Juana Inés de la Cruz.

Other women were noteworthy in this period: in Ecuador, Jerónima de Velasco; in Peru, Saint Rose of Lima (1586–1617); and two poetesses who are known as Clarinda, author of a "Discourse in Praise of Poesy," in tercets; and Amarilis, who sent to Lope de Vega an epistle in the form of a *silva*. But the woman who, after Sor Juana, reached the highest poetic expression in this century is the eloquent nun from New Granada SOR FRANCISCA JOSEFA DEL CASTILLO Y GUEVARA, called MOTHER CASTILLO (Colombia, 1671–1742). By poetic expression we are not referring solely to her verses (some of those attributed to her belonged to Sor Juana) but to certain revelations of her ascetic and mystic prose. She had read from mixed sources: alongside religious books—the Bible, Santa Theresa, St. Ignatius, Father Osuna, and so forth—she read novels and sets of plays which she called "the plague of the soul." She composed her literature from themes and forms of religious and baroque letters, not as a vocation, but under orders from her confessors. One notices a slow progress in her prose, from mannerism and disorderliness in her first pages to the simplicity of her last. She wrote a kind of diary of her intimate devotions—publishers have called it *Spiritual Affections* (*Afectos espirituales*), although it seems that the title in the manuscript is *Spiritual Sentiments* (*Sentimientos espirituales*).

She was twenty-two years of age when she began it—her prose was unsure, affected, exuberant, obscure, laden with rhetorical figures, defective in its expansive moments. Twenty years later she was still writing her diary but the prose was now more moderate. By then she had begun an autobiography that went from her infancy until she gave up the directorship of the convent— the publishers have called it *Her Life* (*Su Vida*). Since it is a work of maturity, the *Life* differs from the *Affections*, not only because she gives us anecdotes and episodes of good and bad convent habits, but also because it is composed with a less luxuriant, less confused prose. Putting to one side the virtues of her prose—which were never excellent—Mother Castillo is of interest to us because her religious sincerity pierced her heavy words like a ray of light. Her religious calling was so intense that she does not resemble anyone in her epoch. In a flight of oratory

Mother Castillo reaches the height of the greatest of Christian themes. She is disorderly, digressive, without doctrinal rigor. But the metaphors shine out from her pages, and as they shine they light up the sentiments of a soul stirred by the joy and the panic of her visions of God. She was *the* mystic of our letters.

C. THEATER

From time to time very talented men visited the colonies from Spain, but their influence was not very great. On the other hand, some writers born in Hispanic America went to Spain and became established there. One example was Father BRUNO DE SOLIS Y VALENZUELA (Colombia, 1616–1677), author of the first Colombian theatrical work. Another American writer made a long visit to Spain and, without saying one word about America, as if he had forgotten it, gave himself to the mother country, where he left the imprint of his genius. He was JUAN RUIZ DE ALARCÓN.

Juan Ruiz de Alarcón (Mexico, 1580–1639) was thirty-three years old when he established himself definitely in Spain. At twenty he left Mexico; he returned at twenty-seven; and lived six more years in Mexico. One does not live his entire youth in his native country in vain. Personal experience is attuned to the frequencies of the local environment. And although the artist may later change his locale and aspire to a more universal expression, the vibrations of that existence, tuned to earlier experiences, can always be heard in his works in a very subtle way. Alarcón's Spanish contemporaries soon detected a certain strangeness in his plays, and later critics have analyzed their non-typical, non-Spanish traits. They have a colonial Mexican character. Although his plays are constructed in the manner of Lope de Vega, they reflect the originality of a new society that is less vivacious and less extroverted than that of the metropolis. Alarcón's characters spend more time in their houses than in the street; duels are avoidable; there is a prudent, reserved, and courteous tone (the Indian gave colonial society a tinge of sobriety); the *graciosos* or comic servants are not as scurrilous, perhaps because the Indian servants in

Mexico were not permitted the familiarities of the servants in Spain. The search for external Mexican elements in Alarcón's theater is difficult and even sterile.The most obvious is a commentary on the water drainage system of Mexico City in *The Man Who Resembles Himself* (*El semejante de sí mismo*). And might it not be that his most apparent Mexican trait is his not wishing to speak of Mexico? One does not live the many years that Alarcón lived in Hispanic-America without being an Hispanic-American; however, when he decided at the end of the sixteenth century and beginning of the seventeenth century, to succeed in the Spanish theater, he did so without having in mind any notions of patriotism. Alarcón had seen some theater in Mexico before going to Spain. Since 1597 Mexico had had a playhouse, that is, a permanent theater, with a building, companies of actors, and a theatergoing public. In this period Alarcón must have had a rough draft of *The Cave of Salamanca* (*La cueva de Salamanca*). But once in Spain he wanted to be a Spanish writer. The Inca Garcilaso, because of the nature of his subject, the Inca civilization, had insisted on his status as a mestizo. Alarcón did not have to speak of his status as a Mexican to engage in theatrical activities in Lope's circle. It is possible, furthermore, that in the aggressive social life of Spain in that epoch, it would have been risky to introduce Mexican themes in his plays—the Spaniards would have mocked such esthetic deformity with the same cruelty with which they had mocked his physical deformity. Alarcón was a hunchback ("a poet between two plates"); and it has been said that his bitterness over this defect (more terrible at a time in history when physical beauty was overly esteemed) created a resentment that finds moral expression in his plays. There is, in effect, an ethical attitude in Alarcón. He ponders the values that orient or should orient human conduct. This moralizing preoccupation was undoubtedly tense in Alarcón's soul, but it was also one of the resonant chords of the Spanish theater of his time. One had to moralize in the theater. And they all moralized; Tirso, later Calderón. Even though Alarcón, in moralizing, followed his own ethical impulses rather than social conventions, the truth is, he did not go very far as a reformer. His morality is the traditional one: honor, loyalty, gratitude, love of one's neighbor. And even the value of his moral characters, both negative and positive, depends more on Alarcón's ability to move the characters dramatically than on the depth of the ideas presented. The liar, the slanderer, the ingrate, etc., have value as artistic characters. They are more complicated than would be necessary for a simple moral lesson. It is the action that moves all the characters of the Spanish play; Alarcón's characters, nevertheless, manage to pause long enough so that we can hear their reasoning. They speak directly to the mind. They are not lyrical. When they become lyrical, it is with moderation. Alarcón gives them commentaries to speak that coincide with our experience of life; that is why his characters' motives of conduct are psychologically true to life. Alarcón constructs his plays with care. Lope and Tirso wrote plays by the hundreds; he, only two dozen. Plays of intrigue, heroic plays. His best productions, character plays like *Walls Have Ears* (*Las paredes oyen*), *The Winning of Friends* (*Ganar amigos*), *Suspect Truth* (*La verdad sospechosa*) —Corneille adapted it in *Le Menteur*—give him an intelligent and modern air. The plays of character development at times take place under marvelous circumstances, such as *Proof of Promises* (*La prueba de las promesas*); at times they unfold in sparkling dialectics as in *It is an Ill Wind That Blows No Good* (*No hay mal que por bien no venga*, 1623?). With this play Alarcón closed his dramatic career. The main character—no stereotype—Don Blas, is one of the few in all of the plays of the Golden Age, who addresses himself directly to the intelligence of the modern reader. Don Blas is so anti-conventional that the sharpness of his dialectics converts this play into the least conventional one of its time. The good sense of the comfort-loving Don Blas surprises and entertains us—at least in the first two acts—because it is not part of a moral lesson, but of a psychological picture.

In the Colonies

More space should be given to Alarcón, but his theater, after all, belongs to Spain. In truth, Spain is the center of all theatrical activity. It is the century of Lope de Vega, of Tirso, of Calderón, whose plays reach the colonies. Companies of Spanish actors bring the latest successes. They present them in palaces and in public enclosures. The audiences applaud. And they read the collections of plays which, from the time of Lope's first one in 1605, are imported from Spain. Plays of the Lope school first, and later those of the Calderón school, influence customs, habits of dress, and manners of speech. The Creoles seldom write for the theater, and when they do, they limit themselves to interludes to fill in the time between the acts of Spanish plays. What colonial writer would dare compete with the masters of Spain? The conformity of court life and of religious life, the lack of stimulus and, naturally, of talent, impoverish the theater. Be that as it may, the productions in Spain and in America move at different tempos. During almost all of the seventeenth century (at least until the death of Calderón) Spain is at its theatrical apogee while the colonies are scarcely producing little occasional pieces; from 1681 onward, the Spanish theater declines while the colonies begin to advance their theater with ambitious plays. In Mexico, prior to Alarcón, we had González de Eslava, already studied in the previous chapter, and after Alarcón, Sor Juana Inéz de la Cruz. But if it did not produce outstanding figures, the Mexican theater did produce an outstanding number of plays. Seldom did one author write more than one play. The normal procedure was for someone to write a playlet to celebrate some event or to honor a particular person, and then he would retire from the theater, never to return to the profession. In reality neither drama nor comedy was cultivated, but rather little exercises in cajolery that were called preludes, dances, interludes, windups, mystery plays, and farces. The most fertile genre was the *loa*, or short panegyric prelude, in which four or six characters presented symbolically either mythological beings or qualities or places. When they represented real men they were usually called "Indians" if they came from America, "gentlemen" if they were from Spain. These *loas* generally celebrated the proclamation of a new king or the welcoming of a viceroy or archbishop.

In Mexico they were composed by Francisco Robledo, Miguel Pérez de Gálvez, Jerónimo Becerra, Alonzo Ramírez de Vargas, Antonio Medina Solís, and others. *The Colloquy of the New Conversion and Baptism of the*

Last Four Kings of Tlaxcala in New Spain (*Coloquio de la nueva conversión y bautismo de los cuatro últimos reyes de Tlaxcala en la Nueva España*), attributed to Cristóbal Gutiérrez de Luna, seems to date from 1619. From 1684 is the unbelievable staging of the life of St. Francis of Assisi, *The Preacher of God and Patriarch of the Poor* (*El Pregonero de Dios y Patriarca de los pobres*) by Francisco de Acevedo. It has already been noted that Bramón included in his *The Goldfinches of the Virgin* a well-structured, well-versified mystery play that made notable use of indigenous scenery and choreography. MATÍAS DE BOCANEGRA (Mexico, 1612–1668), the poet of the famous "Song at the Sight of a Disillusion" (*"Canción a la vista de un desengaño"*), composed in 1640 the three acts of his *St. Francis of Borgia* (*Comedia de San Francisco de Borja*). It is humanist theater in the manner practiced by the Jesuits. In it he has some *décimas* or ten-verse stanzas that recall Segismundo's first soliloquy in Calderón's *Life Is a Dream*, published four years earlier. On the other hand, he introduces native dances and songs. (AGUSTÍN DE SALAZAR Y TORRES, 1642–1675, returned to Spain when he was eighteen years old and there he wrote his plays—like Alarcón he belongs to the dramatic literature of Spain.)

Peru followed Mexico with the same type of theater. The first company of players was constituted in 1599 in Lima, and in the first years of the seventeenth century the *Casa de Comedias* (*Playhouse*) was established. The theater was enjoyed equally by the general public and the aristocratic and ecclesiastical segments. (Friar Gaspar de Villarroel has recorded for us his youthful fancy for plays.) Although in general the works presented came from Spain, there were those by Creole playwrights having local themes; Núñez de Pineda Bascuñán, in *The Happy Captivity*, recounts with special care the episode of his relations with Maulicán's daughter in order to clarify matters, because in Peru, he says, a play had been written and staged that was "quite contrary to the facts, representing these love affairs in a very poetic way." The major figures in this period were Peralta Barnuevo (who, because of the dates of his plays, will be treated in the next chapter) and LORENZO DE LAS LLAMOSAS (1665?–d. after 1705). The latter composed two musical comedies: *The Gods Also Avenge Themselves* (*Tambien se vengan los dioses*, 1698), with an elaborate stage populated by gods, nymphs and shepherds, and *Destinies Conquer Kindnesses* (*Destinos vencen finezas*, 1698), on the love of Dido and Aeneas. DIEGO MEXÍA DE FERNANGIL, of Seville, author of *Antarctic Parnassus* (*Parnaso antártico*), also wrote *The God Pan* (*El Dios Pan*, between 1608 and 1630), a kind of pastoral eclogue treating divine subjects in one act and in verse. Espinosa Medrano and Valle Caviedes, as shall be seen when they are discussed, also wrote for the theater.

To the Colombian theater belongs FERNANDO FERNÁNDEZ DE VALENZUELA (1616–last quarter of the seventeenth century), whose interlude *Laurea Criticizes* (*Laurea crítica*) caricatures various psychological and social types. A caricature of a man of letters who speaks in the language of Góngora is amusing and, in addition, has value as a document in the polemical history of that style. Of greater importance in the Colombian theater is JUAN DE CUETO Y MENA (Spain, 1602?–d. after 1669). In his writings he profited from Lope de Vega, Góngora, Quevedo, and Calderón. It would

indeed be a curiosity if the conjecture were true that Cueto, as he versified
his theatrical "colloquy," *Competition Among Nobles and Discord Reconciled* (*La competencia en los nobles y discordia concordada*, 1662) had
taken into account the mystery plays or *autos sacramentales* of Calderón,
and that the latter, in turn, on writing *Life Is a Dream* (1673), took into
account Cueto's colloquy. If he made an impression on Calderón it must
have been only in the idea of converting the four elements, fire, air, water
and land, into the main characters of an allegory that takes Greek philosophic notions and interprets them in the light of scholastic philosophy.
Cueto's universe was that of Ptolemy; his literature, that of the Baroque.
In his "Song Describing Popa Hill" (*"Canción describiendo el Cerro de la
Popa"*) he distorted in a baroque style the outline of a Colombian landscape. He had his colloquy, *Paraphrasis Panegirica*, performed. A friend
celebrate the verses of this colloquy in the courteous, overwrought, and
adulatory language of the epoch thusly: "thou shall no longer be Juan de
Cueto / for thou shalt be Juan de Mena." Not so—he was and shall be
Juan de Cueto y Mena, one of the many obscure poets who, while cleaving
to baroque techniques, managed with difficulty to come away with one or
two happy images.

IV. 1701-1759

Authors born between 1675 and 1735

Historical framework: The Bourbons take over the Spanish throne. Under Philip V and Fernando VI the Spanish Empire begins its efforts to retain the colonies.

Cultural tendencies: The end of the Baroque. The Rococo. Neoclassicism.

Introduction

From the end of the seventeenth century, France exerted a cultural hegemony over all Europe. Spain received this influence even before the Bourbons entered to govern the country. Undoubtedly the change in dynasties favored such influence. However, more than being Gallicized, Spain was being Europeanized —alongside French influences there were those of Italy and England. But the cultural level between Spain and the rest of Europe was so uneven that Spain's cultural ascension was very slow. In just one generation—let us say from 1680 to 1715—the enlightenment was imposed upon Europe. In Spain, on the other hand, the new spirit, rationalist in philosophy and classical in literature, begins to manifest itself in the third decade of the century. Until then the dominant literature was the baroque. It was natural that the rise of Hispanic-American culture should be even slower. The currents of the enlightenment passed from Spain into America and influenced ideas and customs, but they did not inspire a neoclassical literature until the end of the eighteenth century. In literary progress, then, the colonies lagged behind the mother country. The baroque style continued to be cultivated when al-

ready in Spain it was forgotten or transformed into rococo or remembered mockingly. Lacking great figures—one can scarcely
mention Peralta Barnuevo, Juan Bautista Aguirre, Paz Salgado,
Santiago Pita—we must attempt to paint a broad cultural panorama. Compared with that of Europe, and even with that of Spain,
it is meager. Nevertheless, we cannot dispense with it if we wish
to understand the slow awakening of the spirit of the 1700's. New
lights begin to temper the skies. From the point of view of ideas,
the first rays of the enlightenment filter through the clouds of
scholasticism. From the point of view of *belles lettres*, the warm
colors of the baroque are softened by rococo pinks and cooled by
neoclassical blues. The order of ideas and the order of letters are
not as disparate in reality as they seem to be from the two sentences describing them. There are those wretched encumbrances
that baffle all attempts at classification—the intermediate phenomena: treatises with literary touches and literature for didactic
ends, and the continuation of the baroque throughout the century,
in spite of the attempts of neoclassicism to block its path.

The center of ideas now lies outside of Hispanic culture. What
is happening in Europe (and Spain is the last to find out) is nothing less than the liquidation of Christian cosmology, as it was organized by the churches, and the triumph of a new cosmology
founded on reason and experience. From a bird's-eye view (that
is, a philosopher-bird) the slow and complex process of the decomposition of the authority of the Apostolic Roman Catholic
Church occurred at the same time as the exploration, conquest,
and colonization of the New World: between the fifteenth and
eighteenth centuries. The corrosive agents of this decomposition
in Europe were Protestantism, humanism, and rationalism.
Thanks to the dissolvent action of these three forces, western
culture is radically renewed—the culture of the eighteenth century
is called the enlightenment. The European enlightenment consists
of the belief that men, here, in this real world, can attain a perfection that for scholasticism was only possible to Christians in a state
of grace after death. Newton (nature can be explained rationally) and Locke (we can apply natural solutions to humans things)
are interrated into the enlightenment (nature, reason) and re-

place such previous principles as grace, salvation, and predestination. The Englishmen Newton and Locke did not go as far as their French disciples. The French became the disseminators. In the first half of the eighteenth century—the setting of this chapter— men of the enlightenment like Voltaire and Montesquieu constitute a generation of moderates. They are deists who mock all that displeases them. Only in the second half of the century—the setting of the next chapters—does there appear a generation of radicals. They are too angry to be able to laugh. Years of atheism, years of mechanism. And there will be a third generation (classical rationalists who follow Holbach; sentimental romanticists who follow Rousseau, whose ideal man is a rational and sensitive man, intelligent and good-natured, sound of heart and head) which brought about the American Revolution of 1776 and the French Revolution of 1789 and which will influence the revolutionaries of the Independence of Hispanic-America. But let us not hasten. We are in the period 1701–1759. In Europe, we repeat, there has been a change: life comes down from the Christian, supernatural heaven, after death, to a land where at any moment natural happiness will be attained—a change which implies the doctrine of progress through the radiation of the light of reason. The Roman Catholic Church had always taught; now it had to be taught. And the Church, in fact, cannot help but learn. Reason makes it possible for us to understand the laws of nature. In a universe-watch, created by a God-watchmaker, men live who are capable of reading the movements of its hands. God exists for Voltaire, the deist. But there is no reason to beg Him for miracles —all that is necessary is to understand the watch. (From 1750 onward God will be dispensable—He will be replaced by the goddess of reason.) Ethics will be autonomous. For Christians, man is born in sin; evil is explained by human greed, and the salvation brought by Christ does not imply a cultural policy of environmental betterment. For the men of the enlightenment, the environment is decisive. That is why one must arrange rationally the external circumstances of life so that man can orient himself toward the good. Christianity, obviously, does not disappear. It resists, and continues to appeal to the masses. But nowhere has the Church preserved its power as it has in Spain. The philosophers of the eighteenth century in Europe used to protest because there existed many things that offended reason: all of the medieval past that survived in arbitrary institutions. Moreover, reason—after Descartes, Newton, Locke—claimed the power of organizing human and social affairs. In Spain the new spirit did not go beyond the limits of the Church. The humanitarian spirit prevailed within the Church, in one sector of the clergy and of the laity, a sector not visible or differentiated. Between the mystical heaven of Christianity and the terrestrial heaven that men of the enlightenment fixed in the future, there is in Spain an intermediate heaven, namely, that if society must be improved, it should be done by Christians within the Catholic Church. Of the three agents of dissolution in Europe that changed the conception of the world, Protestantism had no effect in Spain, and humanism and rationalism operated from within the sphere of the Church. Spain was not ready for the leap that Europe had taken, and even the natural and physical sciences continued into the eighteenth century tied to ecclesiastical authority. One must consider, in this period, the labors of a Feijóo, who reconciles religion and philosophy. In Hispanic-America orthodoxy was even more marked—at least here only orthodoxy is manifest. Up to the beginning of the eighteenth century, modern thought, in philosophy and in religion, had not sifted into the Hispanic-American colonies. (Scholasticism will predominate even up to the last decades of the century.) Theology was based on revelation and attempted to demonstrate it rationally. Scholastic rationalism prevailed: the Cartesian type of rationalism was not known, except in very few instances. The sciences depended on theology, and reason on faith. There are only intra-ecclesiastical disputes. Polemics and satires give an illusory appearance of intellectual liberty. It is fundamentally a three-sided family squabble: the Dominican order and its Thomist school; the Franciscan and its Scotist school; the Jesuit and its Suarist school. The Thomists dominated the field of education, and it is natural that some religious orders would be resentful. With so much tension within the Church, it is easy to imagine the resistance to what was openly heterodox. Scholasticism, at first, rejects absolutely all enlightened tendencies; then, it fortifies itself by taking cognizance of its own nature and protecting its weaknesses; finally, several solitary voices, within the Church, are raised against scholasticism. The Inquisition alone cannot be blamed for this misoneism (hatred for the new). Hispanic-American inquisitions did not need to censure Spanish thought because it arrived in the New World already censured by the inquisitions of Spain. The censuring of French and English thought revealed a more spontaneous "holy horror" for novelties rather than a fixed inquisitorial policy. The Inquisition operated on a practical basis, not a speculative one. It prohibited; it did not discuss. Its doctrine was that the great truths had already been discovered and, therefore, there was no progress possible. Hence, the annals of the Inquisition offer nothing of interest for a history of ideas—they only give us data on prohibited ideas. Another repressive force against new ideas was the apologetic literature in defense of the Church and against anything modern. To be a Catholic, it is said, one need not be a philosopher; but if one is a Catholic and a philosopher, he has to be an Aristotelian. We have already noted that there are no fixed boundaries between the genres. Nevertheless, we intend to begin by dealing with written poetry, then written prose and, finally, the activity of the theater.

A. MAINLY POETRY

Baroque

1. *Baroque Poetry* / As we move on to poetry we must first recognize the vitality of the Baroque movement. That it is not a style of decadence is proved by the fact that in America, at least, it exalts the imagination, although poetry does decay in this century.

It is true that there were other types of poetry, for example, popular and Latin poetry. In popular, satiric poetry we have already mentioned Castillo Andraca y Tamayo and his "Couplets of the Blind Man of Mercy" (*"Coplas del Ciego de la Merced"*) and we could couple him with JUAN BAUTISTA MAZIEL (Argentina, 1727–1788), a mediocre and obscure poet (albeit a renowned jurist) who composed one of the first attempts at Gaucho poetry: "A Cowhand Sings in Prairie Style about the Triumphs of His Most Excellent Lord Don Pedro Cevallos" (*"Canta un guaso en estilo campestre los*

triunfos del Excelentísimo Señor Don Pedro Cevallos"). Churchmen produced Latin poetry, for they felt a cordial kinship to this style. The Jesuits
DIEGO JOSÉ ABAD (Mexico, 1727–1779), the above-mentioned Francisco
Xavier Alegre, and RAFAEL LANDÍVAR (Guatemala, 1731–1793)—especially the latter who authored the very important *Mexican Country Sojourn*
(Rusticatio Mexicana)—wrote Latin poetry of marked value; not, however,
pertinent to this history, which is concerned only with Spanish poetry.

Leaving to one side, then, the Latin and popular poets, we
come to the Jesuit father JUAN BAUTISTA DE AGUIRRE (Ecuador,
1725–1786). In the middle of the century, a full century and a
quarter after the death of Góngora and a quarter of a century from
Luzán's *Poética*, Aguirre presents us with a beautiful baroque
flower. He left us scarcely a score of poems. And it is amazing
that in such a small number there should be such variety of tone;
moral, theological, amatory, satirical, lyrical, polemical, descriptive compositions. And such a variety of metrics: sonnets, rhymed
octaves, *silvas* (verses of seven and eleven syllables), *canciones*,
liras (five-line stanzas), ballads, *décimas* (ten octosyllabic
verses), and quatrains. And, finally, such a variety of influences
is apparent: Góngora, Quevedo, Calderón, Rioja, and Polo de
Medina. For Aguirre, poetry must have been a formal type of
entertainment; and perhaps because of this attitude, the baroque
poems, in which his playful disposition and extreme formal style
coincided, are his best. A syllogistic logic runs through his syntax
forcing it to bob and weave striking hyperbaton, ellipsis, constructions based on symmetries and contrasts, and so on. But his logic
colors, sounds, plastic beauty and fragrance appears. At first sight
has exchanged abstractions for metaphors so that a reality rich in
it looks like dynamic poetry. Then one notices that nothing moves
immobile concept (like someone who, in the darkness of a ceme-
—the author has violently discharged a metaphoric light upon an
tery, suddenly casts a light upon a gravestone). But if what matters to us is not the logical meaning of the verses, nor their function
within the allegory, nor the philosophy of the poet, but the very
movement of the metaphor as a meteoric fragment, then we must
indeed recognize a certain dynamism in Father Aguirre. Some
of his images are wrought with all the intensity of authentic poetic
vision: metaphors of a good poet in mediocre poems.

A fellow student of Aguirre was IGNACIO ESCANDÓN (1719), an Ecuadorian by birth although he lived and wrote in Lima. He was a passable poet and his most interesting aspect was his eulogy of Father Feijóo and his plans —unfulfilled—to write a history of Hispanic-American literature. "Southern America," he used to say, "was more abundant in minds than in mines and being a land of men of letters it became a sepulcher to their memory."

A list of baroque poets would be very long. It suffices to mention FRANCISCO RUIZ DE LEÓN (Mexico, 1683), who is still Gongorizing in *La Hernandía, Triumphs of the Faith and the Glory of Spanish Arms* (*La Hernandía, triunfos de la fe y gloria de las armas españolas*, 1755), a tale in twelve cantos and twelve royal octaves about the deeds of Hernán Cortés, and in his poem, *Sweet Myrrh for the Encouragement of Sinners* (*Mirra dulce*); the Jesuit, JUAN JOSÉ DE ARRIOLA (Mexico, 1698–1768), a depicter of local color and a man of culture; the priest, CAYETANO CABRERA Y QUINTERO (Mexico, d. 1775), also adept with words; JOSÉ SURÍ Y ÁGUILA (Cuba, 1696–1762), a popular religious poet, improviser for religious ceremonies and holidays, an eager gleaner of baroque words; LORENZO MARTÍNEZ DE AVILEIRA (Cuba, 1722–1782), also a religious poet, with one or two satirical compositions. The historian Juan de Velasco, of whom we have already spoken, left us a *Collection of Sundry Poetry, Composed by a Man of Leisure in the City of Faenza* (*Colección de poesías varias, hecha por un ocioso en la ciudad de Faenza en 1790*), the first to include Ecuadorian writers. In it are RAMÓN VIESCAS, author of a "Dream at Dante's Tomb" (*"Sueño sobre el sepulcro del Dante"*); JOSÉ OROZCO (1733–1786), author of the heroic poem "The Conquest of Menorca" (*"La conquista de Menorca"*); the brothers AMBROSIO and JOAQUÍN LARREA; and the nostalgic MARIANO ANDRADE (1734). In this anthology of Ecuadorian poets there are satiric, elegiac, and heroic poems in Renaissance and baroque styles. Among the Spaniards (who are also represented) Góngora stands out significantly.

Rococo

2. *Rococo Poetry* / But the baroque slowly becomes rococo. JOAQUÍN VELÁZQUEZ DE CÁRDENAS Y LEÓN (Mexico? 1732– 1786) wrote sonnets with an elegance and sensuality that were more rococo than baroque. FRANCISCO ANTONIO VÉLEZ LADRÓN DE GUEVARA (Colombia, 1721–d. after 1781) was a court and society poet, who bequeathed his verses to viceroys and their wives. He has few Gongoristic traits, and in his verse there is a tone of gallantry; there is also a rococo tone. For example when he sings, "His friend, the beautiful lady, had her hat snatched off by the wind," the attitude is new. The same can be said of his use of mythological themes. The sonnet "to a lady whose mirror, while she was gazing at herself in it, fell and broke to pieces," plays

prettily with eye-mirror images and the Cyclops-Argus theme. His quatrains on the "birthday of a lady" have a rococo grace. In his descriptive ballad of a stroll by the Salto waterfall, there is a feeling for nature and a picture of liberal and mirthful customs of gentlemen and ladies who drink, ride horseback, lose themselves in the woods, etc. This is, indeed, rococo. Rather, one can see in the background the viceregal society that participates in a refined European way, whose style in those days was the rococo.

The word "rococo" has been printed so often in this chapter that it is now time to define it. Rococo style came about in Europe during the first half of the eighteenth century. In Hispanic-America it appeared much later. The word itself, "rococo," was not used in Hispanic-America, but this need not be an obstacle to its use here. Everyone knows that first the changes in style appear, and after a good number of years have passed the changes are described and baptized. The truth is that the word "rococo" became current only after the style to which it alludes had been superseded by a new one: neoclassicism. Rococo, as used in 1754 by the new critics of classical tastes, meant something already outmoded, something that should be ridiculed. But it is obvious that in the Europe of the first half of the eighteenth century, it was a fresh and vital phenomenon. An antecedent to the word "rococo" was *"rocalla,"* which from the sixteenth century meant any outdoor construction or place of luxuriousness and enjoyment: gardens, fountains, grottos, bowers. These architectonic contrivances were elegant, but based on unhewn rock work, incrustations of shells, capricious forms of marine foam and floral boughs. From Italian, French, and German *rocalla* comes the rococo. In the eighteenth century the rococo, essentially a decorative style, softens the baroque. The ostentatiousness, the magnificence, the heaviness, the tragic movement of great masses, the violence of the baroque are converted into a style that is pleasing, playful, pinioned, dancing, dazzling, delicate, apparently frivolous and licentious, always discriminating, always refined, smooth in its undulations, and shimmering with gracefulness in its smallest detail. If the baroque expressed a desperate vision of life, the rococo expressed a life of joy and voluptuousness. The sensual richness of rococo style indicates that men have decided to seek happiness freely. In this sense the rococo accompanies the movement of ideas earlier. Are not libertinism and effeminate delicateness supported by the illuminist idea that, through reason, we discover the naturalness of the sex act, previously considered sinful? One of the rococo elements is the appetite for pleasure. We must remember that, in the eighteenth century, Christian eschatology had been supplanted by another cosmology which promised heaven on earth; and furthermore, it was believed that all men could reach happiness very shortly. Granted that within this idea of terrestrial bliss moral notions were inserted, at the same time, did not this idea release an effluvium of hedonism? Let us recall the scenes of delight in gardens abounding in flirtations, music, and perfumes, that is, Watteau, Fragonard, Boucher, *et al.* Are they not painting pieces of paradise achieved along the line of human progress? In Hispanic-America the rococo manifested itself, as was to be expected, in a mitigated degree—yet its erotic notes of dissipation and love affairs, of tenderness and perversity, of gentility and indiscretion; its landscape tones, in which nature appears as a refuge for gallantry; its moods of intimacy accentuated by proceedings that veil and unveil in ornamental interplay ironies and flights from reality, are found in poets, prosists, and playwrights. Let us not forget that luxury is no longer just a theme in Hispanic-America, but a real experience. The viceregal courts have created an atmosphere of sumptuousness, exquisiteness, and courtship. When the aforementioned Friar Antonio Vélez Ladrón de Guevara describes precious materials, he sees before him the pearl industry on the Colombian coast; and when he refers to the ladies as "madames" he reveals a courtly and Frenchified corner in his mind.

B. MAINLY PROSE

Narratives

1. *Narrative Sketches* / We have alluded to a mass of prose writings in the first part of this chapter. In this section, however—a section more concerned with literary values—very little of the afore-mentioned prose can be included. And whatever is included

will be what is most baroque. In fact, it would seem that what is not baroque is not literature at all.

One must not expect to find the novel here, for the reasons stated in the preceding chapter. In France and in England the novel has to arise amidst the sluggishness and scorn of the erudite and the preceptists, and on arising it does so with the movements taught by *Don Quixote* and the picaresque novels. But despite the fact that the best elements of the European novel will have a Spanish look (like *Gil Blas* by the Frenchman Le Sage and the stories of the Englishmen Smollett and Fielding), Spain does not figure in the shaping of the modern novel. What is certain is that everywhere the novel fared poorly. Philosophers and satirists are in possession. When they wish to rehabilitate the novel, they push it toward genres that are considered more noble, so that they speak of the novel as a "poem in prose"; a heroic-comic poem, for example (this is how they classified *Don Quixote*); or a poem in serious prose, in the manner of Fénélon's *Télémaque*, which had an extraordinary acceptance and was imitated and read everywhere. The first years of the eighteenth century were bleak ones in Spain. No one knew what was happening in the world. Only during the epoch of Charles III will there be a quickened intellectual throb, but still not for the novel. Consequently, it would be too much to expect that there would be novelizing in the colonies.

The lawyer ANTONIO DE PAZ Y SALGADO (Guatemala, end of the seventeenth century–1757) interests us for two works in which satire and anecdote are combined with jocular narrative forms. In *Instruction for Litigants* (*Instrucción de litigantes*, 1742) he attempts to reveal to the general public the secrets of the legal profession. The festive tone, the autobiographical touches, the legal cases, and a certain Quevedo-like glow lend the book a relative legibility. Even more Quevedo-like was *The Flyflap* (*El Mosqueador*, 1742), "to put to flight . . . every kind of fool." The biting description of dullards and the manner of defending oneself against them is witty and expressive. A spiritual autobiography—*The Pilgrim with Guide and the Universal Medicine of the Soul* (*El peregrino con guía y medicina universal del alma*, 1750–1761), by the Mexican friar, Miguel de Santa María, that is, MARCOS REYNEL HERNÁNDEZ— can be placed here.

Chronicles

2. *Chronicles, Treatises, and Didactic Books* / Useful to a historian of Hispanic-American culture, but not interesting to a reader

eager for ideas, are the chronicles, histories, memoranda, critical, theological, scientific, and philosophic treatises that appear in the first half of the eighteenth century. A history of culture has to be constructed from facts: but at times, in order to understand the philosophic renovation of this eighteenth century, one must imagine that there were men whose beliefs fell outside the Aristotelian-scholastic currents, only they could not express them. So the historian finds himself in a difficult position: he must minimize the importance of many of the writings of that century because they are belated echoes; on the other hand, he must lend importance to the void of the non-written, because there, in that silence, new voices are forming that are to burst forth at any moment. In Europe there were new movements; in Hispanic-America, only a few men, who, to make matters worse, did not express themselves. In Europe there were new movements because the changes had borne fruit. It has been said that the seventeenth century was "an age of geniuses." Galileo and Descartes had student experimenters, like Torricelli and many more. In Hispanic-America experimentation was most inferior—Sor Juana makes us laugh with pity when she speaks of her experiments in the kitchen. Nor did Hispanic-America in the seventeenth cenutry have any philosophic geniuses. Thus, the Hispanic world in the eighteenth century was not prepared to take the leap from nature to reason as the enlightenment had done. Our science remained attached to the authority of the Church; and when it broke loose, it did so, not like a ripe fruit falling from the tree, but like a branch cut by a European axe. In Europe the enlightenment felt that Greeks and Romans first, and then the men of the Renaissance and Reformation, had contributed to the exaltation of reason. The Catholic Church, medieval and obscurantist, represented evil for the men of the enlightenment. The enlightenment, like every new religion, needed a devil and the Church was that devil. But in Hispanic-America this was not possible. Everything in Hispanic-American culture was different. Greeks and Romans were known through Church versions; humanists and reformers had not drawn away from the Church. And in comparison with its European counterpart the Hispanic enlightenment did not break with the Church.

We said that, in view of the dearth of great personalities, we would paint a cultural atmosphere. Atmospheres are painted with large brush strokes as in the synthesis given in the pages, above, or with a pointillist technique of light touches, which will constitute the catalog of names we are about to give below. In general, these names mean nothing in the history of literature, but since they are here drawn together they will give the reader the sensation of seeing a laborious group of humans.

Because the majority of the authors were priests, most of them wrote about religion or excelled in sacred oratory. Oratory is the art of using oral language for the practical purpose of persuading the listener. Therefore, it documents not only ideas, but also tastes. And one must study it because it usually slips its linguistic structures into literature. Cultism eventually reached oratory. America also had preachers as bombastic as the one cudgeled by Padre Isla in *Fray Gerundio de Campazas*. However, there were brilliant religious orators like Father Francisco Javier Conde Oquendo (Cuba, 1733–1799). And theoreticians of oratory like Joaquín Díaz Betancourt (Mexico, fl. 1752) and Martín de Velasco (Mexico, fl. 1726). Among the clergy who wrote on ecclesiastical themes let us mention: José J. Parreño (Cuba, 1728–1785); Vergara y Azcárate (Colombia, d. 1761). Of special interest to us is the Jesuit MANUEL LACUNZA (Chile, 1731–1801). He was a "millenarian" or one who believed in the very ancient prophecy that the world would close out its account before the sixth millenium was up. Because the creation of the world, according to Genesis, had taken six days, after six thousand years human history would come to its end—then justice and goodness would prevail over the earth in the seventh millenium. In order to defend the millenarians Lacunza wrote *The Coming of the Messiah in Glory and Majesty* (*La venida del Mesías en gloria y majestad*), with a great apparatus of Biblical erudition and a great display of talent. The redaction was finished toward 1790; it was published in 1811, and many editions followed. Josaphat Ben-Ezra, the "Christian Hebrew," was presented as the author. The work was read with passion. The knowledge it displayed, its novelty, the ordered mastery of its exposition, were virtues that worried the Inquisition. The Church ended by putting it on the Index, not for its beliefs (which were "defensible" for a Catholic) but for minor deviations; for example, the idea that the Church would also fall into betrayal in the days of the antichrist. The prophecy of a kingdom of Jesus Christ on earth lasting a thousand years in a Utopian community with one language, with no discord, and with Hell closed up cannot help but have an aura of poetic charm.

Of the chroniclers and historians, we mention a few: FRIAR DOMINGO DE NEYRA (Argentina, 1684–1757), with one or two good descriptions of his country; Bishop PEDRO AGUSTÍN MORELL DE SANTA CRUZ (Santo Domingo–Cuba, 1694–1768), a passable writer in his *History of the Island and Cathedral of Cuba* (*Historia de la Isla y Catedral de Cuba*); BASILIO VICENTE OVIEDO (Colombia, 1699–1780) who with his *Qualities and Riches of the New Realm of Granada* (*Cualidades y riquezas del Nuevo Reino de Granada*) forms a treasure-trove of things that he not only admires but also tries to put to practical use. JOSÉ DE OVIEDO Y BAÑOS (Colombia, Venezuela, 1671–1738) lived in Caracas all his life and wrote a pleasing and at moments beautiful *History of the Conquest and Population of the Province of Venezuela* (*Historia de la conquista y populacion de la provincia de Venezuela,* 1723), which covered the period from the discovery until the end of the sixteenth century. He worked hard over its composition, making use of other chroniclers and digging up forgotten materials from old archives. He wanted to be truthful, and he was, but his literary style was a pictorial, even musical, prose quivering with baroque. He was baroque, not only in certain occasional phraseology, but in his feeling for spectacular violence, like the scene where the tyrant Lope de Aguirre murders his daughter. JOSÉ MARTÍN FÉLIX DE ARRATE Y ACOSTA (Cuba, 1701–1765) left an apparently disordered and jumbled history, yet with a plan, or at least having a consistent direction—his love of Cuba and his pride in being a Creole of pure Spanish forebears. His *Key to the New World* (*Llave del Nuevo Mundo,* 1761) begins with the Discovery itself, but he only opens up on something when he feels the pulse of his own times. The aristocrat Arrate, hurt because certain Spaniards disparage Cuba, reminds them that they too are disparaged by Europeans for being "backward." In some of the pages he speaks with pleasure of the beauty of the landscape, of fiestas in the country, of court etiquette, the bright life of the city, fashions, refinements and luxuries—an ideal of elegance, of license, of frivolity, ostentation and festivities which, when it becomes more vivid later on, will inspire a rococo style.

Father JUAN DE VELASCO (Ecuador, 1727–1792) is one of the important figures in his country. His *History of the Realm of Quito* (*Historia del reino de Quito,* 1789), although rich in observations and data, is full of legend, fable, and imagination. In it there are giants and amazons. The Andes are the result of the Deluge. Plants and rocks have virtues and vices. As in a novel of chivalry, the Emperor Huaina-Cápac falls in love with Queen Shiri Paccha, and peace is made between two warring nations. The child begotten of this love, Atahualpa, will conquer his stepbrother, Huáscar, an offspring, not of love, but of "reasons of State" between the Inca and the imperial Coya.

FRANCISCO XAVIER ALEGRE (Mexico, 1729–1788) left a copy of the "History of the Society of Jesus in New Spain" almost completed when he was caught up in the expulsion of the Jesuits; in Bologna, Italy, he drew up, "almost from memory," a compendium of the same work. FRANCISCO XAVIER CLAVIGERO (Mexico, 1731–1787) used a good system in his composition of *Ancient History of Mexico (Historia antigua de México)*. He idealized the pre-Cortés Mexico with a modern sentimentalism; although he had read writers of critical thought—Feijóo, Descartes, Newton, Leibnitz —modern preoccupations seem to be absent in his comments on miracles.

There were those who wrote of jurisprudence (MELÉNDEZ BAZÁN, Santo Domingo, d. in 1741) or of science (SÁNCHEZ VALVERDE, Santo Domingo, 1720–1790; FRANCISCO XAVIER GAMBOA, Mexico, 1717–1794; PEDRO VICENTE MALDONADO, Ecuador, 1710–1748) or of philosophy (JOSÉ ANTONIO ALZATE, Mexico, 1729–1799). There were Latinists (JOAQUÍN AYLLÓN, Ecuador, d. in 1712; JUAN B. TORO, Colombia, 1670–1734). JUAN JOSÉ DE EGUIARA Y EGUREN (Mexico, 1695–1763) formulated his very important *Bibliotheca Mexicana* to destroy the "black legend" that Europeans had fabricated against America—confronted with the prejudice that the nature of the New World impedes the development of the spirit, he was going to demonstrate the brilliant and precocious productiveness of Mexican and Venezuelan letters.

In the midst of religious literature—mysticism, hagiography, and so forth—the thought of the epoch falls back on old explanations, even though it has a presentiment of the change in philosophy. Religion, morals, and law traveled together in scholasticism, and now they continue together in their attempts to explain America. What is the origin of America? How is one to understand these lands—unknown to the ancients—within the cosmology and chronology of scholasticism?

Even toward the end of the colonial period, picturesque hypotheses are proposed; for example, those of FRANCISCO XAVIER ALEJO ORRIO (1763), *Solution of the Great Problem of the Population of America Where on the Basis of the Holy Scriptures Is Found an Easy Way to Explain the Transmigration of Men from One Continent to the Other (Solución del gran Problema acerca de la población de América en que sobre el fundamento de los libros santos se descubre fácil camino a la transmigración de los hombres del uno al otro continente)*; or those of ORDÓÑEZ Y AGUIAR, *History of the Creation of Heaven and Earth in Conformity with the System of American Heathenism (Historia de la creación del cielo y la tierra conforme al sistema de la gentilidad americana)*. And one might add the extraordinary explanations of PEDRO LOZANO (Spain–Paraguay, 1697–1752), author of the *Description of the Great Chaco (Descripción del Gran Chaco)*; Father JOSÉ GUEVARA (Spain–Argentina, 1719–1806), revised the work of Lozano after his death. Instead of discovering the distinctive qualities of America, it was customary to sheathe them with European notions. To know America was to interpret it in the light of the Bible and Greco-Latin-Medieval culture. Between the creation of the world and the Deluge—a period of 1656 years, no more or less—the earth was a single, solid continental mass throughout which men were distributed. After the deluge, Noah's Ark arrived at the great island Atlantis, port of call to the New World. Or perhaps the Hellenic god Poseidon was the first inhabitant of Atlantis, and his descendants populated the American lands. The Mayan or Aztec civilizations offer up archeological and folkloric riches that those Spaniards of the first half of the eighteenth century did not know how to value—they tried to force them into a Biblical framework of universal history. Nevertheless, within a few years this Scholastic vision of the world would suffer such a severe blow that it would crumble to the ground, and in its place a rationalist interpretation would be erected. The cleric who best saw the threat, the blow, and the fall, and who most energetically defended the Church, was JOSÉ MARIANO VALLARTA Y PALMA (Mexico, 1719–1790). He denounced those hidden roads down which that impious philosophy was moving and, in doing so, he may have been the first Hispanic-American Scholasticist who expounded a history of ideas. Only, for him, it was the history of Evil. He began writing in Mexico. Having been expelled, together with the other Jesuits, he went to Italy and there he saw triumphant what had been in Hispanic-America only a menace. That is, the modern philosophy seen from the American side was a storm in bloom, and seen from Europe the storm had already destroyed Christendom. Descartes, Gassendi, Copernicus, Newton are the perpetrators of all those infamous, anti-religious principles. He considered Newton the most dangerous because of his theory that bodies had been created from the very beginning by particles of prime matter put into motion. The laws of attraction and repulsion did harm—Vallarta used to say—to the Church's explanation in Genesis. All experimentation was a scandalous departure from theology. And even poetry, when it sings in the name of liberty instead of submission to divine law, was a denial of the faith of Christ. There were more modern trends of thought, but unlike those in the rest of Europe, they did not become separated from the mother Church's apron strings. Yet conceptual thought was becoming more up to date in the colonies. Already under the rule of Philip V and Fernando VI, a change is noticeable. In emulation of France and England, Spain organizes scientific expeditions. In 1736, La Condamine commission, which included French scientists, arrived in Ecuador to measure the degree of earth's meridian. Among the participants were JORGE JUAN (Spain, 1713–1773) and ANTONIO DE ULLOA (Spain, 1716–1795), whose geographical, nautical, cultural, and social observations went into his *Historic Report on the Voyage to South America* (*Relación histórico del viaje a la América meridional*, 1748) and into the almost revolutionary *Secrets Reports* (*Noticias secretas*) whose authenticity has been challenged. The *Historic Report* illustrates that kind of scientific literature in which Alexander von Humboldt would, later on, excel with his *Voyage aux régions équinoxiales du Nouveau Continent*. Ulloa set down in numerous records and reports his experiences of many years in America, in his administrative functions in many locales. His overall view is revealed in the *American Reports* (*Noticias Americanas*, 1772). They were received with praise. A well-ordered and readable global description of the American environment was lacking. Here he gives abundant data on the physionatural characteristics of America and on the many possibilities open to man's labor.

These foreign scientists leave traces: orientation toward intellectual clarity against baroque erudition. Thus, erudition acquired critical sense and slowly converted itself into an anti-Scholastic movement. European philosophy was its nerve center. Even the clergy had to renovate the content of its teachings. Interest in all that was new continued to increase during the second half of the century. For this reason we will study the work of Pablo de Olavide in the next chapter although we might be expected to place him here, since he was born before 1735 (as was José C. Mutis). On the other hand, we bring forth another writer who, since he was born before 1675, should have been examined in the previous chapter, except that he helps us illustrate the cultural orientation of those years, namely, Peralta Barnuevo. And since he created theater, he will serve to head the following section.

C. THEATER

We have said that the predominance of scholastic philosophy over all intellectual life since the Counter Reformation made the penetration of rationalist principles and experimental methods difficult. Even those spirits most avid for knowledge—like the Peruvian PEDRO DE PERALTA BARNUEVO, 1663–1743—vacillate between truth and faith, sallying out to face the ideas of European philosophy and science, but withdrawing not daring to join in the movement that all nations, except Spain, had entered into from the Renaissance to the present. Not only can Peralta Barnuevo be studied under two political regimes (the first half of his life under the Hapsburg viceroys; the second, under the Bourbon viceroys), but his work, although dominated by the characteristics of baroque culture of the seventeenth century, also offers the first fruits of neoclassical "Frenchification" in Hispanic-America. His broad base of knowledge—he was a historian, jurist, theologian, mathematician, engineer, astronomer, dramatist, and poet, apt in several languages—belongs to that type of cultured man whom we have already studied in Sigüenza y Góngora. However, he tends more to the school of the scholasticists rather than to the encyclopedists, though he also anticipated the encyclopedist ideal of the eighteenth century. If for a moment he seems to be a precursor of the latter, it is because of a mimetic phenomenon: as the scholastic traditions with their taste for great syntheses reach the eighteenth century, they resemble illuminist rationalism, like certain butterflies that simulate the leaves they light upon.

Peralta adheres to mysticism in spite of his scientific knowledge —cosmography, mathematics—and in spite of his technical knowledge (he directed the work on the fortifications of Lima). His book, *Passion and Triumph of Christ* (*Pasión y triunfo de Cristo*, 1738), is an expression of a philosophy anterior to that of the enlightenment. Having been disillusioned beforehand by a science of which he saw only the beginnings, Peralta affirms that true wisdom is inscrutable, as inscrutable as God himself. The universe cannot be reduced to human laws. The least forgettable of his literary works are the poem *The Founding of Lima* (*Lima fundada*, 1732) with a few Gongoristic touches; the operetta *Triumph of Love and Power* (*Triunfos de amor y poder*, 1711?), with mythological gods partaking of human love and with a setting more to the Italian taste than that of Lope's time; the play *Affection Conquers Kindness* (*Afectos vencen finezas*, 1720); and a tragedy *Rodoguna* copied from Corneille's *Rodogune*. The influence of Molière's *Les Femmes savantes* and *Le Malade imaginaire* can be discerned in two afterpieces he wrote; this was an early influence since at least one of these was written in 1711.

In addition, he wrote interludes and dances. His most ambitious play was *Affection Conquers Kindness*, a plot in Lope de Vega's style but lacking his poetry, in Calderón's manner but lacking his philosophy. The reader is distracted and loses the threads of this story of love between princes and princesses in a pseudo-Greek world where everyone always speaks pompously. There is not a single scene of real artistic merit. And only a few verses sound well—one admires the variety of metrics rather than of images. All is toned down to crepuscular grays: the lover is not as passionate, the villain is not as depraved; the *gracioso* or comic is not as funny. And though Olimpia, on hearing Roxana's anguish in song, gives the formula of the esthetic catharsis: "After all, evil is not so ugly / when it sings so well; / for groans are other things / when dressed in warbler's clothes"—what is certain is that the play's sentiments are not purified until they attain poetic stature. One of the most vivid passages, Lisímaco's relating his fight with the lion, is entertaining but not moving. There are situations which are pleasant in themselves. Lisímaco and Orondates are walking through a little woods sighing for the love of two princesses who they believe to be dead; upon seeing the princesses they believe them to be visions of a dream; later they see carved on the bark of trees initials that remind them of the names of their loved ones; they decide to follow these markings. Meanwhile, one of the princesses, Estatira, has made her way to a little stream that symbolizes with its crystalline current "the purity of my love, / the constancy of my tear." "Learn from it [Cleone answers her]: don't you see that the stream would punish, with a flood, him who would impede its course?" The two heroes find her there, asleep; the scenes end with intense movement: recognitions, knife duels, abduction in a carriage, pursuit. Songs and dances raise somewhat the lyrical tone of the play.

Since we are on the subject of the theater, let us pause a moment before a curious phenomenon: the abundance of theatrical production in all the colonies, an idea of which can be gathered by this register of authors.

In Mexico, JOSÉ MARIANO ABARCA, PEDRO JOSÉ RODRÍGUEZ DE ARIZPE, FELIPE RODRÍGUEZ DE LEDESMA Y CORNEJO, JOSÉ ANTONIO RODRÍGUEZ MANZO, MANUEL URRUTIA DE VERGARA, MANUEL ZUMAYA, whose opera *El Rodrigo*, the first one composed in Mexico, has been lost; in Colombia, JACINTO DE BUENAVENTURA; in Peru, FÉLIX DE ALARCÓN, PEDRO BERMÚDEZ DE LA TORRE, MANUEL OMS, MARQUÉS DE CASTELL-DOS-RIUS, VICENTE PALOMINO, DOMINGO PRIETO; in Bolivia SALVADOR DE VEGA; in Argentina, ANTONIO FUENTES DEL ARCO, whose baroque *Prelude* of 1717 is the first Argentine theatrical piece.

Of all of these there is none whose vocation is really the theater. Generally they are authors of a single little play (preludes, interludes, dances, farces, afterpieces, colloquies, etc.) or, at best, four or five. Dramas and full-length plays are extremely rare. The preludes were written in verse on the occasion of the installation of a new king, viceroy, or archbishop. Customarily they had symbolic personages (from mythology, like Phoebus Apollo; or of certain qualities, like goodness and wealth) and also "Indians" and "gentlemen" according to whether America or Spain was represented. The taste for theater was shared by all levels of society: aristocratic theater in palaces; popular theater in *corrales* or courtyards; theater for general entertainment in the *Casa de Comedias* or playhouse; religious theater in monasteries and nunneries. Already one can notice in the theater a *costumbrista* trend, *i.e.*, the depiction of local customs and manners, which will be so significant in the years to come. In 1774, for example, an anonymous *Prelude on the Scholar* (*Loa del Licenciado*)—in whose preface Indian speech is imitated—is performed in Lima, at the Viceroy's court. Also in these years, Negro and popular dialects are phonetically transcribed. This cult of the popular and plebeian speech, which we find in the theater as well as in the satire, proves to be the antecedent of the *costumbrista* literature—a literature that will reach its peak during the romantic period (for instance, in the Gaucho literature of the Río de la Plata).

We shall point up only a few of the twenty or so who dedicated themselves to the theater. FRIAR FRANCISCO DEL CASTILLO ANDRACA Y TAMAYO (Peru, 1716–1770) wrote religious, historical and cape-and-sword plays; tragedy, mystery plays, preludes and an *Interlude of Judge and Litigants* (*Entremés del Justica y litigantes*), quite entertaining in its free dialog and in its real-life characters. His pro-Spanish political stand was made clear in the comedy, *The Conquest of Peru* (*La conquista del Perú*, 1747). He presented the whole history in scenes (after Calderón?) in which the Indians receive the benevolent Spaniards with joy. He would burst suddenly into verse, sometimes satirical, sometimes gravely religious or moral in tone. He wrote an epic poem, *Passion and Death of Our Redeemer and Lord, Jesus Christ* (*Pasión y muerte de nuestro redentor y señor Jesucristo*), fables, sonnets, ballads, dirges. In his "Couplets of the Blind Man of Mercy" he was very popular. JERÓNIMO DE MONFORTE Y VERA (Peru) left a very entertaining and worthwhile farce, *Love, the Sprite* (*El amor duende*, 1725), with character types such as the Spanish lover, "cloaked" coquettes, a naive Negro maid; with much action; droll dialog; and with narrow Lima streets as a setting. EUSEBIO VELA (Spain–Mexico, 1688–1737), a continuator of the Calderón school, put on plays in the viceregal palaces. Three have been edited: *If Love Exceeds Art, Neither Art Nor Love Exceed Moderation* (*Si el amor excede al arte, ni amor ni arte a prudencia*), *The Loss of Spain Over a Woman* (*La pérdida de España por una mujer*), *The Apostolate of the Indies and Martyrdom of a Chieftain* (*El apostolado en Indias y martirio de un cacique*). The first portrays the adventures of Telemachus on the isle of Calypso, with great visual apparatus and scenes of magic and enchantment; the second portrays the traditional theme of Rodrigo; the third is an apology on behalf of Franciscan missionaries, Hernán Cortés

and his soldiers, defended by the apostle, St. James on horseback, against
the Devil, mounted on a dragon. Vela does not deal in little things. He lays
hold of the most spectacular techniques possible in the theater: fires, col-
lapsing buildings, all exaggerated to the limit. JOSÉ AGUSTÍN DE CASTRO
(Mexico, 1730–1814), a poet of Calderonian tastes, author of preludes and
mystery plays, is esteemed for his *The Cobblers* (*Los remendones*), a "new
farcette" and *El Charro*, a "new playlet." In the Mexican Castro, as well as
in the Peruvian Castillo Andraca y Tamayo, popular characters speak with
local idioms and slang, a phenomenon which, we insist, will be of major importance when it later becomes a source of a new literature.

One of the most elegant and lyrical plays of this period was *The
Gardener Prince and Cloridano Feigned* (*Príncipe jardinero y
fingido Cloridano*), written between 1730 and 1733, by SAN-
TIAGO DE PITA (Cuba, d. in 1755). Perhaps his theme may derive from the "scenic opera" of the Florentine Giacinto Andrea
Cicognini (1606–1660), *Il principe giardiniero*. However, Santiago de Pita embroidered his plots on the backdrop of the Spanish
theater as developed by the golden-age playwrights. There are
echoes of Lope's lyricism, but even more one hears the formalist
baroque interplay of Calderón and Moreto in every scene. Conceptist and cultist images, twists and turns in versification, situations, conventions, and the like, bring to mind the theater of the
seventeenth century. That century, seen from the eighteenth, is
now a literary background, beautiful in itself but also embellished
by distance. With artistic nostalgia, Santiago de Pita has the
idealized figures of his poetic plays stand out against that gilded
background. He makes literature, then, by profiting from an
already venerable literature; for example, the comic Lamparón's
comparing himself to Sancho Panza and describing his master
Fadrique as another insane Don Quijote. Santiago de Pita's
baroqueness is academic, serene, elegant, sentimental, and
sprouts preferences that later will be characteristic of the rococo:
intimacies in a garden, in a Utopian Thrace, with poetic refinements, aristocracy, women boldly declaring their passions, exaltation of pleasure, action imitating the geometry of a dance, artful
scenery yet taken from nature, and so on. Within the eighteenth
century this play moves along an emotional current and not along
the rationalist one of neoclassicism. Theatrical functions in palaces
tended to be so luxuriant in staging, in adornments, and in music

that by themselves, leaving aside what was being enacted, they record a new spirit.

JERÓNIMO FERNÁNDEZ DE CASTRO Y BOCÁNGEL (Peru, 1689–1737), himself an author of a prelude-operetta, described in *Peruvian Elysium* (*Eliseo peruano*, 1725) a pompous show by Antonio de Zamora: "the orchestra began to ring out the sonorous symphony of violins, oboes and other instruments . . . After a very sweet bass, it ended in the festive happy air of a minuet which serves as a cue to raise the curtain. The stage revealed a luxurious forest and delightful grove . . . One cannot esteem too much the happy shower of lights which, at the soft sounding of a whistle, were thrust down from the backdrop; for it was a veritable inundation of diamonds that drowned our sight in each one of the illustrious actors . . . The rich material of the exquisite and fine apparel, all of sheer fabric, seemed to wish to hide, ashamed at not being able to express more behind the many jewels that covered it. The tufts of feathers and down that filled the air gave off a vague and rich quality of spring . . ."

V. 1759-1788

Authors born between 1735 and 1760

Historical framework: Because of the social, political, and economic reforms of Charles III, the position of Spain and its colonies improves. Nevertheless, the dissatisfaction of the Creoles increases.

Cultural tendencies: Ideas of the Enlightenment. Neoclassicism.

Introduction

The movement of ideas and styles described in the preceding chapter becomes more widespread in this period. The idea of progress begins to make inroads. In general, the Roman Catholic Church did not believe in this concept of progress because what was more evident to it was the idea of retrogression: we have retrogressed from paradise and any betterment on earth is only a preparation for supernatural salvation. The scant attention given to the idea of progress was concomitant with the slight material progress of the Hispanic-American colonies. That is to say, that in Europe, philosophy was elaborating an idea of progress in the face of concrete results of material progress. In Hispanic-America the reverse is true: first we speak abstractively about progress; material progress comes later.

A. MAINLY POETRY

Poetry drags along, its wings clipped. The baroque, after it is sweetened into the rococo, must bow down before neoclassicism.

MANUEL DEL SOCORRO RODRÍGUEZ (Cuba–Colombia, 1758–1818), writes mannerist poetry in the baroque manner. DIEGO PADILLA (Colombia, 1754–

157

1829) is the author of a funeral oration to Charles III. Father José M. SARTORIO (Mexico, 1746–1828) poured his best into poems to the Virgin (and his worst, into verses on current events). He cultivated the fable, a genre typically eighteenth century. If he imitated Iriarte, as did many fabulists of the time, it was for his genre and not for his doctrine. The Argentinian MANUEL JOSÉ DE LAVARDÉN (1754–1809) is the author of "Ode to the Majestic River Paraná" ("*Oda al majestuoso río Paraná,*" 1801), the best poetical composition written in his country prior to 1810. It is a didactic allegory in which the river, a fluvial god, appears described in terms of the local landscape; the river symbolizes the cultural and economic prosperity of the Río de la Plata people. All that is preserved of Lavardén is this "Ode," a "Satire" (1786) against Lima and in defense of Buenos Aires, and a "Philosophical Oration" that he delivered in 1778 at the Royal College of San Carlos. Lavardén's theatrical production has been lost; all we have are works attributed to him but unconfirmed. His tragedy *Siripo* was performed in 1789; there is extant a second act that is said to belong to it. This is doubtful—this second act may belong to a later *Siripo* by another author. The plot, revolving around the chieftain Siripo and Lucía Miranda, is legendary; it was treated by Del Barco Centenera, Ruy Díaz de Guzmán, and other chroniclers. Lavardén remained silent during the English invasions and reconquest of Buenos Aires while many other poets celebrated the victory. Among the Argentines who are to be recorded here because of their dates of birth is the cultured JOSÉ PREGO DE OLIVER, whose hendecasyllables sang praise to the heroes of the reconquest, and the popular PANTALEÓN RIVAROLA (1754–1821) whose octosyllables sang praise to the heroic action of the masses.

Satire / Satiric poetry, especially that directed against the new spirit by the traditionalists, documents the existence in Hispanic-America of a licentious and frivolous society, with court *soirées* and Versaillesque parties, with gallantry and refinements in love and in art. In 1786 there are some anonymous "Venus' Rules for Flighty Girls and Ladies" ("*Ordenanzas de Venus para las majas y chinas de volatería*") in which there is a caricature of the rococo: frothy goddesses, pleasurable art, saucy witticisms, strutting women, impudent conversation, "much laughing, hand gestures, manipulation of the fan," transparent clothes, dances, music and theater, and walks in gardens.

B. MAINLY PROSE

1. Novelistic Attempts

There is nothing to say about the novel. As we have pointed out in preceding chapters, the novel, such as had been created by

Cervantes, was forgotten in Spain. Father Isla, in his *Friar Gerundio*, revealed narrative talent, but unlike Cervantes, he allowed his satire to smother his novel. Since the Spaniards could no longer create a novel in the tradition of Cervantes, they attempted to take possession of Le Sage's *Gil Blas* (and Father Isla, on translating it, said he was restoring to Spain what France had stolen from it). In truth, literary tastes in Spain did not esteem novelists like Cervantes so much as novelists like Marmontel and Florian. The country that had seen the birth of the modern novel, thanks to Cervantes' *Don Quixote*, valued Cervantes for two services alien to art: the ridiculing to death of a literary genre and the defense of the language against translators of French. They did not know what to do with the novel, a genre discredited because it lacked classical antecedents. It was a degeneration of the epic, or not morally edifying, or a frivolous fabrication of falsehoods. What can one say, then, of the novel in Hispanic-America? In Mexico there is FRIAR JOAQUÍN BOLAÑOS' *Death's Prodigious Life* (*La portentosa vida de la muerte*, 1792) in a verbose, truculent, rhetorical prose, padded with sermons, illustrations from religious literature, and symmetrical and contrasting enumerations. With the omnipresence of the "empress of the sepulchers," Bolaños' allegory intended to strike the consciences of contemporary Mexicans, who were, according to him, diverted by trivial pastimes and entertainments. The medieval theme of death, elaborated by the baroque, was being offered to readers living in a rococo age who felt "well situated in the world." So it is not strange if readers did not appreciate Bolaños' work—they found it in bad taste. Even clergymen like Father José Antonio de Alzate Ramírez criticized it as being "prejudicial to dogma and good customs" because death, after all, appears as a burlesque figure and the author seems to adhere to the doctrine of probabilism. Furthermore, he adds, it is "an ill-devised novel." It has little of the quality of a novel. The personification of lady death does not manage to take on life; her visits to men in all walks of life are wanting in adventure. We know for certain that novels were written (several historians have had the manuscripts in their possession), but those manuscripts of novels only prove narrative avocations, since they never made the printing presses: *Fabiano and Aurelia* (1760) by Father JOSÉ GONZÁLEZ SÁNCHEZ.

2. Philosophic, Didactic, and Journalistic Writings

a. *Polemics on the Inferiority of the New World* / In these years the polemics on the supposed inferiority of the New World broke out all over Europe. The French naturalist Buffon was mainly concerned with zoology. The absence of strong and corpulent animals like the elephant seemed to him a proof of the perniciousness of the American climate. The denigration of America by the Prussian abbot De Pauw was anthropological. In his estimation, American man was more recent but at the same time more decadent than men of other parts. He did not believe in the natural goodness of man, but felt that these men, because they did not have the advantage of society, had not been able to develop. Nor did the unhealthy climate favor such development. It was in 1768 that De Pauw declared that the substance of America was weak and that the Indians were degenerate brutes. He conceded the possibility of some progress—"in three hundred years America will look as different from today as it looks today from the time of its discovery"—but that progress would presuppose the de-Americanization of America. Europeans were divided among themselves on the question of the value of the American. While some humanists tended to make a myth of the savage (Montaigne, Rousseau, Herder, Humboldt), others impugned him (Voltaire, Raynal, Joseph de Maistre, Hegel). Since De Pauw also railed at the Spanish conquistadors and the Catholic missionaries, the Roman Catholic Church was the first to react within the Hispanic sphere. In addition to the Spaniards (first the abbot, Juan Nix, and above all Father Feijóo, who exercised great influence in this matter and others), the Creoles also jumped to the defense of America.

The Jesuits, expelled in 1767, felt annoyed at the scorn that Europeans held for America, and at times aroused by nostalgia, were moved to defend their homelands, as in the case of the Mexican ANTONIO LÓPEZ DE PRIEGO (1730–1798). In some 280 *décimas* (1784) he imagined an argument between an Italian who had been in Mexico and a Mexican who had been in Italy and ended with a sonnet censuring those who do not realize "that good and bad are found everywhere." Father Francisco Xavier Clavigero—with whom we have already dealt—wrote his *Ancient History of Mexico* (*Historia antigua de México*, 1780–81) with the intention of refuting the idea of a degenerate America. Father JUAN IGNACIO MOLINA (Chile, 1740–1829), in his *Compendium of the History of Chile* (*Compendio de la historia . . . del reino de Chile*, 1776), answered these European calumnies with pride in his native country and its inhabitants. He would observe that there are more annoying insects in Italy than in Chile. Father BENITO MARÍA DE MOXÓ (Spain–Bolivia, 1763–1816) in his *Letters from Mexico* (*Cartas mexicanas*, 1805) put forth his observations on the landscape in order to undercut the prejudices of De Pauw and his followers. JOSÉ MARIANO BERISTAIN DE SOUZA (Mexico, 1756–1817) continued the *Mexican Library* (*Biblioteca Mexicana*) by Eguiara y Eguren with his own *Library of Northern Hispanic America* (*Biblioteca Hispanoamericana Septentrional*, 1816) not only out of love of learning, but in order to contradict the words of detractors in overseas Spain. Fury subsided with the years, but from time to time voices were raised against the "calumniator and imbecile De Pauw," in tune with the patriotism of the Independence and the romantic feeling for nature: the Argentinian FRANCISCO JAVIER ITURRI, 1738–1822; the Peruvians JOSÉ MANUEL DÁVALOS, HIPÓLITO UNANUE, 1755–1833, and Manuel Lorenzo Vidaurre; the Colombians DIEGO MARTÍN TANCO and Francisco José de Caldas; the Mexican Friar Servando Teresa de Mier; and the Honduran JOSÉ CECILIO DEL VALLE, 1780–1834.

Whether they were defending themselves against the vilifications of the Europeans or whether, along with the polemics, they were expressing confidence in the intelligence of the Creoles, it is certain that during these years one of the preoccupations of writers was with American progress.

b. *Expulsion of the Jesuits* / There were those who reacted against progress and there were those who supported progress. In this balance of forces the position of the Jesuits was a curious one. In 1767 Charles III ordered that the Jesuits in America be expelled. They departed in flocks. And perhaps because they wrote their works in exile, and at times in Italian or Latin, they have not been considered part of the history of Hispanic-American letters. To be sure, their importance in a purely literary history is not great, but it is indeed in a cultural and political history. The humanistic culture of the Jesuits was like a bridge between the baroque and the neoclassical. As antiroyalists and cultural restrainers, the Jesuits gave a new direction to Spanish intellectual traditions. They came to a *rapprochement* with the Creole bourgeoisie; they sympathized surreptitiously with the cause of national autonomy and diffused some of the philosophical and scientific ideas of the enlightenment.

We mentioned several of these Jesuits in the preceding chapter and at the beginning of this one: Francisco Xavier Clavigero, Francisco Xavier Alegre, Rafael Landívar, Manuel Lacunza, and others. Other writers born after 1735 could be added: PEDRO BERROETA (Ecuador, 1737), poet; ANDRÉS CAVO (Mexico, 1739–1803), historian; MANUEL FABRI (Mexico, 1737–1805), biographer of the brothers of his order; JUAN LUIS MANEIRO (Mexico, 1744–1802); PEDRO JOSÉ MÁRQUEZ (Mexico, 1741–1820), who combined his concern for archeology with esthetics; and many others. The expulsion of the Jesuits damaged literary culture but in the long run permitted the unobstructed expansion of the modern spirit. As antiroyalists and conservers of cultural life, the Jesuits formed the ideological root for the revolution of the colonies against the metropolis. Certainly, their modern spirit made the Church a more effective force, and without them there was more intellectual liberty.

c. *Scientific and Didactic Activities* / In sacred oratory the Church cried out with no restraint: Father JUAN BAUTISTA BAREA (Cuba, 1744–1789), Father RAFAEL DEL CASTILLO Y SUCRE (Cuba, 1741–1783). But modern voices were also heard. A defense of ideas—dedicated to "Mexican youth"—was undertaken by the Jesuit ANDRÉS DE GUEVARA Y BASOAZÁBAL (Mexico, 1748–1801). He extolled Descartes, Galileo, Bacon. FRANCISCO ANTONIO MORENO Y ESCANDÓN (Colombia, 1736–1792) was one of those who executed the order for the expulsion of the Jesuits. He proposed an important educational reform, promoting the study of the physical and natural sciences in order to correct "futile questions of scholastic theology." He advised theologians to begin studying "in order to flee from the superstition and credulity into which the masses easily fall." In philosophy, he used to say, "eclecticism . . . experience and observation must prevail." JUAN BENITO DÍAZ DE GAMARRA (Mexico, 1745–1783), who was not a Jesuit, but who was far from Descartes, imported eclectic philosophies (or at least seventeenth- and eighteenth-century philosophies of which the eclectics partook). His *Errors of Human Understanding* (*Errores del entendimiento humano*, 1781) criticizes formal scholasticism and proposes a practical logic. There was scientific activity. JOSÉ CELESTINO MUTIS (Colombia, 1732–1808) was one of the greatest naturalists of his time. He maintained an epistolary correspondence, in Latin, with his European colleagues, Linnaeus, Bergius, Willdenow. Linnaeus, in a letter dated 1774, called Mutis "immortal"; and when years later Alexander von Humboldt arrived in Colombia he was amazed at the library of Mutis, this "venerable 72 year old clergyman": "Outside of Banks' in London, I have not seen a botanical library as large as Mutis'." He fought against the intellectual lethargy of Spain and its colonies, expounding scandalous things like the Copernican system!

ANTONIO DE ALCEDO Y BEXARANO (Ecuador, 1735–1812) wrote a notable encyclopedia of Hispanic-American subjects—*Geographico-historical*

Dictionary of the West Indies or America (*Diccionario geográfico-histórico de las Indias Occidentales o América*, 1786–1789). Physicists and mathematicians like José Ignacio Bartolache (Mexico, 1739–1790); ethnographers and archeologists like José Domingo Duquesne (Colombia, 1748–1822) and Antonio León y Gama (Mexico, 1735–1802) point to a new intellectual tension. The new critical, didactic, and constructive spirit of the Enlightenment first appeared in reforms of intellectual life: the founding of library gazettes, greater participation in social affairs, care of libraries, translations, bibliographies. For now the beginnings of an argumentative, satirical, or pedantic epoch are seen which at least have a solid direction in historical scholarship. In history we might cite Ignacio José Urrutia y Montoya (Cuba, 1735–1795); the deacon Gregorio Funes (Argentina, 1749–1829); and Antonio del Campo y Rivas (Colombia, b. in 1750), of whom we have a local *History* charged with a humanitarian spirit that condemns the conquistadors as "destroyers of the human species" and denounces their cruelty for which "humanity is horrified" (notice the word "humanity").

d. *Thought of the Enlightenment* / The most fruitful changes during this period are found in the field of thought. These are the years of the intellectual beginnings of the autonomist movement. The Creoles travel to Europe and return with revolutionary pamphlets and ideas. Sailing ships arrive laden with seeds of the enlightenment.

Encyclopedism, openly rooted in the philosophy of the French Enlightenment, was cultivated by Pablo de Olavide y Jáuregui (Peru, 1725–1804). Already noted for his intellectual brilliance and capacity for action, he went to Spain in 1752 to defend himself from accusations that dishonored him. He was incarcerated. Later he made a fortune and enjoyed the protection of the court. In France he thrust himself into the turbulent life of the salons, where he came to know artists, writers, and philosophers: in rococo art, Boucher; in neoclassical literature, Marivaux, Marmontel; in ideas of the enlightenment, Diderot. He struck up friendly relations with Diderot, D'Alembert, Voltaire. Back in Madrid he started a literary salon like those in Paris and constructed a private theater for which he translated and adapted Racine's *Phèdre*, Voltaire's *Zaïre*, Regnard's *Le Joueur*, Maffei's *Merope*, etc. He frequented Jovellanos' literary circle. In 1776 a satire directed at Olavide appeared: *The Enlightened Century: Life of Don Cherrytree, Born, Reared, Educated, Exalted and*

Died in Accordance with the Lights of the Present Age. Published as a Model of Customs by Don Justo Vera de la Ventosa (*El Siglo Ilustrado. Vida de Don Guindo Cerezo, nacido, educado, instruido, sublimado y muerto según las luces del presente siglo. Dado a luz por seguro modelo de las costumbres por Don Justo Vera de la Ventosa*). Following the form of the picaresque novel, the author, a Spaniard, invented a character through whom he mocked, episode after episode, the ideas of Olavide. Jailed, condemned, and harassed by the Inquisition, he fled to France in 1780. The revolution having broken out, he became one of the adopted citizens of the republic. But in time he came to abhor the republic. Experiencing an inner, personal crisis, Olavide, with bowed head, began to meditate over the frailty of human presumptuousness and to write poetry on sacred themes—about nine thousand verses of fiery religiosity. A little after 1794—the year he was taken prisoner in Orléans, a victim of the Jacobean terror—he returned to the Catholic faith and wrote *The Gospel in Triumph of the History of a Philosopher Undeceived* (*El Evangelio en triunfo o Historia de un filósofo desengañado*, 1797). He created a novelesque plot interwoven with autobiographical episodes. A philosopher stops at a monastery by chance. Through the preachings and example of one of the monks he repents of his wickedness. Upon rejoining society he readjusts his life and his family's in accordance with Christian norms. Letter-writing formed part of the literary mode of the epoch. Epistolary novels, like Samuel Richardson's *Pamela,* Rousseau's *La Nouvelle Héloïse*, Goethe's *Werther*, were being read. Consequently, Olavide resorted to this technique to illustrate the controversies of the philosopher in him, his moral crisis, and his conversion. Olavide's theological knowledge was weaker than his religious conviction. His prose is tinged with sentiment and fantasy; it is a prose that, despite his return to Spanish faith, preserves the twists and turns learned by having read so many French writers. His repentance was extended to his verses. *The Spanish Psalter or Paraphrastic Version of the Psalms of David, the Canticles of Moses, Other Canticles and Some Prayers of the Church* (*El salterio español o Versión parafrástica de los Salmos de David, de los cánticos de Moisés, de otros cánticos y algunas oraciones de la Iglesia*) served the cause of faith, but not of poetry. In the same fashion the hendecasyllables of his *Christian Poems (Poemas cristianos)* alienate the poet, but not the moralist. This was the last of his writings. And so ended, on the plains of conservatism, traditionalism, and Catholicism, the man who in his youth had been an eminent figure of the enlightenment.

In secret meetings the Creoles aired the equalitarian preachments of Rousseau. Philosophy and politics conspired to change the colonial order and even to overthrow it. One of the most outstanding personages of the enlightenment was the mestizo FRANCISCO EUGENIO DE SANTA CRUZ Y ESPEJO (Ecuador, 1747–1795). He possessed encyclopedic knowledge. While in philosophy he was imitating some of the sensualist ideas, in politics, whether he knew it or not, he was preparing for American independence. Documents reveal that in Quito the revolutionaries of 1809 were accused of being "inheritors of the seditious plans of an old inhabitant named Espejo who died years ago in that capital." The writings of Espejo moved from hand to hand. He would accuse colonial education of being "a slave's education." Neoclassicism like sixteenth-century Erasmianism was an attempt to Europeanize the Hispanic world. And it is strange that now, as in the sixteenth century, the satirical dialogs in the manner of Lucian should be the genre preferred by the new spirit. Espejo wrote the *New Lucian or Awakener of Minds (Nuevo Luciano o Despertador de ingenios).* It consists of nine conversations between the characters Murillo and Mera (the latter is the spokesman for Espejo) on such topics as rhetoric and poetry, philosophy, plans of study, and theology. The purpose of the work is to examine and criticize the mental climate of the colonies. It is the best exposition of colonial culture of the eighteenth century. In it he reviewed the colonial poets. He wrote other works which continue the *New Lucian.* He directed, and wrote in its entirety, the first Ecuadorian newspaper *First Fruits of the Culture of Quito (Primicias de la Cultura de Quito).* Also in a mocking vein (although different from that of Espejo) is the *Guide for Blind Wayfarers . . . Taken from the Memoirs of Don Alonso Carrió de la Vandera . . . By*

*Don Calixto Bustamante Carlos Inca, alias Concolorcorvo (Laza-
rillo de ciegos caminantes . . . sacado de las memorias que hizo
don Alonso Carrió de la Vandera . . . por Don Calixto Bustamante Carlos Inca, alias Concolorcorvo).* Although Concolorcorvo really existed and did accompany Carrió de la Vandera, he
had nothing to do with the composition of the book. It was all a
hoax. ALONSO CARRIÓ DE LA VANDERA (Spain, *ca.* 1715–d. after
1778) printed it clandestinely in Lima, in 1775 or 1776, put
down Gijón as the place of printing, moved the date up to 1773,
and pretended that Concolorcorvo had taken it from the reports
of voyages that he had dictated to him. Why? Carrió de la Vandera, who had been settled in Lima since 1746, was commissioned
in 1771 to inspect and reorganize the stage posts between Buenos
Aires and Lima. Involved in some sort of misunderstanding with
a postal administrator, he may have decided to guard himself
against a direct attack by publishing his observations as if someone else were doing it. Carrió gave this explanation in one of his
letters: "I disguised my name so as not to find it necessary to give
away all the copies. Your grace knows how dry a diary may be,
particularly in sparsely populated areas, so that it behooved me to
dress it up according to local tastes so that wayfarers might amuse
themselves during their stopovers and that their travels might
become less rigorous." The *Guide*, in fact, is conceived as a traveler's manual, including some documentation, chronicle, popular
traditions, local customs, jokes, anecdotes and dialogs, all with a
certain novelistic flavor. One picaresque element is that of having
Concolorcorvo speak in the first person: "I am Indian through
and through, although I shall not vouch for my mother's tricks.
Two princess cousins of mine preserve their virginity, much to
their regret, in a convent in Cuzco where they are maintained by
the King, our lord. I find myself resolved to solicit the job of dog
beadle for the Cathedral of Cuzco in order to enjoy ecclesiastical
immunity." His intention was to educate, to reform. Carrió is
familiar with Greco-Roman and Castilian literature (Cervantes,
Quevedo, Gracián, Feijóo), but he is not bookish. On the contrary, he describes directly the American reality he sees around
him. He is a very Americanized Spaniard who critically over-

comes all provincialism—superiority lies in civilization, not in this or that nation. His criticism at times runs against Spanish administration; sometimes he is anticlerical. With smiles and irony he chastises Spaniards, Creoles, mestizos, and Indians. There is sympathy for the well-bred man, be he Spaniard or Creole. From here he runs rapidly down the scale: Gauchos, mestizos, Indians, Negroes. The *Guide*, for the most part, is a very lively description of the trip from Montevideo to Lima, passing through Buenos Aires, Córdoba, Salta, and Cuzco. The picaresque tone, the rhythm of the action, the description of customs, and the art of surprising the reader in an unexpected situation makes the reading entertaining at times. In this travel diary (for this is what the *Guide* is) the eye picks out singular things: the couplets sung by the *gauderios* or gauchos, the sale of Negroes, the differences in customs from one locality to another.

Among these travelogs (although it must be noticed that their purpose was scientific) one should mention those of FÉLIX DE AZARA (Spain–Argentina, 1746–1821), who looked at nature and man in the light of the progressivist ideas of the enlightenment, as he revealed in his very interesting *Report on the Rural State of the Río de la Plata in 1801 (Memoria sobre el estado rural del Río de la Plata en 1801)*.

In the last twenty years of the eighteenth century the intellectuals and the cultured urban citizenry—like Espejo, Nariño, Rojas y Salas, Gual y España—realized that they had better take advantage of the times and control the new social changes. More significant than literary activity (which bore the neoclassic stamp on it and which was channeled into typical neoclassical genres) was the intellectual life in the universities, in the press, in literary clubs, in French books, in polemics between the Jansenists and sensualists. The active philosophy of the French Revolution was more influential than written philosophy. Literary history at times tends to appropriate great political figures that in reality do not belong to it, but because they were "men of letters" (in the broad sense that this term has in Spanish America) the inclusion is permitted and justified. This is the case of FRANCISCO MIRANDA (Venezuela, 1750–1816). His importance is political because the historical events of the movement of independence rise from his intrigues and struggles, but it is proper to consider his writings in that they expose an original spirit. Without having any literary ambitions he recorded here and there what he saw, thought, heard, and read. His keen and concise comments are as excellent as his documentation of those years of crisis.

e. *Journalism* / A note or two on journalism, an activity typical of the eighteenth century, is in order here. In the sixteenth century printed sheets carrying European news appeared. In the seventeenth there were journals, issued irregularly, such as the first *Gaceta de México* of 1667. But it was in the eighteenth century that periodicals emerged everywhere and changed intellectual life. Of those dedicated to literature and to the sciences, the ones published in Mexico by José Antonio Alzate (1729–1799) and José Ignacio Bartolache (1739–1790) are noteworthy. In Colombia Francisco Javier Caro (1750–1822) published a pleasant *Diario* (1783) in which bureaucratic life was ridiculed.

C. THEATER

Because of its social character, the theater is an index of the refinement with which the customs of the capital cities of Spain and of Europe were imitated. Pablo de Olavide had been charged with the construction of a new playhouse (the old Colosseum had been destroyed in an earthquake), and he built such a sumptuous one that it reflected all the brilliance of the rococo age. Here, the celebrated Creole actress Micaela Villegas, known as Perricholi, reigned from 1760 onwards. She was the mistress of the Viceroy Manuel de Amat y Junient; and her bearing, her coquettishness, her rakish elegance gave the colonies the same tone of beauty and pleasure that Europeans enjoyed in their courts. In the second half of this century interludes and farces brought on a new way of describing customs. The slackening of the mining industries in Mexico and Lima, the centers of court theater, coincided with the establishment of theaters and opera houses financed by landowners and businessmen who were fond of entertainment, in cities showing economic growth: Havana in 1776, Buenos Aires in 1783, Caracas in 1784, Montevideo in 1793, Bogotá in 1793, Guatemala in 1794, La Paz in 1796. Works in pretentious neoclassic fashion were produced; however the Creole farcists multiplied and instead of putting *majas* and the Madrilenians of the Spaniard Ramón de la Cruz on the stage, they presented the popular types from the different regions of Hispanic-America, for example, *The Love of the Farmer's Daughter* (*El amor de la estanciera*), an anonymous farce in verse, composed between 1780 and 1795. It lacks literary worth, and its value as a picture of customs is marred because the author could not have chosen more vulgar expressions even had he wished to mock Argentine country life and people. The practical joke played on the Portuguese is not worse than that played on the two gauchos and their wives. The girl is also a vulgar type. The historian, however, must be alert to this literary activity which devoted itself to depicting popular types, ways of life, slang expressions, and dialogs among humble people: alert, because from this will spring what will later be called Gaucho literature. It is this literary activity, and not the songs of mythical minstrels, that becomes the source of the "singing gaucho" image as created by Hidalgo, Ascasubi, Hernández, and other poets of the people. In 1780 the anonymous play *Ollantay* was presented in Peru, but it does not concern us because it was the Quechan language. Although it was based on an Inca legend, the structure and conventions are Hispanic. It has historical importance because it coincided with the rebellion of Tupac Amaru II.

VI. 1788-1808

Authors born between 1760 and 1780

Historical framework: Under the inept rule of Charles IV Spain takes a purely defensive position and begins losing her colonies. Because of the Napoleonic invasions, Charles IV abdicates in favor of his son Fernando VII: the days of the Spanish empire in America are over.

Cultural tendencies: Literature carries a Gallicized, neoclassical stamp. Rationalism is colored by subjectivism.

Introduction

A history of literature intent on adjusting itself to its own material—the record of man's effort to express himself in beautiful words—should close its eyes to what was the most important element of this last period of the eighteenth century, which was not literature, but the movement of philosophic ideas and the preparation for political independence. At any rate, it should point out only what most approximated literature. Let us examine, then, in the foreground, those writers who want to go into literature—poetry, imaginative prose—without, however, refusing to glance at their ideas, however lacking they may be in literary values. It is the ideas that are important here. Remember that we are on the threshold of independence, and it is more necessary now for us to understand the ideological basis of our revolutions.

Hispanic-American readers, with patriotic impatience, may wish to have the distinctiveness and originality of their respective countries presented, and if that be the case, we may be reproached for the attention given to European styles and ideas up to now in these pages. But the study of literature, in order to aspire to universal norms, does not need to pay too much attention to those characteristics of American society which might just as well be found in books on ethnography. The Europeans brought to the New World their wealth of culture; and though they adapted themselves to the environment and their children, and grandchildren, and great-great-grandchildren were Americans, European culture did prevail. Even though they live in a different historic setting from the European, European influences never cease. The ties between the metropolis and the colonies are close. The lack of direct communication is compensated for by the idealization of the European culture which is not known first-hand, and by the desire to belong to the best-known culture. In the eighteenth century, for example, just when a more original expression of American experiences was to be expected (because the colonies now seemed distant from the first Spanish settlers and from the initial founding of cities and institutions) a new Europeanizing wave came again to conceal the undeveloped indigenous culture. Constant waves of immigration, technical and administrative progress, commercial activity, movements of armies and navies, and the like, continue the cultural contacts initiated in the early years.

A. MAINLY POETRY

During the last thirty years of the colony, Mexico was a thriving humanistic center. Classicism, even though it only reflected light, had warmth. At least it warmed the hearts of many versifiers. Horace, Vergil, Ovid, Catullus, Martial, and even the Greeks were translated, imitated, and commented on copiously. The only person from the epoch of Charles IV who was a writer by vocation if not by talent was FRIAR MANUEL DE NAVARRETE (Mexico, 1768–1809), a poet of Mexican landscapes who was more refined in his neoclassic culture than he was perceptive in his observations. He began publishing his verses in 1806. He promoted the Mexican Arcadia (one of the many academies of the period), whose members assumed the names of shepherds in imitation of the anacreontics of Meléndez Valdés. The latter taught him to sweeten his erotic verses, and also to read Young, whose *Night Thoughts* he imitated in "Nights of Sorrow" (*"Noches tristes"*) and in "Moments of Sorrow" (*"Ratos tristes"*). In this way he moved from the soft pastoral poetry of his youth to the elegiac poetry of the disenchantment of his later years. In "Eucharistic Poem of Divine Providence" (*"Poema eucarístico de la Divina Providencia"*) there are reminiscences of Fray Luis de León. Similar to him is MANUEL JUSTO DE RUBALCAVA (Cuba, 1769–1805), a classic poet, moderate, decorous. In his *silvas* he sang of Cuban fruit, in imitation of Vergil ("Eclogue") and the Spanish poet José Iglesia de la Casa. His sonnet "To Nise Embellishing a Flowerpiece" (*"A Nise bordando un ramillete"*) is among his best. MANUEL DE ZEQUEIRA Y ARANGO (Cuba, 1764–1846), like other neoclassical poets, wrote didactic, heroic, and satiric poems. He succeeded, however, in his bucolic meters. We are referring to his ode "To the Pineapple" (*"A la piña"*) where he sings of the pleasures of the tropics. With trappings taken from mythology he composes a kind of fantastic biography of the pineapple, from its birth to the time when, adorned on earth by Poma and Ceres, it is borne by Ganymede to Olympus where it triumphs among nectars and aromas and is celebrated by the gods. This artfulness, so typically neoclassical, acquires a native, Creole emotion when the poet boasts with pride about the pineapple, "splendor of my country." He followed in the steps of Meléndez, Cienfuegos, Quintana. One of his most poetic inventions occurred not in his poetry but in his life when, having gone insane, he believed that his hat made him invisible. GRACILIANO AFONSO (Canarias–Puerto Rico, 1775–1861) translated Anacreon from the Greek and composed more or less original anacreontics.

The fable, that old moralizing and practical genre, was transformed in the eighteenth century into ideological discussion. Animals spoke like philosophers as in the fables of the Spaniards, Iriarte and Samaniego. In Hispanic-America the genre and not the philosophy was imitated by JOSÉ NÚÑEZ DE CÁCERES (Santo Domingo, 1772–1846); DOMINGO DE AZCUÉNAGA (Argentina, 1758–1821), a skeptical spectator of the society in which he lived, who introduced animals and local matters in his fables;

FRIAR MATÍAS DE CÓRDOVA (Guatemala, 1768–1828), the author of a notable fable, "The Attempt of the Lion and the Success of His Undertaking" (*"La tentativa del león y el éxito de su empresa"*); and RAFAEL GARCÍA GOYENA (Ecuador–Guatemala, 1766–1823), in whose thirty or so fables one glimpses certain ideas that were new in the Hispanic-American continent.

In the last years of the eighteenth century, satiric poetry, the anonymous as well as the known, is charged with the stormy air of social and political questions. Poetry acts as a barometer of the great changes that are impending. Satiric aggression was used principally by the defenders of traditionalism, who were losing ground against the advances of modernism. But satire was also a channel of revolutionary unrest. The poems of derision were generally anonymous, but some names are preserved: MARIANO JOSÉ DE ALVA Y MONTEAGUDO (Cuba, 1761–1800) and his festive glosses; Father ÁLVARO MONTES DE OCA (Cuba, 1768–1848). The great influence on satiric poetry in America was Quevedo: his themes, his formulas, his language, his moments of appetite for the world and his satiation with it. A Quevedo disciple was ESTEBAN DE TERRALLA Y LANDA, an Andalusian who lived in Mexico and later in Peru where he satirized local customs in his ballads, *Lima Inside and Out* (*Lima por dentro y fuera*, 1797), a bitter work, disordered and resentful. In *The Life of Many or a Week Well Employed by a Lima Dandy* (*Vida de muchos o sea una semana bien empleada por un currutaco de Lima*) he noted down day after day the emptiness of life. But whose? That of a typical fop? We suspect it was his own life. He was an egocentric who blamed the Creoles for his economic and social failures. He felt persecuted. What was happening was that he could not learn to adapt. He joined the Spaniards in their anti-Creole attitudes. He was not very intelligent and was blind to the great historic changes of his time. Let us call a halt on poetry of circumstance, which is where all poetry comes to a halt; for instance, the enormous number of verse compositions to which the English invasions of Buenos Aires gave rise.

B. MAINLY PROSE

1. Imaginative Prose

There are no novels, and what follows now is a continuation of the history of a genre absent in Hispanic-America, which was begun in previous chapters. A type of realist narration nourished by national traditions was cultivated in Spain throughout the eighteenth century. But it did not have literary quality. It was merely a picture of customs, satirical or ironic. Everyday reality did not seem worthy of artistic seriousness. The best Spanish writers had no wish to write novels, and the public had no wish to read books that reflected the trivial circumstances of Spanish life. They translated more than they wrote. The translations, to select the best among the dregs, were of Swift, Fielding, Goldsmith, and Richardson (if not Richardson at least one of his continuators, Frances Sheridan, whose *Memoirs of Miss Sidney Bidulph* was translated by JACOBO DE VILLAURRUTIA, 1757–1833, only he did it from a French version and entitled it *Memoirs for the History of Virtue* [*Memorias para la historia de la virtud*]); those of the German Campe and Goethe's *Werther;* those of the Frenchmen Marmontel, Florian, Mme de Genlis, Ducrai-Duminil, Saint-Pierre's *Paul et Virginie* and Chateaubriand's *Atala* (the latter by the Venezuelan Simón Rodríguez); those of the Italians Della Croce (*Bertoldo*) and Count Zaccharia Serinam. All this translation activity was carried on despite the animosity of the literati, the court circles, and the Inquisition (in 1799 an order from the council prohibited the printing of novels). Of course, the cultured minorities read in the original those novels not translated, like those of Ann Radcliffe, Defoe, Rousseau, Voltaire, Diderot. Within her borders, then, Spain was moving in a void and those who wished to breathe the air of the novel had to turn to foreign sources. European narrative currents placed great emphasis on emotion, morals, psychological analysis, conversation, the monolog, the epistle, and philosophy. There was an eruption of sentiment, tearful virtue, feminine themes, exoticism, travails, fantasy, the supernatural, literary trickery, deism, and pantheism. In this climate the new Spanish novelists, Montengón, Martínez Colomer, Mor de Fuentes, languished and failed. All this came to the colonies much later, much confused, much weakened. Consequently, one must not expect in Hispanic-America a novelistic production in tune with the times.

Novelistic traits are barely found in the priest, JOSÉ MARIANO ACOSTA ENRÍQUEZ (Mexico; his literary works are from 1779 to 1816). He included Cervantes, Quevedo, and Torres Villarroel in the plot of his *Dream of Dreams* (*Sueño de sueños*) and with them he undertook a voyage to the netherworld, presenting death in an allegorical form. Acosta Enríquez narrates in the first person, and with his three admired writers he converses about the changes in fashions and speech, about old age, medicine, and death. Retinues of people of every class appear and personifications of popular sayings and moral symbols pass by in review. There is no narrative skill in them. Even the theme of *Dream of Dreams* is not new. Quevedo had written "Dreams" and Torres Villarroel had imagined a dialog with Quevedo. To this company Acosta now adds Cervantes—he was not the first in gathering this group, because in 1728 Nicolás de Molani Nogui had published a *Plaint Made by Don Quixote de la Mancha at the Court of Death Against Don Francisco de Quevedo on the First and Second Part of the Visions and Visitations of Don Diego de Torres* (*Querella que Don Quixote de la Mancha da en el tribunal de la muerte contra Don Francisco de Quevedo sobre la primera segunda parte de las visiones y visitas de Don Diego de Torres*). But, despite all, this little work is interesting for its information on the literary tastes of the eighteenth century. He must have written it in 1801: he speaks of "the end of the century just over, called the century of light," and the most recent book he mentions is the translation of Richardson's *Clara Harlowe*, of 1798 (and it may even be possible that the *Robinson* he speaks of is the translation of Campe's *The New Robinson*, in which case the date is 1800). From the threshold of the nineteenth century he glances back at the history of Spanish narrative and points out the literary fortunes of Cervantes, Quevedo, and Torres Villarroel, adding interesting notes on the dominant tastes of the eighteenth century. He informs us that the many translations from the French are changing the language of the writers. Among the books that are "running through Mexico similarly to yours"—he tells the three Spaniards—he lists those of the Frenchmen Bottens, Fénélon, Le Sage, Mme de Genlis; of the Englishmen Fielding (Henry as well as Sarah), Richardson; of the German Campe; and of the Italian Serinam. Among the Spanish novels, Acosta mentions Montengón's and *The Town's Entanglements* (*Los enredos de un lugar*, 1778) by Fernando Gutiérrez de Vegas, which he feels is the best. Acosta tells us that the hero of this novel, the licentiate Tarugo, resembles Don Quixote.

2. Discursive Prose

Religious, Philosophic, and Political Ideas / Sacred oratory, even though it may soar esthetically, continues to be bound by the mental attitude of the clergy: e.g., Father JOSÉ POLICARPO SANAME Y DOMÍNGUEZ (Cuba, 1760–1806), famous for his "sermon of the cloud," given in Santo Domingo. There is abundant religious literature, reverently leaning toward its own traditions and dogmas, like *Spiritual Watering for New Plants* (*Riego espiritual para nuevas plantas*) by Mother MARÍA PETRONILA CUÉLLAR (Colombia, 1761–1814). In a simple and spontaneous prose she attempts to direct novices and nuns. However, in general, the most significant pages, within religious themes, were those that carried on the discussion of the new ideas. JOSÉ AGUSTÍN CABALLERO (Cuba, 1762–1835) was a man of the Church, except that he attacked scholasticism and expounded on Locke and Condillac. Furthermore, his *Elective Philosophy* (*Philosophia electiva*) was a systematic formulation of anti-scholastic thought. In the face of the advances of this modern philosophy, scholasticism, though ever resisting, was receding. An illustrative case is the course on ethics given in Buenos Aires between 1793 and 1795 by MARIANO MEDRANO. His method was still scholastical, though not strictly so, and the doctrine professed follows that of Aristotle and Thomas Aquinas, though not to the letter. Medrano, as a Catholic and monarchist, resists the thought of Hobbes, Locke, Rousseau, and others, but in his resistance he feels the force of their blows and retreats from his own dogmatic line; and in this way the new ideas advance in the classrooms of San Carlos. In reality scholastic philosophy (which was decadent toward the end of the eighteenth century, especially in the Río de la Plata area) was counterproductive. In 1793 when the flames of the French Revolution were lighting up the American colonies and Miranda had launched his campaigns of emancipation, Medrano wished to convince his Creole students of the absolutist rights of the Spanish monarchy. He defamed Las Casas; he cloaked the theological thought of Vitoria; in short, he cut the only emotional ties that the Creoles could have felt for their Spanish past. A few years later these Creoles would be the leaders of the movement for independence. There were friars who, already undermined by some encyclopedist ideas, accepted independence as inevitable and even worked together with the patriots. In Colombia the enlightened CAMILO TORRES (1766–1816), author of *Record of Grievances* (*Memorial de agravios*, 1809), had a clear idea of the importance of Hispanic-America in the world economy and knew that the anti-liberal errors of Spain were going to incite independence. JOSÉ FÉLIX DE RESTREPO (Colombia, 1760–1832) was a supporter of the educational reforms of Moreno and Escandón. He was not an encyclopedist, but rather a "Christian philosopher" who abandoned Aristotelian methods and adopted experimental ones. For him, the sciences were not enemies of religion. He fought for the abolition of slavery, was in favor of independence and against Spanish "despotism" and "tyranny." TOMÁS ROMAY (Cuba, 1764–1849) was a progressive, scientific, and constructive soul, but with a good literary education. FRANCISCO ANTONIO ZEA (Colombia, 1766) was a mind possessing literary sensitivity (some verses have been attributed to him) and even in his descriptions of the "endowments" and "witcheries" of botany there is a loving view of nature, related to that of the rococo. The fact is that the pages of studious and thinking men are saturated with the sentimentalism of the age, as in the *American Letters on Politics and Morals* (*Cartas americanas políticas y morales*, 1823) by MANUEL LORENZO DE VIDAURRE (Peru, 1773–1841) and in one of the greatest scientific spirits of his time, FRANCISCO JOSÉ DE CALDAS (Colombia, 1771–1811). The eighteenth-century style of the "sensitive man," quick to tears, is seen in Caldas' letter to his teacher Mutis, concerning Humboldt's rebuff to him, or in the letters to his sweetheart. It is the influence of the exclamatory letters in Rousseau's *La Nouvelle Héloïse*, a literary novelty. Caldas was a naturalist with literary talent and his descriptions of nature, e.g., that of Tequendama, have the value of art. His prose is akin to that of Feijóo, Jovellanos, and Quintana, although that terrible landscape through which he moved apprehensively is wont to inspire in him expressions of powerful pathos. "Reason, experience are my light," he would say; but he also received light from his heart. Light is the key word. He published his *New Granada Weekly* (*Semanario de la Nueva Granada*, 1808–1809) to "promote incessantly the enlightenment and the happiness of its peoples." When independence failed he was shot by Enribe, the one made famous by the phrase: "Spain does not need learned men." Nor does the figure of ANTONIO NARIÑO (Colombia, 1765–1823) belong to literary history, because he produced no literature. Nevertheless, he lived the literature of others, and he should be mentioned here, if only as an example of an Hispanic-American intellectual during the last years of the colony. Nariño's private library was the richest in the Viceroyalty of New Granada. He discussed these books, many of them prohibited, with his friends; and he used to print on a hand press selections of his readings to give to his friends. He translated the *Déclaration des droits de l'homme* (1794), which had great repercussions since it prepared for the uprising of the colonies.

JUAN EGAÑA (Peru–Chile, 1768–1836) left us a book of memoirs, *The Chilean Consoled in Prisons* (*El chileno consolado en los presidios*, 1826). He was one of the Creole encyclopedists, author of a dramatic poem and also a jocular one, but when Marcó del Pont deported him to the island of Juan Fernández he wrote his memoirs in prison.

Without belonging entirely to the world of letters, the figure who ornamented the literature of this period with the most original coloration is FRIAR SERVANDO TERESA DE MIER (Mexico, 1763–1827). The great event of his life, the cause of his misfortunes and indirectly of his autobiographical pages, and even of his political thought, dates from 1794, and it occurred within the cultural life of the Church. We refer to his sermon denying the popular tradition of the Virgin of Guadalupe and affirming the preaching of the Gospel in America by no less than Apostle St. Thomas himself, before the arrival of the Spaniards. Mier lamented the preference given to Spaniards. He loved his native land. In the way Spain invented its Apostle St. James, he decided (after hearing Borunda and not being quite convinced) to invent a St. Thomas Apostle for Mexico. Here his misfortunes were born: if Mier had been right, we Spanish-Americans would not even owe our faith to Spain. Mier was not in disagreement with the Church, but with Spain. Had he persisted in this thinking, Mier would be one of many ecclesiastical minds who still insisted on an extravagant view of the world even after the triumph of the enlightenment. But he grew in human stature because of the cruel persecutions he suffered, and as he grew more and more aware of the world, he embraced political causes that placed him in the historic line of independence. Nevertheless, one must not lose sight of the fact that Mier had his head filled with ideas from the past, that he defended Catholic faith against heretics (Jansenists, deists, atheists) and, in the final instance, although he may have associated himself with the efforts of independence, he justified his action not with the principles of the political philosophy of the enlightenment, but with the myth that St. Thomas had preached in America: "in the same way that St. Thomas prophesied the coming of the Spaniards, he also predicted the end of their domination, and this more or less is the moment." This myth (like the one about the Apostle St. James in Spain which, incidentally, he links with his own) sets Mier apart from the new intellectual movement. But he was not a misoneist, and at times he criticized friars for their narrow views. He had the cosmic vision of a priest, although not the temperament of a priest. He lack humility, meekness, and serenity. And this psychological conflict gave birth to his originality as a person and to the contradictions in his literature. Literarily Mier exists through his memoirs which belong to the eighteenth-century cycle. His autobiographical pages, which have been collected by editors under the generic term *Memoirs*, make Mier known to us in his grievous contacts with eccleciastical life. But his work gains literary interest when he raises his sight and looks at the reality of the countries in which he lives. The *Accounts (Relación)*, for example, give a good description of France, Italy, and Spain. Here is Mier the writer. Mier said that the translation of *Atala* which appeared under the name of S. Robinson, pseudonym of Simón Rodríguez, was his. Be this as it may, there are no Chateaubriand traits in his literature or in his make-up. He did not create artistic prose. Nor did he try to describe natural landscapes or artistic monuments. Either he speaks of his own misfortunes (insisting always that he is persecuted because, as an Hispanic-American, his intellectual superiority is intolerable to the Spaniards) or he describes the most immediate social circumstances, those involving his travels. He generally reflects on differences in customs; in so doing, his attitude is influenced by eighteenth-century traits (the understanding of things regional, popular, and unique). His prose moves rapidly but with dignity. From time to time, there is a happy epigram. At times, with a stroke or two, he paints a character that deserves to live in a story. There is wit, occasionally sarcasm, and, at times, violent polemics. Whether his memoirs are novelistic or not could be argued—no one will argue that he, Friar Servando, was not a novelistic hero.

The time he spent in London (1811–1816) was important to the formation of his political ideology. Inspired by the example of the institutions of the English monarchy, he wanted absolute independence for the Spanish colonies in America (*Letters from an American*) (*Cartas de un americano*). Later on, in his admiration for the political regime of the United States, he embraced republicanism, moderating it with theological and even fantastic ideas from his own "Instructive Statement on Politics" (*"Memoria politico-instructiva"*).

Among the intellectuals who prepared the way for the May revolution in what today is Argentina, the two minds best informed on the political doctrines of the enlightenment were Belgrano and Moreno. In MANUEL BELGRANO (1770–1820) these doctrines were tempered by the influence of Italian economists like Genovesi. MARIANO MORENO (1778–1811) translated Rousseau's *Social Contract*, toning down the chapters on religion.

3. Journalism

Journalism becomes more intense and intervenes more effectively in the ideological and social transformation of the epoch. Occasionally these periodicals opened their pages to literature and even to literary criticism, as when Manuel del Socorro Rodríguez came to the defense of the literary activities of New Granada by answering a reader who believed that verses should not be published in New Granada because it was literarily inferior to Mexico and Peru.

C. THEATER

During these years, 1789 to 1808, the establishment of theaters continues—details have already been given. A greater index of the growing interest in theater, however, is what is happening in cities where it had existed many years earlier. The score of plays that were presented each month in Mexico and in Lima were by Spanish authors—the Hispanic-Americans devoted themselves more to farces and short pieces. In truth the men of the theater of those days were more play-adapters than playwrights. For their adaptations they preferred successful authors. The repertory of the Mexico City and Lima theaters was almost the same as that of Madrid. It seems that as the theaters began to sustain themselves as public entertainment, the most recent authors became the leading ones. Calderón, inevitably, was the god—he headed all the repertories. Others from the Golden Age appear repeatedly: Moreto, Rojas Zorrilla, Mira de Amescua, Vélez de Guevara. On the other hand, Lope, Tirso, Alarcón were not considered because their school seemed too remote. The taste for the modern element centered in the recent authors of the eighteenth century: Iriarte, Jovellanos, Ramón de la Cruz, García de la Huerta, Moratín, Moncín, Valladares, Cañizares, Bances Candamo, Arellano, Zamora. The works of non-Spanish authors that were given were the Frenchmen Racine, Molière, Beaumarchais, Jean Baptiste Rousseau, and the Italians Goldoni, Metastasio, Apostolo Zeno. In a history of theatrical taste throughout the eighteenth century, in its transition from baroque to neoclassicism, minor and obscure figures are of special interest. These are figures of little significance when seen from the highest perspectives of literary history (history should move from peak to peak), but yet they reveal a process of the modernization and even Americanization of the theater.

In this sense certain little works that were performed on occasion are of interest, such as *The Mexican Lady in England* (*La Mexicana en Inglaterra*, 1792), *La Morbella* (1792), and *American Loyalty* (*La lealtad americana*, 1796) by FERNANDO GAVILA, an actor in the company at the New Colosseum in Mexico. The taste for the lyrical genre, operas and musical dramas, was a novelty in Mexico. Other Mexicans were: JUAN DE MEDINA (fl. 1796), MANUEL QUIRÓS Y CAMPO SAGRADO (fl. 1792), DIEGO BENEDICTO VALVERDE (fl. 1790), JOSÉ MARÍA VILLASEÑOR CERVANTES (fl. 1809), and JUAN WENCESLAO BARQUERA (1779–1840). In 1791 the *Peruvian Mercury* (*Mercurio peruano*) of Lima was urging "a little modern taste in the preference for pieces" and above all, that sensible people refrain from joining in the applause that the "low-class plebeians" gave to the interludes. But that is the way one of the most successful playwrights, the actor RAFAEL GARCÍA ("Chicho"), entertained with his scurrilous farces and interludes. There was also theater in other parts of Hispanic-America: FRANCISCO COVARRUBIAS (Cuba, 1774–1856), JUAN FRANCISCO MARTÍNEZ (Uruguay, fl. 1807), JUAN ANTONIO TRIS Y DOYAGUE (Chile, fl. 1792). The most outstanding figure was that of CAMILO HENRÍQUEZ (Chile, 1769–1825), a boisterous patriot, who, having rooted himself in Buenos Aires, wrote politico-sentimental dramas. One is *Camille or the Patriot of South America* (*Camila o la patriota en Sudamérica*), an example of bad theater, where there is an attempt to teach the people tolerance and liberty. This Chilean friar was a liberal. He used to say, "Voltaire, Rousseau, Montesquieu are the apostles of reason." He took part, as a journalist and as a versifier, in the political progaganda favoring independence.

PART TWO
One Hundred Years of the Republic

VII. 1808-1824

Authors born between 1780 and 1800

Historical framework: Wars of independence, which end in the triumph of Creole arms.

Cultural tendencies: Neoclassicism and the first indications of English romanticism.

Introduction

Since history is pure flux, each of its periods is one of transition. In the period 1808 to 1824 the transition referred to in the previous chapter continues: within the enlightenment ideas become more liberal, literary forms more varied, and individual styles more emotional but the enlightenment itself is moving along new roads and, when least expected, it will be seen conversing with voices that are already romantic. Since shortly we will leave the enlightenment and come face to face with romanticism, it is fitting that we should do justice to the former. In the realm of action, the culture of the enlightenment made noble efforts to regenerate Spain and its colonies. It helped to lift ideas out of scholastic quagmires and affirmed humanitarianism, liberty, progress, reason, and the study of nature. In the realm of literature, it achieved the virtues of clarity, order, equilibrium, and universality.

Neoclassical Liberalism

Neoclassicism was the literary face of the enlightenment. But in neoclassical themes, like that of nature, for example, one notices that the writers go beyond rational limits and give us emotional vistas. Nature (once held suspect by traditional Christianity) is venerated more and more and is not looked upon as sheer mechanism (as by the rationalists), but as an organism with purpose. Another theme of neoclassical literature was politics. From the old Latin word *liberalis* (befitting a man of free birth) comes the adjective "liberal," and it was precisely in these years that the Spaniards and Hispanic-Americans, convened in the Parliament of Cádiz, hypostatized that adjective into a political concept. From here the slogan "liberalism" (already used by 1814) was coined to characterize the system of beliefs opposing the absolute power of state and Church. The political themes of neoclassical literature were, then, those of liberalism. Liberalism was the political expression of the desire to give man dignity, which at bottom implied the faith that man was capable of dignity. Liberty and progress were, therefore, the keys to the epoch. Liberalism gave vitality to literature. Literature had often been a mere academic, rhetorical exercise for frivolous entertainment. Now the cultured minorities made literature a vital act. Neoclassicism, in this way, acquired new impetus. The intellectuals felt responsible for the liberty and progress of American society. Thanks to liberalism the poets, teachers, writers, and orators were able to give philosophic meaning to a revolution and a declaration of independence which broke out before the colonies were prepared for them. Though it is true that there were economic, social, and political forces that moved in that direction, it is also true that the Napoleonic invasions of Spain precipitated events and forced the colonies to improvise the emancipation. When the insurrectional movement began in 1808 many of the intellectuals we have studied in the colonial period were still living and writing. And there were also old or middle-aged men who were just beginning to write. But we turn our attention here to the literary contributions of the younger men.

Parenthetical Remarks on the Language

Since this chapter opens up the period of independence and republicanism in our history, we shall pause a moment to say something about the language. After all, the history of Hispanic-American letters is the history of the use that Hispanic-Americans have made of the Spanish language. Naturally, this language was not a loan from Spain. It was brought here by Spaniards who came to see the New World, settled here and raised families. These Spaniards and their descendents were as much the masters of their language as those who remained in Spain. Language is the property of the person who speaks it, not of a geographical tract of land. Was a special Spanish language created in America? Did that supposed "American Spanish" constitute a linguistic unity, or was it rather a panorama of diverse linguistic regions? If an American Spanish was formed, was it able to function harmoniously with the Spanish spoken in Spain, or did it gradually begin to deviate toward a future independence? No one contests that there are universal norms; nor does anyone contest that each person speaks in his own way. But, between an abstract language in general and a concrete individual way of speaking, how shall we characterize the Spanish language, spoken by Hispanic-Americans, which has produced the literature we are studying?

One principle of differentiation is based on the fact that Spaniards from the lowlands, such as Andalusia, colonized lands in America that were predominantly lowlands, such as the Antilles, the coasts and plains of Venezuela and Colombia, the Argentine and Chilean coast lines; while Spaniards from the highlands, like Castile, colonized predominantly highlands, like Mexico or the countries of the Andes. But the differences between this land and that land do not destroy the fundamental unity. Nor do differences in geography, or a series of local political events, native substrata, or ways of life with their respective characteristics. Furthermore, all of these differences prolong real or potential trends in the Spanish language of Spain. In the sixteenth century the speech of Castile and that of Andalusia were not as different from each other as they are today. On being transplanted to the New World, they levelled out, and from there, through the lips of the conquistadors, they spread out over the continent. Today the most notable linguistic region is that surrounding the Caribbean: Puerto Rico, Santo Domingo, Cuba, the coast of Venezuela, the Atlantic coast of Colombia, the Gulf of Mexico and Central America. Ever since the sixteenth century, then, there has been a levelling process in the language spoken in Hispanic America. Even in colonies that sprang from currents of conquistadors independent of those spreading out from the Antilles (such as Río de la Plata) or in later colonies common linguistic traces can be found. Thus, unifying traces appear all over America. First, in the sixteenth century, came the *seseo* (the pronunciation of *c* before *e* and *i* and the letter *z* like *s*). Then, in the seventeenth and eighteenth centuries, the dropping of "*vosotros*" and its pronominal forms. The first colonies had become societies of the people and these gave the language its levelling drive. At times the unifying elements that appeared in the seventeenth century were alien to Spain, like the combinations of "*vos*" and "*tu*" (forms of the second personal pronoun) in "*vos eras*" ("you were") and "*te quiere a vos*" ("he loves thee [you]"), that became prevalent from Tabasco to Río de la Plata and Chile. There is unity and diversity of language within America, within the whole Hispanic linguistic realm. The unity in America is not less solid than that in the Iberian peninsula. The unity exists not only in what is peculiarly Hispanic-American (*seseo, loismo* [the use of "*lo*" as a masculine pronoun in the accusative case], the dropping of "*vosotros*"), but in the total phonetic, morphologic, and syntactic system of the Spanish language in general.

We shall study the great figure of Andrés Bello in this chapter. He was the author of a *Grammar of the Spanish Language Destined for the Use of Americans* (*Gramática de la lengua castellana destinada al uso de los americanos*, 1847), the best of all times in all countries. He defended the rights of Americans to participate in the unceasing life of the language, although this did not mean that he preached an independence of idioms. On the contrary, his program was the unification of the language, in Spain and in all the Hispanic countries. Whether or not this good intention is maintained, Bello said, depends on us. It is in this that Bello differs so much from the partisans of individual national languages (who became more and more vociferous from the beginning of romanticism), as well as from those who, like Cuervo (later), believed that the fragmentation of the language is inevitable, as was the case with Latin.

A. MAINLY POETRY

Neoclassical Poetry / José Joaquín de Olmedo (Ecuador, 1780–1847) wrote some ninety poetic compositions, few of which could be saved by a demanding reader. They cover a long period, from 1802 to 1847, with long intervals in between because his poetic capacity and even his calling would fail him. He was always a neoclassical poet, imitator of the Greeks and Romans, and in his enraptured moments he was close to Meléndez Valdés, Cienfuegos, and Chateaubriand (whose *Atala* he versified in "Indian Song" [*"Canción indiana"*]); generally, he was in line with Quintana and Gallego. There are two of Olmedo's poems that rise above the level of his times, even beyond America. "The Victory at Junín: Song to Bolívar" (*"La victoria de Junín. Canto a Bolívar,"* 1825), and "To General Flores, Victor of Miñarica" (*"Al general Flores, vencedor en Miñarica,"* 1835). The historic importance of both events shook the poet Olmedo and impelled him to work with all the strength of his art, a grandiloquent art not only because it was a deliberate imitation of the eloquence of his great models but also because his soul tended to the emphatic; and so we have the case of a poet composing coldly, astutely, slowly, with much care and retouching, who achieves fiery and stormy effects. Because of these odes Olmedo passes as an ardent and vehement person while down deep he was sober, moderate, pensive, sensible. Thanks to the correspondence between Olmedo and Bolívar and the variants between editions, the genesis of the "Victory at Junín" is known. It seems that Bolívar asked him to sing the praises "of our latest triumphs" (although he urged that his name not appear). Olmedo began to conceive his poem when he was apprised of the battle of Junín (August of 1824); but it was the victory at Ayacucho (December 9 of the same year) that inspired a grandiose ode, with Bolívar as the hero, of course, but constructed in such a way that not only Junín (where Bolívar fought) figures in it, but also Ayacucho (where Bolívar was not present). To unite the two battles in the same tale, he resorted to an old trick in the epic book—a supernatural apparition that prophesied, after the victory at Junín, the more decisive victory at Ayacucho. It is Huayna-Cápac, the last Inca to rule over the undivided Empire. The discourse that Olmedo puts in the mouth of the Indian is typical of the humanitarian philosophy of the epoch. Olmedo did not advocate the restoration of the Incas, far from it. But the men of his generation (both Creoles and Spaniards) had acquired a sentimental attitude toward the Indians which helped them to condemn the cruelties of the conquest and, while they were at it, agitate against political absolutism. Basically, the chant of independence follows the liberal thinking of the Spaniards themselves who, on the other hand, were sanctioning Las Casas and writing historical novels and dramas with indigenous themes.

Another political characteristic of those years was that Olmedo (or better, Huayna-Cápac) speaks of the peoples of America as "of one family and a single people." The genuine feat—he says— is not in defeating Spain, but in creating an Hispanic-American federation of hard-working and free provinces. Olmedo demanded so much of himself that he became discouraged with the imperfections of his verses and came to believe that he had failed. Nevertheless, "The Victory at Junín" is one of the best odes in our literary history. His verses flow like powerful waves of music, and the reader yields to the enchantment of his interplay of sounds —resonant in verses like "the horrendous thunder that in clamor explodes," soft as in "sonorous murmur and niveous foam," always vivacious, light and sinuous. His was not empty eloquence. He unfolded his verse with solemnity and one fears that this might end in mere pomposity, flatulence, and wordiness, but the surprise comes in the conciseness with which he has selected each word, each rhythm, each image. His is a verbal economy in a genre and style that tend toward extravagance. Olmedo expressed his feeling for landscape and thus the poem, epic in its inspiration, didactic in its purpose, quivers with lyricism. This lyrical accent was what was newest and what was most American. Once his imagination was struck by a ray of color from the landscape, the poet would begin to elaborate his impressions, animate and personify things so as to convert them into storybook personages. Olmedo was the poet not only of the last wars of independence but also ten years later he was to write about the civil wars. "To General Flores, Victor at Miñarica" is an even more accomplished ode than that offered to Bolívar because of its delicate sounds, its evolved and original images, the spontaneity with which the verses flow and the feelings that are laid bare. But General Flores was of lesser political stature than Bolívar, and Olmedo regretted having dedicated verses to him. It is not difficult to imagine the feelings of horror at the anarchy and fratricide that were beginning to dismember the great and united Hispanic-America of which he had sung earlier.

Andrés Bello / Higher yet in literary rank was ANDRÉS BELLO (Venezuela, 1781–1865). His early education was religious though tempered by the tastes of the enlightenment. He read the Latin classics with relish (at the age of fifteen he was translating one of the books of *The Aeneid*); he enjoyed Cervantes and Calderón; his knowledge of French and English opened before him a panorama of the great social and cultural movements of Europe. He stood out early because of his broad intellectual curiosity and his literary proclivities. His first poetic exercises are pure experimentation. Traits from Horace and Vergil and from the Italo-Spanish school of the sixteenth century join the neo-classical esthetics—prosaic, didactic, scientific—of the eighteenth century.

Poetry, stimulated by the ardor for construction, attempts to rectify the intellectual backwardness of the Spanish-speaking nations. And this patriotic, progressivist ideal takes all activities in tow, so that lyricism, too, falls behind. His sonnet "To the Victory of Bailén" ("*A la victoria de Bailén*," 1809)—which Bello always valued among his better poems—closes the first period of his life. Then in 1810 he went to England as an aide to Bolívar and López Meléndez, both delegates of the Caracas revolutionary junta; and he spent his second period, until 1829, in London (the third was to be his Chilean period, from 1829 to 1865). Bello had never been a revolutionary. He was more in sympathy with an enlightened monarchy. From 1810 to 1829 he was alone in Lon-

don, in the midst of the splendor of European culture, and began
the study of languages, literature, philosophy, history, sciences,
law. It was the most fertile period of his life. In his *American
Library* (*Biblioteca Americana*) he published the "Address to
Poetry" ("*Alocución a la Poesía*," 1823), fragments of a poem
that Bello intended to entitle "America." It is a neoclassical *silva*,
but within this tradition the poet sings with a new spirit. He
invokes poetry to leave the courts of Europe and to come to the
nascent nations of America where nature and history will be
more propitious to it. In the midst of the wars of independence,
therefore, the poet launches a program for literary independence.
There is here an American feeling of nostalgia and love—above
all, the feeling for an epoch just beginning.

The Hispanic-American armies were fighting in the name of
liberty and progress against the despotism and the inquisition of
Fernando VII. They were horrifying wars like all wars (Bello was
never a bellicose poet), but they opened up the way for the creative forces of history. Humanity was shaking off the yoke of the
past, and the battles in America were "instances of the great
struggle for liberty, that was beginning." The universal triumph
of that historic urge, although certain, was still far off. Radiant
with the resplendence of liberty, America bared its beauty and
was becoming worthy of poetry, a poetry whose voice, though
educated in Europe, would sing of native themes. The "Address"
of 1823 set an original course in literary history, not only for
Hispanic America, but also for Spain, urging poets not to be led
astray by rhetorical imitations. Bello profited by his classics and
continued his study of them, but his purposes were new. Even his
invocations to the muses—so rhetorical—took on the value of an
esthetic manifesto. Three years later he published in the *American
Repertory* (*Repertorio Americano*) his *silva* "To Agriculture in
the Torrid Zone" ("*A la agricultura de la Zona Tórrida*," 1826).
It was conceived on the same plan as the "Address," but the poet
could not fuse both *silvas* because basically they were of different
poetic stress. The battles of Junín and of Ayacucho had ended the
wars of independence, and Olmedo had set the events to poetry.
Reconstruction had to take place. Let the people put down their

arms and take up their plows. The theme of the glorification of country life as opposed to city life was a classical one; and the reminiscences of Vergil, Lucretius, and Horace are evident. But Bello has affection for the country, because it is the home*land* he loves most. His preachings, aimed at dignifying the populace, become dissolved in a genuine feeling for the tropical landscape. The Bello of the *silva* "To Agriculture" had found the way leading to the expression of the newness of America which he understood because it was his. His poetic language, nevertheless, resembled the traditional one. There was a descriptive-didactic school derived from the Romans, continued by the humanists of the Renaissance, cultivated by those Jesuits who versified in Latin, and enlivened by the naturalism of men like Humboldt whom Bello met in Caracas. The ideas of the enlightenment also inspired him to write prosaic and moralizing verses about peace, work, virtue, reconciliation with Spain, political unity of Spanish-America. It is to "agriculture," a practical activity, and not to "nature" as landscape, that he dedicates his poem. This is neoclassical. But that abundance of images, that impetuous enthusiasm for description, that pride in American fruit and its indigenous names, that nostalgia saturating the entire poem, overflowing its moral and intellectual molds and rising in a lyrical tide, isn't this new to our literature? For this reason the images on American plants, which in the "Address" were dispersed, but in the *silva* "To Agriculture" are developed, enriched, brought into play with one another, acquire not only more beauty but also more meaning. This is where the poet crystallizes his rich vein of feeling. As he embraced his own intimate and American world, Bello was approaching the romantics. However, let us beware. If what moves us most in the "American *silvas*" is their lyricism, it is because this lyricism is closer to present-day tastes. But Bello remained true to his neoclassical poetics and from that esthetic position corrected his own impulses. There are other poems that belong to this period: among the best, the "Letter Written From London to Paris From One Hispano-American to Another" ("*Carta escrita desde Londres a París por un americano a otro*"), a moral epistle to Olmedo in which Bello feels exiled not

only from America but from the world; and in tercets rich in
patriotic feeling, he laments what would become obvious in the
years to come—that independence had brought neither virtue,
nor the dream of happiness. In London Bello cultivated the
friendship of Blanco-White, Puigblanch, José Joaquín de Mora,
and other Spanish liberals. Blanco-White, the leader, tried to have
his friends break away from neoclassical rhetoric. The example
of English poetry, fresh, sincere, inspired by the beauties of nature,
by folklore, by the simple life and by the immediate reality, had
its effects. The first romantic budding in Spanish literature appeared, as a consequence, in *London*, but being a literature written
by *émigrés* (and sometimes in English) it had no influence in
Spain; therefore, it is not registered in literary histories. In any
case, it was a romanticism so different from that which prevailed
after 1834 (when the *émigrés* educated in France returned to
Spain) that it is not generally referred to as such. Bello could not
be an exception to the change in literary tastes of the London
émigrés. Romanticism in the English pattern must have influenced his description of the beauties of his land. Still, during his
years in London he did not write romantic poetry. Once he became established in Chile, in 1829, he immediately published an
article on the poetry of Fernández Madrid (a fellow expatriate in
London) and in it he referred to the new literary movement, that
of the Spanish *émigrés* of 1823—a movement far removed from
Meléndez Valdés and Quintana. But the romanticism that caught
fire in Spain was that imported from France. The liberals who had
discovered in London the value of original poetry, devoid of imitations from French classicism, were displeased with this new
Gallicization of Spanish letters. Their reaction seemed anti-
romantic, but in reality it opposed what was insincere in the new
fashion. Bello understood the ideals of romanticism, but he was
prepared to resist the new mode. He denounced the fancy dress
of the Gallicized romantics. He translated Victor Hugo (as he
had translated Byron earlier) and he even took advantage of the
translation of the *"Prière pour tous"* (1830) in order to pour
into it his own intimate feelings—the "Prayer for All" (*"Oración
por todos,"* 1843) is an adaptation more than a version. It is the

old Bello translating the young Hugo, or is it the classicist Bello paring down the imagination of the romantic Hugo? At any rate, in it one sees Bello in the midst of the romantic current, but resisting. The same could be said of his translation of *"Les Djinns"* (1828) in "The Jinns" (*"Los duendes,"* 1843).

The arrival in Chile of the Argentinians Sarmiento, Alberdi, López—above all, Sarmiento—shook literary life violently. These Argentinians had learned their romanticism in French books; and a polemic was kindled in which Bello appeared as a classicist. Nevertheless, in his famous inaugural address at the University of Chile in 1843, Bello demonstrated that he was the most understanding of all. He had known romanticism at its English sources —he was just questioning the superficiality of the improvisers. Mischievously (he had a fine sense of irony) he unmounted the romantic springs and mechanisms of the machine and then mounted them again, demonstrating in this way that he understood its functioning. In 1846 (more or less) he created an image of the romantic fashion in a composition he called "The Fashion" (*"La Moda"*) revealing all its secrets. It is a poetics in reverse, noteworthy because Bello ridicules not from the outside but from the inside and understands completely. When Mitre went astray in his composition "To the Chilean Condor" (*"Al cóndor de Chile,"* 1849), Bello ridiculed the lack of logic in its romantic style in his own "The Condor and the Poet" (*"El cóndor y el poeta"*). Proper construction was his law and for this reason his greatest achievements were in this line. He wrote legends (at least one, "The Outlaw" [*"Proscripto"*]) in the romantic fashion. But this was not his forte. He was a civilizer, a master builder of nations. He was also a thinker and his last work, *Philosophy of Knowledge* (*Filosofía del entendimiento*), gives him a unique place in the philosophic panorama of Hispanic-America. Although in it Bello refers only to psychology and logic, it is sufficiently systematic to be incorporated in the history of ideas. Bello's thinking no doubt reflected European tendencies. He sought a deviation from what he considered the dominating philosophies of his time: the Scotch schools (Reid, Dugald Stewart, Brown) and the eclectic (Cousin, Jouffroi). He found it in the lessons learned in the English philosophy that preceded the Scotch (from Hobbes to Hume, especially Berkeley). He gathered from eclecticism elements of Kant, and acknowledging the positivism that was rising before him he proposed to reduce the "powers of the soul" to intellect and will. He divided the study of the intellect between psychology and logic (he did not achieve a formulation of the dichotomy between moral psychology and its practice in ethics). Everything he said had already been thought before, but he thought about it again. And the energies which he exerted on these already-discussed ideas created a very personal shade of meaning especially visible since it is Bello, the philologist and writer who is communicating his experiences. *Philosophy of Knowledge* is, in short, an exceptional book in the Spanish language of those days.

More Neoclassical Poets / In Buenos Aires—as in other cities of Spanish America—the revolution of 1810 against Spain was waged with Spanish political formulas (Jovellanos provided some of them); and the first poems sung to liberty, resounded with the neoclassical ideals in vogue in Spain. There undoubtedly existed the will to create a new nation and to give that nation its own literary expression. But the truth is that when the themes of the war of independence were discussed in literary circles, these themes did not inspire a new poetry, but seeped into traditional poetic forms. A part of the great abundance of patriotic versification, beginning in 1810, was collected into two books: *The Argentine Lyre* (*La Lira argentina*) and the *Collection of Patriotic Poetry* (*Colección de poesía patriótica*). An examination of the verse production of these fifteen years barely saves several names from oblivion. VICENTE LÓPEZ Y PLANES (1787–1856), who had already documented in more than a thousand hendecasyllables "The Argentine Triumph" (*"El triunfo argentino"*)—a triumph over the English invaders—now wrote a "Patriotic March" (*"Marcha patriótica"*), one of many that circulated in those days, which was later converted into a national anthem. ESTEBAN DE LUCA (1786–1824) also wrote a patriotic march, odes to Creole victories and to liberty in America, and elegies to the death of our heroes. His "Song to the Victory of Maipú" (*"Canto a la victoria de Maipú"*) and his "Lyric Song to the Liberty of Lima" (*"Canto lírico a la libertad de Lima"*), though his best, are spirited only in their civic intentions. Neoclassical rhetoric had clipped their wings.

The man who rises above all this drabness and reaches a level close to that of the great neoclassical poets of Hispanic-America (Bello, Olmedo) is JUAN CRUZ VARELA (1794–1839). His youthful poem "Elvira" gives him kinship with the erotic poets Cadalso, Meléndez Valdés, and Arriaza. Although in his early years as a poet Varela believed he would consecrate himself not to themes of blood, carnage, and wars, but to "tenderness, laughter, and amusement," he joined before long the chorus of patriots, and sang to the triumph of Maipú (1818), to the death of Belgrano, to the freedom of Lima, and so on. Rather than poetry, it was declamation; not even impassioned declamation but the cold academic type, typical of the neoclassical period. From 1820 on Rivadavia, first as governmental minister and then as president, gave unity and impetus to the enlightened culture of his epoch, and Cruz Varela was to become the official poet. Whoever looks back to these brief years of the Rivadavia epoch will perceive a Utopian luster that was soon to be dulled by civil wars and barbarism. There was trust in reason as an instrument of public welfare. The life of the people had to be regulated and, in keeping with rational norms, progressive institutions of universal value had to be founded. Cruz Varela became the poet of Rivadavia's administration. Like all neoclassicists he was a reader of Vergil (later he was to translate fragments of *The Aeneid*), and from the episode of Aeneas and Dido he wrote a three-act tragedy; or rather, an elegy, because what stands out in *Dido* (1823) is the sadness and death of the abandoned queen. Years later he wrote another tragedy, *Argia*, inspired by Alfieri and, like Alfieri, he disguised his hatred of tyrants in the old clothing of classical antiquity. The theater in the Río de la Plata area was then "a practical school of morals." The Society of Good Taste in the Theater (founded in 1817) intended to protect the public from the "corruptions" and the "absurdities" of Lope de Vega and Calderón. Cruz Varela's two tragedies raised standards in the Río de la Plata theater, but in truth contributed nothing that had not been done before in Spain. With his "Song to Ituzaingó (*"Canto a Ituzaingó"*) he returned to the war theme. But now the battle was against Brazil, not Spain. The poets of the war against Spain had become muted. Cruz Varela was the solitary figure; he wrote of the new enemy emulating Olmedo's "Victory at Junín." In 1827 Rivadavia fell; Dorrego was shot in 1828; and in 1829 a dictator who was to dominate the country until 1852 entered the scene: Juan Manuel de Rosas. Cruz Varela fled to Motevideo and there he died. A few months before his death his "swan song" was heard: "The 25th of May of 1838 in Buenos Aires." It was political, civic poetry, vehement in its invective against Rosas. For the vigor of its images and for the repudiation of the sham neoclassicists it is among the most original and moving that he wrote. His tercets beat in time to the rhythm of his soul, nostalgia, contempt for Rosas, and the dignity of the defeated. He does not fling insults; he takes his leave sadly.

Everywhere there was cultured poetry in neoclassic form, with themes taken from the philosophy of the enlightenment, at times mocking and satiric in tone, but always moralizing. Examples are: SIMÓN BERGANO Y VILLEGAS (Guatemala, 1781–1828), who was condemned by the Inquisition for being an "agitator of pernicious and seditious ideas," wrote fables, rondels, a "song to vaccine" and a *"silva* to political economy"; Father JOSÉ TRINIDAD REYES (Honduras, 1797–1855), the first poet to appear in his country, wrote some political satires called "whens" because "when" was the first word of each refrain. His patriotic poetry follows the line of Quintana. His best efforts were "Pastorals," versified theatrical pieces of popular inspiration. And JOSÉ MARÍA SALAZAR (Colombia, 1785–1828), a neoclassical lyricist, author of patriotic songs, but also the author of an *Ode to the Death of Lord Byron (Oda a la muerte de Lord Byron)*. This is the place to consider those who wrote national anthems. We have already

mentioned Lopez y Planes for Argentina. Let us add BERNARDO DE VERA Y
PINTADO (Argentina–Chile, 1780–1827) for Chile, whose national anthem,
except for the chorus, was superseded by another by Eusebio Lillo.

Popular Poetry / Alongside this urbane, cultured, academic poetry, attention was given to a poetry that expressed the voice of the common people.
MARIANO MELGAR (Peru, 1791–1815) was without doubt an educated
mestizo. He barely had time to express his own erotic inspiration because
he died at an early age; furthermore, part of his poetry was destroyed precisely because it dealt with love. Of what remained we can recognize neoclassical preferences: fables, translations and imitations of Vergil, and
translations of Ovid. But, in the most sentimental vein of the neoclassic
style, Melgar succeeded in two things: first, in singing to a love he actually
experienced; and second, in molding that song into the short meters of the
Quechua ballads. Melgar's *"Yaravíes"* are not poetically important, but that
indigenous melody, a melody of the strophe and of the emotions, was something new. He launched a mestizo poetry which the romantic poets later
would carry through as they returned to nature and native themes. Melgar,
because of his vernacular tone—remember his *palomitas*, "doves"—is outstanding among other Peruvian writers of his time: e.g., the satiric poet
JOSÉ JOAQUÍN DE LARRIVA (1780–1832), who, after having made fun of
Spain, would make fun of the new republics.

Origin of Gaucho Literature

During the wars of independence, the most significant phenomenon in the trend toward the creation of a poetry of the people
was the emergence in Rio de la Plata of what has come to be called
"gaucho literature." The word "gaucho" appeared in Rio de la
Plata around 1790 with a negative connotation. A gaucho was a
vagabond, a knife-wielder, an outlaw, a rustler. There is no doubt
that, out of all the pastoral nomadic people scattered about the
plains, the word applied to those elements of humanity whose in-
subordination and unwillingness to exert themselves were most
alarming to law-abiding citizens. But before long the word took on
a more favorable meaning. In the first place the peasant masses
began to take an active part in the historic life of the nation and,
since 1806, the time of the English invasions, they had demonstrated a sense of loyalty and patriotism. They understood the
political significance of the revolution of 1810 and they came to
the defense of the ideals of independence and democracy even
when some people in the capital were vacillating. During the siege
of Montevideo (1812?) the Spaniards showed their contempt

for the army of patriots by calling them "gauchos." The word was used by the patriots in an affirmative and defiant sense, as in the case of the "gauchos" of Güemes. Already the noun "gaucho" had appeared in an occasional song or farce, but it did not actually exist yet in literature. The person who deliberately created the literary figure that from that time on would represent the "gaucho genre" was BARTOLOMÉ HIDALGO (Uruguay, 1788–1822). Hidalgo was not a gaucho, but rural and urban characteristics co-existed in him as they did in all the inhabitants of the Rio de la Plata area. He knew the peasant and was familiar with his idioms. Following the cult of the plebeian that stemmed from the eighteenth century (as we have already pointed out in previous chapters in our study of local customs, theatre with dialog in dialect, popular satire), Hidalgo decided to use the gaucho song as political propaganda in the service of the movement for independence. Something similar had been done in Spain as a national reaction against the French, except that in Rio de la Plata the figure was naturally the rural man, the peasant. This does not mean that the anonymous songs of nomads roaming the pampas attained literary status directly. What Hidalgo did was to create, through traditional literary channels, a literary gaucho. Whatever artistic value lies in the genuine songs of those who populated the pampas belongs to folklore, not to literary history. Concolorcorvo, who heard them around 1776, called them "horrible ballads of the carousers." The task of literature would not be to gather up the poetry of the gauchos, but to build a tradition artistically elaborated by men of culture who sympathized with the people and addressed themselves to them, trying to speak their language. Hidalgo's importance lies in his being, if not the first, at least one of the first to discover for poetry the value of the rural people of America. He made use of the melody of one of the dances in vogue at that time, the *cielito*, of the dialogs of the local theatre, of the rural dialect, and of contemporary civic and political issues, to mold a new type of literature. In his "*cielitos*" and "dialogs" he succeeded in capturing the tone of the peoples' improvisations. In his verses the gaucho is not a wandering minstrel, but a citizen who comments on the political reality of the wars against the Spaniard in a spontaneous and plebeian style, rugged but new to the neo-classic literary scene.

Assuming the point of view of the gaucho, he puts into poetry the feelings of the people of the countryside in the wars of independence and in their struggles for freedom. In the *"cielitos"* he sings about the militant ideals of the struggle against the power of Spain from 1811 to 1816. He sings about love of country, hatred of tyrants, and he encourages the gauchos to struggle against the partisans of Ferdinand VII. He no longer restrains himself in his "dialogs." They have the years 1821–1822 for a background. Hidalgo contemplates the conflicts of his country and evokes the glories of independence. He desires to inspire pride in the Creoles by giving them a vision of the deeds of the patriots of May. And because the "dialogs" reflect his great seriousness, they give us the best of Hidalgo. Read the "Report Made by Gaucho Ramón Contreras" (*"Relación que hace el gaucho Ramón Contreras"*). This is *"costumbrismo"* (the portrayal of local customs in the arts), but it is made complex by the artistic device of the con-science-mirror of the protagonist. Hidalgo immediately won the acclaim of the populace, both in the city and in the country. Two of his gaucho works appeared in *La Lira Argentina* in 1824. In this first collection of poetry from Rio de la Plata, he seemed to be taking a very modest step, but it led to a revolutionary destiny, for it opened the way to an American form of expression. We shall meet the followers of Hidalgo and we shall see his humble invention curiously transformed during the romantic period.

Pre-Romanticism

In this period we have seen the first romantic sparks flying in the Hispanic cultural skies, wafted by winds from Spain. The words "romantic," "romanticism" were already known as synonyms for picturesque, extravagant, absurd. What is important in literary history is the use of these words to designate a new esthetic current. And naturally this defining or characterizing use of the term comes after the new literary current has been in existence. The word "romanticism," in this sense, belongs to the nineteenth century, but the literature to which it refers comes from the eighteenth. The concept "romanticism" as opposed to "classicism" is used with complete awareness of its importance, in Germany from 1802, in France from 1816, in Italy and Spain from 1818, in England from 1823. These definitions were disseminated thanks to the efforts of August Wilhelm Schlegel. As we said when studying Bello, there were curious contacts between liberal Spanish and Hispanic-American *émigrés* in England and English romanticism. The English writers whom now we call romantics constituted a group possessing a coherent vision of poetry, imagination, nature, and spirit. Their style, rich in metaphors, symbols, myths, at times obscure, mysterious and even mystical, was new. The mechanical concept of the universe was rejected in favor of the graphic and creative power of fantasy. The simplest and most humble aspects of the world are saturated with metaphorical light. With his songs the poet participates in the infinite and eternal forces of the universe. Nature appears as an animated, organic, living totality in such a way that the poet, as he celebrates its purpose, identifies beauty with truth. One notices how this romanticism, seen in England and quickly felt by all other European literatures, awakens a new sensibility even in minor Hispanic-American figures.

JOSÉ FERNÁNDEZ MADRID (Colombia, 1789–1830), who was called "the Sensitive One," was one of the first to cultivate a poetry with themes of home, with overtones of meditation, and with feelings for nature which he must have read about in England, because in France it appeared at a later date. He was also a reader of Chateaubriand. He had *Atala* staged in the form of a tragedy. With the landscapes of *Atala* in mind, he composed "The Mountain Rose" (*"La rosa de la montaña"*). English poetry was enjoyed not only by the *émigrés* in England, but also by those living in the United States. JOSÉ ANTONIO MIRALLA (Argentina, 1789–1825), translator of Thomas Gray's "Elegy," had lived in both countries. Young and the false Ossian were other influences that arrived from England, directly and indirectly. They affected not only verse but also a type of poetic prose: ruins, tears, remembrances, solitude, melancholy, a nature convulsed by the anguish of men, become manifest even in discursive prose. In a university discourse JOSÉ MARÍA GRUESSO (Colombia, 1779–1835) gave definitions like this: "The murmuring of a fountain is the sweet smile of a nymph; the trills of little birds, the weeping of Philomela; the dew that humidifies the fields, the tears of Endymion; and the rustling of the trees, the sighs of the god of the woods." He wrote poetry. "The Nights of Geussor" (*"Las noches de Geussor"*), in which he speaks of little "romantic" woods, derives from the nocturnal aspects of the *Nights* by Young. And, in fact, his friend Ulloa called him "the Hispanic-American Young." FRANCISCO ANTONIO ULLOA (Colombia, b. 1783) wrote in artistic prose in which the reading of Fénélon, Ossian, Saint-Pierre, and Chateaubriand can be detected. His sentimental letters were in keeping with the times: tears, tender friendship, kisses. He translated "A Night" from Ossian's poetry, and in a sugary letter he dedicated to Gruesso "those beauties worthy of sensible hearts and of sad melancholy that have drawn from your soul such tender and pathetic sighs." The literary phenomena just alluded to are not openly romantic, but they prepare us for the coming of the new style.

B. MAINLY PROSE

1. Novel

From the Mexican group of the period of independence— ANDRÉS QUINTANA ROO (1787–1851), FRANCISCO MANUEL SÁNCHEZ DE TAGLE (1782–1847), FRANCISCO LUIS ORTEGA (1793–1849), JOAQUÍN MARÍA DEL CASTILLO Y LANZAS (1781– 1878) and others—we will feature the oldest and the best: JOSÉ JOAQUÍN FERNÁNDEZ DE LIZARDI (1776–1827). He started by writing plebeian verses (in general, satiric), which he printed in pamphlets to be sold in the streets. However, from 1812 on, he wrote prose works, for which he had a brilliant talent. He had been educated within the currents of the liberal thinking of the enlightenment. He seemed to have been indifferent to independence, but his liberalism was authentic—the evil did not lie in the fact that the colonies belonged to Spain, but in that its institutions transgressed against reason and liberty. He accused the Church of responsibility for the ignorance of the people, he welcomed the abolition of the Inquisition, he attacked the vices of the powerful, and he insisted on the necessity for a radical social reform. The triumph of the absolutist reaction in Spain restored the Inquisition and Lizardi had to conceal his ideas, but he did not acquiesce. When the censor condemned his newspaper articles Lizardi decided to take refuge in a new type of literature. It was a fortunate decision. Thanks to it the first novel in Hispanic America appeared: *The Itching Parrot* (*El Periquillo Sarniento*), published in 1816 in three successive volumes (because of official prohibition, the fourth volume appeared posthumously). Why were no novels produced during the three-hundred-year colonial period? We have already answered this. The fact is that suddenly the genre was born in Mexico, robust and yelling with originality. It was born resembling its mother—the picaresque novel. There is a striking resemblance in its outward appearance: narrative in the first person, descriptive realism, a preference for everything sordid, successive adventures in which the hero goes from master to master and from trade to trade, sermons to make it easier to swallow the bitter pill. But the soul of the new offspring was different. Lizardi continues to display the optimism of eighteenth-century rationalism; thus, in spite of appearing to be a picaresque writer in his descriptions of the bad customs of the city of Mexico, he did not create a *pícaro* or rogue. Periquillo is not a *pícaro*, but a weak character thrown among bad influences. Lizardi's achievement was to fill the emptiness of the hero's will with the social seaweed and rubbish left by the undertow of his time. Lizardi's affiliations are with the eighteenth century; therefore, his novel shows more kinship to the picaresque genre of Le Sage, Father Isla, Torres Villarroel than to that of the baroque. Where can we place *The Itching Parrot* within the tradition of the Spanish novel? The national, satiric, and realist novel continued to be written in Spain from 1700 to 1808; however, from 1785 the new European novels of Richardson, Goethe, Mme De Genlis, and others were being read. But this modern, sentimental, and pre-romantic novel would bear fruit in the following period, from 1824 onward. In *The Itching Parrot* there are sentimental episodes of this type, with the persecution of virtuous men, unfortunate women, sex accepted as a normal force, and so on. We should recall the story of Don Antonio (Vol. I, chaps. xix–xxi), or that of the ragpicker (Vol. II, chap. iv). From an overall point of view, however, *The Itching Parrot* lies within the realist tradition. It is a realism that does not take its themes seriously, but rather reduces them to the stylistic plane of the comic. The misfortunes that befall our protagonist are due to his incapacity to live in accordance with rational and virtuous norms. Periquillo is the sandwich man who moves about in Mexican society calling attention to the evils of that society. That is, he moves along the avenues of the ideas that

Lizardi held on social life. Each chapter is a step in the development of a philosophy. The intention is to demonstrate that when a boy falls, weak in character and badly reared because of his mother's snobbery, he falls into the miseries of a cave of thieves, a hospital, prison, the travails of a scribe, barber, apothecary. Lizardi aspired to something more than a description of society—he wanted to improve it. He was not one of the "enlightened philosophers" (those who broke with the Church), but a "Christian philosopher" (those who proposed reconciling Catholicism and liberalism). Unfortunately he was more of a moralizer than an artist and sacrificed narrative freedom. Even leaving aside his moral sermons, his aim at reform is so obvious that it appears in the very construction of the episodes. Let us recall in the early chapters the three schools Periquillo attended in succession: the first, with a good but ineffective teacher; the second, with an effective but bad teacher; and the third, a synthesis of all the pedagogical virtues that the author offers as a solution. This means that Lizardi does not deny that there may be paths open to good; but he does wish to show the grossness, the typical, the ordinary in the life of his time. This is the attitude of a depicter of customs, not a detractor of values as in the picaresque. We have given *The Itching Parrot* some consideration because of its historical importance, but Lizardi's masterpiece was *Mr. Dandy the Showoff* (*Don Catrín de la Fachenda*). Here he has learned the art of storytelling without being distracted by digressions. It does not have the color variegation of the vignettes of *The Itching Parrot*, but it has more of the novel—the action moves more gracefully from episode to episode, and is conceived in more balanced proportions. He tells his story like Cervantes, whom he imitates—the end of chapter III where he abruptly cuts the scene leaving Tremendo and Modesto with their sabers raised, to take it up again at the beginning of chapter IV when they furiously discharge their blows, is a parody of the fight between Don Quijote and the Biscayan, also interrupted by the changing of chapters (a parody, in turn, of the *Araucana*). It harks back then to a picaresque past. But what is certain is that *Don Catrín* is of value for its novelty. Its theme is the life of a Mexican youth, well-groomed and of good family, who because of his ancestry, disdains honest work and as a consequence falls with the speed of a suicide falling from a tower. In his falls the poses he strikes are these: soldier, swindler, gambler, comedian, servant in a brothel, assailant, and beggar. The adventures are entertaining, and the irony with which they are narrated is among the finest in Hispanic-American literature of the day. The didactic intention is evident: the characters have symbolic names; the dialog is generally channeled along typical notions of good and evil, of intelligence and stupidity, of maliciousness and virtuousness; the threads of the plot, manifesting the reformist philosophy of the author, are interwoven in symmetries and in contrasts. In spite of all this, Don Catrín takes on life as a character. We see him; we hear him. We would recognize him if we saw him in the street. He exists. He is a type, we admit, but sufficiently concrete and individualistic for us to feel his presence as if he were a neighbor. In his death throes, with gaping mouth, Catrín remains faithful to his way of being.

It is possible that the reader of today may become annoyed at the constant intervention of Lizardi's irony in Catrín's autobiography. Although the story is told in the first person, the reader is aware of two narrative focuses: one is the protagonist's point of view, the other is Lizardi's, also seen through the protagonist, thus making for an ironic, squint-eyed view. This novel is also notable for its style which moves at the tempo of a yesteryear's nobleman but is, nevertheless, agile and youthful. Witticisms sound like phrases we have read in good Spanish literature; but they were not just added, they were born on the lips of the characters created by Lizardi. Artistically inferior are his other two novels: *Little Miss Quijote and Her Cousin* (*La Quijotita y su prima*, 1818) and *Sad Nights and Happy Days* (*Noches tristes*, 1818). In addition he wrote sketches of customs (he was one of the precursors of the genre in America), fables, and theatrical pieces. His novels are the most original produced in America during the years that the colonies were struggling for their independence.

Also autobiographical, picaresque, and depicting social customs was *The Wandering Christian* (*El cristiano errante*, 1847) by ANTONIO JOSÉ DE IRISARRI (Guatemala, 1786–1868). Under the pseudonym of Hilarión de

Altagumea he published another sketch for a novel: *History of the Heroic Epaminondas of Cauca* (*Historia del perinclito Epaminondas del Cauca*, 1863). The hero's travels through various Hispanic American countries are a satire on customs, political events, and even historical personages, like Simón, Bolivar's teacher. The intent is to denounce the errors of the liberal ideology represented by Epaminondas. He was a brilliant polemicist, conservative, monarchist, antiliberal, restless, an untiring traveler, a rancorous personality, and a man of great human interest. He is also the author of *Satiric and Burlesque Poetry* (*Poesías satíricas y burlescas*, 1867).

The Hispanic-American novel anticipated the Spanish novel in another direction—the historical novel. In 1826 *Jicoténcal* appeared in Philadelphia, by an anonymous author. It was the first historical novel written in Castilian in the nineteenth century. Its subject matter was American (the conquest of Mexico) and it preceded by two years the first historical novel by a known Spanish author. Is it legitimate to include *Jicoténcal* in a history of Hispanic-American literature? It has been said that its author was a Mexican. This is difficult to prove. His censure of Hernán Cortés is not inspired by Mexican patriotism, nor much less, by a pro-Indian spirit, but by the rationalist, humanitarian, and liberal ideas of the enlightenment. The author, whoever he was (one of the writers to whom the novel has been attributed is P. Felix Varela, Cuba, 1788–1853) selected Tlaxcala as his setting and Jicoténcal as his hero, because this reality lent itself better than any other to his Francophile ideology. Tlaxcala becomes the republic; Cortés and Moctezuma the despots; the young and the old Jicoténcals symbolize liberty, virtue, and reason; Teutila, innocence. Even American color is lacking in *Jicoténcal*— conventional landscapes, few indigenous words, barely a trace or two of local customs in the marriage ceremony of Jicoténcal and Teutila. It is a discursive, not a descriptive novel, and the discussions interpret the events of the Mexican conquest in European terms. The author is more liberal than patriotic, more rationalist than pro-Indian. It is not a romantic novel. Offhand, there are no traits of Walter Scott. There is no storytelling; there is sermonizing. Its sentimentalism derives rather from the pre-romantic historical novels of France: Marmontel, Mme de Genlis, Mme Cottin, Chateaubriand, a sentimentalism always directed by reason, more rococo than romantic.

2. Miscellaneous Prose

By way of marginal activity several grandees wrote good prose, like JOSÉ CECILO DEL VALLE (Honduras, 1780–1834), framer of the declaration of independence for Central America and author of beautiful descriptions of nature; VICENTE ROCAFUERTE (Ecuador, 1783–1847), president of the republic, who continued writing while in office; and General JOSÉ MARÍA PAZ (Argentina, 1782–1854), author of some excellent *Memoirs* (*Memorias*), written in a manly, plain, objective style, that were true to military facts, and novelistic in the expression of strong sentiments of disillusion. BERNARDO DE MONTEAGUDO (Argentina, 1785–1825), one of the founders of the *Sociedad Patriótica Literaria* (Literary Patriotic Society) (1812) in Buenos Aires.

The liberal ideas of the *Encyclopedia* had wielded their influence since the eighteenth century, but the violence of the French Revolution, Jacobinism, and the general excitement, gave way to an irrational, sentimental, and therefore, almost romantic element. Rousseau—one of the sources of French romanticism—inspired the men of the independence. Miranda had read him; Simón Rodríguez, Bolívar's teacher, taught him; and SIMÓN BOLÍVAR himself (Venezuela, 1783–1830) was nourished so much by Rousseau that, without being a writer, he is one of those who best represented him. Some of Bolívar's pages approach literature, like "My delirium in Chimborazo" (*"Mi delirio en el Chimborazo,"* 1824) or the penetrating perceptions of the "Letter from Jamaica" (*"Carta de Jamaica"*), or his preamble to the constitution of Angostura, his proclamations and letters. His two critical letters to Olmedo with regard to the composition of the "Song to Junín" not only interpret literature, they create it. They are refined, penetrating, ingenious, sincere, lively. Bolívar understood the relatedness of heroic greatness to independence. "If I were not so good and you were not such a poet," he says, "I could come to believe that you had wanted to write a parody of the Iliad with the heroes of our poor farce." As for the appearance of the Inca Huaina Capoc in the song, Bolívar joked about it with exquisite humor, giving documentary proof of how little the pro-Indian movement meant in the ideology of the emancipators. His genius for action bridled his Utopian imagination, and his prose trotted, spirited and checked, with beautiful gambols. But Bolívar was more a theme than an author, because the wars of independence were described in poetry; and Bolívar was the hero.

C. THEATER

The struggle for independence during these years was particularly harmful to the development of the theater. Let us focus our attention on MANUEL EDUARDO DE GOROSTIZA (Mexico, 1789–1851), a talented neoclassical playwright of the Moratín school. Absent from Mexico since childhood, his work belongs to the Spanish theater. Already he had produced his best works when, in 1833, he returned to Mexico. But his plays—for example, *With You, No Matter What* (*Contigo, pan y cebolla*)—which were performed in Mexico since 1833, without a doubt opened a new epoch of the theater. ANASTASIO M. DE OCHOA Y ACUÑA (Mexico, 1783–1833) who left the manuscript to a novel of sorts—*Alexander and Myra's Letters* (*Cartas de Odalmira y Elisandro*)—was a jocose poet and wrote two plays. FRANCISCO DE COVARRUBIAS (Cuba, 1775–1850); LUIS VARGAS TEJADA (Colombia, 1802–1829).

VIII. 1824-1860

Authors born between 1800 and 1835

Historical framework: Dismemberment of the colonies into national segments; anarchy, rule of the petty dictator; struggles between absolutism and liberalism.

Cultural tendencies: Romanticism in two forward movements. From *"costumbrismo"* (the depiction of local customs) to realism.

Introduction

Following the example of all Europe, Hispanic-American literature became romantic. Yet the conversion to the new trend was not as simple as one might expect. We have already seen how some earlier neoclassicists ended by accepting the stimulation of the new esthetics (Bello). Now we shall see that the opposite happened: some young men went about still hanging on to neoclassical skirts as if unaware of the change (Baralt). Along with these were those who vacillated, now toward academic traditions, now toward artistic liberty, resisting the advance of romanticism by feigning indifference, or by going along with it almost without realizing it (Heredia). But those who gave equilibrium to the period are those writers who were fully conscious of the new concepts of life, art, and history.

In the preceding chapter some allusions were made to the first indications of romanticism: the propagation of Schlegel's definitions in Spain: the emigration of Spaniards and Hispanic-Americans to London, where they were witnesses to the new mode; the influence exercised by France. In this chapter France's influence will be affirmed. In effect, the first Hispanic-American generation of romantics, who know what they want and act with a polemical program, abandon their mother Spain and adopt France as their stepmother. This occurs especially in the more aggressive countries like Argentina toward the middle of the century. Later the Hispanic-American will realize that France was not a mother, but a good aunt, and will embrace Spanish romanticism. This is why romanticism, speaking neither French nor English, but Spanish, came late to the slow-paced countries. European romantic literature entered America already Hispanicized. It was not so much that French influence had diminished, since this was not to happen until the twentieth century, but that Spanish influence had increased.

We have then, two romantic generations: the first is the one that gives significant works prior to 1850, such as Sarmiento's *Facundo;* the second is that which begins to produce after 1850, for example, the serial stories with which Alberto Blest Gana initiates himself into the genre of the novel. If, roughly speaking, we date the first generation according to the writers born between 1800 and 1825, and the second generation according to the writers born between 1825 and 1850, it will be evident that not all of the second generation will fall within the confines of this chapter. Here we will study a few of the writers of the second generation; and the rest, because of their long lives or because of their impact on literary development, will be placed in the next chapter. Because it was a vital, changing, expansive, and long-lasting movement, romanticism cannot be easily enclosed within chronological limits. One could even outline more than two romantic generations— doesn't romanticism reach our own times, in continual transformations?

On the Threshold of Romanticism / The golden key that opens this chapter is JOSÉ MARÍA HEREDIA Y HEREDIA (Cuba, 1803– 1839). As a child Heredia was already translating Latin writers, studying in them his first lessons on literary composition, and was imitating French and Spanish neoclassicists. His elders were doing the same thing—translating and imitating. When he arrived in Mexico at the age of sixteen, the humanism he found there had lost its spiritual force and had been reduced to prescribing norms for art and to paraphrasing, without art, a past from which no one could receive inspiration. Heredia never forgot his apprenticeship in Latin letters—even in his poetry written at full maturity, in moments of great sincerity and lyricism, his verses contain classical reminiscences; hence, the reader will recognize in "my sepulcher shall not contain me completely" from "Poetry" the *"Non omnis moriar"* of Horace. He received his neoclassical influence from the poets who revived the old school of Salamanca: Meléndez Valdés, the best lyricist of his time, Cienfuegos, Jovellanos, Quintana. He began writing in a literary gamut that extended from sweet and melancholy eroticism to social and philosophical poetry. Examples from English and French literature indicated that he was going in the right direction; and by translating and imitating Ossianic poetry, Chateaubriand, Byron, Ugo Foscolo, Lamartine, and perhaps Victor Hugo (whom he never cited, yet whose works he possessed) he was able to tinge his own verses with imagination, melancholy, and romantic anguish. This dolorous tone in his poetry is what is most valuable in it. His was the humanitarian philosophy of the enlightenment: peace, liberty, justice, rational order, progress. He would meditate on and exalt these themes using the declamatory gestures of a Quintana.

When he returned to Cuba he conspired in favor of its independence and became an heroic poet. Nevertheless, his originality does not rest on his patriotic fervor, but on nostalgia—a more intense form of love of country. In him, nostalgia manifests itself in the evocation of landscapes and loves. He was homesick for Cuba. He had lived only for a short time on the island and for this reason idealized it. A feeling of absence and of being far away constitute the leitmotiv of his literature. He created innumerable verses to "the day of departure" from Cuba which was like one of those mental traumas from which one never fully recuperates. He suffered exile more as a lyricist than as a citizen. He did not feel at home anywhere, either in Mexico or in the United States. The truth is that even in Cuba he was not happy. He had no roots anywhere. He loved his country, but had never taken root there. Nothing could make him happy, because his unhappiness was in his own soul. His greatest inspiration (if not in his life, at least in his poetry) was love. His first love, naturally, had been in Cuba. He was never to forget it. It was the constant theme of his writing. It was refracted and given iridescence in conventional literary language, but the force of that persistent ray of light could not but be recognized: to love and not to be loved in return, jealousy, the preference of love to fame, the desire to keep his loved one from undergoing the harm of being tied to such an unfortunate life as his own. The Cuban landscape was vividly pervaded by his enamored spirit and was therefore evoked by the exile as part of his tender love. Later circumstances were to bring him to write about the necessity of war against the Spanish oppressor (it has been mentioned that Heredia was a civic-minded, patriotic poet). But more powerful in his lyricism than that of abstract notion of a free fatherland is his sense of nostalgia. Heredia was unadaptable but in his unadaptability he yearned for quietude. At times his theme of peace, developed as a civic virtue, uncovers in its harmonics the real feeling of the poet: peace, yes, but above all, to be left in peace. This ideal of the tranquil life is as obsessive in him as is the love of women and the recollection of the beauties of his homeland; all this rises together before him like a mirage before a man lost in a desert, like the dream of a sad and solitary man.

Of all the poets of neoclassical background, Heredia is the one who speaks most about himself. He was the most lyrical of all. After the critics had defined Bello as the poet of "Address to Poetry" and of the *silva* "To Agriculture," and Olmedo as the poet of "The Victory at Junín" and of "Victor of Miñarica," in order to maintain the symmetry, they had to present Heredia as the poet of "In the Temple of Cholula" (*"En el teocalli de Cholula,"* 1820) and of "Niagara" (1824). But an anthology of Heredia would be more extensive than that of Bello or Olmedo—he succeeded in achieving lyricism more often and left several compositions as good as (and perhaps better than) the two mentioned above. The poem that best situates Heredia in literary history is "In the Temple of Cholula," of which there are two versions, one from the 1825 edition and the more polished and augmented one of the 1832 edition. The melancholy, the sight of ruins, the comparison of the monument to the volcano, the musing over nature, history, and the feeling of time, are indications of a fresh imagination. The perception of each shade of color, of the outline of each thing, appears with extraordinary clearness; and yet, such precise description, which makes us feel as though we were endowed with another pair of eyes, is not physical: there is no exterior reality except that of the soul in anguish, which contemplates, feels itself alive, and meditates. His poetry is more philosophic than descriptive. Dusk is a movement of shadows in the intimacy of a consciousness that has escaped from its own time.

In his song to "Niagara" he infuses nature again with lyricism; the poet is awed by that natural wonder, and others even greater: God, Time. And in this expansion of the self, the desire for his beloved and the nostalgia for Cuba increases. With what force Heredia breaks the neoclassical framework of this poetry and gives vent to his (romantic?) emotions in "Misanthropy" (*"Misantropía"*), "Lovelessness" (*"El desamor"*), "On My Birthday" (*"En mi cumpleaños"*), "To the Star of Venus" (*"A la estrella de Venus"*), "Return to the South" (*"Vuelta al sur"*), "Deceits" (*"Desengaños"*), "Pleasures of Melancholy" (*"Placeres de la melancolía"*), "Hymn to the Sun" (*"Himno al sol"*), and "Hymn of the Exile" (*"Himno del desterrado"*)! When we say that he broke the neoclassical framework of his poetry we refer to the rationalistic, didactic inner form of classicism because, insofar as it relates to the standards of versification, he maintains those of his epoch. If we expand the concept of romanticism Heredia falls within it, because of the overtures of sensibility to nature, to ruins, to exile, to suffering. Heredia also wrote drama, criticism, and short stories. The best story is "History of an Italian Highwayman" (*"Historia de un salteador italiano,"* 1841). Even in a prose that is tightly restrained, it has romantic force: the setting is in the Abruzzi, exotic to a Cuban; the theme, the Italian youth who becomes a bandit in despair of love; the angelic woman; the contrast between the purity of Rosa and the brutality of the bandit captain; the passion of the young man (who does the narrating), and the final act of wishing to be her first executioner since he had not been her first lover (symbol: the captain possesses her in life, deflowering her; the young man possesses her in death, planting a dagger in her heart; love and death).

JOSÉ JOAQUÍN PESADO (Mexico, 1801–1861) was a mediocre poet who never rose to great heights; yet he never wrote a poem that was really bad. There is dignity in his measured, certainly heavy, slow, sure, movements. He knew a good deal of literature (he read Latin, Italian, French) and before setting up a verse he must have rapidly reviewed his readings. At every step we find reminiscences of the Bible, of the Greeks and Romans, of Dante and Petrarch, of Tasso, of Fray Luis de León, without counting the translations and imitations that he himself indicated. He was more meditative than lyrical, but his abstractions move so well within each strophe that they seem like cold daughters of his fantasy. Better than his love poems, "To My Loved One at Early Mass" (*"A mi amada en la misa del alba"*), are his sacred ones; and better than these are the sonnets and descriptive ballads, "Places and Scenes of Orizaba and Córdoba" (*"Sitios y escenas de Orizaba y Córdoba"*). Better yet, and of more significance to our literary history, was his collection *The Aztecs* (*Los aztecas,* 1854). Here he attempted to revive indigenous Mexican poetry. An Indian translated old poetical traditions of Nezahualcóyotl for him which Pesado transformed into Spanish verse. It represents the efforts of a cultured poet; Horace can be recognized in his *Nezahualcóyotl;* and in his poem on the "Vanity of Human Glory" (*"Vanidad de la gloria humana"*) one recognizes the Medieval pattern *"Ubi sunt qui ante nos in mundo fuere."* But the desire to express in poetry the soul of the Indian will appear more and more in Hispanic-American literature. In the cultivation of neoclassical Mexican poetry, one might mention MANUEL CARPIO (1791–1860) together with Pesado. He was his elder in years, although his poetry came later. It came later partly because, although he went about with his eyes fixed on God, the stars, and the Bible, he was pedestrian and his feet trampled in rubbish. He could describe and narrate, but there was no music in his work. Other names will appear further on, at the point in our history where neoclassicists and romanticists encounter one another.

Of the three poets that Venezuela offers in the first years of the independence, Fermín Toro, Juan Vicente González and RAFAEL MARÍA BARALT (1810–1860), the one most addicted to neoclassical tradition was the latter. His cold precepts, his cold verses, his cold historical depictions, his cold disdain of cosmopolitan culture, and his cold academic knowledge take the spice out of his work, and today no one would touch it. His thinking was liberal; his literature, conservative. On the other hand, the other two poets harmonize the classical tastes of the classroom with the new taste for history, local color, emotions, and intuition and, therefore, are the forerunners for the younger Venezuelan romantics, José Antonio Maitín and Abigaíl Lozano. JUAN VICENTE GONZÁLEZ (Venezuela, 1811–1866) was the first prose writer of merit in Venezuelan literary history. He cultivated the poetic prose that was being stylized in the eighteenth century; and in fact, his *Messenianas* are adaptations of the elegiac *Messenianas* of the abbot Jean-Jacques Barthélemy. He was also a historiographer of passionate prose, similar to his contemporary, the Argentinian Sarmiento, who had the ability to feel the turbulence of the masses. His *Biography of José Félix Ribas* (*Biografía de José Félix Ribas*) evokes, with graphic violence, the beginnings of Venezuelan independence. González skirts history and enters romantic literature as an arm of the sea invades the land. FERMÍN TORO (Venezuela, 1807–1865) esteems neoclassical literature enough to continue it in his anacreontic verses "To the Nymph of Anauco" (*"A la ninfa de Anauco"*). But his feeling for history, developed through his reading of men like Chateaubriand, brought him close to romanticism. He was the first Venezuelan to approach the new esthetics so closely, while maintaining an equilibrium with traditional forms. He wrote an "Ode to the Torrid Zone" (*"Oda a la zona tórrida"*) which was reminiscent of Bello's *silva* in more than just the title and had a greater capacity for responding with wonder to the legend and nature of America. In his "Song to the Conquest" (*"Canto a la conquista"*), also classical in form, the Indian is not only a spectacle but also a spectator, for Toro imagines him in the act of watching those who in turn are describing him. Unfortunately, his poem "Hecatonphony" (*"Hecatonfonía"*) remained unfinished, but the cantos we have breathe the mystery of the Mayan ruins: "Each sign is a mystery, each ruin a problem." "There is horror, sublime horror / in this region of terror." He carried this very romantic feeling for the past to the historical novel. In *The Widow of Corinth* (*La viuda de Corinto*) he presented the struggle between Mussulman and Christian, although the tragic love he is relating is independent of the historical framework. In *Sibyl of the Andes* (*Sibila de los Andes*, 1849) he wished to exploit the American theme, but his efforts did not reach completion. Another novel was *The Martyrs* (*Los mártires*). He wrote "sketches of local customs" because it was the fashion—*Customs of Barullópolis* (*Costumbres de Barullópolis*). This genre descends from the eighteenth century carrying its rationalistic and didactic philosophy with it, but the moment comes when it sheds this burden and turns romantic. Fermín Toro wrote a humorous article, "A Romantic" (*"Un romántico"*), in which one can see that romanticism was new to him. In describing a madman who recites evil and incestuous verses at midnight, Toro has him say: "I am a romantic!" and then adds: "I was amazed; never had I heard that word"; "since that moment I tremble whenever I hear the word romantic." Writers interested in the customs of different countries have left jocular portraits of this new human type, with his manners, gestures, and words. Romanticism, then, was a theme in the "sketches of local customs." Later, the sketches themselves will be romantic.

Many of the patriots who had fought in favor of independence, or those who had expected great forward strides after the battles of Junín and Ayacucho, became quickly disillusioned. Hence, a critical, mocking, bitter, though not reactionary, literature emerged. Certainly reactionary was the implacable FELIPE PARDO Y ALIAGA (Peru, 1806–1868). His family, monarchist and haughtily aristocratic, had emigrated to Spain after the achievement of Peruvian independence. There Felipe was educated, during the dark ages of the despotism of Fernando VII. On his return to Peru, Felipe Pardo was displeased by republican institutions and liberal principles and attacked them furiously in the name of a decrepit order. He did not understand the meaning of the social changes of his time, and consequently his satiric verses, his famous rondels, his plays, his sketches of local customs have lost all of their vital significance, despite the skill with which he wrote them. He was against equality of races, against social justice, against political liberty. It was shocking to him that instead of a hereditary king—a Spanish one, naturally—there should be a "czar of three tinctures, Indian, white, and black, / who governs the American continent, / and calls himself the Sovereign People." He deplores the law that sees as equals a white man of good family and "the black man who yokes up your oxen / and the one who irrigates your cornfields." In his satiric poem, "Political Constitution" (*"Constitución política,"* 1859) he ridiculed democratic citizenship. His education was neoclassical: that of the "enlightened despot," that of rhetorical authorities. He began writing odes of an academic pattern. He admired Quintana; on the other hand, he found sentimental "pastoral or bucolic" poetry tiresome. His soul was devoid of lyricism. That is why he succeeded in his satire ("The Snout" [*"La Jeta,"* 1834]), in didactic plays (*Fruits of Education* [*Frutos de la educación*, 1829], *An Orphan Girl in Chorrillos* [*Una huérfana en Chorrillos*], and *Don Leocadio*) and in his articles on customs ("The Mirror of My Land" [*"El espejo de mi tierra,"* 1840]). He wanted to be caustic: "If my truths burn, so do cauteries, but they cure." But Pardo did not have remedies to cure the ills of an independent America—he believed in the colonial past. Instead of cauteries he applied vinegar to the wounds. His scorn at least permitted him to see the defects of the first republican period with clarity. These defects, it may be said in passing, were inherited from the colonial period. His moralizing intentions are evident. His talent is also evident. But he is lacking in the tenderness which gave greatness to the style of other writers of customs. He imitated the romantic Béranger; he cited Byron; he paid tribute to Zorrilla in "a homage of admiration to the new characters of the Castilian poetry of this young priest of the muses." But he was not a romantic—his articles on local customs, "A Voyage" (*"Un viaje"*), "The Promenade of Amancaes" (*"El paseo de Amancaes"*), do not feel the fascination of the original landscape, nor the historical movement of the life of the people.

Of the same literary stature as Pardo, and in the same satiric vein, was MANUEL ASCENCIO SEGURA (Peru, 1805–1871) who wrote another type of sketches of customs, satires, and comedies. They were adversaries. Before all else, Segura felt the Peruvian reality as his own: "In spite of my misfortunes," he says, "I have not yet lost my attachment to the things of my land." With his mocking but understanding smile, Segura joins the historic march of his country: hence, the "national" quality of his literature. The dialecticism, which coming from Pardo's derisive pen was used to humiliate the Peruvians, in Segura fulfills the function of creating sympathy for the Creole. He is full of life, clear-minded, witty, fond of meandering and prying. While he is describing the customs of his time, he is constantly talking about himself, because although he may be laughing, he is part of what he is describing. He identifies himself with the people; he *is* the people. One of his themes is his own career as a writer—he tells us how and why he writes. He does not take himself seriously; although half-jokingly, he asserts that his writings follow "the spirit and tendencies of his age." His tone is conversational and thus enriches his prose with lively and capricious expressions. His epigrams do not become brittle. In his festive verse—certainly he was more festive than satiric—Segura showed facility in giving fluidity to his wit and in making it flow in a variety of meters. *"La Pelimuertada"* (1851) was his best poem. But it is his theatrical pieces in verse that give him importance in our literary history. One of the first was *Sergeant Canuto* (*El sargento Canuto*) of 1829. He wrote a total of fifteen plays, of disparate value. His esthetic compass ranges from the farces of Ramón de la Cruz to the works of Bretón de los Herreros. *The Resigned Man* (*El Resignado,* 1855), *Ña Catita* (1856), *A Toy* (*Un juguete,* 1858), *Episodes of Amancaes* (*Lances de Amancaes,* 1862), *The Three Widows* (*Las tres viudas,* 1862) laid the foundation for the Creole theater of Lima. To ask for deep dramatic conflict, new theatrical situations, fine psychological analyses would be asking too much. But the dialog incessantly crackles with mirth and imagination. In spite of a conventional verse and a conventional theater —monologs, asides, mechanical entrances and exits, and traditional intrigues—the characters are real. They are real as social types, not as individual characters, but at any rate, real. His works contain a popular realism, at times uncouth, like Ña Catita's intestinal discomposure, and at times they are written with the touching power of folklore, as when Ña Catita squats to separate two straws that have fallen to the ground in the form of a cross: "Nothing . . . just that there's a cross here. / Don't step on it." Themes treated are marriage, the political shenanigans of Lima, the abuses of newspapers, factious military personnel, and the mania to enter the civil service.

In tranquil, correct, and elegant epic octaves JOSÉ BATRES MONTÚFAR (Guatemala, 1809–1844) released a throng of dynamic images at full speed. He knew how to tell a story, and the best he wrote were three spicy tales, "False Appearances," "Don Pablo," and "The Clock," grouped together under the curious title *Traditions of Guatemala* (*Tradiciones de Guatemala*). The plot is disclosed quickly and deftly; that his talent was primarily narrative is proved by the fact that the best passages are those in which the poet entangles his plot, and keeps us waiting, filled with curiosity, until the final disentanglement. But he was dynamic in other respects; for instance, in his imagination, which infuses even inanimate objects with movement, life, scope, and gestures. In "Don Pablo," for example, the dialog between the moon and the lamppost ("Now all reigned in peacefulness and repose, / now the moon was submerging in the west / and in the tremulous light that it cast / the dying lamppost bid it its last") is one of the innumerable lyrical notes in his poetry. The lyricism is in step with the narrative; its voice is tempered to the jocular tone of the situations and characters described. This produces one of the effects (may we be permitted to say "*à la* Heine"?) of José Batres' verses; it seems as though the poet were ashamed of having uncovered his lyrical tenderness and, quickly interrupting himself, makes a wry face and laughs. This may cripple his expression. No doubt. But remember that the minor genre in which he wrote—humorous short stories in verse—was a stumbling block in literature. Batres Montúfar was a solitary, timid, cultured, skeptical, ironic man. His good humor does not sound like a jester's jingle bells—it is silent, like an intelligent smile. The false values of the mealy-mouthed atmosphere in which he lived wounded him profoundly and painfully; but his heart bled honey. He criticized the hypocrisy, the ignorance, the violence, and the stupidity of the men and institutions of his time. His most woeful sentiments were expressed in poems like "I think of you" *("Yo pienso en ti")*, an anthological gem. Also from Guatemala was the good poet JUAN DIÉGUEZ OLAVERRI (1813–1865). Although GABRIEL GARCÍA MORENO (Ecuador, 1821–1875), scarcely belongs to literary history, his political importance threw a sidelight on his belligerent activity both as a prose writer and as a satirical poet. Let us insert an eccentric here who actually does not fit anywhere in the history of literature: EMETERIO VILLAMIL DE RADA (Bolivia, 1804–1880). He tried to prove with ridiculous scientific verbiage in *The Language of Adam* (*La lengua de Adán*) that the first human dialog had been spoken in the Aimara language, since Adam and Eve were Bolivian and the Garden of Eden was in Tiahuanaco. His suicide put an end to a life so unbalanced that it has a fascination, as if it were not the life of an author, but that of a literary character.

Romanticism

Before presenting the different literary groups, let us take note of their general characteristics. Romanticism chose the closest wellspring, which was the ego and its circumstances. From this spring, flowering in a definite place and at a definite time, emerges a literature that attempts to free itself from the authorities of the past. More concerned with voices of his individual life than with the counsels of universal reason, the romantic writer feels himself to be the center of the world, but at the same time, a creature of that world. It is a vague feeling of harmony between the subjective and the objective that expresses itself in undefined effusions. Romanticism affirms free and spontaneous inspiration, emotional impulses, historical conditioning in lives of men and people, literature as an evocation of a nationalistic past and also as propaganda for a liberal future. In American children we recognize the faces of their European fathers. In America, however, cultural phenomena take on special patterns. In the first place, the Creole romantics lacked a great domestic literature. They did what they could to safeguard the few literary monuments they remembered, and when they battled for a new style it was because they had put themselves, mentally, in the old world. They joined the ranks of distant armies. At home there were no enemies: colonial works and writers could not impose norms nor dominate literary creativity. Everything, then, had to start from scratch.

Creole romanticism was more a civilizing activity than a school of *belles lettres*. The weapons, no matter how literary they may have appeared, were used outside of literature, in the war between tradition and progress, Hispanicism and Europeanism, masses and minorities. In general, the Atlantic coast of the continent was more aggressive in its romanticism than the Pacific coast. In the region of the Río de la Plata the colonial past was poor indeed and, as Bello observed in a letter to Mier in 1821, Buenos Aires was the city where the least reading was done. For that very reason they were not as conservative there as in Peru or Mexico: literature surged forth there with the same impetus as the desire for national independence. Violence was evident in polemics and doctrinaire manifestoes that were lacking in other countries. While the Río de la Plata generation was more cosmopolitan than traditional, the Romantic models of the other countries were generally those of traditional Spain. Some of the Spaniards who visited or settled in America were promoters of their national literature: José Joaquín de Mora, Fernando Velarde, Sebastián Lorente, Juan Bautista Arriaza, García Gutiérrez, Zorrilla. Nor were the Hispanic roots weakened in those colonies that did not become independent, like Cuba and Puerto Rico, in spite of the growing prestige of French and English literature. A map of European influences in Hispanic America would show these names with frequency: the Spaniards Larra, Espronceda, Zorrilla; the Frenchmen Hugo, Lamartine, Chateaubriand; the Englishmen Byron, Walter Scott; the Germans Goethe and Schiller (who were known indirectly); and the Italians, only occasionally Manzoni and Foscolo. Not all romantics knew they were romantics. In order not to be confused with the traditionalist romantics who focused on the Middle Ages, religion, legend, and egotism, there were many who militated within a social, democratic, progressive, prophetic, liberal, collectivist romanticism and denied they were romantics. Thus arose burlesque parodies by romantics against romanticism. These were quarrels between brothers and some of them renounced the family name.

The social romantics, especially in the Río de la Plata, were shunning their Spanish past, defending the right to an American

language, and promising a national literature, based above all on
the new landscape and on the new way of life. Linguistic nationalism was more radical in Argentina than anywhere else. The romantics of the ego as well as the romantics of society imposed
their terminology: meditative, horrible, prophetic, nefarious,
somber, deliriums, ruins, or proscripts, lights, progress, socialism;
and, naturally, American words that designated native things of
the land: neologisms, archaisms, indigenisms. The indifference
to things Spanish and the admiration for things of other European
countries and, above all, the penchant for improvisation had as
a consequence the acceptance of many foreign words, especially
French, into the language. The emphasis on emotion, the inac-
curacies of thought, and the carelessness in writing left their mark
on romantic syntax. The preferred forms in verse were the sonnet
and the ballad: in general the ballad was preferred in regions
where the cultured minorities were proud of their Spanish past:
Mexico, Cuba, Colombia. Metric forms were enriched, especially
in strophic combinations. In order to give variety to a composition
and in order to diversify the movements of a theme, the romantic
poets mixed measures with notable frequency. Together with this
polymetrics there were renovating attempts at unearthing or inventing meters. These attempts, if they were not far from those
made by the Modernists at the end of the century, in some cases
anticipated Rubén Darío, for example, in Gertrudis Gómez de
Avellaneda, José Eusebio Caro, and others. With these varied
meters poetry could now keep time with the off-beat palpitations
of life rather than with the beat of ideas. Literary genres acquired
new meaning. Many theatrical pieces were written but few were
performed—nor were they of much value. On the other hand,
prose displayed all its strength. "Beautiful prose thrusts itself into
the future / and verse in obscurity lies dethroned!" exclaimed the
Peruvian Salaverry in his sonnet "Verse and Prose" (*"Verso y
prosa"*). He exaggerated, but certainly with romanticism prose
assumed literary dignity in novels, short stories, newspaper serials,
sketches of social customs, essays, memoirs, travelogs, and even
prose poems. The sketch of customs, a reforming genre in the
eighteenth century though in the nineteenth century it was in

sympathy with local color, became dynamic and was converted into the short story. The local customs of these "sketches" entered into the composition of realist novels. Historical and romantic narratives were more abundant. Political novels were not lacking, nor were curious allegorical novels.

Within the vast repertory of themes in the world of romanticism, the most typical ones in Hispanic-America were the natural landscape, human types, ways of living under different social circumstances, and history. In those countries having large indigenous masses there was an idealization of the Indian: an evocation of a distant Indian, of the pre-Colombian age, of the conquest, and of the colony. In Argentina, on the contrary, literature was hostile to the Indian. The treatment of the close-at-hand, real, contemporary Indian was not very romantic. In the nineteenth century there were few writers (González Prada was one of the first) who saw him as a social problem. History was cultivated with profusion in novels, dramas, and in prose and verse legends. Even a genre was invented—the "tradition," with Ricardo Palma heading a school of forty imitators. A strange aspect of romantic historicism was the works—in their majority theatrical, although there were narratives as well—that presented episodes of literary life about characters who were real writers, e.g., Cervantes.

Argentinian Romanticism / We pause in Argentina because, unlike other Hispanic-American countries, it had a clearly romantic generation. 1830 is the boundary year. Until this year the educated men of Buenos Aires lived in the rationalistic and humanitarian "Age of Reason." The May revolution, the Independence and the first political and cultural organization of the republic from Moreno to Rivadavia were carried on under the sign of the enlightenment. From 1830 on, Buenos Aires came under the influences of French romanticism, and the generation of Echeverría, Alberdi, Gutiérrez, López, Sarmiento and Mitre was formed, all agreeing to justify the total break with Spain, to express the new emotions aroused by the American scene, and to put a liberal political system to the test.

Of the young men who had not become involved in the civil

wars between federalists and centralists (known as *Unitarios*), but whom the tyrant Rosas had forced into exile, ESTEBAN ECHEVERRÍA (Argentina, 1805–1851) was the standard-bearer. In 1825 Echeverría left for France. At the time, he was twenty years old and had lived tempestuously, without having been ensnared in the rationalist nets that his teachers at the School of Moral Sciences of Buenos Aires had stretched out for him. Through what he revealed later in his writings, and from the information left by his friends, we infer that Echeverría attentively observed, during the four years in Paris, the synthesis of romanticism and liberalism that was being produced precisely at that time. But of the rich canvas that France presented, Echeverría profited only from a few aspects. Between 1826 and 1830 important books appeared by Vigny, Hugo, Lamartine, Musset, Sainte-Beuve, Dumas. But more than these Frenchmen, it was the English and German who had influenced them, who oriented Echeverría's tastes. He studied the philosophy of history and society which, evolving from the German historical school from Herder to Savigny, lent new accents to the French thought of Leroux, Guizot, Lerminier, Cousin, and others. Echeverría left Paris, if not educated by romanticism, at least with his mind sharpened by his romantic readings. By then he had projected two romantic formulas upon the Argentinian reality: political liberalism, which came to justify the break of the American colonies with Spain and advocated the continuance of the revolutionary line of May, 1810; and sympathy in the arts with the way of life of the people, through which he discovered the possibilities of an autochthonous literature based on the historical and geographical peculiarities of the pampas. Although the first formula was the more significant in the history of political ideas of Argentina, in a literary history we are obliged to refer only to the second. He had no calling or genius for poetry. He fulfilled, nevertheless, the function of a forerunner in the external history of our literature. *Elvira, or the Argentine Bride* (*Elvira, o la novia del Plata*, 1832) was the first seedling transplanted directly from France, independent of Spanish Romanticism; *The Consolations* (*Los consuelos*, 1834) was the first volume of verses published in Argentina; "The Captive," one of the compositions in *Rhymes* (*Las rimas*, 1837) was the first work that displayed with skill the aim of a poetry that looked to the local scene, tradition, local color, the people, and history. In the immense pampa the Indian was seen as the appraiser of civilization.

The young set, dissatisfied with academic "good taste," became enthusiastic about Echeverría. They believed that with "The Captive" (*"La cautiva"*) national literature had been established. Its simplicity sounded like sincerity to them; its emotional abundance, poetic richness. This consecration no doubt flattered Echeverría. His life had been difficult—it would be so to the very end. He was poor, sickly, tormented. These were his misanthropic years; and the literary reputation he earned from 1832 to 1837 must have alleviated his sadness. But, as his friend Gutiérrez noted, he felt more like the "hero of a novel," and reputation was not enough—it had to be glory, glory, and nothing else! "I renounce reputation," he wrote to Gutiérrez in 1836, "glory, yes, I would want if it were given me . . ." Today Echeverría is one of the glories of Argentine history, not because of his verses, but because he put his reputation as a versifier—that reputation that he renounced—to the service of the political regeneration of his country. Because of his literary reputation, young men followed the battle standard that he had once raised. From then on his prose works would surpass his poetry. He was, indeed, a better prosist than a poet; for this reason, *The Slaughter-House* (*El matadero*, 1837–40) takes a place of honor in literary history. It is a sketch of customs of extraordinary realist vigor, differing from what had been written earlier because of the intensity of pathos and climax. As a sketch of customs it has a political and reformist purpose: to expose the despicable rabble that supported Rosas. But suddenly certain figures take on life and the sketch becomes a story. Then, in spite of the muckiness of the description, the romantic outlines become clear: the contrast between the horrifying note about the child whose throat is cut and the humorous note about the Englishman knocked down in the mud; a feeling for the "picturesque" and the "grotesque"; an aura of misfortune, fatality, death; the literary beautifying of the ugliness of the riffraff by comparing it with extreme ugliness; the curious spectacle of hundreds of "African" Negroes; the presentation of the young "Centralist," the gallant hero who loudly hurls challenges at society, in counterpoint as in a melodrama with musical background of guitars and popular song, and who, before he can be assaulted, dies of indignation, bursting into "rivers of blood." In other, more serene prose writings, Echeverría left lucid road signs that led out of the mire in which "federals" and "centralists" were having their disputes. Echeverría had a serious plan. Aware of the respect in which he was held, he decided to rally all youths around a clear doctrine. Thus the Young Argentina or the May Association was constituted in 1838; it branched out quickly throughout the remotest corners of the country. Thanks to Echeverría and his May Association, Argentine romanticism became the distinctive feature of the Hispanic American literary movement that swept a whole generation into its orbit. Romantic voices made themselves heard here and there through all Hispanic-America; it was only in Argentina however, in the decade of 1830, that there arose a generation of young romantics, educated by the same books, tied together by the same vital attitude toward historical reality. Witnesses to the calamities of their fatherland, they were friends who, in their assiduous personal associations, concurred in fundamental points of view, worked and talked together in clubs and newspapers, and while sounding the death knell of past norms, expressed the repertory of their own yearnings in a new style. Echeverría gave them their initial discipline. The work they accomplished is amazing. Argentina has never again had such a group of men thinking great thoughts.

In addition to Echeverría, some of the most important authors in Hispanic-American literature came from this group: Sarmiento, Mitre, Alberdi, Gutiérrez, López. To these names can be added the best lyrical poet of those years: Mármol, another exile from Rosas, unattached to the association but personally associated with the members. Furthermore, Argentinian exiles brought their romantic ideals to Uruguay and to Chile, and from there launched forceful literary movements. As important as was the purely literary contribution of this generation—novels, dramas, poems,

essays, sketches of customs, history—it cannot be abstracted from
political action. That philosophic thought be applied to social reality and literature be employed in the service of justice is characteristic of Hispanic-American culture. These Argentinian writers who banded together in 1838 will formulate the constitution,
will become members of parliament and ministers and, at least two,
Mitre and Sarmiento, will become presidents of the republic.

When Echeverría returned from Paris laden with novel ideas, JUAN
BAUTISTA ALBERDI (Argentina, 1810–1884) was among those who understood the romantic writers most lucidly. The capacity to understand was his
forte. He was more or less cold, reflexive, observant, careful, adaptable, and
more understanding toward romanticism than enthusiastic about it. He
preferred a literature that reflected society and educated the people.

He signed articles on local customs with the pseudonym of Figarillo. The
truth is that Fígaro [Larra] had an influence on all Argentinian romantics.
Perhaps Larra is the only Spanish writer who figures in the spiritual formation of this group, otherwise so attentive to France. Once he was in Montevideo, Alberdi continued to cultivate this type of critical, mordant, and
moralizing literature: not only sketches of customs, but also theatrical
pieces, which are valuable not for their art, but as documents of his political
activity. In reality, the figure of Alberdi was growing in political and not
literary stature, and his most important writing, *Bases* (*Las bases*), which
had a decisive influence on the spirit of the framers of the constitution of
1853, for example, does not belong in this history. More interesting,
literarily, is what Alberdi wrote when he became enmeshed in a merciless
controversy with Sarmiento. Alberdi's *Letters from Quillota* (*Cartas
Quillotanas*) and Sarmiento's *One Hundred and One* (*Ciento y una*) barely
clarify their respective points of view on national organization—basically
they were in agreement. But in their personal antipathies they expressed
themselves with such vehemence that at times their letters took on literary
value: above all, those of Alberdi—who never was as good a writer as
Sarmiento—because they displayed his fencing skill in polemics. His long
absence, since 1838, weakened his grip. From Europe his thrusts were no
longer hitting the target. He was only successful in theoretical works. But
the work written in those years that most merits attention here is his *Daylight's Pilgrimage* (*Peregrinación de Luz del Día*), an allegorical novel on
Argentine politics. Truth (i.e., daylight) escapes from the horrors of Europe
in 1870 and expects to find honor, tranquillity, and decorum in the New
World. Daylight scarcely disembarks in Buenos Aires when he comes across
his old enemies, who also had fled Europe in order to settle in South America: the hypocrite Tartuffe (Molière), the intriguing Basilio, and cynical
Figaro (Beaumarchais), the rogue Gil Blas (Le Sage), the seducer Don
Juan (Tirso). He will also meet Don Quijote, Sancho, etc. While arguing
with them, daylight, chagrined, discovers that the Argentina of Sarmiento,
who was president at the time, had betrayed the ideals of liberalism. This
allegorical novel, showing signs of improvisation and defects of a writer
not cultivated as such, but containing a few aphoristic phrases of great

strength, can amuse one who is interested in the clues and can recognize the allusions to the political scene of those days; as pure literature, it will put one to sleep. In it Alberdi lost his coldness and, disillusioned by the liberals, expressed with original images and ingenious phrases his morose feeling as an exile. Unfortunately, he did not sufficiently elaborate his allegory, which even lacks unity. Rather than a novel, it is the outline of a novel. It is painful or at least tiresome to read because one keeps stumbling over masses of rubbish. But it has the merit of not resembling anything written during this period.

Alberdi's most intimate friend was JUAN MARÍA GUTIÉRREZ (Argentina, 1809–1878), a student of literature more than a writer. When he wrote his poems, sketches of customs, and novels, he put more care in his expression and this immediately set him apart from the disorderliness of his colleagues. His attitude was one of respect for the literary past, an attitude which was to change him eventually into a historian and critic of literature, as can be seen in the stamp of neoclassicism which still marks him. The volume of his *Poems (Poesías,* 1869) leaves no doubt that its author was addressing himself to a cultivated public—he was aiming high. He wrote sketches of customs; his best known, "The Ant Man" (*"El hombre hormiga,"* 1838), is not noteworthy. But noteworthy was *The Captain of the Patricians (El capitán de patricios),* an idyllic novelette written with all the romantic formulas of a tearful literature: an ideal love in a paradisiacal San Isidro, the summer-resort town near Buenos Aires, between an angelic lady and an archangelic patriot, interrupted tragically by the wars of independence. Yet, Gutiérrez' imagination does cut a swath in all that borrowed material and does manage some lyrical raptures that are surprising for having been written in those days. Although published in 1874, it had been written in 1843. Amidst the alluvium of sketches of customs that covered Hispanic-America, the majority of which were coarse and unpolished and always realistic in style, the poetic prose of *The Captain of the Patricians* had the merit of putting forth an aristocratic ideal of expression. The fact that poetic language ages quickly does not subtract from its merit: whoever has sufficient literary education can salvage sincere lyrical expressions from outmoded styles. Gutiérrez was a man of exceptional intelligence, but one who consumed himself in an obscure task: to present and study the then immature Hispanic-American literature. There can be no great critic without a great literature. And Gutiérrez, who had an extraordinary aptitude for criticism, could not surpass the stature of the literature to which he dedicated himself.

BARTOLOMÉ MITRE (1821–1906) is another of those Argentinians of this same generation who exalted the country through his great deeds, but who sacrificed his literary talent to action. His youthful *Rhymes (Rimas,* 1854), his drama, *Four Eras (Cuatro épocas,* 1840), his novel, *Solitude (Soledad,* 1848), and his essays on literary criticism give evidence of Mitre's multiform talents. Nevertheless, his best contribution to the field of letters lies in his historical works.

Domingo Faustino Sarmiento / When in 1838 some of the young men who had studied in Buenos Aires returned to San Juan with the books in fashion—books by Lerminier, Leroux, Cousin, Sis-

mondi, Saint-Simon, Jouffroi, Quinet, Guizot—DOMINGO FAUS-
TINO SARMIENTO (Argentina, 1811–1888) allowed himself to be
infused with the new current of ideas. But Sarmiento's originality
rests in his having intimately fused the romantic philosophy of
history with the intuition of his own life as part of that history. He
felt that he and the nation were one and the same creature, dedicated to an historic mission within the process of civilization.
Owing to this, his writings, since they are always political acts,
have a peculiar autobiographical tone. In his first autobiography,
My Defense (*Mi defensa*, 1843), forged in Chile like a weapon,
Sarmiento shows himself fighting with all his might against poverty, backwardness, ignorance, violence, injustice, and anarchy.
His phrases are refracted into two beams: one that illuminates the
impulse of creative will, and the other the inertia of adverse circumstances. The reader will quickly notice that this polarization
has a philosophic meaning: it alludes to the conflict between
spirit and matter, liberty and need, history and nature, progress
and tradition. And in fact, when Sarmiento passed from the feelings in his own personal life to interpreting the public life of Argentina, the confidential material of *My Defense* was converted
into a political formula: "civilization and barbarism." *Civilization
and Barbarism: Life of Juan Facundo Quiroga* (*Civilización y
barbarie: Vida de Juan Facundo Quiroga*, 1845) is not history,
nor biography, nor novel, nor sociology—it is the vision of a
country by a young man anxious to act as a transforming force
from within. "The evil that afflicts the Argentine Republic is its
size," he says. The cities are islets of civilization; the pampa envelops them and engulfs them like a sea of barbarism. From the
countryside come the gauchos, knife in hand: they are simply
savage manifestations of nature, without any historic initiative.
The men of the city are those who promote progressive phases in
the operation of civilization. In this setting, and with these actors,
the political drama from 1810 has taken place in two acts: (1) the
May revolution and independence stood for the struggle of European and liberal ideas that settled in the cities against the absolutism of Spain that no longer created spiritual values but ruled
with the weight of tradition; (2) then anarchy took over because,

from the immense plains of the country, resentful hordes were loosed upon the cultured cities. Argentina, said Sarmiento, was dominated by such somber figures as Juan Facundo Quiroga and Juan Manuel de Rosas. With Facundo dead, Rosas had to be overthrown. But that would not be sufficient. After all Rosas was only an incarnation of this barbaric reality. It was reality itself that had to be transformed. Now the author turned to the public and proposed a political program of national reconstruction: public education, European immigration, and technical-economic progress. This dialectic was so simple that Sarmiento himself found it insufficient, and as he went along in the book, he had to complicate it with paradoxes, omissions, and reservations that contradicted his thesis. The countryside was not so barbaric; the cities were not so civilized. Furthermore, Sarmiento sympathized esthetically with the gaucho customs that in the name of political principles he disdained. "Facundo and I have affinity," he once exclaimed. And the intellectual gaucho that was Sarmiento—"I am Doctor Montonero, the mobster Doctor," he said on another occasion. He had a profound sympathy for the other real gaucho, Facundo, his brother Cain. Within the dynamic scheme with which Sarmiento gave meaning to his perception of the country —civilization against barbarism—the terrible shadow of Facundo took on a powerful artistic reality because he was not simply a rhetorical theme, but a pathetic presence in Sarmiento's bosom. In this sense Facundo is an imaginary creation of Sarmiento's. He impresses us as a living personage precisely because what gives him life is the imagination of the author. And the exaggerated strokes with which Sarmiento paints the criminality, lasciviousness, courage, and primitivism of Facundo do not come just from the political intention of denigrating him, but also because, for the Romantic Sarmiento, all of nature, including Facundo, was shaken by something tremendous, fascinating, and catastrophic; and Sarmiento's apprehension of the horrible mystery of barbarism gave his piece a tremolo of melodrama. Nevertheless, his Facundo, with all the fantastic and exaggerated elements that one could wish for, was real.

Subsequent investigations have rectified some of the details of the picture; even Sarmiento corrected himself several times. But it is essentially what he saw in 1845. In *Facundo*, Sarmiento revealed his literary talent. This was even more apparent in the epistolary book that followed, *Travels* (*Viajes*, 1845–47), because here the pleasure of narrating was greater than political motivation. These letters are so imaginative that they are considered among the best prose of the time. At each step they take us by surprise with their sharpness of observation: they have merit as sketches of customs and landscapes of France, Spain, Africa, Italy, and the United States. Even more surprising than the observations made is the observer who is making them. In no other book does Sarmiento's soul open so widely and deeply, with his enthusiasms and depressions, his solemnity as a prophet, and his humor. He feels like an actor in the world he is describing; his letters, then, are the fragments of a virtual novel. Furthermore, they carry an implicit philosophy of history. Not only did he have a gift for metaphor that enabled him to reveal his intimate self in concrete images, but also one for abstraction, which elevated minutiae to universal categories. On the road of civilization, Sarmiento tells us, nations run, become tired, sit in the shade to doze, or else strike out with a desire to arrive before the others. They are like people. And what matters is not what they have been in the past, but the impetus they carry. Sarmiento becomes disillusioned with Europe, which is too quiet, and proposes as a model the civilization of the United States, which advances with the strides of a giant and promises political liberty and economic well-being. His memoirs in *Provincial Memories* (*Recuerdos de provincia*, 1850) continue those in *My Defense*. But eight very intensive years have transpired. His rovings through Europe and the United States have given him a favorable perspective from which to understand Spanish America. Now he is more man, more writer. He is conscious of his mission and addresses a public that will survive him. His style is more personal. He writes his memoirs not only from the political need to answer Rosas' calumnies with a self-portrait that reveals him superior to Rosas, but also to abandon himself to the sweetness of evocation. He looks around him and sees a procession on the march—it is the march of civilization on

Argentinian soil. He mixes with the multitude. And what a pleasure it is for him as he recognizes his own family in that great dispersion of people driven on by the good wind of the spirit! In his rich, full, and colorful experience of an "I" excited by the commotions that come down from the past, there is also the consciousness of a providential mission to fulfill. He lived not only his own individual life, but also the life of the people, of mankind, and even of God, inasmuch as from Sarmiento's point of view history was the development of a divine plan and he felt himself an agent of history. In 1851 Sarmiento left Chile to join Urquiza's army, which in the Battle of Caseros (1852) defeated Rosas, and thus began a new cycle in Argentine history—that of organization. Disillusioned with Urquiza whom he only partly understood, Sarmiento left Argentina. Once in Chile he wrote the *Campaign of the Grand Army* (*Campaña en el Ejército Grande*, 1852), another of his good books, which is as pleasant as the intimate diary of a novelist, despite the disorderly mixture of documents, anecdotes and personal effusions. What he wrote later—discourses, commentaries, proposals, and pamphlets which fill several volumes of his works—is less valuable. It is understandable. From 1862, which is the date of the unification of Argentina, to 1880, which is the date on which the city of Buenos Aires became the federal capital, Sarmiento is seen in the role of governor. His judiciousness as a governor was less inspiring than his passion as an expatriate.

A new group, the "men of 1880," is beginning to receive the influence of new cultural ideas. They are reading Darwin, Spencer, Taine. Now it is believed that the methods of the natural sciences can explain even spiritual phenomena. Sarmiento had always been a fancier of the spiritual goals of history. But, because he was so bent on achieving practical results from action, his romantic way of thinking was becoming more and more empirical and reached a meeting ground with positivism which offered a mechanization of the correct historical evolution. When at the height of his life Sarmiento wanted to organize his ideas on history in a systematic way, he wrote the outline of a positivist book: *Conflicts and Harmonies of the Races of America* (*Conflictos y armonías de las razas en América*, 1883). It was the last and the

worst of his sociological works, because of the scientific preten-
tiousness of its disconnected verbiage. The thesis—if there is one
—is the racial inferiority of Hispanic-American society. Intuitive
ardor was his forte, not science. He would set upon reality, enraptured, and attack it from within with such a will to possess it,
to personalize it, to change it, that when he sought to describe it,
he realized that he was both subject and object. For this reason
his style is autobiographical and his autobiographies are national
histories. Sarmiento only used to write when he had something to
say. His habits were those of the journalist and not the writer. Occupied with many tasks simultaneously, his manipulation of words
was another way of working. They struck like waves. And if they
seemed to withdraw somewhat abated, it was like the undertow of
the sea, which quickly returns and with greater impetus. He
reaches expressive fullness effortlessly; and even in his moments
of carelessness his creative genius spills over.

Historical Novel in Argentina

Another important person in the group exiled by Rosas was VICENTE
FIDEL LÓPEZ (1815–1903). In his *Autobiography* (*Autobiografía*) he tells
how, as of 1830, there was in Buenos Aires "a torrential ingress of books
and authors that had never been heard of before. The works of Cousin, of
Villemain, of Quinet, Michelet, Jules Janin, Merimée, Nisard, moved
among us producing a fantastic following of new ideas and preachments
about romantic, classical, eclectic, Saint-Simonist schools and writers . . ."
López gave himself, body and soul, to the study of the philosophy of history.
With this preparation he wrote a historical novel on the effects in Lima of
Francis Drake's piratical expedition of 1578 and 1579: *The Heretic's Bride*
(*La novia del hereje*). In his epistolary prolog of 1884 he says he wrote the
novel at the age of twenty-five (that is, in 1840) and that he published it later
as a serial in a Chilean newspaper. In the same epistolary prolog he expounded the romantic conception of the historical novel better than anyone
of his Hispanic-American generation. Its point of departure was a profound understanding of the historical nature of man. Our existences are
fixed in the framework of time: a past clings to our backs, and with it we
move out into the future. In addition to existing, we coexist with our society.
If one human action affects the collective development, we call it historical.
But certainly every action, no matter how private it seems, is historical,
since we are at every moment subjects of history, agents of a spiritual
process. What we know from documentary evidence of the past helps us to
imagine that which we cannot know, but which we can intuit vividly—all
human drama being one. The novel, containing what we know and what we
can imagine, saves the past. There is, therefore, no conflict between actual
deeds and the atmosphere with which our fantasy envelops them. With this

theory, López wrote one of the most interesting historical novels of Hispanic-American romanticism. He puts into motion the pendulum of Spain in the sixteenth-century world and describes her colonizing enterprise in Lima: rivalries between the Church and state and between the various religious orders, the Inquisition, customs of the middle class and of the aristocracy, the attitude of the Spaniards toward the English Protestants, peculiarities of the coastal seamen and of the homosexuals of Lima. His point of view is that of a liberal nineteenth-century Creole who makes use of colonial literature, like Centenera's poem, but who has respect for the apologias furnished by English letters on behalf of Drake and other pirates. Writing from a historical base, López devoted greater attention to its novelistic aspects. His interest lies in the narrative, integrated in the historical; the narrative is not merely the rear guard or the appendix to history, but has a dignity of its own. Oxenham's raid is historical, but its purpose— the seizing of two women—is novelistic. As in Walter Scott, the historical personages (Drake, Oxenham, the Viceroy Toledo, the archbishop Mogrovejo, Sarmiento de Gamboa) remain in the background, and the principals (Henderson, María, Father Andrés, Mercedes) are fictitious. The tone is always romantic: opposed loves between the heretic Henderson and the Catholic María, contrasts in black and white between hero and villain, deaths of atonement; nocturnal encounters, intrigues and vengeance, naval battles, inquisitorial trials, limpid idyllic scenes and scenes of local color, heroic sacrifices, espionage, secrets pathetically revealed, yearnings for freedom, and nature in solidarity with the human drama, as in the scene of the earthquake. Finally, Henderson and María escape from the claws of the Inquisition, reach England, and live happily ever after. The marriage between Drake and Juana (the daughter of a Spanish priest and a Peruvian descendant of the Incas) is a fiction that brings to the fore López' interest in showing the good relations between English pirates and Hispanic-Americans. The blackness of the novel is not in the pirates, but in the diabolic Father Andrés, the character of greatest strength because, precisely in him, López discharged the frightening darkness of his creation. The evocative vignettes of colonial Lima and the speed of the action maintain the reader's interest despite the ponderousness of the prose. Inferior were his "historical short stories," *The Insane Woman of the Guard* (*La loca de la guardia*), that move along the road of San Martín's liberating army, and his epistolary novel, *The Great Week of 1810* (*La gran semana de 1810*). The name of López is best defended by his work as a historian.

Parenthetical Remarks on the Theme of the Pirate / If we have spoken more about López' historical novel, *The Heretic's Bride*, than of his admirable *History of the Argentine Republic* (*Historia de la República Argentina*), it is because our obligation is literary. But even in his novel, what is interesting is its philosophy of history, so typical of romantic liberalism. One way of proving this is to compare the judgment on piracy formulated by López with that put forth by the colonial writers. The French pirates during the Franco-Spanish war of Charles V and Philip II against France (1520–1559); the English corsairs during the struggles of Philip II against England (1568–1596); the Dutch freebooters during the hostilities of the low countries against Spain until the Peace of Westphalia (1648) and, finally, the buccaneers and sea-robbers, who up to 1750 were masters of strategic points in the Caribbean, all undermined Spain's power in the New World. Our writers painted them in narrative poems, theatrical works, and chronicles as Protestant heretics, agents of the devil, the scourge of God, enemies of truth, justice, religion, property, commerce, social order, monsters of infamy and cruelty. Cristóbal de Llerena, Juan de Castellanos, Silvestre de Balboa, Martín del Barco Centenera, Miramontes y Zuázola, Rodríguez Freile, Oviedo Herrera, Sigüenza y Góngora, Bishop Lizárraga, and scores of others let fly with their pens when they described the depredations of the "Lutheran" pirates. The most respected for his exploits was Drake (about whom Rodríguez Freile would say, that because he had been a page in the court of Charles V, he was very "Hispanicized"). At times they express admiration for the pirates; at times they put the blame for piratical successes on the ineptitude of the Spaniards; but in general, the tone is always one of horror and condemnation for the heresies and ravages of the pirates. In passing they record unwillingly that Negroes, Indians, and certain Creole groups sympathized with the pirates expecting that "the English" might bring freedom to colonial life. This identification of piracy with freedom will encounter its true place in romanticism. Like Byron, like Espronceda, the romantics exalt the titanic life of the pirate and convert him into a hero of liberty: the pirate had been the first to challenge the religious, political, and economic absolutism of Spain, from which the romantic liberals had just emancipated themselves. And so, in the historical novels of the nineteenth century, a series of idealizations of the pirate emerges. The series is opened by López' *The Heretic's Bride.* It is followed by Justo Sierra O'Reilly's *The Freebooter* (*El filibustero,* 1841), Coriolano Márquez Coronel's *The Pirate* (*El pirata,* 1863), Eligio Ancona's *The Freebooter* (*El filibustero,* 1866), Vicente Riva Palacio's *The Gulf Pirates* (*Los piratas del golfo,* 1869), Alejandro Tapia y Rivera's *Cofresí,* 1876, Francisco Añez Gabaldón's *Carlo Paoli,* 1877, Soledad Acosta de Samper's *The Pirates in Cartagena* (*Los piratas en Cartagena,* 1885), Francisco Ortea's *The Treasure of Cofresí* (*El tesoro de Cofresí,* 1889), Carlos Sáenz Echeverría's *The Pirates* (*Los piratas,* 1891), Santiago Cuevas Puga's *Shackles and Hangman, Other Pirates in Penco* (*Esposa y verdugo, otros piratas en Penco,* 1897), among others.

Other Argentinian Romantics / Among the enemies of Rosas—called the "banished ones"—there were only two important poets, Ascasubi and Mármol, each of whom was different. HILARIO ASCASUBI (Argentina, 1807–1875) was the one who dug deepest into the popular vein. He was a man of the city, but of all his rich experiences, early trips to Europe, revolutions, wars, newspaper campaigns, he elected as the theme of his satiric poetry the experience of the countryside and its people. He has been compared with Jasmin, the Gascon dialectical poet, celebrated by the French romantics. But Ascasubi was versifying the language of the gauchos after the example of Hidalgo. The difference was that Hidalgo's figures were outlined against a neoclassical background, while in Ascasubi there is a concentration of reflections of romanticism; the dream of a national literature, in the rustic language with accents of local color; sympathy for the folklore of the people, with a preference for their songs; a belief in the myth that poetry had its origin in anonymous bards; the ennoblement of the gaucho. In *Paulino Lucero* the gauchos are centralists, enemies of Rosas. They chant their love of liberty, their hatred for tyranny. The tone is somber and horrified by so much crime. Read *"La refalosa"* in which we see Ascasubi's hatred for Rosas come back like a boomerang, expressed in the hatred of a Rosist for Ascasubi, a transposition of hatred similar to that in *The Slaughterhouse* (*El matadero*) by Echeverría. (The title *"La refalosa"* [meaning "The Slippery One"] refers to a popular song and sliding dance. According to other interpretations it also means "blood" because dictator Rosa's bullies used to play the tune while cutting off the heads of liberals and these victims slipped on their own blood in a gory dance of death.) In *Aniceto the Rooster* (*Aniceto el Gallo*) his attitude is relaxed and festive. Rosas has been deposed, and Ascasubi, who stood on the side of Buenos Aires against the confederation, now derides the political inconsistencies of Urquiza. (He had used the titles, *Paulino Lucero* and *Aniceto el Gallo* as pseudonyms.) His most important work, reflexive and not burlesque, was *Santos Vega or The Best Twins* (*Santos Vega o Los mellizos de la flor*), whose action takes place in the last thirty years of colonial life, although the reality described belongs to the country and city of the middle of the nineteenth century. Anachronisms break the historical illusion that the poet wished to create. But colonial life was not much different from the life that Ascasubi knew, not to mention the fact that time increasingly blots out differences that do exist. For this reason, what remains in the book is an evocation of rustic life formed by Ascasubi's cherished vision. At times it seems to be a book of miscellaneous recollections, organized into the form of a novel in verse. In 1851 he published a few fragments, then interrupted the composition. Twenty years later he took it up again; it was published, complete, in 1872. Ascasubi narrates that a Cordovan friar narrates that Santos Vega narrates the history of two brothers, Luis, the bad one, and Jacinto, the good one, but deals particularly with the bad one. In Mitre this Santos Vega was a legendary minstrel. In Ascasubi he was on the contrary an old *"escrebido y letor"* (colloquialism meaning a man who is able to read and write) who is reputed to be a singer, although we never hear him sing, merely narrate. (Pedro Obligado, whose image of Santos Vega was close to that of Mitre, was to write his own "Santos Vega" refuting the debased image that Ascasubi gave him.) As for the theme of the "bad one," we know that it was common in ballads and melodramatic and pseudo-historical serials. They moralized; they played on the reader's emotions. The customs and landscapes of the Pampas are put into poetry. Ascasubi evokes a reality that has disappeared, detail by detail. He describes everything as it lay before his eyes—the dawn, the dance, the advance of the Indians, the tasks and feasts of the country people, the cattle moving over the pampas, the rustic psychology (for the first time, that of the rustic woman) in scenes of precise contours and colors. He felt the adventures of men of action, he felt the dangers of the frontier, but he did not know how to construct a novel in verse. The composition is very defective. His work has little value, but it has the merit of having made the voice of the gaucho acceptable even to cultured people in the cities.

JOSÉ MÁRMOL (Argentina, 1817–1871) wrote his first verses on the wall of the cell where Rosas had caged him in 1839: the emphasis with which he related this circumstance over and over was typically romantic. Everything he wrote was typically romantic: verses, dramas, novels. And the circumstance was always the same—the tyranny of Rosas. When Rosas fell, the poet became mute. The poems that Mármol presented at the poetry competition of 1841 in Montevideo carried an epigraph by Byron; and Byron's *Childe Harold's Pilgrimage* inspired his first important work—the twelve *Songs of the Pilgrim* (*Cantos del peregrino*). Naturally, this was not the only influence. There was that of Lamartine, Zorrilla, and Espronceda. But Byron was for Mármol the last great poet that Europe had given: "Song died with Byron," he says in the first verses of his poem. However, one must not forget the influence of his friends, Alberdi and Gutiérrez, who had composed a type of poetical diary on their voyage to Europe, "Eden" (*"El Edén"*). On remembering the poems inspired by the sea, Mármol cited *Childe Harold*, although it is possible, as Gutiérrez suspected, that "Eden" (a Byronian work, anyway) might be a closer source. Mármol began writing the *Songs of the Pilgrim* during his trip to Chile in 1844. The ship left Rio de Janeiro and descended to Cape Horn but, drawn to the Polar Zone, it could not reach the Pacific and had to return to its point of departure without making any stopovers. In the *Songs*, the poet duplicates himself—both he and his character, Carlos, recite. They are one and the same lyrical person, but each song by the pilgrim Carlos is preceded by a narrative prolog. While the songs strictly maintain the same elegiac tone, the prologs tend to change to a festive one. Mármol would rebel romantically against the classical tradition of pure genres. All in all, the poem has "system," as Mármol himself says. Nothing happens in the *Songs:* the poet, alone, in mid-ocean, meditates on man and on the lot of his country, evoking American scenes and contemplating the beauty of the sea, of the night, and of the clouds. But there is order: "decrepit Europe" is compared to an America open to the future; he remembers his youth, his first love; he describes the tropical landscape he sees before him, and that of Argentina which he sees in nostalgic visions; as they sail along the Argentinian coast he thinks of the horrors of the tyranny. And so the *Songs*, which are a miscellany of evocations, develop, like a travel diary. Furthermore, there is a lyrical sequence of thought. In his round-trip voyage, from the tropics to the South Pole, there is no one but Mármol, singing about exterior scenes (skies, coasts, sea) and about interior ones (nostalgia, indignation, rapture in the face of beauty): his soul lifts all themes to a high point of imagination. No doubt Mármol is verbose. Owing to the excessive facility of his improvisation, he is incorrect in his extremely varied versification. At times he is prosaic, at times declamatory; but his undisciplined lyricism is of value because his imagination was extraordinary.

Another collection of his verses was *Harmonies (Armonías,* 1851–1854). With some of these he gained his greatest popularity because of their violent disdain of Rosas. Disdain more than hatred. In any event, the hatred of one who disdains from the depths of his being. Rosas was belittled forever; in fact, a man who could be disdained in this fashion could not possess any greatness. The drums of Mármol's poetic damnation of Rosas deafened his readers so that they did not hear the lyrical, more intimate strings that also formed part of his orchestra. Mármol was no less important in the history of the novel than in that of poetry: his *Amalia* (1851–55) was a serial based on truculent adventures occurring in Buenos Aires during the abominable years of the Rosas tyranny. It is therefore a political novel; and, as Mármol had lived and suffered under the Rosas regime, it is an autobiographical novel too. He seems to have taken on a double identity in the two characters, Daniel and Eduardo, some of whose adventures Mármol had experienced. In spite of the exaggerated colors, of the overwrought contrasts, of the belligerently feverish fictional elements, *Amalia* succeeded in being truthful to the political picture it presented. He intended, as he explained in his prolog, "to describe in retrospect personages who live in the present." Ten years separated the narrator from what he narrated, but he created such an illusion of greater distance that some critics consider *Amalia* a "historical novel." Nevertheless, the past was recent; in fact, it was not a past. The author viewed matters, not from an historical perspective, but from a political one; he objectified contemporary reality into historical form, not because it was actually "history" but because, deep in his heart, he felt it was superannuated. The dialog has extraordinary vivacity; the characters live; and although many of the novelistic situations bear the mark of the romantic serial, they do succeed each other dynamically. And the reader, no matter how much he smiles, does not put down the book. Mármol was less fortunate with his dramas of 1842: *The Poet* (*El poeta*) and *The Crusader* (*El cruzado*).

Uruguay and Chile / When they went into exile, the Argentinian romantics took their ideals and their libraries with them. In Montevideo, Argentinians and Uruguayans identified with the same cause. It would be idle to differentiate them into national groups: nationality was not felt as it is today. Alongside the Argentinians, the Uruguayans also sought a Creole form of expression. None of them left an outstanding work: neither the critic ANDRÉS LAMAS (1820–1891) nor the poets ADOLFO BERRO (1819–1841) and JUAN CARLOS GÓMEZ (1820–1884).

The Argentine *émigrés* also initiated the romantic movement in Chile. Sarmiento and López had arrived with new ideas: they were the agitators. We have already studied Andrés Bello, who, because of his superior culture, was above all the polemics on the language and on romanticism that took place in 1842. From this date the so-called generation of '42 derives its name, a group formed by Bello's sons, Carlos (1815–1854), Francisco (1817–1845), Juan (1825–1860), and Emilio (1845–1875), and also by his spiritual children. Some Chileans satirically resisted the ideas of Argentine romanticism: Jotabeche, Sanfuentes.

Other Chileans, Lastarria, for example, and also the liberals who were closer to Mora than to Bello, sympathized with the new mode. J. J. Vallejo, known by the pseudonym JOTABECHE (1809–1858), wrote such animated sketches of customs that they seem like stories. SALVADOR SANFUENTES (1817–1860), as a disciple of Bello, read a good deal of the classicists and even translated Racine. His verse legends are also in classical style. Yet, there is a feeling for the Hispanic-American past, an idealization of the Indian, a taste for violent, passionate contrasts, an art of narrating adventures that, if it were not for the author's academic attitude, could be associated with the beginnings of Chilean romanticism. His best legend is "The Carillon" (*"El campanario,"* 1842), on tragic loves in the colony. He published other stories in verse, and one drama. The Indianist theme that he dealt with in some of these legends, *"Inami," "Huentemagu,"* have a Chateaubriandesque stamp. JOSÉ V. LASTARRIA (1817–1888) did not surpass Jotabeche as a depictor of customs, but he was the superior storyteller: "The Beggar" (*"El mendigo,"* 1843). In his "Speech on Literature" (*"Discurso literario,"* 1842) Lastarria advised young writers to observe the immediate Chilean reality. Then, he proceeded to follow this advice. His narratives tend to be loaded with political intentions—e.g., his *Don Guillermo*, 1860, is more libel than novel—or in any case, it makes observations on the historical and popular life of Chile. In his old age he gathered up his narrative works in *Yesteryear and This Year: Novels of Hispanic-American Life (Antaño y ogaño. Novelas y cuentos de la vida hispanoamericana,* 1885). In one of his first stories, *The Lieutenant Alonso Díaz de Guzmán* (1848), there appeared the figure of Catalina de Erauso, the Lieutenant Nun. In his last years Lastarria was still able to publish one good story, "A Daughter" (*"Una hija,"* 1881), in which he showed sympathy for the Negro in his clash with the white man. One of the books of this generation most read today is that of VICENTE PÉREZ ROSALES (Chile, 1807–1886)—*Memories of the Past (Recuerdos del pasado,* definitive edition 1886). Written in good, pleasing prose, these memoirs, with the passage of time, have been converted into history, and the book, into one of the masterpieces of Chilean literature. WENCESLAO VIAL GUZMÁN (Chile, 1822–1864) made an arrangement of these memoirs to make a novel of them, including letters, in *The Life of a Friend (La vida de un amigo,* 1846).

Bolivia / Four minor poets make up the frame of Bolivian romanticism: MARÍA JOSEFA MUJÍA (1813–1888), whose muse is sorrowful; RICARDO JOSÉ BUSTAMANTE (1821–1886), a poet of the hearth, of homeland, of nature; MANUEL JOSÉ TOVAR (1831–1869), who attempted the Biblical theme of the Genesis in the poem *The Creation (La creación)*; and NÉSTOR GALINDO (1830–1865), a bard of melancholy voice.

If these poets stand out, it is not for any brilliance of their own, but because we see them against a dark background, that of the cultural backwardness of their country. MANUEL JOSÉ CORTÉS (1811–1865) and MARIANO ROMALLO (1817) remained in the darkness. Some of these poets composed drama in verse, generally on historical subjects. If we would like to toy a little with the wild idea of a Bolivian Pirandello of these years, it would be interesting to attend *Plan of a Play (Plan de una representación,* 1857) by FELIX REYES ORTIZ (1828), a dialog between students who are preparing a dramatic presentation—in other words, a play within a play.

Mexico and Cuba / Independent of the romantic movement that had been projected from Buenos Aires into Montevideo and Santiago de Chile, more romantics sprang up in other parts of America. In a short time the wave covered all the countries in which Spanish was spoken.

In Mexico, the romanticism of FERNANDO CALDERÓN (1809–1845) moved in great noisy strides across the boards of the stage, yet fell over its feet whenever it wished to go over to lyrical poetry. His dramas, in verse, were inspired by the remote past of exotic lands—a typically romantic genre which was propagated all over Hispanic America (one instance among many: in 1842, when Calderón produced *Herman or the Return of the Crusader* [*Her-*

man o la vuelta del cruzado] in Mexico, Mármol, at the other end of the continent, in Argentina, produced another drama on the same theme, *The Crusader* [*El cruzado*]). His play *None of the Three* (*A ninguna de las tres*), in which he presents Mexican characters and criticizes the excesses of romanticism, was exceptional. Of course, even in his tragedies there is a love of country and an aversion to tyranny that, although dissimulated under European disguises, reflect his Mexican attitude toward the dictator Santa Ana. In this libertarian nationalism he is following Alfieri, whose *Virginia* is present in Calderón's *Death of Virginia* (*Muerte de Virginia*). In Calderón's dramas there is a certain indifference to Mexican themes. Not so in the author to whom we shall now pass, although the latter eludes, if not Mexico, at least his epoch.

IGNACIO RODRÍGUEZ GALVÁN (1816–1842), inferior to Calderón as a dramatist—he too cultivated historical dramas—surpassed him as a lyricist. Effusive, wailing, he swells like a river, and the waves of desperation, anger, complaint, and consternation pound and abuse the great themes. His moods, at times delirious, contradicted the scene and the story (see his *Prophecy of Guatimoc* [*Profecía de Guatimoc*]).

There was resistance against romanticism, not only on the part of conservatives, traditionalists, and Catholics, but also on the part of an atheist and liberal reformer with classical tastes—IGNACIO RAMÍREZ (1818–1879) whose pseudonym was The Necromancer (*El Nigromante*). He was one of the noble figures in the struggles known as the reform, but the work that bears on literary history is of little note. Nevertheless, in his humanist and scholarly poetry suddenly there is a blaze of passion, hatred, and sarcasm, whereupon one recognizes the intimate life of the author, much more romantic than in his verses, in its titanic negation of God, of Spanish traditions, and of the ruling political order. Honorable and reformist like Ramírez, but without culture, without spirituality, and romantic in his negligence of style, if not in his sensibility, was GUILLERMO PRIETO (1818–1897), poet of the masses, robust and picturesque, author of a popular and sentimental *Book of National Ballads* (*Romancero nacional*) and also of *The Holy Mondays of Fidel* (*Los San Lunes de Fidel*), a collection of interesting sketches of customs. As in all Hispanic-America, the romantic novel of Mexico preferred historical subjects (JUSTO SIERRA O'REILLY, 1814–1861; PASCUAL ALMAZÁN, 1813–1855; JUAN A. MATEOS, 1831–1913); and adventures and love episodes (FERNANDO OROZCO Y BERRA, 1822–1851; FLORENCIO M. DEL CASTILLO, 1828–1863). The robustness with which the genre of the novel had been born in Lizardi was in part inherited by the hair-raising and scrurrilous MANUEL PAYNO (1810–1894). He wrote the type of novel called "serials" with no other purpose than to amuse his readers. He had the defects of the pulp narrator: glibness, truculence. But from *The Devil's Tiepin* (*El fistol del diablo*, 1845–46) to *The Bandits of Río Frío* (*Los bandidos de Río Frío*), his best book, he composed a lively canvas of local customs. His observations were penetrating, but his documentary material was constructed following romantic conventions. Because of his feeling for adventure and his observations on contemporary life, sometimes ironic, he can still be read with pleasure.

Another of the Lizardi heirs was JOSÉ TOMÁS DE CUÉLLAR (1830–1894). In the light of his lantern—*The Magic Lantern* (*La linterna mágica*) is the title of his collection of novels—Cuéllar roguishly projects Mexican types and customs. LUIS G. INCLÁN (1816–1875), who knew Mexican country life better than anyone else, uses this knowledge to build a novel of adventure, *Astucia, Chief of the Fraternal Order of the Leaf, or the Cowboy Smugglers of the Bough* (*Astucia, el jefe de los Hermanos de la Hoja, o Los Charros contrabandistas de la rama*, 1865–66). The reader who, with piqued curiosity, is able to follow the successive episodes without tiring, can be grateful to Inclán's basic art of narrating. To bring to a close the Mexican romantic scene, one must observe that one of the themes was its Indian past. After the serious efforts to gather up the traditions of Nahuatl culture, undertaken by Olmos, Sahagún, and others, interest fell off. If the baroque writers of the seventeenth century, such as Sigüenza y Góngora, turn their attention to the indigenous past, it is to pause before the picturesque or to create fantasy from history. Clavigero, Veytia, Boturini, writers of the enlightenment, profit in the eighteenth century from what already had been said in the sixteenth century without adding new views. It is with romanticism that literature opens up to the old indigenous culture: granted, that through that open door, fantasy, improvisation, and facile enthusiasm go in and out. Bustamante, Roa Bárcena, José Joaquín Pesado, Rodríguez Galván, Peón Contreras, Calderón, Chavero, for example, reelaborated the most popular chronicles without coming into contact with the primitive texts.

In Cuba, Diego Gabriel de la Concepción Valdés, known as PLÁCIDO (1809–1844), was not far in his precepts from those writers born in the eighteenth century, for example, Quintana and Martínez de la Rosa, whom he admired. He was an obscure figure lacking the enlightenment of a literary education and, what is more serious, an original imaginative style. He versified with facility: ballads like the "*Jicoténcal*"; erotic sonnets like "The Flower of the Cane" ("*La flor de la caña*"); anacreontic, legendary, civic, epigrammatic compositions. In nothing was he able to go beyond his mediocrity, although occasionally he touched certain zones of his inner self, as in this image from his sonnet "Fatality" ("*La fatalidad*"): "Devoid of any clemency of pity / thou hast with spines encircled me, blind Deity, / As a font whose marge displays for its array / the thorny, pungent cacti and wild maguey." His compatriot JOSÉ JACINTO MILANÉS Y FUENTES (1814–1863), on the other hand, sounded the two characteristic notes of romanticism: rebellion and the resurrection of the Golden Age theater. His best years as a poet were those from 1835 to 1843, after which he became hopelessly insane. But even during those years of mental lucidity, the poetic light was intermittent. With many of his compositions—festive, of local color, descriptive, social, amatory—he sank into the shadows of other poets. He wanted to think and to be: to think, in the sense that the Victor Hugo or Espronceda type of romantic gave to this vague elocution; to be, "the bard who illumines the people." It is possible that Milanés may have reached the crowds through these paths. His most worthy attribute, however, was his lyricism: the tenderness, the ingenuity, the complaint of his unwilling solitude, the delicate amorous sentiment. He also wrote for the theater. His most serious effort was the drama in verse *Count Alarcos* (*El Conde Alarcos*, 1838), whose theme comes from a sixteenth-century ballad already dramatized by Mira de Amescua, Lope de Vega, and Pérez de Montalbán.

More lyrical and powerful than the voices that had been heard in Cuba—Plácido and Milanés—was that of GERTRUDIS GÓMEZ DE AVELLANEDA (1814–1873). Educated in the personal though still neoclassical poetry of Meléndez Valdés and Quintana, she never freed herself from those bonds and, at her height, continued to admire Gallego and Lista. Her romanticism, therefore, was eclectic. The veil with which women cover their most ardent feelings and the veils that grandiloquence placed about the nakedness of her soul never succeed in veiling her sincerity. Her lyricism is not the serene jet from a garden spout, but a force of nature in freedom. She loved with a daring vigor, so intense that she could not be happy. The loves of Avellaneda, turbulent in her and in the Spanish society of her time, for she had lovers as well as husbands, usually were soothed by pure religious devotion. And she was even at the point of becoming a nun. She wrote poems on faith. This was a passionate, vehement woman, carried away by pleasure, depressed by sadness, and at times serenely peaceful. She always felt urged by a necessity for expression that caused her to meditate carefully on the workings of art, and reach a clear esthetic conception. We refer not only to those poems in which she sings to art, but also to those in which she sings to the virtues of clarity, formal perfection, and a careful style. At times, she was too careful retouching the re-editions of her lyrical verses (the first in 1841; the second 1850; the third 1869–71) and this academic touch-up de-petaled the rose. Nevertheless, because of her awareness of art, none of her sentimental outbursts became maudlin but were converted into elegant stylization. Though her heart is rent, Avellaneda does not disfigure her own image. Even if she is a romantic, she preserves something of the academic "good taste" in which she was educated during the waning years of its vogue. The Spaniards consider her among their Parnassians. And they are justified, for it was in Spain that she lived, published her poetry, and triumphed. But she also belongs to the literary history of Hispanic-America, not for the mere accident of her birth, but because she had already written poems before leaving Cuba and always felt nostalgic ties and love for Cuba. One of her noteworthy sonnets is precisely one in which she records her sorrow on leaving her homeland—"On Departing" (*"Al partir"*). And Cuba, which on her lips was always "my homeland," is present in many of her compositions. She wrote dramas (*Baltasar*) and novels (*Guatimozín*). Generally, they take place in times and places unknown to her. On the other hand, her novel *Sab* (1841) is based on things she saw in Cuba. Its theme is slavery—a mulatto slave, Sab, falls in love with the daughter of his master—and the novel, though romantic, has excellent descriptions of Cuban reality.

Having mentioned Avellaneda's fiction, let us pass on to the Cuban novel, whose chief promoter during these years was DOMINGO DELMONTE (Venezuela–Cuba, 1804–1853), although he himself did not write novels, only Creole ballads (*Romances*). Young Cubans who read romantic authors (from Walter Scott to Victor Hugo and Honoré de Balzac) met in Delmonte's house. And from these meetings came the first narrations. The themes were the Indian, Negro slavery, local customs, and the historical past. RAMÓN DE PALMA (1812–1860) published a short Indian story, *Matanzas y Yumurú* (1837) and two other short novels, of which *Cholera in Havana* (*El cólera en la Habana*, 1838) was the better. The fashionable historical novel, put in vogue by Walter Scott, prompted JOSÉ ANTONIO ECHEVERRÍA (1815–1855) to publish *Antonelli* (1838). His protagonist is the Italian architect Antonelli, whom we see in Havana in the year 1560, constructing the Morro castle by special request of Philip II. With these very thin threads of history the novelist, in a most romantic fashion, weaves his tragedy. Antonelli woos in vain the angelic Casilda, Lupercio's betrothed. His soul is agitated and possessed by contradictory passions: love and hate, pride and despair, generosity and jealousy, scruples of conscience and homicidal impulses. The night of the feast in the Morro castle, Casilda and Lupercio fall victims to an Indian's vengeance. Antonelli, who has prompted the Indian to commit the crime, now collapses to the ground, overcome by remorse. The tale includes all the romantic themes, such as the ominous bird, the solitary, nocturnal walks, the battle between angel and demon which

rages within each man's soul, mysterious shadows, secret amorous rendezvous, serenades by moonlight, duels, violence, tears, fainting spells and
tender dialog, conflict between the nobility and the commoner, condemnation of the superstitious fanaticism of Philip II, readings from Dante . . .
Aside from those moments when Echeverría interrupts the thematic flow
of the novel with explanations, reflections, or conversations with the reader,
the prose style is also romantic by virtue of its sentimentality.

Notable in the history of the novel was CIRILO VILLAVERDE (Cuba,
1812–1894). In ten years of continuous literary activity, he wrote almost a
score of romantic narratives that do not amount to very much: incestuous
love affairs between brother and sister or between father and daughter,
deaths, disasters, superstitions, violent passions, sketches of customs, melodrama. His best work *Cecilia Valdés or The Angel's Hillock* (*Cecilia Valdés
o la loma del ángel* [an English translation has appeared under the title *The
Quadroon*]) was published in its first part in 1839 and revised and completed
in 1879; the version of 1882 should be considered as definitive. It is a pulp
novel with a coarse plot: the loves of the beautiful mulatto Cecilia and the
young master, Leonardo, who do not know that they are brother and sister;
when he is about to marry another woman, Cecilia incites an admirer of hers
to kill him. Villaverde plotted his novel with real persons, with customs
obvious to all, with observations on different social classes and races, from
domineering Spaniards to Negro slaves, with dialog where different manners
of speech are heard, with reflections on the most somber aspects of Cuban
life. Realist art? That is what the author boastingly declared. His readings
had been from the romantics (Chateaubriand, Saint-Pierre, Scott, Manzoni,
James Fenimore Cooper, Dickens), but he leaned toward realism. It was
not so much that he was a realist; rather, one might say, that with the failure
of the novel as art, what is left to interest the readers is the crude reality,
without novelistic refinement. What most attracts our attention are the
sketches of local customs dispersed here and there. Villaverde, because of his
interest in describing the customs of colonial Cuba in the 1830's, painted a
convincing picture, though at times painful, as in his references to slavery.

One of the problems which most preoccupied the young writers of Delmonte's group was slavery. In spite of the legal abolition of slave trade
(1815 and 1817), it was still practiced. Thus, there arose in protest the
abolitionist literature: *Petrona y Rosalía* (1838) by FÉLIX MANUEL TANCO
Y BOSMENIEL (Colombia–Cuba, 1797–1871) and *Francisco* (written in
1839; published posthumously) by ANSELMO SUÁREZ Y ROMERO (1818–
1878). The latter, which Delmonte ironically subtitled "the sugar plantation
or the joys of the fields," records the ugliness and ignominies of slavery,
life in sugar refineries, and the customs of the peasant; and his intensity in
documenting has given realist energy to the still-romantic prose of the
author. *Francisco* began a cycle of anti-slavery novels: we have already
mentioned Avellaneda's *Sab* and we could add ANTONIO ZAMBRANO's *The
Negro Francisco* (*El negro Francisco*).

Regional novels full of social criticism and moralizing purpose, but far
below the standards of Cirilo Villaverde, were those of JOSÉ RAMÓN DE
BETANCOURT (1823–1890), *A Charity Bazaar in 183 . . .* (*Una feria de la
caridad en 183 . . .*, 1841), ESTEBAN PICHARDO Y TAPIA (1799–1879), *The*

Fatalist (*El Fatalista*, 1856), RAMÓN PIÑA (1819–1861), *Honest Jerome* (*Gerónimo el Honrado*, 1859).

Sketches of customs were the most abundant; and in Cuba, along with the aforementioned writers, JOSÉ VICTORIANO BETANCOURT (1813–1875) and, better yet, JOSÉ MARÍA DE CÁRDENAS Y RODRÍGUEZ (1812–1882) did the honors.

Venezuela and Colombia / No doubt, Cuban romanticism spreads out and reaches Venezuela. Among the most renowned Venezuelans of the first generation, the one who stands out is JOSÉ ANTONIO MAITÍN (1814–1874), famous for the "Funeral Chant" ("*Canto Fúnebre*") in memory of his wife. During these years there is not an elegy that outshines this one in sincerity, sweetness, circumspection, and simplicity. Then ABIGAÍL LOZANO (1821–1866), skillful in words best forgotten, and CECILIO ACOSTA (1818–1881), esteemed as a thinker but estimable for his poem "The Little White House" ("*La casita blanca*").

Passing from Venezuela to Colombia we meet a select group of writers. In poetry, JOSÉ JOAQUÍN ORTIZ (1814–1892) wrote neoclassical patriotic odes; he was the first to eulogize the recently created Colombian flag; and JULIO ARBOLEDA (1817–1861), poet and soldier who composed an epic-legendary poem on colonial subject matter—*Gonzalo de Oyón*. It was lost: all we have is an unfinished version.

Along with these men stands a superior poet—JOSÉ EUSEBIO CARO (1817–1853). His life was a short-lived flame, but intense and brilliant. This flame was fed by the culture of his time and by his own combustible and violent temperament. Although he was not a philosopher, his works are on fire with the ideas of his time. He began as a skeptic, a rationalist, a utilitarian, through his readings of Voltaire and the encyclopedists, Bentham and Destutt de Tracy. Then he returned to the Catholic faith, impressed by Balmes, José de Maistre and Bonald, only to turn to Comte's positivism and, in turn, to Christian tradition once again. In these changes one can see a search for a moral, worthy, and decent position. Each one of his poems was a moral act, either because of its civil theme, or because of his urge to achieve sincerity. As a lyrical poet he figures in the purest and happiest vein of romanticism. He had formed his style following the lead of the Spanish authors from all ages, and also of the classic writers of Italy and France. The romantics, above all the French and English, helped him to discover his lyrical direction. Caro's lyre lacked none of its strings, not even the political and philosophical. Themes that usually invite an impersonal treatment, in him sounded personal.

He is always at the center of emotion; he always draws from his own interior. Political invective, moral meditation, landscape description, and didactic purpose do not deflect him from his lyrical position. Here, as well as in his intimate themes of love and family, we recognize the sincere and fiery temper of a soul that wishes to be alone and to express something original. Because even though Caro was a fighter in the political anarchy of his day, he always listened to the inner promptings of his own personality. He was an exile, and the exiles of Hispanic-America were banished because they had a living interest in their society. It was society that exiled them and not the romantic yearning for solitude, as in the case of many Europeans. In Caro we have both conditions: the exile by force of circumstances and the exile who is a loner, an exile by choice. He began by clothing his poetry in loose, free, and flowing meters, somewhat after the manner of Quintana, Gallego, and Martínez de la Rosa, thus moving comfortably, as in the *silva* "The Cypress" (*"El ciprés"*), in a slightly declamatory posture, to be sure, but with that attitude of giving himself to the reader that characterized all his works. Later on, following the English more than the Latins, he imitated the classical hexameter, combining it at times with the hendecasyllable. Evidently, he was seeking his own rhythms; and in this third manner of versification, he punished each line with unusual accents, perhaps stiffening the flow of the words, but enriching the poetic language.

In prose, the most abused genre was the sketch of customs which, in certain cases, became short story and even novel. José Manuel Groot (1800–1878) was one of the first to cultivate it. Pages of memorable descriptive achievements are contained in *Bunkhouse Notes* (*Apuntes de ranchería*) by José Caicedo Rojas (1816–1897). The first Colombian novel was historical: *Yngermina, or The Daughter of Calamar* (*Yngermina or la hija de Calamar*, 1884) by Juan José Nieto (1804–1866). It goes from 1533 to 1537 and tells about the subjugation and revolt of the Calamar Indians; the local customs come from a chronicle by Friar Alonso de la Cruz Paredes, but the novelistic apparatus is geared to European romantic models, like those of Walter Scott. Eugenio Díaz (1804–1865) author of sketches of customs and historical narrations, also wrote novels; one of these, *Manuela*, is more effective in its realist description of country life than in the emotional description of love.

Other Countries / In Guatemala the best prose writer was Salomé Jil (1822–1882), an anagram of José Milla. He evoked the colonial past in a series of historical novels: *The Nazarene Trees (Los nazarenos), The Governor's Daughter (La hija del adelantado), The Inspector (El visitador).* In general, the real and fictitious characters converse convincingly. This idealization of the past is of least interest today; on the other hand, we increasingly esteem his activity as a painter of his time. His *Sketches of Customs (Cuadros de costumbres),* more good-natured than satirical, animate the society in which he lived, save it from oblivion, illumine it with the grace of art. They have, at moments, the movements of a short story, and they have even created a popular character, Juan Chapín.

Romanticism comes to the Dominican Republic with MANUEL MARÍA VALENCIA (1810–1870). But the Dominican poets of this generation never reach full vigor: FÉLIX MARÍA DEL MONTE (1819–1899), NICOLÁS UREÑA DE MENDOZA (1823–1875), JOSÉ MARÍA GONZÁLEZ (1830–1863), FELIPE DÁVILA FERNÁNDEZ DE CASTRO (1806–1879), JAVIER ANGULO GURIDI (1816–1884), FÉLIX MOTA (1829–1861), MANUEL DE JESÚS DE PEÑA Y REINOSO (1834–1915) and JOSEFA ANTONIO PERDOMO (1834–1896).

The Second Romantic Generation

We have seen how the first shoots of romanticism, transplanted from Europe, took root in various countries. Now we shall study the writers who began to write after Hispanic-America had cultivated its own romanticism. In certain areas like Peru, Ecuador, Puerto Rico there was no romanticism other than that of this second generation.

A. MAINLY POETRY

From the grape cluster of Peruvian poets—JOSÉ ARNALDO MÁRQUEZ (1830–1903), MANUEL ATANASIO FUENTES (1820), MANUEL NICOLÁS CORPANCHO (1830–1863), CLEMENTE ALTHAUS (1835–1881), we shall pick only two: Salaverry and Cisneros. CARLOS AUGUSTO SALAVERRY (1830–1891) wrote about a score of dramatic works, in verse and in the romantic manner, but he was a poet, not a dramatist. His lyricism was irascible, for that was the mode, but in his most sincere moments he succeeds in expressing himself in correct verses. LUIS BENJAMÍN CISNEROS (1837–1904) was esteemed as a romantic poet and disregarded for his romantic novels which, nevertheless, have the merit of presenting for the first time in Peru the middle class, superficial in its aspirations to wealth and ostentation (Julia) and frustrated by civil wars (Edgardo). Ecuador's vintage gave us NUMA POMPILIO LLONA (1832–1907), modern in his sorrow, traditional in his sonnet form; and JULIO ZALDUMBIDE (1833–1887), meditative, contemplative, elegiac, religious.

In Puerto Rico MANUEL A. ALONSO (1823–1889) initiates interest in local customs and things Creole: he collected popularly inspired verses and prose in *The Rustic (El Gíbaro,* 1849). He was, then, the first chronicler of

the national character. His attitude is gay, but moralistic. From his recollections (he was in Spain at the time) he reconstructed typical pictures of
local customs: weddings, dances, cockfights, horse races. Because even his
poetry resorts to phonetic orthography in order to imitate the speech of the
Puerto Rican peasant or *jíbaro*, his work is also a linguistic document.
ALEJANDRO TAPIA Y RIVERA (1826–1882) poured his romantic wine into
poetry, novels, and dramas. He was a propagator of uncomfortable ideas,
like the heretical one of *The Sataniad, Grandiose Epic Dedicated to the
Prince of Darkness* (*La Sataniada, grandiosa epopeya dedicada al Príncipe
de las Tinieblas*). He would rewrite history artistically in his dramas and
novels. His themes were not always on Hispanic-America, although two
certainly were: *The Quadroon Woman* (*La cuarterona*, 1867) which deals
with racial prejudices, and his novel *Cofresí* (1876) on the Puerto Rican
pirate of the same name. He wrote curious allegorical and philosophical
novels. What is read today with pleasure is *My Memoirs* (*Mis memorias*).
Two other Puerto Rican poets were JOSÉ GUALBERTO PADILLA (1829–1896),
patriotic, classical in his tastes; and SANTIAGO VIDARTE (1827–1848), a romantic versifier, a disciple of Espronceda, melancholy and pessimistic in
tone, dealing in themes of love, religion, and nature.

All of the writers about whom we will now speak were aware of their
romantic antecedents in their own countries, and their works represent in
some a continuation, in others, a reaction to this past, and in still others, a
leap forward. We shall see those who leaped farthest in the next chapter.

In poetry, there were the slow-paced young Mexicans ALEJANDRO
ARANGO Y ESCANDÓN (1821–1883) and JOSÉ MARÍA ROA BÁRCENA (1827–
1908). The latter, who as a lyrical poet is barely passable, was inspired by
indigenous legends in the colorful life of the people, by Mexican scenes, and
even by the fantastic ballads in prose of Nordic literature which made such
an impression on our romantics. His short stories should be studied. The
Venezuelans twist romanticism so that we see them stretching out early
toward English, German, and Italian poetry (JOSÉ ANTONIO CALCAÑO,
1827–1894, and JUAN VICENTE CAMACHO, 1829–1872) and toward the
native landscape (JOSÉ RAMÓN YEPES, 1822–1881). The Cuban JUAN
CLEMENTE ZENEA (1832–1871) finds his way into anthologies by way of
his elegiac "*Fidelia.*"

In Colombia GREGORIO GUTIÉRREZ GONZÁLEZ (1826–1872),
like others of his compatriots, was formed in the school of the
Spaniards Zorrilla and Espronceda, and of the Venezuelans Maitín
and Lozano; above all, the school of Zorrilla, though not all of
Zorrilla's poetry, only the most tearful. But even in his youthful
poems, in which his dependence on Zorrilla is most clearly evident,
he achieved such simplicity of style and such sobriety of emotion
that his sin of imitation is attenuated. Moreover, he seems to have
been so aware that his lugubrious and vexing poems were the artificial fruits of the fashion of the day that even while he wrote

them he censured and even ridiculed them. The truth is he preferred the sober verse of a more sentimental vein, sincerely felt.
That is why, though he followed in Zorrilla's wake, he digressed
for moments toward a more intimate expression which years later
Bécquer would cultivate with genius. Let us say that his preference
was "realist," a condition which made him reach greater poetic
heights, and which assured him a place of honor in our literary
history. I am referring to his *Memoir on the Cultivation of Maize
in Antioquia* (*Memoria sobre el cultivo del maíz en Antioquia*,
1866). Here Gutiérrez González retires from the literary society
of his day and takes refuge in one of the primitive woods of his
country to compose, not only his most extensive poem, but also
the strangest and most original of his generation. With a humorous
wink he pretends to present to the School of Sciences and Arts a
Scientific Memoir (*Memoria científica*). Since he wishes to be
understood by the people, he declares that his instructions will be
precise, clear, and methodical: "The not-too-Spanish words I use
/ in my writing will not be underscored / for since I write only for
Antioquia / I do not write Spanish but Antioquian." And in fact,
the poetic language of the *Memoir* is so rich in indigenous and dialectical words that even the Colombians of Bogotá must have recourse to the linguistic notes that two friends of the poet added to
the edition of his complete works. Yet, the *Memoir* is not a poem
that lives exclusively in one province of America. True, its theme
is regional: Gutiérrez González describes how thirty peons and
the landowner search in a woods for terrain adequate for the cultivation of maize; how they fell trees and burn the ground; how
they build their huts, sow, irrigate, and defend the seed from the
birds; how maize grows; how it is harvested and cooked. But the
art of looking at and idealizing every detail in a lyrical image,
the emotion felt for the customs of a simple people and the contrast between life in the open and life in the city were the refinements of a very cultured poet. In this picture of agricultural labors
we do not see the *Georgics* of Vergil—as we did in Andrés Bello
—but the direct observation of nature by an imaginative writer.
The narration moves in a clear line; and undoubtedly many of its
hendecasyllables are incorrect, heavy, and even prosaic. Never-

theless, how remarkably stylizing is Gutiérrez González' attitude!
He looks down from above, as if he were visiting the earth from
another planet; and from this distance (not with the eyes of the
peon) he is filled with wonder at the strange beauty of each movement below.

In Chile there was a group of poets: EUSEBIO LILLO (1826–1910), author
of the national anthem, GUILLERMO MATTA (1829–1899), a prolific writer
on civic themes, polished in his tastes, who in his later years translated the
Parnassian Heredia; and, the best, GUILLERMO BLEST GANA (1829–1904).
He was romantic from beginning to end. In *Poems* (*Poesías,* 1854) he
weeps over an amorous disillusionment. Of course there is much mournful
art in his weeping. He is a lad who has read many lines of lachrymose literature. And with the passing of years, he himself will laugh ironically at the
youthful poetry of suffering. He had translated Musset; and, like Musset, he
considered himself to be suffering from the *mal de siècle.* Later he became
more tranquil and abandoned the pose. If earlier he had written in an
exalted state an anthological piece, "No, All Does Not Perish" (*"No, todo
no perece"*), now he writes a compassionate one, equally anthological, "The
First Kiss" (*"El primer beso"*). Blest Gana, in his period of maturity and
sincerity, gave proof that his melancholy was his own and not that of the
Europeans he had read. That is to say, in his last years of poetic production
he gave expression to the disenchantment and sadness which as a youth he
had seen imperfectly in his own depths. As a good romantic, he wrote a
Chilean historical drama in verse on *Almagro's Conspiracy* (*La conjuración
de Almagro*). He also wrote narratives. Difficult to classify is the Argentinian CARLOS GUIDO Y SPANO. He lived from 1827 to 1918, and covered,
thus, a great stretch of literary history. He never went below the surface of
a mitigated but elegant Attic, refined, sober romanticism. His first book,
Leaves in the Wind (*Hojas al viento,* 1871) is a collection of compositions
dating from 1854: tender, candid, with sentiments of family affection, containing reflections more or less philosophical, or civic themes lyrically
treated, as in his famous "*Nenia*" dedicated to Paraguay and written on the
occasion of its devastation by war. Many of his poems, like "Myrta at the
Baths" (*"Mirta en el baño"*), "In the Cherry Trees" (*"En los guindos"*),
"Marble" (*Mármol*"), have plastic qualities. His precise mention of the
color of things underscores this poetic plasticity. Because of his cold polish,
his visual sensitivity, and the reminiscences of the *Greek Anthology* (*Antología griega*)—which he translated in part—Guido y Spano has been
associated with the Parnassian ideals of the modernists. His second book
of verses, *Distant Echoes* (*Ecos lejanos,* 1895), abounds in verses on current
events.

B. MAINLY PROSE

The ideas of interesting men like the Chileans FRANCISCO BILBAO
(1823–1865) and BENJAMÍN VICUÑA MACKENNA (1831–1886) and the

Venezuelan ARTÍSTIDES ROJAS (1826–1894) were naturally expressed in prose. It is the art of prose that interests us here, even though that art, as in the depicters of local customs, may be rudimentary. In Colombia the writers interested in local customs used to meet regularly. Out of the meetings of this group came the journal *El Mosaico* (1858–1872). Juan de Dios Restrepo, better known as EMIRO KASTOS (1827–1897), believed that his sketches of customs lacked brilliance because, above all, one had "to respect the truth" (as if truth could not be brilliant!). The trouble was that Kastos was more an observer than a man of imagination, and although he possessed a certain dry humor, he had no desire to give color to his pages. He was disillusioned with man to the point that, in his derision, he no longer saw any hope for improvement: "*A Bottle of Brandy and Another of Gin*" (*Una botella de brandy y otra de gin*), "*Los Pepitos.*" The local color in the work of JOSÉ MARÍA SAMPER (1828–1888) had a certain charm, but not much.

JOSÉ MARÍA VERGARA Y VERGARA (1831–1872), enlivener of the literary movement in Bogotá, was a sentimentalist whose sentimentalism learned its mode of speech in the books of Chateaubriand. In his letter "A little handful of grass" (*"Un manojito de hierba"*) (pulled from Chateaubriand's grave during his trip to Europe) Vergara y Vergara wrote with lyrical tension or with essay-like delivery. Like many other writers—and this is one of the unfortunate phenomena of our literature—Vergara y Vergara put his greatest effort into writing on non-American themes; when he wrote about America, on the other hand, he scribbled in haste. It is to be lamented that his sketches of customs do not have the artistic dignity he could have given them. For example, in "The Three Cups" (*"Las tres tazas"*)—each cup serves to recall the fashions, ridiculous to his way of thinking, of the social gatherings in Bogotá: chocolate in 1813, coffee in 1848, tea in 1865—the theme is more interesting than the literary solution. The fact is that, aside from Chateaubriand, he preferred the less elevated company of Fernán Caballero and Trueba: and his depictions of customs place him even below this level. JOSÉ MANUEL MARROQUÍN (1827–1908), who tried his art of versifying in "The Puppy" (*"La perrilla"*), earned his fame as a narrator in *The Moor* (*El moro*, 1897), the story of a horse narrated by the horse: an equine autobiography in the manner of Anna Sewell's *Black Beauty*, rich in observations of local customs. He compiled his sketches of customs in several books, one of which was modestly titled *Nothing New* (*Nada nuevo*, 1894).

The novel put a definitive frame around the subject matter of the sketches of customs. The local customs in these sketches were shreds from the picaresque novels of Spain which had influenced the English (Addison, Steele), the French (Jouy, Mercier), and Spanish (Larra) prosists; transformed in this way, these sketches on customs had their effect on the Hispanic-Americans. But within the novel there is a clearcut difference between eighteenth-century sketches of customs—let us say, *A Town's Intrigues* (*Los enredos de un lugar*) by Gutiérrez de la Vega—and the nineteenth-century

ones—let us say, *The Devil Loads the Weapons* (*El diablo las
carga*) by the Venezuelan ROS DE OLANO, 1802–1887—because
in the nineteenth century, the writer becomes more interested in
the plot of the novel than in the atmosphere. Moreover, the plot
and the environment interest him more than social satire. The
serial-type novels (in France, e.g., those of Sue, Dumas, Ponson
du Terrail, Paul Féval) accustomed readers the world over to absurd episodes, to the most complicated and unending plots, contrasts between angelic and sinister persons, passions, violence, and
exaggeration. Although in Hispanic America they were not always
written in serial form, this type of novel was also cultivated.

Sue's *The Mysteries of Paris* (*Los misterios de París*) was followed by
The Mysteries of Santiago (*Los misterios de Santiago*, 1858) by JOSÉ AN-
TONIO TORRES (Chile, 1828–1884). A little novel of adventure, with a complete string of romantic traits, is the one by MARIANO RICARDO TERRAZAS
(Bolivia, 1833–1878): *Mysteries of the Heart* (*Misterios del corazón*,
1869). In these novels there is a mixture of historical, erotic and, with
curious frequency, anti-clerical adventures as in *Father Horán: Scenes of
Cuzco Life* (*El Padre Horán. Escenas de la vida cuzqueña*, 1848). It was the
first Peruvian novel. It was written by NARCISO ARÉSTEGUI (Peru, 1826–
1869) and based on a real murder. In 1836 a priest had stabbed a young
girl. The story is realistic and the purpose is reformative, but the realism
becomes lost in a tangle of loose strands (love and lust, class conflicts, religious fanaticism, revolutions, etc.) and the author's purpose of reform
harms the novel by introducing excessive sociological developments (like the
defense of the native peasants against the unjust tax laws). Just as Arestegui
started a cycle of literature in favor of the native masses, the liberal FER-
NANDO CASOS (1828–1882) did the same thing for the masses of enslaved
Negroes in *Elena's Friends* (*Los amigos de Elena*, 1874), a corrosive novel
on contemporary politics. (A curious fact: Ricardo Palma figures in this
novel in the person of Edgardo Dátiles.)

Another of the romantic genres, as we have seen, was the historical
novel: JUANA MANUELA GORRITI (Argentina, 1819–1892); SOLEDAD ACOSTA
DE SAMPER (Colombia, 1833–1913); NEPOMUCENO J. NAVARRO (Colombia,
1834–1890); DANIEL BARROS GREZ (Chile, 1834–1904); JOSÉ ANTONIO DE
LAVALLE (Peru, 1833–1893); FRANCISCO MARIANO QUIÑONES (Puerto Rico,
1830–1908). Of the army of novelists of these years, we shall pause before
but a few of them, if only to give an idea of what was being novelized, and in
what way. There was only one outstanding novelist, Alberto Blest Gana,
and he will be reserved for the end of the list.

One who attracts attention in the genre is VICENTE RIVA PALACIO (Mexico, 1832–1896). He was a man who studied the archives not so much because he was studious as because he was a collector of anecdotes. He knew
the colony like the palm of his hand, and especially what happened behind
the closed doors of the Inquisition. Nevertheless, his novels are more like

serial adventures than lucid evocations. *Martín Garatuza* (1868) is perhaps better than *Nun and Wife, Virgin and Martyr (Monja y casada, virgen y mártir)*; *The Pirates of the Gulf (Los piratas del Golfo)*; *The Return of the Dead (La vuelta de los muertos)* and the rest of his works, although not much better. He displayed his humor and talent writing on the past traditions of Mexico; these were better constructed than Palma's Peruvian traditions since they were more like short stories—his posthumous collection was called *The General's Stories (Los cuentos del general,* 1896). However, his best stories are not those in which he attempted to add wings to the massive colonial chronicles, but those that relate happenings and events that he knew from more immediate sources. His years in Madrid left a mark on his style. He was, after Roa Bárcena, the founder of the Mexican short story. It is possible that posterity will keep his short stories and not his novels. Meanwhile, he had the good humor of story-tellers. He would search books for events, little fables, amusing cases, especially about enamored nuns and monks, all part of a folklore that he would make fun of, in his conversation more than in his literature.

EUSTAQUIO PALACIOS (Colombia, 1830–1898) is the author of *The Royal Ensign: Chronicle of Eighteenth-Century Cali (El Alférez Real. Crónica de Cali en el siglo xviii)*, a romantic novel, not so much for its historical evocation (for after all, that past was quite recent—1789—and Palacios gathered it without effort) nor for its descriptions of local color, although these provide most of the interest the novel may have today, but for the melodramatic and maudlin seal impressed on it by the nineteenth-century novelistic tradition. Waves of sentimentality cover the thick, heavy dialog. It lacks subtlety; it lacks shading. For this reason the situations are sentimental, but sentiment is missing. The novelistic construction is naive and predictable. The author displays his materials with such candor that the novel becomes so translucent as to permit the reader to see through to its denouement. The love of orphans, the villain, the foreboding of a mystery in Daniel's life, and the revelation of the secret marriage of his parents, the parallelism between the tender loves of Inés-Daniel, on one hand, and Andrea-Fermín, on the other, the happiness that is showered on all at the end, must have enchanted the contemporary reader: today we are disillusioned by the psychological superficiality of those characters who nonetheless speak eloquently.

The old romantic sentimentalism inspired many idyllic and historical elaborations, like *Cumandá* (1879) by JUAN LEÓN DE MERA (Ecuador, 1832–1894). Of the romantic novels of this epoch, it is the one that can least defend itself from the changes in taste. It has become irremediably old. Even when it was conceived in 1871 this type of novel was outdated; it was derived from the *"poèmes en prose,"* a genre that from Fénélon to Chateaubriand had included in its narrative the language, and even the subject matter from poetry (Homer, Milton, Gessner, Ossian, etc.). The poetic vein remains fresh in *Cumandá:* it moistens with lyrical metaphors the description of the jungles, mountains, and rivers of eastern Ecuador and the sketches of customs of savage natives. No doubt the settings and scenes of this virgin America are what Europeans admired and what made them consider *Cumandá* one of our principal works. But, when all is said and done, it is a novel; and judging it as such, it is false from its very first line. The action occurs in 1808, but it stems from the uprising of the Guamote and Columbe Indians in 1790. The reader immediately guesses that the lovers Cumandá and Carlos are sister and brother, separated in infancy by the tragic events of the rebellion. With one blow the interest of *Cumandá* as a novel of adventure is destroyed. But Mera's worst offense as a narrator is his overflowing sentimentalism, at once conventional and swollen. Instead of inviting the reader to enter imaginatively into those unfortunate loves, thus creating the condition that will involve him emotionally, he weighs the reader down with heavy sentimental bundles, prepared, condensed, and wrapped with the trademarked ribbon of effete romanticism. Hence, there is not a single moving character, a single convincing episode, a single dialog that records the living speech of the people. Everything is absurd, even ridiculous. Mera's attitude toward the Indians of his own country—European in literature, Spanish in politics, and Catholic in metaphysics—also falsified what has been called, for some reason, "Indianism," in *Cumandá*.

The romantic novel idealized the Indian by presenting him as a poetic, exotic, legendary, or historical personage. Anselmo Suárez, Gertrudis Gómez de Avellaneda, Rosa Guerra, José Ramón Yepes, José María Lafragua, Eligio Ancona, Ireneo Paz, J. R. Hernández, Manuel de Jesús Galván, Ramón de Palma y Romay, Alejandro Tapia y Rivera, and others wrote romances with Indian characters. Mera perhaps approaches the more recent Indianist novel because of one particular: when he alluded to the violent protest by the Indians against the injustice and abuse that the despotic landowners subjected them to, he implanted a social theme that in time was to be the most important within this genre. We repeat then, *Cumandá* is worthwhile as a poetic exercise on an American theme, that is, as a point of contact of the novel with the Indianist poems that Mera himself had written. *The Virgin of the*

Sun (*La virgen del sol,* written in 1856, published in 1861) is a
verse legend in which the historical facts dealing with the crum-
bling of the Inca empire before the advance of the Spaniards serve
as a framework for the novelistic embroidering of loves and vengeances. In "Indigenous Melodies" (*"Melodías indígenas,"* 1858)
he also harks back to the Indian past. "I have also tried to make
myself Indian," he tells us in the prolog. Rather, he has disguised
himself as an Indian. Down deep, he had no feeling for the Indian.
At most it was a pretext for his European-styled texts. Mera tried
his hand at sketches of customs. His *Ecuadorian Novelettes*
(*Novelitas ecuatorianas*) especially "Between Two Aunts and an
Uncle" (*"Entre dos tías y un tío"*) describe an Ecuadorian scene
which we are able to recognize.

JOSÉ MODESTO ESPINOSA (Ecuador, 1833–1915), author of *Miscellany*
(*Miscelánea*) and *Sketches of Customs* (*Artículos de costumbres*), was an
accomplished narrator of local scenes.

In Uruguay, if any writer is to be mentioned, it must be ALEJANDRO
MAGARIÑOS CERVANTES (1825–1893). His lyrical poetry is trivial. No better, but at least more typical, was his verse legend *Celiar* about tragic loves
that are placed at the end of the eighteenth century. In *Caramurú* (1848) a
snarled-up novel about a gaucho during the period of Portuguese domination in 1823, a coarse and pulp-serial romanticism wastes even what might
have been worthwhile: customs and local color.

In Chile MANUEL BILBAO (1827–1895), to propagate his liberal, anti-
clerical ideas, used the technique of the serial novel. In *The Elder Inquisitor*
(*El inquisidor mayor,* 1852) he painted the colonial atmosphere of Lima,
the city in which Bilbao initiated his literary career. Another novel, one of
adventure but quite historical, was *The Pirate of Guayas* (*El pirata de
Guayas,* 1865).

The best novelist of this generation was another Chilean, AL-
BERTO BLEST GANA (1830–1920). He lived in France between
1847 and 1851; there he read Balzac and began his vocation as a
novelist. He wrote several novels in which, not unlike Balzac, he
presented a cycle of Chilean life from independence to the beginning of the twentieth century, with the social movements of the
middle class, political marriages, the customs of Santiago, the
power of money, the conflicts between "status seekers" and the
oligarchy, the political tumults. Balzac was not his only model; he
even cites Stendhal, when the latter was scarcely known in the
Hispanic world. He was one of the first realists in Spanish letters:

Galdós was to write shortly thereafter. His work as a novelist might be divided into two periods. From 1853 to 1863 he wrote ten novels; he then produced, in addition, a drama and various articles of customs and chronicles. Between 1864 and 1897, a long silence. And from 1897 to 1912 only four novels. The important ones from the first period are *The Arithmetic of Love* (*La aritmética del amor*, 1860), *Martín Rivas* (1862) and *The Ideal of a Profligate* (*El ideal de una calavera*, 1863). Blest Gana himself gave the formula for his realism: "The painting of verisimilar incidents, provided there is nothing extraordinary and if the coloring is alive and true, can be of as much interest to the reader as the uncommon events with which many modern novelists have corrupted the tastes of the unlettered" (1861). With this condemnation of the pseudo-Romantic serial writers Blest Gana laid out a new course for the Hispanic-American novel. He was strongly determined to be a novelist addressing himself to Chilean readers. His purpose was to novelize ordinary life, and in order to accomplish this, he had to restrain his own feelings. Blest Gana, who was not championing a cause, understood and sympathized with his fellow citizens. And his characters, who are grouped according to their affluence, show no real conscious class struggle. In *The Arithmetic of Love*, the protagonist is a young man who wishes to live well, but who does not have the money to finance such a life. He wavers between cynicism and virtue and after many misfortunes ends up by marrying his first sweetheart, the poor but loyal Amelia. *Martín Rivas* was better. But Blest Gana still makes stereotypes out of his characters, insisting that they speak and act as he wants them to. The procedure is mechanical, so that he mechanizes all of his figures, which move without acquiring the dimensions of real characters. The interest in *Martín Rivas* lies in the changing situations, in the weaving of the plot, where Martín, Rafael, Leonor, Edelmira, Chilean society, and the mutiny of 1851 are drawn in filaments of vivid color.

Two social classes, that of the big houses and that of a modest pension are involved in amorous intrigues. Realism? Yes, because the romantic narrative style now disdains excessive sentimental effusion—"without any affectation of sentimentality," says Blest

Gana—and instead describes bourgeois life more effectively, with coolly humorous scenes. But this is still not the realism of those novels with which he will break his long silence. *The Ideal of a Profligate* continues the procedure referred to, although improving it. The same combination of novelistic episodes with historical episodes—the protagonist is shot after the mutiny of Quillota. The same picture of youths from an impoverished middle class, having ambitions and promiscuous loves. But Abelardo Manríquez is now different from Martín Rivas, not only in his moral conduct but in that, as a character, he has more life, more novelistic authenticity and complexity. In his second period Blest Gana wrote *During the Reconquest* (*Durante la Reconquista*, 1897), *The Migrants* (*Los trasplantados*, 1904), *Crazy Estero* (*El loco Estero*, 1909) and *Gladys Fairfield* (1912). With the exception of the last, these are Blest Gana's best. For its theme and its art, *During the Reconquest* is the best of all. Earlier, Blest Gana had used historical episodes in order to accelerate the denouement of his novels; now the whole novel is made of history. It is one of the best historical novels of Hispanic-America and, according to some, if not his masterpiece, at least it is his most ambitious undertaking. It harks back to the years 1814–17, from the eve of the battle of Rancagua to that of Chacabuco. He interweaves many novelistic intrigues in a rigorous historical tapestry which he copies from Barros Arana's *General History of Chile* (*Historia general de Chile*) and colors it with his own observations on Chilean society which had not changed much in the few decades that had passed. In *The Migrants* he illuminated in a crude light, sometimes derisive, sometimes tragic, the family life of some rich Hispanic-Americans living in Paris. Dazzled by false lights, they look down upon their native lands and, in turn, are looked down upon by the European aristocracy. *Crazy Estero* is perhaps the most graceful, delicate, entertaining, and refined of Blest Gana's novels. It consists of adventures and loves—back in the Santiago of 1839—tinged by the nostalgia with which the aging Blest Gana evokes the years of his childhood and youth. In 1864 he established himself in Paris, and from then on Chile became for him a fond memory.

The autobiographical talent of LUCIO VICTORIO MANSILLA

(Argentina, 1831–1913) assures him of a higher place than many of those writers with less talent who consecrated themselves to the more sacred genres: poetry, drama, novel. This does not mean he did not work in literature: he translated a novel by Vigny and another by Balzac; he translated, with Dominguito Sarmiento, Laboulaye's *Paris in America* (*París en América*); he wrote a play about local customs, *An Aunt* (*Una tía*, 1864); a romantic drama, *Atar Gull*, 1864; a collection of maxims, *Moral Studies* (*Estudios morales*, 1864); a pretentious historicopsychological essay, *Rozas*, 1898, and others. But his natural gift was autobiographical; it is dispersed throughout pages which remain fragmentary despite the author's having bound them in volumes: *Between Us: Thursday Chats* (*Entre nos. Causeries del jueves*, 1889–90), *Portraits and Recollections* (*Retratos y recuerdos*, 1894), *My Memoirs* (*Mis memorias*, 1911), *Brief Pages* (*Páginas breves*). Of all this literature, the most important book, and one of the most original in America, was *An Excursion Among the Ranquel Indians* (*Una excursión a los indios ranqueles*, 1870). He had been named frontier commander of Río Cuarto, Córdoba by President Sarmiento in 1868. It meant the continuation of the conquest of the desert from the Ranquel Indians. Mansilla signed a treaty with them but since the Indians were distrustful of the good faith of the Christians, and with reason, he decided, courageously, to visit the encampment of the Indians, unarmed, in order to convince the Indian chieftain. He lived among the Indians, and the chronicle of those days does not have an equal in our literature. In this book there is political intent: to mock the institutions of our civilization by contrasting them with the forms of sociability in the wigwam village of the Ranquel Indians. "Like Gulliver in his travels to Lilliput," Mansilla says, "I have seen in my travels to the land of the Ranquels the world such as it is." But his political thought which was against "strong governments," against a "civilization having no clemency" for the Indians, against the corruptive barbarism of the Christians, did not take a Utopian form as in Swift nor an allegorical one as in *Daylight's Pilgrimage*, which Alberdi was publishing that very year in order to rail against similar evils. Rather, it was embodied in his descriptions of the life of the Indians. In time, the political allusions weakened, but as a result,

Mansilla's value as a narrator increased. The human groups he describes are complex: Indians, mestizos, renegades, white adventurers or outlaws, captured women. Mansilla looks upon them as a portion of Argentina, a portion in which the evils from the city operate: many of the whites are worse than the Indians. Each life is a drama. Mansilla presents it dramatically. And the pampa setting, which Echeverría had idealized and which Sarmiento had described without having seen, in Mansilla is real. His air of naturalness, which at times becomes a disregard for literary form, had the virtue of avoiding oratorical style.

C. THEATER

Theatrical production could be counted in titles by the hundreds. We have already seen that among the writers included in this chapter there were some who contributed to the theater. It would be impossible to give an account here of such abundant productivity. Let it be enough to mention a few thematic preferences: themes on European history, with a romantic touch of medievalism (Milanés, Fernando Calderón, José Marmol). Themes on Hispanic-American history, from the conquest to the episodes that rose from independence. Themes of recent American politics (HERACLIO C. ALMAGRO, Uruguay, 1838–1867, *Camila O'Gorman*). Themes on the Indian, idealized by romantic fantasies (JAVIER ANGULO GURIDI, Dominican Republic, 1816–1884, *Iguaniona*; PEDRO P. BERMUDEZ, Uruguay, 1816–1860, *El Charrua*; SALVADOR SANFUENTES, Chile, 1817–1860, *Cora or the Virgin of the Sun* [*Cora o la virgen del sol*]). Themes on local color, the richest source (M. A. Segura and Felipe Pardo y Aliagam were the most important).

Unclassified names: JOSÉ ANTONIO CISNEROS (Mexico, 1826?) advanced toward a more realistic concept of the theater, with plays in prose, natural dialog, no asides, no monologs: *Mercedes* (1860).

In Chile the first theatrical plays to present a real picture of the nation were those of Alberto Blest Gana: *The Head of the Family* (*El jefe de familia*) and Daniel Barros Grez: *As in Santiago* (*Como en Santiago*).

IX. 1860-1880

Authors born between 1835 and 1855

Historical framework: Just as we can define the previous period as anarchic, in spite of the efforts of the people to give themselves a constitution, we can define this period as one of achievement in the field of organization, although anarchy continues to gnaw at the insides of Hispanic-America.

Cultural tendencies: Second romantic generation. Intellectual, scholarly, critical attitude. Early fruits of the Parnassians and the naturalists.

Introduction

The authors whom we studied in the previous chapter had kindled their torches in the great romantic bonfire of 1830; then they passed them on to younger men; and in this way, while romanticism remained in the past, romantic torches were still burning in many hands at the beginning of the second half of the century. In some instances they were extinguished: it was clear that several writers turned toward the light of humanistic literature. The truth is that romanticism no longer has its earlier theoretical splendors. Now it is nothing more than a calm practical exercise. It becomes romantic literature without the belligerent display of its esthetic formulas. Since authors have to write with more discipline, with more scholarship, they seek the manner of the classicists and the philologists. The themes of this second generation of romantics are the usual ones: the sadness of defeated titans, popular speech and habits, indigenous legends of extinct peoples, history. Occasionally perhaps there appear in the form of new themes the nostalgia for home, inspired by many years of exile, or civil war. Romanticism's sketches of customs end by becoming realist in technique. At the end of this period there will be writers who will cultivate letters for their own sake and begin to bring to America the first indications of the new literary movements of Europe, such as Parnassianism and naturalism. We will attempt to harmonize the literary development by grouping writers like musical chords, and by combining these chords according to their national keys. Of course, there will be dissonances. The first chord will be from Mexico, and from there we shall move down toward Argentina.

A. MAINLY POETRY

(i) *Mexico* / As elsewhere, we find in Mexico during these years poets who stuck to tradition. The tradition was classical, Vergilian in spirit, in *Murmurs of the Forest* (*Murmurios de la selva*) by Bishop JOAQUÍN ARCADIO PAGAZA (1839–1928), a craftsman of the lovely details he observed in the country. The tradition of the productive JUAN DE DIOS PEZA (1852–1910) was Spanish romanticism, grandiloquent in public themes and eloquent in his domestic tenderness: *Songs of the Home* (*Cantos del hogar*, 1884). Also romantic in the Spanish manner, though more lyrical, was MANUEL ACUÑA (1849–1873), author of "Nocturne" (*"Nocturno"*), which was inspired by an amorous sentiment and written on the eve of his suicide as a farewell to life and love. Acuña was a poet of liberal ideas in politics and positivism in philosophy. "Before a Cadaver" (*"Ante un cadáver"*) is a curious example of how Romantic lyricism makes its way through the themes of scientific materialism, in those years new and provocative. Another romantic in the Spanish manner was MANUEL M. FLORES (1840–1885) the erotic poet of *Passion-flowers* (*Pasionarias*). On the other hand, AGUSTÍN F. CUENCA (1850–1884) was able to see the position from which, years later, the innovators were to appear.

(ii) *Central America* / DOMINGO ESTRADA (Guatemala, 1850–1901) was a romantic of modern tastes, an admirer of Martí, a translator of Poe. MANUEL MOLINA VIGIL (Honduras, 1853–1883) sank romantically to liberty, love and death.

(iii) *The Antilles* / LUISA PÉREZ DE ZAMBRANA (Cuba, 1835–1922) was the author of the best elegies of her generation. In the Dominican Republic the first lyrical voices of quality are heard: those of JOSÉ JOAQUÍN PÉREZ (1845–1900), author of *Indigenous Fantasies* (*Fantasías indígenas*), SALOMÉ UREÑA DE HENRÍQUEZ (1850–1897) concerned with civics and civilization, and the emphatic FEDERICO HENRÍQUEZ Y CARVAJAL (1848–1951). The patriot MANUEL RODRÍGUEZ OBJÍO (1838–1871) could also be listed. In

Puerto Rico, there are two romantics: one with a French education, José
de Jesús Domínguez (1843–1898), author of *Elegiac Odes* (*Odas elegi-
acas*) and *The White Houris* (*Las huríes blancas*); and the other, more
important, a romantic in the Spanish manner, José Gautier Benítez
(1850–1880), serene, melancholic, Becquerian, with his themes of love and
country; and we might even add the name of Lola Rodríguez de Tió
(1843–1924).

(iv) *Venezuela* / The Venezuelans were Jacinto Gutiérrez Coll (1836–
1903), who knew the Parnassians in France, and Antonio Pérez Bonalde
(1846–1892). What unknown affinities made Pérez Bonalde translate
Heine and Poe? We don't know. They were so secret that they did not reveal
themselves in his original poetry. Nevertheless, his having translated Heine
and Poe, who a few years later would be rediscovered by the "Modernist"
generation, has occasioned the belief that the elegiac Pérez Bonalde was a
precursor of that poetic tone, rich in shades and exquisiteness, that prevailed
from 1890 on. A precursor? Perhaps. But why not say he was a straggler?
Poe and Heine had entered Spanish literature before Pérez Bonalde was
born. The preference for the Germanic, with its predilection for things mysterious, legendary, supernatural, is noticeable already in the decade of 1840.
Bécquer himself, who manifested this better than anyone else, came later.
Because of his Nordic, misty romanticism, Pérez Bonalde was considered a
"strange one," a modern, almost a modernist. But his books of poetry,
Strophes (*Estrofas*, 1877) and *Rhythms* (*Ritmos*, 1880) do not belong to
the cycle that Darío's *Azure* opens. His best tone was the nostalgic one. His
"Return to the Homeland" ("*Vuelta a la patria*") is a beautiful romantic
evocation of his town and family.

(v) *Colombia* / In Colombian romanticism, which generally
played in the octave that goes from Chateaubriand to Victor Hugo,
Rafael Pombo (1833–1912) sang with personal impetus. He
lived the longest of the Colombian poets—seventy nine years—
and was the most fecund—over four hundred poems without
counting translations, fables, and stories in verse. Many years,
many works, in which one can naturally point out several stages.
From 1851 to 1853, in the first onrush that smacks of Zorrilla and
Byron, his poems are more sentimentalist than sentimental, although the plaintive notes are usually subdued owing to the moral
temperament of the man. In his second phase, during his residence
in the United States, he reaches his fullness. His travels, the experience of a foreign culture, his relations with distinguished
people, his friendship with Longfellow and Bryant, the study of
classics and moderns which contributed to his skill as a translator,
and the maturity of his years, all gave flexibility and strength to his

verse, from the ode to the epigram, from love elegies to philosophic meditations, from landscape description to civil and jocular themes. His third phase goes to 1912. It is upon his return to Colombia and the decadence of old age that his poetry becomes more rationalistic, and the modes of versification become fixed: the sonnet was the preferred form of his later years. But these phases are entirely comprised within the romantic orbit, without a tinge of neoclassicism, without an indication of the modernism to come. One theme dominates his poetry: love, which inspires him from his youthful "The Glass of Wine" (*"La copa de vino"*) to the senile "Avisag." The love of a bachelor for all women and not for one; the love of real and ideal women, angelic and sensual women, women of all races and ages, and in "Elvira Tracy" even dead women. Eroticism of the flesh and of the imagination tormented him as much with the vision of beauty as with the vision of his own failure. He even indulged in false feminine poems (*"Mi amor"*) that deceived readers into believing that hidden in Colombia, was an ardent Sappho: Edda la Bogotana. Later Pombo confessed his fraud by writing "Edda," one of his better known poems. His sentiment for women went hand in hand with his sentiment for landscape—after all, woman and landscape were for him spectacles of nature. He would go to nature not as a gardener who arranges it in pretty shapes, but as one restrained and distrustful of the force of art: "Put up your lyre, poet, / put up, painter, your palette, / and your chisel, sculptor; / nature is better / than the sign that interprets it." In "Prelude to Spring" (*"Preludio de primavera"*) it is nature that is worthwhile: at its feet, the life of man is small and only inspires melancholy. This meditation on our destiny as men, whenever he contemplated nature, tended to overwhelm his spirit.

Since Heredia, Niagara Falls has always been an obsession in Hispanic-American poetry; when Pombo in "At Niagara" (*"En el Niágara"*) began to describe that "museum of cataracts," "factory of clouds," "a sea staved in by the weight of its waves," he showed a visual strength more powerful than anyone else's. What he saw is here in his verse: the reader sees Niagara again because it lies before his eyes. Torrential poetry, like Niagara itself. He did not

adhere to the graphic element only, and one might add that this is
the least important in Pombo's poetry. Misanthropy is pleased to
depreciate man as it exalts nature. Why fear nature?: "the gravest
evil it does is a good: it offers us a grave, a bed for the tired." Man:
"there is the monster," "there is the asp at whose contact I shud-
der," "atrocious grafting of angel and devil." "For me," he ends by
saying, "life is a sarcasm." There was within Pombo a Leopardi,
and he gave us his desperate note. At twenty-four years of age, he
wrote sixty-one *décimas* "The Hour of Darkness" (*"La hora de
tinieblas,"* 1864), which, for the sincerity of its doubts, is blasphe-
mous to one of religious conscience, profound and anguished to all.
Pombo, on the strength of his Catholicism, recanted in old age,
but what he had said remained said, and his work is a high point
in the history of our literature. He was one of the best lyricists of
his generation; but the waters are so boisterous that the undulation
of his verse becomes rough, turbulent, and broken, and so our ears
at times suffer from the noise. Because of his achievements we
must forgive him his failings.

After Gutiérrez González and Pombo, the worthiest poet is
DIEGO FALLÓN (1834–1905), who gave his idealistic visions of
nature a concrete shape in classicist poetry (see his ode "To the
Moon" (*"A la luna"*). With EPIFANIO MEJÍA (1838–1876), with
his realist poetry, CANDELANO OBESO (1840–1884), with his
"black poetry," and RAFAEL NÚÑEZ (1835–1894) with his poetry of ideas, we can close the list of Colombian poets of the second
romantic generation.

After them came others, disciplined through their contacts with the
classicists and philologists. In Colombia, a conservative and traditionalist
country, pedagogical norms have always been overbearing. The Spaniards
had not participated in the march of modern linguistic history, which was
primarily German, with French and Italians bringing up the rear. After *el
Brocense* (Francisco Sánchez de las Brozas) there was a long interruption,
until the Colombian RUFINO J. CUERVO (1844–1911) became the great
linguistic leader—the Spaniard Menéndez Pidal would come later. Inclined
also toward the study of language—although more a grammarian than a
philologist—was another illustrious Colombian, MIGUEL ANTONIO CARO
(1843–1909) who brought to literature his seriousness as a scholar. He was
an excellent representative of the flourishing of humanism in Colombia in
those days. His closeness to Horace, Propertius, Catullus, and, above all,
to Vergil—he translated *The Aeneid* admirably—left its mark and counter-

mark in every verse. His verses sprang from wisdom and are technically irreproachable, but they are cold, as if born in the damp basement of literary history. They lack grace and feeling. The poet goes about on his knees because his religion is not the defiant titanism of the romantics, but a humble and resigned Catholicism. His sonnet "To Himself" ("*A sí mismo*") is propped on Caro's two knees, one classical, the other Catholic. His thought was academic, not critical; in other words, he succeeded as a critic when his materials were academic, but he did not understand the new values. In time, his constant rejection of what he did not understand separated him from the literature of his time. He remained like a classical statue: in a statuesque style he wrote one of the best poems of his age—"To the Statue of the Liberator" ("*A la estatua del Libertador*").

(vi) *Ecuador* / The Ecuadorian CÉSAR BORJA (1852–1910) was somber in his sentiments, luminous in his images.

(vii) *Bolivia* / LUIS ZALLES (1832–1896), DANIEL CLAVO (1832), MERCEDES BELZU DE DORADO (1835–1879).

(viii) *Chile* / In lyric poetry, JOSÉ ANTONIO SOFFIA (1843–1886) was one of those minor poets, moderate, simple, acceptable to good families. His *Lyrical Poems* (*Poesías líricas*) date from 1875; his *Leaves of Autumn* (*Hojas de otoño*) from 1878. Bécquer had just given Spanish romanticism its softest note. Soffia preferred that softness. Softly he sang of love—above all, of his wife—of nature, loneliness, mystery, death, virtue, his native place, God. In narrative, descriptive and dramatic poetry, CARLOS WALKER MARTÍNEZ (1842–1907) achieved merit for his themes dealing with American ethnography, colonial history and episodes from independence. ESTEBAN MUÑOZ DONOSO (1844–1907) came out suddenly with an ambitious epic poem, *La Colombia*, which extols the discovery of the New World and includes Columbus, his men, God, Lucifer and Archangel Gabriel, American scenes, Indian tribes, the intrigues of conquistadors and prophecies that apply to the modern era. PEDRO NOLASCO PRENDEZ (1853–1906), an eloquent extrovert set to meter historical episodes and grandiose panoramas (as in his eulogy to the Andes mountain range). DOMINGO ARTEAGA ALEMPARTE (1835–1880), author of odes to love and sorrow. LUIS RODRÍGUEZ VELASCO (1838–1919), sentimental and evocative in his *Lyric Poems* (*Poesías líricas*). EDUARDO DE LA BARRA (1839–1900) is remembered not so much for his poetry as for his studies of meter (and still more for the pages in which he helped Rubén Darío).

(ix) *Argentina* / The chords of Argentina are still waiting for us to play them. First of all, let us strike the chords of a guitar, from poets turned gaucho. Before going on to the works culminating in "gaucho poetry," the reader should re-read what has been said in preceding chapters about the movement concerned with local customs, a movement that had been paving the way since the eighteenth century for the arrival of Bartolomé Hidalgo. It was through Hidalgo that the image of the gaucho became a symbol of the Creole peasants as opposed, not only to foreigners, but also to the young lordlings of the city. Both partisans and adversaries put out news-

papers and pamphlets in which the rural idiom was imitated. Even the
most cultured writers, moved by moral passion in the midst of civil wars,
attracted by the rugged spectacle of the country (which, in another sense,
was there, invading the city) and, above all, carried away by the romantic
idea of a literature based on local color and the speech of the people, they
began to make a myth of the gaucho. We have already seen that Hidalgo's
gaucho was not a sudden portrayal of an alleged minstrel of the pampas,
but a figure created by artists and having antecedents in the literature of
local customs. But the romantics began to change the image of the gaucho
from the somewhat uncouth figure of political verse into a noble myth. Sarmiento, in *Facundo*, created the singing gaucho. Ascasubi, aware of the importance of "gaucho poetry," pursued the idea of a great work along this
line, which resulted in his *Santos Vega*. Mitre, in his *Rhymes*, elaborated on
the legend of Santos Vega, "the untaught bard of the pampas." Finally,
two remarkable poems were to emerge from this glorification of the gaucho:
Fausto and *Martin Fierro*. Afterwards the gaucho theme was to be reproduced in every genre with such proliferation that it is impossible to follow
here its development step by step. In the novel, *Don Segundo Sombra*, by
Güiraldes, the gaucho was eventually to dissolve into pure idea.

ESTANISLAO DEL CAMPO (Argentina, 1834–1880) was a
cultured city man, who knew how to write lyrical poetry in the
romantic manner of his time. Nevertheless, his place is among the
gauchesque poets. We have seen already how, first Hidalgo, and
later Ascasubi, although both city men, had lived in the country
with the peasants and had written poems in the rustic idiom. In
1857 Del Campo started his literary life by writing gaucho verses
in imitation of Ascasubi. Del Campo responded to the satires published by Ascasubi under the pseudonym of *Aniceto el Gallo*
(Aniceto the Rooster), signing his responses with the pseudonym,
Anastasio el Pollo (Anastasio the Chicken). Ascasubi would
imitate the gauchos and Del Campo would imitate Ascasubi. Del
Campo would not have gone very far had it not been that, in his
gaucho imitation, he created a burlesque imitation of Gounod's
Faust, which, in turn, was an operatic imitation of Goethe's *Faust*.
Del Campo put his point of view into the rustic idiom of a narrator who tells about an encounter between the peasant Laguna
and Anastasio el Pollo. In the course of the dialog el Pollo tells
Laguna, in detail, from the moment he entered the theater until the
final curtain fell, everything he has seen in the Colon Theatre,
which has just shown the Italian version of Gounod's *Faust*. The
story of Faust, Marguerite and Mephistophiles is recreated

through the impressions of the two friends. The situation was comical in itself, first because of the contrast between the cultured, sophisticated, Europe-loving bourgeois world of the Colón theater and the two gauchos who had come from a distance to visit the city; and then because of the contrast between Gounod's opera and Goethe's drama. Del Campo's parody sprang from a humorous view of the world. Of course it would be impossible for a peasant to buy a seat in the Colon theater; and then, hearing an opera in Italian, to be able to understand it enough to narrate its plot, without even realizing that it was an artistic performance and not real life. The conventions that Del Campo uses are incredible, and it is not worth while making an inventory of their improbabilities. Del Campo observed with irony the oscillation between truth and fantasy, the gaucho and the European, the vital reality and the artistic artifice. He communicates with the public with a wink of complicity. But el Pollo and Laguna are also communicating with each other in a subtle game of ironic complicity. Peasants enjoy a story as they enjoy lies. Laguna admires his friend's inventive faculty and eggs him on to further invention, and finally ends by paying his expenses at the inn, which is how the public has always treated its entertainers. El Pollo is a buffoon. What is meant as a joke, then, should never be taken literally or seriously. The joke began by inverting the theme of world-as-theater. Ever since Plato the comparison of the world to a theater and of man to an actor has been a universal part of literature. Conscious of the decrepitude of this metaphor, Cervantes inverted it and gave us the episode in which Don Quixote, as spectator, takes seriously Maese Pedro's presentation. This inversion of the formula produced humorous effects. Instead of showing us the world as a stage contemplated by a brilliant god, which had been the idea of pagan philosophers and Christian preachers, Del Campo shows us the theater as a world contemplated by a gaucho. The contrast between the reality of the gaucho and the artifice of European art was effective.

At times he falls into verses displaying his poetic erudition, but they are not his best. His best verses are those in which he achieved a traditional poetic style, with epigrammatic wit, imaginative vivacity, sympathy for the way the peasant feels, and fluidity in his

scenic descriptions. Del Campo played the guitar with the technique of the lyre, and the lyre with the technique of the guitar, and
managed to achieve the music of a lyric guitar.

Artistically, Del Campo was superior to his model, Ascasubi.
Nevertheless, he would be surpassed later by another poet of the
gaucho, Hernández. With the publication of *Fausto* (1866) the
question of whether there existed a "national literature" was revived in Buenos Aires. A balance sheet is drawn up and there are
those who, in 1870, say that such a literature does not exist. Might
Fausto perhaps be "national literature"? Is the external description of language, clothing, customs, folklore, sufficient to consider
a literary work "national"?

JOSÉ HERNÁNDEZ (Argentina, 1834–1886) lived in the midst
of these discussions. He was a man of letters who sympathized
with the cause of the gauchos and distrusted the Europeanist spirit
of the statesmen of his day. He must have been fed up with hearing
the same remarks: gaucho literature did not have literary merit, it
was only enjoyable in works like *Fausto*. And he probably felt
resentful since his own preferences had no place in the scale of
values of his time. What is certain is that he decided to join the
gaucho series by writing a poem also: *Martín Fierro* (the "Departure," 1872; the "Return," 1879). His intentions were serious. In
the depths of his verses there is a muted polemic against the Europeanist group that is indifferent to the gaucho world, or against
Europeanists who believed that *Fausto* was the measure of what
gaucho literature could produce. Hernández breaks out in song,
fully aware of his sober mission, and above all, quite cognizant
that there are those who do not believe in him or in the gaucho
literature of which he is capable. He reproaches the gauchesque
poets for a task half done. Hernández realizes that he himself is
bringing something new and more complete. And in order to record it, he imitates with more talent than the others the authentic
voice of the gaucho. *Martín Fierro* then, has a twofold public—
cultured readers and gauchos. With the same words he offers two
distinct messages. From the cultured readers, he demands justice
for the gaucho. As for the gauchos, he attempts to give them moral
lessons to better their condition. In other words, *Martín Fierro* was
a political poem when read in the city and a pedagogical poem

when read in the country. However, in miming the gauchos with the intention of bettering them morally, Hernández achieved something ingenious: an emotional and imaginative identification with the world of the gaucho. His *Martín Fierro* became an outstanding example of an individual poet who allies himself with popular poetry, re-elaborates its material, exalts it poetically, and allows the profound voice of an entire society to be heard in his own voice. *Martín Fierro* is not an epic poem. It is a popular poem in which the poet, with all deliberation, puts his song in the service of an oral tradition. The impulse is individual; the source is popular. Hernández does not adapt the poems of others—he invents everything, but in the spiritual attitude of a legendary *payador* or gaucho balladeer. For this reason, his *Martín Fierro* seems to derive from an anonymous people. For this reason the gauchos read it as their own. For this reason the traditional elements are not brought from the outside, but felt and conceived by an Hernández transformed into an ordinary inhabitant of the pampas.

He was, then, a cultured poet with a traditional manner. The cultured poet is easily recognized in the skilled construction of the poem and in his intentions toward social reform which give coherence of plot to the adventures and value to the protagonist as a type and as a symbol. The traditional manner is that of improvisation. Hernández had observed the country men with keen attention. He had lived with them and imitated them. Saturated with the gaucho spirit, Hernández makes believe he is improvising: "the couplets spring from me / like water from a fountain." It's not true—the emendation of the manuscripts and the study of the systematic lines in *Martín Fierro* reveal the arduous task involved in its composition. One of *Martín Fierro's* stylistic traits is that Hernández writes with self-constraint, attuning his voice to that of the gaucho he carries in him. He knows that his cultured voice would cripple the poem, that it is the voice of the gaucho that will give it its quality. He does not write in a prevalent gaucho dialect, but rather in a normal Spanish language which he fashions from within with a gaucho's outlook on life. It is an individual, energetic, creative language, rich in folklore but with no frontiers between what he gathered and what he invented.

The seven years between the "Departure" and the "Return"

accentuate the poem's intention to promote reform. The conduct of the gaucho Fierro is motivated by different reasons. In the "Departure" Hernández raises a series of sociological situations within which he moves the anarchic, proud, and maltreated figure of the gaucho. The point of departure, then, is logical and constructive, and belongs to one who has studied social reality and proposes to disseminate his political message. There are allusions to the doctors of Buenos Aires, to Sarmiento's politics, to the government's abuses. Allegorically, Fierro flees with no other hope than that offered by the Indians who live beyond the pale of civilization. In the "Return," Fierro reappears, but with a European and progressivist vision of work: "for the land gives no fruit / if not watered by sweat." "Vandalism is ended." Now he avoids fights and explains why earlier he had killed; they are legal justifications which show that Hernández, down deep, was a conservative who respected the law, the reason being that, by 1879—Avellaneda is the new president, Sarmiento no longer holding the reins—Hernández recognizes "society" as legitimate, which earlier he had condemned in the "Departure." There are two moralities in the "Return": the one that Hernández proposes and one that the cynicism of the old man Vizcacha documents as a reality, the first morality having ideal goals and the second, opportunistic ones. Hernández' idealism and Vizcacha's realism. An Argentina with a program and an Argentina without morals. Lights and shadows. Civilization versus barbarism: here is where Hernández, the enemy of Sarmiento, in the end agrees with him. *Martín Fierro* is one of the most original poems emanating from Hispanic romanticism. Its strophe, keeping within romantic metrics, indicated an effort to avoid classical rigor without being dragged under by traditional currents: octosyllabic verses organized in sextets, with the initial verse free of rhyme, the four following lines in rhymed couplets, and the last one rhyming with the second and third (abbccb). The poem had the traits of the "romantic school": literature as an expression of society; local color; nationalism; sympathy for the people; the exotic theme of Indian customs; the exiled and doleful hero as the victim of society; Fierro's noble friendship with Cruz; the novelistic episodes of violent contrasts as in the death of Vizcacha, the fight between the Indian and Fierro in front of the woman, the child whose throat is cut, and the happy meetings of Fierro with his children and with those of Cruz.

OLEGARIO ANDRADE (Argentina, 1839–1882) clings more to the forms of romanticism than Hernández did. Of Andrade's two epochs—that of Entre Ríos, 1855–75, and that of Buenos Aires, 1876–81—the second is the one that counts, for it was then that he wrote his best poetry. "The Condor's Nest" (*"El nido de cóndores"*), "The Lost Harp" (*"El arpa perdida"*), "San Martín" and others, possess the mark of "titanism," a characteristic of Romanticism; and in fact, the symbol of Titan appears in "Prometheus," his "song to the human spirit." Andrade's creative imagination was more epic than lyrical. He prefers to relate what took place in the world to that which takes place in his soul. Nevertheless, what Andrade objectifies best are metaphors, that is, lyrical visions: visions with amplifying crystals that magnify everything beyond measure. Robust, sensational metaphors constructed with such a desire for clarity that they generally appear in the form of comparisons and similes with the structural links "like" and "as" in plain sight. They are the metaphors of a visual poet who pours his inner world into a mold of things that lie before the eyes of everyone—plastic metaphors. Although one may recognize their kinship to the metaphoric language of romanticism (Victor Hugo's, especially), Andrade's metaphors are not adopted children, but the natural children of his fantasy. They have the same features, like the members of one family, but each one lives its own life. Andrade writes from the position of one ready to leap. He is obsessed with space, with heights. He leaps upon great themes—progress, homeland, the future, liberty, human destiny—from hyperbole to hyperbole. Resonant poetry, round but not hollow, or at least no hollower than the breast from whence the strength of song emanates; always affected, partly because art is affectation; grandiose for its grandiloquence, but not great; because in spite of everything Andrade was not a great poet. He lived bewildered by the peal of his own declamations and the declamations typical of the journalism of his age: Andrade paid dearly for not knowing how to forget that he was a journalist when he wrote poetry.

The terminal date for this chapter is 1880. And it happens that in Argentina those who were between thirty and forty years of age were called "men of the year '80": 1880 was the year of the federalization of Buenos Aires which gave the country its definitive organization. Because of its political significance, historians have chosen the eighties as a literary landmark. The only trouble is that during this period of time—ten years before, ten years after—writers of different generations converge. Men like Vicent F. López, Bartolomé Mitre, and Lucio V. Mansilla are still influential figures. Yet the representatives of the eighties are O. Andrade, E. Cambacérès, E. Wilde, L. V. López, M. Cané, R. Obligado, J. A. García. The common features which bind them are the feeling of belonging to families that had helped to build the nation or that deserved to govern the republic; coupled with the awareness that the social and political transformation of Argentina was thwarting their ambition and forcing them to fail; and a skepticism and sterility, which sought a mode of expression in a fragmentary literature of ironic and autobiographical tone. Here we shall deal only with the poets; of the prose writers we shall have more to say later on in the chapter.

The lyricists who had the best reputation at this historical juncture were Guido y Spano, Andrade (already studied), and RICARDO GUTIÉRREZ (1836–1896). To these were added the new poets Obligado and Almafuerte. The poetic work of RAFAEL OBLIGADO (1851–1920) is very scarce; he wrote only one book, *Poems (Poesías,* 1885) augmented in the second edition of 1906, and even in it moments of excellence are scarce. But in Argentina he was considered "the national poet," in part because he insisted on themes and attitudes along the Echeverría-Ascasubi-Hernández line, at a time when the country was putting a cosmopolitan mask on its Creole face. Having taken refuge in a simple poetry—nature, the past, affection for regional types, folklore—he seemed original to his friends and readers. What was original, nevertheless, was his writing this kind of poetry in the face of the waves of immigration, of technical-economic progress, of the imitation of European styles, ideas, and customs, of the ambition for material wealth. The exaltation of nationalism was what gave fame to Obligado. Of his poems, some legendary, others historical, others intimate, time has saved his *Santos Vega,* the *payador.* First Bartolomé Mitre, then Ascasubi, and later Eduardo Gutiérrez in a novel, had already written about this *payador.* Obligado had heard his peons tell how Santos Vega had been outsung by the devil, and from that time on had wandered over the countryside like a soul in purgatory. With material taken from literature and folklore he wrote his poem: not in a Creole dialect but in very precise, very lyrical language, made subtle with shimmering images of mystery and, within the scope of romanticism, disciplined through a great deal of literary study. The poem is not pure poetry, nevertheless, for it contains moral preoccupations, patriotic lessons, and even an allegory: in the section "The Death of the *Payador"* Ragged John, the stranger, symbol of progress, industry, science, and European imagination, diabolically triumphs over Santos Vega, symbol of moribund Creole tradition. In adding a new canto in 1887 ("The Hymn of the *Payador"*) to the three in the first edition, he accentuated his patriotic intent.

Among the "men of 1880," Cané, Obligado, Oyuela, *et al.,* we cannot include Pedro B. Palacios, better known by his pen name, ALMAFUERTE (Argentina, 1854–1917). The former were cultured, rich, sober, influential, elegant, satisfied, conventional, Europeanized. Almafuerte was swimming against the current. And later when the "men of 1880" were succeeded by those "modernists" clustered about Rubén Darío, Almafuerte remained once again outside the group: on one occasion he asked for recompense "in the name of Hispanic-American letters, which I have saved from decadence and effeminacy." Indeed, he could not be a "decadent," that is, one of the new poets who admired Verlaine, for the simple reason that his voice was that of another decadence—romanticism. Literally speaking, he was ill-mannered; in order to enrage the esthetes he made believe he was worse than he was. The first impression that one receives on reading him is that of the deformity of his verses. But he who perseveres in reading him will discover a poet of vigor, even more, a poet of spiritual complexity. Defective and unequal, his poetry reflects the character of a very singular person. He was a blasphemer. He was misanthropic, misogynous, megalomaniacal and messianic; eccentric through and through, with misguided aspirations to being a prophet and philosopher, stentorian in voice, delirious, furious, haughty, rude, and grotesque. But he was a lyricist with a new voice in our literature. That voice resounded, augmented by continuous hyperboles. He directed himself to the rabble, to the "vile sweaty multitude." He was not a poet of the masses, despite the fact that his popularity came from the lower classes, but an aggressive individual. At first glance his style seems to be popular claptrap, vulgar expression, related to the tango dives and the low-life toughs of the slums; but if the style is carefully observed it reveals a desire to renovate poetic language, to adopt new meters, to invent words, to seek a certain perfection in an incessant correction of the work itself. He had bad taste, but was individualistic in the brazen sincerity with which he renounced the conventions of his time and dared to confess his anguished vision of life. Everything for him was a failure: himself, man, the universe, God. His pessimism, his disdain, his anger are deep-rooted. Almafuerte found failure at the very root of existence, and no one has given finer poetic utterance than he to the ugly, the obscure, the poverty-ridden, the aborted, the sordid, and even the repugnant. He expressed his somber humor in generally epigrammatical prose: *Evangelics* (*Evangélicas*). Since it is the function of prose, more than that of verse, to articulate thoughts with rigorous logic, it is in his prose that the contradictions in Almafuerte's logic appear. He believed and disbelieved in the dignity of man; he believed and disbelieved in God and in a universal truth; he believed and disbelieved in moral progress; and on and on. The robustness of his thought was in its onslaught; the direction did not matter. It was badly articulated thought, but rich in insight into the wickedness of man and the falsehoods of society. He is one of the few Argentinian poets of the nineteenth century esteemed by those of the twentieth: Lugones admired him and some of the young writers of today still admire him.

B. MAINLY PROSE

Certain names are lacking in our panorama of poetry. It is not that they have been forgotten, but they stand out as writers of prose and, as such, they will be studied farther on: Isaacs, Palma, González Prada, Varona, and Sierra. The prose of this generation is extraordinary; if, in addition to those names, we add Montalvo, Hostos, and others to come, it will be evident that we stand before the best prosists of the nineteenth century.

1. Novel and Short Story

Some of the writers whom we shall examine cultivated the historical novel. In their majority, these novels fell beyond the pale of literature—they were wild, truculent, coarse serials, even less artistic than the serial novels of the Spaniard Fernández y González. In the last decades of the century one notices the tendency to apply the techniques of realism to the evocation of the past. As in Europe, after Walter Scott and Manzoni come the realists Flaubert and Georg Ebers, so in Spanish America the novelists promised themselves, above all, to be faithful to the truth, at least the truth as they came to know it in the books at hand. To fix the details of the transition from the romantic novel to the realist is impossible. Nevertheless, it is clear that scrupulous insistence on being faithful to historical reality was restraining the flights of fancy more and more. The romantic philosophy of history was succeeded by positivism.

(i) *Mexico* / One of the best novelists of this generation is the Mexican, IGNACIO MANUEL ALTAMIRANO (1834–1893). As with others, political agitation often took Altamirano away from literature. He was a worthy poet—*Rhymes* (*Rimas*, 1880) in that he kept all of his sensory organs open to the world, and had a high quality of perception. Although the literary language of his epoch was a weighty encumbrance to his creative spirit, he would frequently free himself from its weight and arrive at a true image. His grasp of things was that of a novelist. He started to write *Christmas in the Highlands* (*La navidad en las montañas*, 1871) with a "sketch of customs" in mind; but it did not end up as such. It is, rather, a little sentimental novel, with landscapes, action, and stereotypes embellished with the artificial light of literature—of literature and not of folklore. When a child recites a Lope de Vega ballad, the priest expresses his satisfaction that children are learning poetic Spanish compositions and not "the very bad verses" of popular ballads. These complaints against the debasing of good poetic Spanish tradition in the bad couplets of the people were heard in many romantic writers: Tapia y Rivera, in his *Cofresí*, laments that verses by Calderón had wound up deformed in the mouths of the popular balladeers. The Indians become "real shepherds similar to those who appear in the idyls of Theocritus and in the eclogues of Virgil and Garcilaso." The loves of Carmen and Pablo follow romantic conventions. The technique of the narrative —one narrator introduces a character, who in turn relates another episode, and on and on—is not that of the "sketch of customs." Altamirano militated in favor of the Mexican reformation; and he created as a protagonist a perfect priest, exceptional, unique, an ideal image who, because of the clearly delineated contrast with the clerics of those days, must have flattered the liberals more than the Catholics. But Altamirano's importance in the history of the novel rests on *Clemencia* (1869) and, above all, on *The Blue-Eyed Fellow* (*El Zarco*). The first is a sentimental, romantic novel, psychologically false, in no way set off from the great mass of novels of a similar type that was produced in those years. Set in the last weeks of 1863 and the beginning of 1864, when Maximilian's French army was forcing the Mexican patriots into constant retreat, *Clemencia* relates the unfortunate loves of four youths in Guadalajara: the blond Flores and the brunette Valle, the blond Isabel and the brunette Clemencia. The two women, one angelic, the other ardent, both love Flores, who is physically handsome though morally base. Valle, on the other hand, is physically repulsive, but morally superior. Flores betrays the patriotic cause and is about to be shot; but Valle, who loves Clemencia, sacrifices himself, helps his rival to freedom, and dies in his place. Only then does Clemencia realize that she should have loved Valle. She withdraws from the world and enters a convent.

In *The Blue-Eyed Fellow* the imperfections of a posthumous manuscript are scarcely noticed, even though it did not receive the benefit of the final retouches that the author, who was so careful in his style, could have given it. *The Blue-Eyed Fellow* is an episode of Mexican life in 1861–63 when, at the end of the civil war between liberals of the reformation and the pro-clerics, groups of cold-blooded bandits terrorized the tropical zone. Several characters are taken from real life: the blue-eyed fellow, Salomé, Martín Sánchez, the great Benito Juárez. In the composition we note romantic concessions: the play of symmetry and contrast between the good Pilar and Nicolás, and the evil Manuela and the blue-eyed fellow; the ominous owl that chants on the branch where the blue-eyed fellow will be hanged. But it is a realistic novel. When he describes the landscape, and he does it beautifully, he does not associate it with the moods of the characters. "An indifferent nature followed its normal course," he comments during one of the most dramatic moments. He describes the bandits' den in full color, but it is not the "local color" of the romantics. Further, Manuela's love for the bandits—nourished by romantic books—is presented with ironic observations. There are allusions also to the inverisimilitude of *Atala* and *Paul et Virginie*. Altamirano's attitude is that of the moralist. At times his feelings intervene too peremptorily, and the novelist defines a character before he has presented him, and judges him without giving us time to see him live. Nevertheless, Altamirano's desire to understand and explain good and evil made him one of the most penetrating novelists of this generation. His psychological analyses are complex, precise, cogent. *The Blue-Eyed Fellow* is noteworthy for the attention focused on the souls of its characters—one sees them in intimate conflicts with pros and cons. And in these souls changes take place; they are souls that mature, and the transitions are there to be seen. Furthermore, he knows how to tell a story. The episodes are well linked: the thread of the action runs rapidly and the reader's attention does not wane.

One of Altamirano's friends was JUAN DÍAZ COVARRUBIAS (Mexico, 1837–1859), and like him, a romantic and a liberal. He dedicated to Zorrilla his somber and sepulchral poetry. He wrote several novels: *Gil Gómez the Insurgent or The Physician's Daughter* (*Gil Gómez el insurgente o La hija del Médico*), set amidst the wars of independence; *The Middle Class* (*La clase media*), in which he exalts the virtues of the bourgeoisie and criticizes aristocratic groups; *The Sensitive One* (*La sensitiva*); and *The Devil in Mexico* (*El diablo en México*), "sketches of customs." This latter work is a good literary exercise. The breakup of the theme—the disillusionment of love—into romantic, ironic, and realist planes is varied and apt: narratives, local customs, letters, intimate diaries, little homespun philosophies. The author describes the landscapes, and even the moods, in romantic rhetoric, but is capable of subtleties. His characters read Byron and George Sand, but the author is aware that romanticism is a style, that is, a way of life in the past, and in the midst of his sugary poetic effusions, he laughs mockingly on seeing the triumph of what he calls "positivism." In the wind-up, the "devil," an anti-romantic devil, mocks the lovers by separating them and coupling them in unexpected pairs.

In the historical novel: ELIGIO ANCONA (1836–1893), IRENEO PAZ (1836–1924), EULOGIO PALMA Y PALMA (b. 1851), CRESCENCIO CARRILLO Y ANCONA (1836–1897), JUAN LUIS TERCERO (1837–1905). The realist novel, seasoned to the Spanish taste and not in the raw realism of the French, had good representatives. JOSÉ LÓPEZ PORTILLO Y ROJAS (1850–1923), author of poetry, drama, essay, excelled in short stories which were recently gathered—*Complete Stories* (*Cuentos completos*, 1952). In one of them, "In a Stagecoach" (*"En diligencia"*), he judges the state of literature as it appeared to him: two young men decide to win over a woman through literature, one considering Zola and naturalism to be in the vanguard as the only school worthy of the century, and the other defending the romanticism of sentiment and tears. López Portillo y Rojas, of course, left romanticism, but did not go into naturalism. His purpose was to be a nationalist—to create Mexican literature. What he did was follow the footsteps of the Spanish regionalist. Nevertheless, he felt a genuine sympathy for the more destitute social classes of Mexico, and this is preserved in his novels *The Parcel of Land* (*La parcela*, 1898), *The Forerunners* (*Los precursores*, 1909) and *The Weak and the Strong* (*Fuertes y débiles*, 1919). The first of these is the best.

In EMILIO RABASA (1856–1930) the sketches of customs of the romantic years now unfold more ambitiously and give us functional characters and problems within a social and political reality which is then studied. Of his five narrations, the novel *The Uprising* (*La bola*, 1887) and the novelette *The Three Years' War* (*La guerra de tres años*, 1891) are the best. He denounces the afflictions of our countries—bossism, militarism, clericalism, bureaucracy, corruption, politicking, and so on—and he does it mordantly. Alongside those named we must cite RAFAEL DELGADO (1853–1914) who, when he wanted to be a realist, was impeded by his excessive sentimentalism.

In the *Woodlark* (*La calandria*, 1891), *Angelina* (1895), *The Rich Relatives* (*Los parientes ricos*, 1903), and *Ordinary History* (*Historia vulgar*, 1904) a romantic gust keeps the description of regional customs fresh. He was also a short story writer, poet, and theatrical author.

(ii) *Antilles* / NICOLÁS HEREDIA (Cuba, 1852–1901), a realist in *A Man of Business* (*Un hombre de negocios*, 1882), achieved his best novel in *Leonela*, in which elements of naturalism mingle with passionate romantic fluorishes. The historical novel was also cultivated in Cuba: RAIMUNDO CABRERA (1852–1923) and EMILIO BACARDI (1844–1922). In the Dominican Republic we have FRANCISCO GREGORIO BILLINI (1844–1898), who wrote about the social life of his island in his novel, *Baní or Engracia and Antoñita*, but with a syrupy sentimentality. He was a poet and dramatist, but it is his pages on local customs that have interest for us today. It is in the historical novel, however, that we find the greatest Dominican figure.

MANUEL DE JESÚS GALVÁN (Dominican Republic, 1834–1910) novelized history in *Enriquillo*. He had been educated in the tradition of academic classicism and his cultural limits were Jovellanos and Quintana, Scott and Chateaubriand. In evoking the Spanish colony of Santo Domingo (1502–1533) Galván subjected the march of his novel to norms of historical accuracy; he sacrified the artistic value of the narrative each time he had to choose between his imagination and his documentation. Even in those cases where he found no documents, instead of inventing, he interrupted the narrative. He substantiated historical truth on original documents, even to the point of transcribing entire pages of Las Casas and of explaining episodes with lessons in history. It is amazing that Galván should have succeeded in achieving a novel of such literary quality, in spite of the difficulties of his complicated historical theme and of his academic method. The Indian had become extinct in Santo Domingo as a consequence of Spanish political action, so that the Dominicans, standing up to Spain, invoked the Indian as a symbol of the spirit of liberty. National restoration motivated the support of indigenous elements. Galván, in the midst of this flowering—José Joaquín Pérez had just published *Indigenous Fantasies* (*Fantasías indígenas*, 1877)—began his novel by also idealizing the Indians. The first part of *Enriquillo* was published in 1878, the completed edition in 1882. However, although Galván feels the pull of the romantic sympathy for the Indian, he does not allow himself to be dominated by it. He notifies us explicitly that he is on the side of European civilization: "We beg the reader to believe that we are not attached to the Indiophilic mania. We shall never overpass the limits of just compassion . . ." There is, then, a difference in attitude between Galván and the other indigenist writers of his time. Father Las Casas became the doctrinal axis of Galván's novel; his writings were followed to the letter, at times textually. But Galván did not interpret Las Casas' preachings as proof of the moral turpitude of Spain, but as a noble example offered to the world by Spain. After all, Las Casas was a Spaniard; and the strength of his invectives redeems Spain. Galván called his novel a "legend." A romantic title. But his prose, rather than resembling that of other writers of "legends," such as the romantics Zorrilla and Bécquer, resembles that of the neoclassicists Jovellanos and Quintana. This is why the dominant framework of the novel *Enriquillo* consists of a logical, clear, ample, serene style of writing, with a minimum of regionalist and indigenist idioms and a reluctance to abandon the norms of "good taste." Nevertheless, typically romantic embroideries abound on this classical canvas. Above all, embellishments on the theme of love: impossible loves like that of Grijalva and María de Cuéllar who both die of sadness, and the constantly interrupted idyl of Enriquillo and Mencía. In these pages the readers of 1880 must have found new stimuli for the emotions engendered by previous romantics. And, as in all romantic literature, they must have felt the contrast in Valenzuela's lustful outrage of Mencía's honor. These contrasts of romantic mores between heroes and villains that Galván loves to etch until he succeeds in portraying Pedro de Mojica are perhaps the best study of perversity in all Hispanic-American romanticism.

Another romantic touch was the animation of Nature as a confidant of human passions. Also romantic was the heroic ideal —liberty or death—which appears with typical emphasis; living for fame and posterity; the technique of weaving the threads of the action into a plot rich in coincidences, disguises, sudden sentimental outbursts, rendezvous at night, with repentances and final atonements. The characters live original lives, with the exception of Las Casas. This is understandable; Las Casas is not a novelistic personage but a dedicated historical figure, and Galván preferred to show his known characteristics, without re-creating him imaginatively. Enriquillo, on the other hand, lent himself to unrestricted psychological elaboration. He is not a symbolic hero but a mestizo of flesh and blood and soul. We see him in his youth, grieved by his orphanhood, respectful toward the Spaniards who are rearing him, always compassionate with the maltreated Indians. He tolerates jokes and even impertinences because he sees the good side of things. As he grows, his idea of justice grows within him, and once, upon seeing the Spaniards beat the Indians with rods, he feels the first throb of a new calling: to defend those of his race. We see how Enriquillo becomes increasingly understanding by looking within himself. The evil of others sharpens the consciousness of his own virtue and of his duties as an Indian; a few steps more and Enriquillo discovers that "death is preferable to the humiliation of the soul." This discovery humbles him: he knows that the great tests will begin now precisely because he has discovered his moral law; now he believes only in rebellion, and he rebels. Even in minor characters, Galván indicates subtle psychological changes. The life that Galván was able to infuse into his characters is so great that the dialogs acquire a real dramatic quality.

In Puerto Rico the Spaniard MANUEL FERNÁNDEZ JUNCOS (1846–1928) gave us descriptions and reports of the island that are full of elementary realism.

(iii) *Venezuela* / EDUARDO BLANCO (b. 1838), JULIO CALCAÑO (1840–1919), JOSÉ MARÍA MANRIQUE (1846–1907), were historical narrators.

(iv) *Colombia* / JORGE ISAACS (Colombia, 1837–1895) was born exactly one hundred years after Bernardin de Saint-Pierre; but his *María* (1867) belongs to that literary family that was founded by the novel *Paul et Virginie* at the end of the eighteenth century. In *Paul et Virginie*, Saint-Pierre had created the idyl of innocent creatures who, in the midst of a nature equally innocent, love each other with a love that death will seal with absolute purity. Years later Chateaubriand, with that same sentimental tendency to idealize love and to discover a new geography, wrote *Atala:* again the purity of first love, now in the lonely regions of the forests of America, between two youths whom death consecrates as virgins. So in writing "that dialog of immortal love impelled by hope and interrupted by death," Isaacs was following an erotic star that once before had led an entire caravan. But it was Chateaubriand who taught Isaacs to orchestrate his vague eroticism esthetically. For this reason, when Efraín reads the novel *Atala* to María, he records very significantly that María "was as beautiful as the creation of the poet, and I loved her with the love he had imagined." Even more—the reading of Chateaubriand heralds for Efraín and María the sad denouement of the idyl they are living, as if *Atala*, in a subtle way, were the libretto of a drama that they are performing. As he "Chateaubriandized," there was one thing that Isaacs felt sure about—his vision of the scene. Chateaubriand had written about an ideal America; Isaacs describes a concrete America in which he loved, worked, and struggled. For a Frenchman, the American setting of *Atala* was exotic; for Isaacs that America was his own land. Consequently, *María* has a national significance that is lacking in *Atala*. In *María* the colorful image of our American life is given back to us—Americanism, not exoticism. But exoticism was such a typically romantic trait that Isaacs refused to renounce it and hence gave us the story of Nay and Sinar in an African setting. Africa was for Isaacs what America was for Chateaubriand. Isaacs' descriptions were not realist: he looked upon the landscape with eyes already accustomed to the romantic mode. Just enjoying nature was, in itself, a romantic disposition. Isaacs knew, therefore, that the landscape was a great literary theme. And he developed it as a mood, in the romantic manner. "If happiness caresses us," says Efraín, "nature smiles upon us." Contrasted with the garden landscape where María strolls, Isaacs describes nature without María as disarrayed, terrible, foe-like. Paradise and purgatory. When the novel of hell, of the green hell of the jungle, emerges in America later, men are esthetically worth less than the serpents.

Another of the discoveries of romanticism that influenced Isaacs was local color. When Isaacs began writing, all Colombians, some more, some less, were writing or reading recollections of city, country, and family life. Isaacs succumbed to the vogue. But sketches of customs, which are apt to have a bitter flavor when they appear in detached articles, take on a sentimental prestige that sweetens them when they are incorporated in novels. In *María*, even mocking touches are affectionate. The novel is weakened somewhat by these dissonances between the idyllic notes and the notes on customs.

Yet, there are compensating and appealing scenes in the evocation of José's highland farm, the tiger hunt, the loves of the young girls, Tránsito's wedding and Feliciana's burial and, above all, the rustic picture of delicious Salomé, painted in the center like a mulatto nymph, innocent, playful, and sensual. This happy feudal society in which masters, peons, and slaves live together without sordidness is as idealized as the loves of the two young masters. The romantics had falsified the idea of man; and Isaacs describes the feelings of María and Efraín in the false fog of these notions. María was born as an abstraction, but the sincerity of the author was humanizing her. This María was a lyrical synthesis of Isaacs' love experiences, the ideal of his early years, the imaginative focal point where that great diffused light of real remembrances and longings would be concentrated. Although Isaacs pushed his eroticism to the point of molding it into the literary category of the woman-seraphim, he had more than enough rich amatory experience—experience that was real, diversified, concrete in its details —to save his idyl.

He liked women and knew how to create distinctive types. It is obvious that he felt a strong attraction toward all the women of the Cauca. Isaacs invested Efraín with his own virility. In spite of the delicacy of his love, Efraín is fully aroused by all of María's little exposures of flesh and completely alert to them. María also feels an attraction for Efraín. It is not always literature that unites them, but love. If Efraín's arm brushes against her body, a blush reddens her face. Kisses flutter timidly, without ever alighting, but always seeking each other. The idyl between María and Efraín repeated old vignettes, but the sincerity of tenderness created the miracle of such fresh expression that it seemed original. The rites of an amorous fetishism—the exchanging of flowers, of locks of hair—the coquettishness and innocence with which María hides or abandons her hand to the caresses of Efraín, the using of the child John as a household cupid, the landscape as confidant, the pre-enjoyment of sadness while enjoying happiness are moments sincerely lived, sincerely expressed. The first letter that María writes to Efraín is so authentic that one is surprised to find it in a book; and the last pages are to be remembered always as among the best in the Spanish literature of its time. The stream of poetry that runs through the work is not continuous, but it lasts long enough to have a place in the history of our artistic prose. On the other hand, in his verses which treat of narratives, remembrances of childhood, patriotic songs, moral reflections, and landscapes, a profound lyric vision very seldom appears.

Before writing his novel, *Transit* (*Tránsito*), LUIS SEGUNDO DE SILVESTRE (1838–1887) had evidently been in transit through Isaac's *María*. Among the historical novelists we list: FELIPE PÉREZ (1836–1891), MARCO ANTONIO JARAMILLO (1849–1904), JESÚS SILVESTRE ROZO (1835–1895), FRANCISCO DE PAULA CORTES (b. 1850), TEMÍSTOCLES AVELLA MENDOZA (1841–1914), CONSTANCIO.FRANCO VARGAS (1842).

(v) *Peru* / RICARDO PALMA (1833–1919) was the great figure of lagging Peruvian romanticism. He wrote dramas in verse which he condemned later as "abominable monstrosities" and many verses (four volumes) which he called, with manifest disinterest, "rhymed lines." In the entertaining, confidential notes of *The Bohemian Life of My Time* (*La bohemia di mi tiempo*, 1887) Palma tells of the romantic literary excesses of the years 1848 to 1860. Disappointed and mocking, Palma withdrew from romanticism; but only after he had lit one of his torches there to illumine romantically the Peruvian past. The romantic sympathy for the past took possession of certain literary genres. A born narrator, Palma must have felt the attraction of all of them: the historical novel, the sketch of customs, the legend, the short story. He did not submit to any of them, but taking a little from here and a little from there, he created his own genre—the "tradition." Already in 1852 he was writing stories on traditions; ten years later these "traditions" were taking on definitive character and, from 1872, the long series of *Peruvian Traditions* (*Tradiciones peruanas*), in perfect form, were published. From 1872 to 1883 there were six series which were followed by others with different titles: *Old Clothing* (*Ropa vieja*, 1889); *Moth-eaten Clothing* (*Ropa apolillada*, 1891); *Knick-knacks and Traditions and Historical Articles* (*Cachivaches y Tradiciones y artículos históricos*, 1899–1900); *Appendix to My Latest Traditions* (*Apéndice a mis últimas tradiciones*) already in print in 1911. (We have read the manuscript of "Off-Color Sauce" ["*Tradiciones en salsa verde*," 1901], still unprinted, and scarcely printable because of its pornography.) With the years, Palma became aware of his originality and recorded the formula for his invention in several places: in his letter to Pastor S. Obligado, in the prolog to Clorinda Matto de Turner's *Traditions*, in the introduction to his *Old Clothing*, in the frequent allusions to his theory and to the method of the traditionalist, diffused in the *Traditions* themselves. From these we extract one: "A dash or two of lies, and an equal dose of truth, no matter how infinitesimal or homeopathic it may be, a good deal of nicety and polish in the language, and there you have the recipe for writing Traditions . . ." The socio-geographical-historical-psychological tapestry he offers us in his *Traditions* is quite extensive: from the beggar to the viceroy; from Tucumán to Guayaquil; from the time of the Incas to contemporary events in which Palma himself had a role; from the idiot to the genius.

But in the center of the tapestry, and woven with a fine thread, is the resourceful viceregal society of eighteenth-century Lima. The sources are numberless and at times unrecognizable: edited and unedited chronicles, histories, lives of saints, books on travel, pasquinades, wills and testaments, tales by missionaries, convent registries, verses, and, in addition to the written word, the oral one of the proverb, the cliché, the couplet, superstition, legend, popular stories. The structure of *Traditions* is also complex. The combination of historical documentation and narrative action is unmethodical, shifting, free. At times there is no structure at all; the events erode and smother the narrative. Or, in one tradition, there are many other minor traditions inserted one within the other. The granary of plots, situations, and interesting characters is so abundant that a whole family of short story writers could feed there. One sentence might be the kernel of a possible story. Even Palma's spirit unfolds on two planes. He was in Herderian sympathy with the voices of the people, but also indulged in Voltairian mockery of them. But the person who influenced his humor was not so much Voltaire as Balzac and his *Contes drolatiques*. He has the multiplicity of perspectives of the bantering skeptic, and even his protestations of impartiality—"I don't subtract or add anything"—are ironic needlings at the absolutism of Church and State.

He was a liberal, and only took seriously the right to a free conscience, and the sovereignty of the people and the moral values of goodness, honor, and justice. His dominant tone is one of mischievous, picaresque jesting. He even keeps a smile on his lips when he relates the poetic miracle of "The Scorpion of Friar Gómez" (*"El alacrán de Fray Gómez"*) or the dramatic sacrifice of "Mother Love" (*"Amor de madre"*). This latter "tradition," one of his best, aroused the enthusiasm of Benito Perez Galdós so much that, according to what he tells in a letter, it gave him the desire to write a drama "like *El abuelo*." Nevertheless, because of that semi-mocking, semi-compassionate smile of Palma's, "Mother Love" would be more suitable to the grotesque theater of the Italians Chiarelli and Pirandello than to drama in the manner of Galdós. The Palma vein is tragi-comic farce, not tragedy. Despite his carelessness, he was a good narrator. He knew how to keep us waiting for the denouement. There is not a single virtue of the short story writer that Palma did not have. He presented his characters gracefully, especially the women; he selected strange conflicts, tangled them, and then untangled them. But there is not quite a single "tradition" that is really a short story. His joy at being an antiquarian causes him to collect facts; and to make room for them, he interrupts, deviates, and constantly alters the course of the story. His handling of historical facts keeps his hands so occupied that he cannot give the action that final tweak for a surprising wind-up. He is attracted not only by the action, but also by the historical atmosphere in which it occurs; and that atmosphere is composed of particles of archival dust. The facts float in the air, loosely and wildly. As with Montalvo, Palma's prose is something of a linguistic museum in which words and tropes are squeezed into the smallest spaces. However, in contrast to Montalvo, Palma's language is more American and more colloquial. In this instance Palma, who as a member of the Peruvian Academy, corresponding to the Spanish Academy, had worked in lexicography, responded to a linguistic theory: that the vocabulary is enriched by allowing free entry to Americanisms, archaisms, neologisms, cultured and popular words; but that one must conform to the syntax studiously and zealously. In *Traditions* the oral and written language, the Spanish and Hispanic-American language, the popular and cultured language constantly interchange thrusts, movements, cadences, words, and syntax. Since these undulating ideals of expression had joined, separated, and then joined again in literary history, even Palma's artistry has a good deal of the colloquial, and in turn, his manner of conversing, a good deal of literature. On the whole, his prose is enchanting for the way it vitalizes hackneyed expressions and raises popular expressions to the category of artistic monuments.

MERCEDES CABELLO DE CARBONERA (1845–1909) sought a formula for a novel that would surpass both romanticism, which was incapable of seeing the real world, and naturalism, which was incapable of entertaining sympathy for human feelings. She found it in realistic novels (influenced by the scientism that had attracted Zola) which vigorously analyzed the decadence of Peruvian society. Her best novels are: *Blanca Sol*, in which she created a convincing character, a haughty lady of Lima, who is blinded by the false lights of luxury and descends indolently and voluntarily at the same time from lover to lover until she reaches the depths of degradation in the company of loose women; and *The Conspirator* (*El conspirador*), in which she abandons the perspective of the omniscient author and speaks through her protagonist, a political leader, whose monologs also reveal the decadence of the era from within.

(vi) *Bolivia* / SANTIAGO VACA GUZMÁN (1847–1896), whose best novel, *His Excellence and His Worship* (*Su excelencia y su Ilustrísima*, 1889), not only records, historically, the enmity between the governor and the bishop in sixteenth-century Paraguay, but also, philologically, resorts to the prose of that epoch. Other novels by Vaca Guzmán: *Bitter Days* (*Días amargos,* 1886), a "psychological analysis of the neurosis of the suicide," and *Without Hope* (*Sin esperanza,* 1891), a case of conflict of conscience in a man of the church who has an earthly love, a more violent conflict than the one in its possible model, *Jocelyn* by Lamartine. The best novelizer of history in Bolivia, and one of the best in all Hispanic-America, was NATANIEL AGUIRRE (1843–1888), whose novel *Juan de la Rosa* (1885) evokes episodes of the history of Cochabamba between 1810 and 1812. The subtitle reads: "Memoirs of the Last Soldier of the Independence." In reality the narrator is relating his childhood, so that the struggles for independence appear as seen through the eyes of a twelve-year-old. Since Aguirre's object seems to have been to fill in the missing knowledge about the heroic resistance of Cochabamba against Goyeneche, he stuffs the story with didactic pages and puts excessively conventional discourses in the mouths of his characters. As a novel, it strikes false notes. Aguirre writes an adorned, academic, and careful prose. But he composes carelessly. Some of his techniques of composition are those of the romantic or serial novel; for example, the mystery of the identity of the narrator's father, the contrasts between villainy and virtue, the beauty of the women. Aguirre's liberalism and patriotism are obvious; still, in *Juan de la Rosa* there is not a vivid description of the Bolivian people. The Indians are scarcely pointed out in the distance, although in the most sentimental passages one always hears the singing of the *yarvíes* and *huaiños*. Another Bolivian historical novelist: MARIANO RICARDO TERRAZAS (1833?): *Mysteries of the Heart* (*Misterios del corazón,* 1869).

(vii) *Chile* / Chilean themes, similar to those of Blest Gana with even more love incidents and with the same recognition of the power of money, tempted other novelists. None of them bested the master. ADOLFO VALDERRAMA (1834–1902) wrote about an ill-fated love in the provinces in his epistolary novel *María.* ZOROBABEL RODRÍGUEZ (1839–1901), in a prose that revealed his study of the Spaniards and his pleasure in words for their own sake, depicted landscapes and love scenes in *The Cave of Mad Eustaquio* (*La cueva del loco Eustaquio,* 1863). VALENTÍN MURILLO (1841?) wrote *The Straw Hat* (*El sombrero de paja,* 1887). MOISÉS VARGAS (1843–1898) wove scenes of local customs into *Episodes of Christmas Eve* (*Lances de Noche Buena,* 1865). ENRIQUE DEL SOLAR (1844–1893) wrote *Legends and Traditions* (*Leyendas y tradiciones*), less novelistic, but superior to his novel *Two Brothers* (*Dos hermanos*). Only one author rose above the surface of such a mediocre level: VICENTE GREZ (Chile, 1847–1909), who was also a poet and dramatist. Of all his novels, *A Wife's Ideal* (*El ideal de una esposa,* 1887) is notable for the analysis of the jealous passions of a married woman. This novel not only introduced a new theme that surprised readers not accustomed to such intensity in a woman's hatred as that displayed by Faustina, but it also presented a true-to-life psychological analysis. LIBORIO E. BRIEBA (1841–1897) distinguished himself in the serial novel. He found a lode in the episodes that followed the disaster of Rancagua in

1814, that is, the government of the reconquest and later the liberation of Chile by the army of the Andes. *The Talaveras Family* (*Los Talaveras,* 1871) was the beginning of a long cycle. While presenting the abhorrent phalanx of the fanatic ex-monk who served Spain, Brieba instilled moral and patriotic lessons. Another serialist was RAMÓN PACHECO (1845), who exaggerated the anticlerical sentiment of the epoch in *The Jesuit Underground* (*El subterráneo de los jesuitas*, 1878).

(viii) *Uruguay* / EDUARDO ACEVEDO DÍAZ (1851–1921) novelized the independence and the civil wars in *Ismael* (1888), *Nativa* (1890), *Cry of Glory* (*Grito de gloria*, 1893) and *Lance and Sabre* (*Lanza y sable*, 1914). The first three form a triptych and place Acevedo Díaz among the most energetic novelists of America. Of this triptych of novels, the first is the principal one, still romantic in its heroic and mythical exaltation of the gaucho formation of the country, but written with powerful, observant, realist art. Life in the city, and above all, in the midst of nature, the sufferings, the violence and the aspirations of an unpolished people, the onslaught with which men act on reality and create history, the colorful customs, the highlights of the soul, carry Acevedo Díaz' mark of narrative ability. *Ismael* takes place in the time of Artigas, from the preparations of the Creole uprising against the Spaniards to the battle of Las Piedras and the expulsion of the patriotic friars from Montevideo in 1811; *Nativa* skips the period that goes from Artigas' rise to his fall and brings us to a minor episode during the Brazilian domination in 1824; in *Cry of Glory* he tells of the liberating crusade of the *Treinta y Tres Orientales* up to the gaucho battle of Sarandí in 1825. *Lance and Sabre* is not linked with the others, but it completes the historical picture with the first civil wars. He wrote other novels: *Solitude* (*Soledad*) is the one with the most literary value, the one with the best prose, the one most in tune with the artistic tendencies of the European novel of his day.

(ix) *Argentina* / There was a group of prose writers who knew, and some of them practised, at least two of the current French styles: Parnassianism and naturalism. This was the "men of '80" group in Argentina. They had the air of dilettantes, as if intellectual curiosity were a luxury. They were generally distinguished for their fragmentary, sundry, opinionated prose. They also contributed to the more imaginative genres: the novel, the short story, the drama, and poetry. SANTIAGO ESTRADA (1841–1891), although his talent was that of chronicler and critic, wrote several "fantasies" with poetic intent. LUCIO VICENTE LÓPEZ (1848–1894), author of various titillating stories in the manner of Daudet or Dickens, left in *The Great Village* (*La gran aldea*, 1884) a novelistic description of "Buenos Aires customs." Badly constructed, carelessly styled, it nevertheless has a certain enchantment because during the twenty years in which the action occurs the Argentinian capital had grown and changed dizzily, and López was its best chronicler. MIGUEL CANÉ (1851–1905) defined his own literature in the titles of his books: *Light Prose* (*Prosa ligera*), *Literary Chats* (*Charlas literarias*), *Notes and Impressions* (*Notas e impresiones*). Capriciously he lighted on many themes with agile intelligence, and his entertaining autobiography, *Juvenilia* (1884), is noteworthy precisely because it is the record of life in a boarding school, suffered and enjoyed by an intelligent lad. He had a deep romantic fund of pessimism, sadness, egocentrism, desires for adventure, and preoccupations with time. EDUARDO WILDE (1844–1913) gave a finer expression to the ironic, humorous attitude of the "men of '80." His intellectual work is so abundant and his jocular tone is so persistent that the more fantastic, imaginative, intuitive portion of his work—his stories, poematic prose, and autobiographical pages—are overshadowed. He was an improviser; and defects in style are more annoying in him than in his contemporaries, because in Wilde they interrupt an admirable capacity for original phrasing. He had a rare sensibility and knew how to express it in images so audacious for his time that they remind us of the influence the Parnassians were exerting in Buenos Aires in the decade of the eighties. Read in *Prometheus and Co.* (*Prometeo y Cía.*) the stories: "The Rain" ("*La iluvia*"), "Tini," "The First Night in the Cemetery" ("*La primera noche del cementerio*") and you will discover the potentiality of a great writer. His autobiography *Downstream* (*Aguas abajo*) with its recollections of his childhood in Bolivia where he was born, is one of the most delightful of that generation of Argentinian autobiographers. Ironically enough, the best of all these Gallicized Argentinian writers was a Frenchman: PAUL GROUSSAC (1848–1929). He had come to Argentina when he was eighteen, and there learned Spanish, which he used admirably. He was a teacher of critical severity, of disciplined study, of intellectual sternness. From 1880 Buenos Aires was reading poems and stories of the French Parnassians; furthermore, these Parnassian writers—Banville, Mendès, Silvestre, Coppée, France—were contributing directly to Buenos Aires newspapers. And Paul Groussac was one of the first to study them in America. In a series of articles, "*Medallions*" ("*Medallones*," 1884) he commented on the work of Leconte de Lisle. Other Argentinians were also doing so—Domingo Martino, Martín García Merou—but since they are younger we shall refer to them later. Although one can find in Groussac an occasional touch of Parnassian beauty, he sought in the novel—*Forbidden Fruit* (*Fruto vedado*) —in short stories—*Argentinian Tales* (*Relatos argentinos*)—and in the drama—*The Crimson Banner* (*La divisa punzó*)—a vigorous, human, and personal form of expression. He was not a "modernist"; yet Rubén Darío was later to recognize him as one of his masters of "modernist" prose. When Groussac published *Forbidden Fruit* (1884) he had lived in Argentina for eighteen years, which was precisely his age when he arrived in Argentina; and because he wanted to master Spanish, although the Argentinians of his generation were slipping into French, he, a Frenchman, developed a purer, more Hispanic, more correct prose than the native Argentinians. His novel is divided into two parts. The first in Buenos Aires, in the northern country, and in Tucumán; the second, aboard ship, with a stopover in Rio de Janeiro, and the finale in Paris. It is an autobiographical story of an adulterous love affair. Marcel Renault, the protagonist, repeats some of the real-life events of Groussac himself. And he put forth the psychological problem of double nationality. Groussac also showed a preference for complicated psychological cases in his *Argentinian Tales* (*Relatos argentinos*). As the title indicates, the stories are Argentine in locale, at times in the nationality of their protagonists and in the situations in which they are involved. But the psychological analysis makes European stories out of them in the sense that it reveals depths and intricacies that Argentine literature of that time did not usually have. The Frenchman Groussac put his Europeanism to the service of Argentine themes. The best story is "Number 9090," more of a novel than a short story because the psychological analysis of Daniel de Kergoet's conscientious scruples dominates the situation of the story which is about the changing of one lottery ticket for another. *The Crimson Banner* (1923) is a drama in three acts with Rosas and his daughter as the key characters. At the end Manuelita sacrifices her love for Thomson and remains with her father, who needs her and takes advantage of her. The contrast between Rosas and Manuelita is adroit: Rosas is barbaric, intuitive, cunning, crafty, energetic; and Manuelita the incarnation of nobleness, docility, pride, and tenderness. Groussac does not intervene in the work; he does not take sides. He is a dramatist who can be impersonal himself to create persons.

The most talented novelist of this Argentinian group was EU-GENIO CAMBACÉRÈS (1843–1888). Like many of his colleagues —Cané, Wilde, López—he was a man of the world, of vast reading knowledge (especially in French), a skeptic, scoffer, conservative, with all of the refinement that his trip to Paris and the leisure of the aristocratic clubs of Buenos Aires offered him; and together with this, he enjoyed the direct experience of country life. In demure circles, his four novels caused as many scandals; and it seems that at his death he left a fifth novel unpublished, which his wife hastened to burn at the behest of her father confessor. They were naturalist novels, in the manner of Zola. Nevertheless, Cambacérès was not overpowered by his model; he profited from Zola not so much from the technique of the experimental novel, as from the example that it was legitimate in art to unveil the sordid conditions of human life. Candid, intelligent, free, agnostic, daring, he had no illusions about how little man matters. His moral sense— shown in the cynical and brutal behavior of his principal characters—challenged the conventional lies of society, but with a tired, grumbling gesture he dropped his arms, recognizing that the power of nature lowers us to the level of animals. With bitterness, almost in anger, he describes human indignities. And to make them more painful, he chooses wickedness, sickness, corruption, vice, adultery, failure, death. The repugnant description of Paul's syphilis, in *Sentimental Music* (*Música sentimental*), was a proof that the novelist was not willing to let himself be frightened by bad taste; and, in fact, his vigorous naturalism subjects us to sexual scenes that were new to our literature. Its theme is not love; it is the tedium that comes after the orgasm. Not only was he truculent in his novelistic situations; his prose itself violently assaulted the reader: his was the graphic, evocative, conversational language of Buenos Aires where Creole idioms, Italian and French expressions, and metaphoric innovations are thrown together as in a gutter. *Without Direction* (*Sin rumbo*), his best novel, documents the complexity of the Argentinian reality of those years: there are shacks where the red paint of Rosas' epoch could still be seen; there is an old man who fought against Rosas; there are contrasts between the refinement, the culture, the art, the gay adventures, the nightclub life in the capital, and the hard country labor in the province of Buenos Aires. The character Andrés is one of the best delineated psychological studies in the Argentine novel.

In the field of the historical novel we have EDUARDA MANSILLA DE GARCÍA (1838–1892).

2. Essay

Some of the poets and narrators we have presented were also distinguished men of thought. Now we shall give special attention to those who preferred to express themselves in the various media of the essay, the treatise, the study, the chronicle. Sometimes all the essays of an author bear the unique stamp of great artistic quality (Montalvo, for example). However, sometimes there are writers whose literature and thought have other key values. These men are more thinkers than artists. Since we seek esthetic values, it will not be surprising that, even among these, the more serious thinkers, we should wish to dwell on the literary aspect of their work (Sierra, Varona, Hostos, Gonzáles Prada).

JUSTO SIERRA (Mexico, 1848–1912), a disciple of Altamirano, became, in his turn, a teacher. Such is history, a relay of torches passed from generation to generation. Sierra was, above all, a maker of men, and today his written work is of less importance than his tutelage. He labors as an historian, essayist, educator, orator, politician, storyteller, poet. Here we look at his minor side: that of the man of letters. Minor because it did not grow in proportion with his public stature; he did not attain the full stature of

a master. He went into letters drawn by romantic voices, the robust one of Victor Hugo, the muted one of Musset, and from
Spain, the intimate voice of Bécquer. His poetry, collected posthumously, his gracefulness, freshness, elegance, and it is not uncommon that some of it (*"Playeras,"* for example) is judged as
anticipating Modernism; there is also (in "The Bucolic Funeral"
[*"El funeral bucólico"*], for example) the perfect art of picking
up classical themes and inviting them to walk down the avenue of
fashion. Justo Sierra's poetry became prose in the double sense
that, for one, it fell into prosaic forms and, secondly, it rose toward
the Bécquer-like *Romantic Stories* (*Cuento románticos*) collected
in 1896. He knew European literature: the French Parnassians,
D'Annunzio, Nietzsche. And he approached the new Hispanic-
American poets with a greeting of sympathy and recognition. His
prolog to the poetry of Gutiérrez Nájera is a landmark in our literary criticism. At the same time, it is luxuriant prose, imaginative,
lyrical, and charming. He did not always write in this fashion. He
was not an esthete, but a servant of practical programs and ideas
akin to "positivism."

Of the two major Cuban figures of the last third of the nineteenth century, MANUEL SANGUILY (1848–1925) and Varona, we
shall dwell only on the latter. As a thinker ENRIQUE JOSÉ VARONA
(1849–1933) felt comfortable astride French positivism and English empiricism. Although bound by the dominant ideas of the
nineteenth century, the fact that Varona was skeptical about the
welfare achieved by man, and yet energetically directed his own
conduct toward superior moral values, gives a personal tone to his
philosophy. Basically, he was confident that man, when he let himself be carried away by the illusion of liberty, could better the
world. It was an illusion of liberty, because Varona was a determi-
nist, an agnostic inclined toward the sciences; and man appeared
to him as a creature capable of redeeming himself within the evolution of nature. Cuba had had its philosophic careerists: Félix
Varela, José de la Luz y Caballero, José Manuel Mestre; but
Varona was the first Cuban to convert philosophy into rigorous
discipline. Nevertheless, he was more successful in his fragmentary reflections than in his systematic works, such as the three

volumes of *Philosophic Lectures* (*Conferencias filosóficas*), for example. The aphorism is the best vehicle for a relativist. And those in *Linked Aphorism* (*Con el eslabón*) offer pages of great penetration and beauty. His brief essays, collected in *From My Belvedere* (*Desde mi Belvedere*) and *Violets and Nettles* (*Violetas y ortigas*, 1917), must count among the best in our literature. One could extract from them integral theories (for example, his relativist esthetic theory), but his charm is in the sprightliness with which he goes from subject to subject. His poetry was youthful. He began with patriotic verses— his "Ode at the Death of Gaspar Betancourt Cisneros" (*"Oda a la muerte de Gaspar Betancourt Cisneros"*) is of 1867—and ended the bulk of his poetic activity with *Poems* (*Poesías*, 1878) and *Cuban Landscapes and Narrations in Verse* (*Paisajes cubanos y narraciones en verso*, 1879). He was a prosaic poet, with the prosaic quality of Campoamor, although "Wings" (*"Alas"*) and "Berceuse" show such a restlessness for wandering, for achieving impossible perspectives, for yearning to be something else, and for living away yonder where one dreams, that they are equivalent to poetry. "Wings" belongs to his *Poems* and "Berceuse" to *Of My Recollections* (*De mis recuerdos*) which he published in 1919 under the pseudonym of Luis del Valle. It was a theme he felt intensely, and it would reappear in *Little Poems in Prose* (*Poemetas en prosa*, 1921). He valued the Parnassians and the symbolists; but he referred to the "Modernists," and also to the "futurists" and "cubists" who came after him, with irony because, in his opinion, "they go about wishing to say what they never finish saying."

Among the writers of essays and treatises in Puerto Rico— CAYETANO COLL Y TOSTE, 1850–1930, and SALVADOR BRAU, 1842–1912—one stands at the peak: EUGENIO MARÍA DE HOSTOS (Puerto Rico, 1839–1903). Similar to other civilizers that we have mentioned and will mention, Hostos preferred action to art. In his concern for his conduct, he was careless with his literature. We cannot grant him the same place in literary history that he would deserve in a gallery of great American teachers. He differs from Bello, Sarmiento, Montalvo, Varona, González Prada, Martí —all builders of nations—in that he came to abhor his literary vocation and renounced it. In *Social Morals* (*Moral social*, 1888), his most important work, he wrote three chapters against literature. He used to say that he disdained it in the name of morality and logic. His attitude is strangely incomprehensive, narrow, and dogmatic. Is there in his rancor against novels, dramas, and even poetry, a wounded vanity, a feeling of failure, the haughtiness of an apostate? In his youth, Hostos had ambitions of literary glory; except that a "crisis of character"—to use his own words—came to enrich his life through generous struggle and to impoverish his pen through didactic functions. In Spain, where he was to live from 1851 to 1869, he wrote brief lyrical tales, prose ballads that followed the fashion that imitated Hoffmann, Gessner, Ossian. And above all, he produced a poetic novel, *The Peregrination of Bayoán* (*La peregrinación de Bayoán*, 1863). Considering its merits in style, imagination, and sincerity, it is really lamentable that Hostos did not persist in this genre. It is a strange novel. According to one of its first readers, the Spanish novelist Nombela, the style was "absolutely new" in Hispanic letters; and, in truth, it was not the current prose. In the prolog to the second edition of 1873, Hostos tells us of the process of its creation, the circumstances in which he composed it, and his moral and political intentions. One need not dwell, however, on what Hostos says: in 1873 he considered that "letters are the vocation of the indolent or of those who have already finished their life's labor," and he exaggerated the value of *The Peregrination of Bayoán* as a doctrinaire work that combated Spanish despotism in the Antilles. Undoubtedly, it contains some serious thinking: the liberty of his fatherland, the unity of Puerto Rico, Cuba, the Dominican Republic, and Haiti, duty before happiness, the claims of justice and truth. But the message is diluted in an intimate diary of extraordinary lyricism, because that is what *The Peregrination of Bayoán* is, an intimate diary. Unfortunately, its didactic purpose, the allegories, and the novelistic episodes cripple the artistic quality of this intimate diary. It is the diary of Bayoán; and Hostos, who appears as the editor of these intimate pages, reconstructs the novelistic action when the diary is interrupted, and even intervenes in the plot. All of the characters have symbolic names: Bayoán is the name of the first aborigine of Borinquen, that is, of Puerto Rico, who doubted the immortality of the Spaniards; Darién, the loved woman, is the indigenous name of the most beautiful region of Cuba; her father Guarionex bears the name of a powerful Haitian chieftain at the time Columbus reached the island. And Hostos informs us that the three characters "represent in this book the union of the three great Antilles." The value of *The Peregrination of Bayoán* lies, in spite of the author, in his poetic vision of the landscape and of life, and in the new aspects of his prose. His outlook was typically romantic. To suggest sources, if necessary, those that would have gratified Hostos might be Goethe (*Werther*), Foscolo (*Jacopo Ortis*), Byron (*Childe Harold*). Many of the situations in the novel (Darién's illness and death), many of the themes (solitude, exile, dolorous love, the titanism of the hero who challenges his times, the feeling for nature), many of the procedures (emotions, characters, and deeds drawn in clear-cut contrasts of black and white) are of the romantic school.

But Hostos is original because, through self-contemplation, he discovered very personal nuances in the depths of his soul. From these depths, touched thus by the spirit, there arose impetuously an exclamatory, throbbing, vivid, voluptuous, passionate, variegated, morbid, rich, and imaginative style. It does not succeed as a novel: it is foggy in its symbols, broken in its narrative, out of proportion, in any case. It would have been better if *The Peregrination* had presented Hostos' intimate diary in all its starkness. But some pages undoubtedly have a vigorous brilliance. He never wrote like that again. It is strange that Hostos, who was so effusive in *The Peregrination*, so sentimental in the story of his loves, *Inda* (1878), so bland in his *Stories for My Son* (*Cuentos a mi hijo*, 1878), should believe that the most important thing was to be a "logical man." He sacrificed his inner self, which was rich and complex, to a logical activity that did not carry him very far. He was not a philosopher, despite his yearning to be a systematic thinker. He managed to construct an abstract prose, hardened by symmetries and oppositions in the manner of the Krausists and the positivists. But he had no aptitude for theory, and his thought, although noble, had a short radius. His first contacts with philos-

ophy had been his knowledge of Krausism. The influence of the
German Krause on the generation of 1868 in Spain: Sanz de Río,
Salmerón, etc., is now well known. But Hostos followed one of the
currents added to the repertory of ideas of the Spanish Krausists:
positivism, with its trust in reason and the experimental sciences.

In order of merit, the best prosist is JUAN MONTALVO (Ecuador, 1832–1889), one of the best in the Spanish language. A
great many of his works derive from the struggle against the evils
of Ecuador, which are the evils that prevail in our America: anarchy, military bossism, the fanatical desire of the clergy for
power, the ignorance of the masses, despotism, administrative
corruption, rudeness, injustice, poverty. But Montalvo's political
literature does not have the turbulence that could be expected
from such a combative life. He made politics out of literature; and
his literature was made with skillful language. In his preoccupation with language, Montalvo would even become distracted from
the theme upon which he was writing. His interest was not so
much on the ideas, but on the musical and plastic richness of the
language. He thought more with words than with ideas. Although
it was the essay that gave him best results, Montalvo vacillated in
his literary career by writing poetry, short stories, and dramas. He
never valued his own verses. On the contrary, he came to believe
that he had a gift for narrative. He wrote a few short stories that
had unity. They do not have the quality of the illustrative "episodes" (cf., *Seven Treatises—Siete tratados*), of the anecdotes at
the service of his discourses (cf., *Orations Against Catiline—Las
catilinarias*), one of his allegories and parables (cf., *Moral Geometry—Geometría moral*), of the stories on Ossianic poems or
Greek legends, and so on. These pages are more like unrelated
exercises of narrative ability which never developed completely.
What is certain is that Montalvo was not interested in giving accounts of actions, but in delivering discourses. Even in *Chapters
that Cervantes Forgot* (*Capítulos que se le olvidaron a Cervantes*),
which constitute a novel, what can be salvaged are the interpolated
essays, or those put in Cervantes' mouth. In writing the book
Montalvo's attitude was that of the essayist and not that of the
narrator. Instead of telling us about the adventures of Don Quijote,

he substitutes for them essays on insanity as a source of adventure, on the virtue of water, tears, decorum, and poverty, the value of action, his respect for trees. His tale breaks off and disappears. What remains alive and warm in the book are the essay fragments, alien to the environment of Don Quijote. The same can be said of his dramas, which do not exist in themselves, except as vehicles for pieces of discursive prose. And since what we are hearing is the voice of the author-ventriloquist that apparently comes from the mouth of each puppet, stage dialog is not dialog at all, but a monolog in various voices. The poet, the narrator, the dramatist are shadows of the essayist.

The best of Montalvo's literature, then, is his essays. But to point out which are his best is difficult. There are essays which, as brief discursive units, are quite good. Notice, for example, many of those in *The Spectator* (*El espectador*). They are short, simple, effective, agile. But it seems that this type of minimal essay did not satisfy him. He strove for more ample and complicated compositions, opulent architecture, "treatises." Montalvo wrote articles spontaneously, but he considered them of little consequence and regarded them only as elements of larger "works." Thus the miniaturist leaped into the composition of the vast mosaics of his *Seven Treatises*. The more literary airs he put on to capture imaginary readers, the more precious his style became, the more his composition went out of control. He would improve the fragments and cripple the totality. In the *Seven Treatises* there are many moments of brilliance, many rhythms, much wealth of metaphor and aphorism, many techniques, and a great frequency of felicitous poetic devices; but each treatise is not a fluent unit, created from within, but a scaffolding—at times clumsily erected—upon which are placed paintings barely connected to each other. On the other hand, in the short essays of *The Spectator*, these paintings appear in isolation. But his having left them in that state indicates that Montalvo had not much interest in them and did not "work them out" for us artistically; and, in fact, they are simple and wanting in thought and in imagination.

When he looked into his own life, Montalvo generally focused his esthetic eye on experiences that lent themselves to romantic

adornment, on experiences of resentment, displeasure, indignation, horror, hatred, and on experiences stimulated by literature.
Consequently, there is in his prose a principle of differentiation between the modal qualities of the beautiful, the truculent, and the
traditional. When the solitary Montalvo—that Montalvo who is
aware of the exquisiteness of his sensibilities—set out to express
his intimate emotions, he tended to give us a poematic prose.
However, it was a romantic prose, oriented toward the "poem in
prose," approaching the "modernism" of the following generation.
His yearning for solitude, and within that solitude the desire to
enjoy the landscape and his own melancholy, was a retractable,
timid, nervous moment of his soul. Except that that soul did not
find peace in withdrawal: it felt permanently offended by the
world, and at the slightest humiliation, sometimes without any humiliations, it leaped into the arena ready to fight. Just as he found
the esthetic formula for his exquisiteness, which was that of the
poem in prose, he found for his defamation of men and things, for
his fits of tragic, pessimistic, disillusioned or sarcastic humor, the
esthetic formula of the insult. The resentment that burned in his
viscera swirled in the air like smoke until it entered the spotlight
of defamatory literature and became diatribe. In his seclusion as
well as in his exasperation Montalvo took pleasure in remembering glorious scenes and in visualizing himself as a person of fantasy. In this way his experiences were shaped into patterns,
themes, models, ideals, and reminiscences of certain forms of artistic expression that had already been consecrated by history.
When he related anecdotes of his own life, he usually enriched
them with recollections gathered from books; or conversely, he
projected an autobiographical meaning to his bookish recollections. It would be interminable to enumerate the literary traditions
that find a place in many of his pages. The past constantly oozes
from every word. Montalvo's prose is one of the richest in nineteenth-century Spanish.

Perhaps Montalvo's greatest expression of energy, and the most
amazing, is his having invented, in a little corner of America, a
personal language: a language kneaded with the clay of many centuries of literature and kneaded for the love of the language itself.

He had the extraordinary gift for coining phrases, for avoiding the well-trodden path, and for finding marvelous expression, for evoking a reality with the slightest touches of imaginative prose. From this need to twist and complicate his expression, he achieved, with more frequency than his Spanish-speaking contemporaries, stylistic fragments of the first order.

Although he had written verses when he was twenty, MANUEL GONZÁLEZ PRADA (Peru, 1848–1918) did not bulldoze his way completely into literature until after 1880. Until his death he was the most gifted writer of his country, feared and hated by many, surrounded by a few disciples. After his death his stature gradually assumed giant-like proportions: his books continue to win disciples. He broke, violently, not only with the little lies of our civilization, but also with the large ones. He rejected the Spanish absolutist tradition, he denounced the Catholic church for its responsibility for iniquities in the world, he condemned unjust privileges—property, state, military—he ridiculed literary academies and priggish pens, he chastised the optimism of fools, he cursed cowardice and carnality. Our literature had had tremendous polemicists: Sarmiento, Montalvo. But González Prada's protest was even more terrible because it dealt blows not against persons and parties, but against the whole of the ruling order. He was an atheist, an anarchist, a naturalist, a partisan of the Indian and the worker. His only conservative impulse was that of the nationalist: so long as frontiers exist, he used to say, we must hate the enemy who crosses them. This was purely an emotional impulse, if one remembers that the frontiers in Hispanic-America were not definitely fixed and that conflicts were between brothers who spoke the same language. His intellectual makeup had been formed by reading the men of the Enlightenment, some Hegel, Schopenhauer and Nietzsche, a little Guyau and Renan, and a good many, almost all, of the positivists: Comte, Spencer, Darwin, Claude Bernard. He spurned metaphysics and embraced the natural sciences, whose influence is noted in his preference for biological and physical metaphors. He differed from other supporters of science, however, in placing liberty and equality above order and hierarchy, and disputed with positivist sociologists who spoke of the racial inferiority of the Indians and the inevitable failure of the Hispanic-American countries. He ended by exalting anarchist ideology more than the belief in science. In Marx he saw "one of the greatest social agitators of the nineteenth century," but he felt closer to Proudhon, Tolstoy, and Kropotkin. His sincerity became a style of writing; there is not, in these years, either in Spain or America, a prose as sharp and incisive as that of González Prada. He scorned the limp language of the Castelars and the Valeras and, going his own way, he discovered areas in our language that were still erectile. The importance of González Prada in Hispanic-American literature is due more to his prose than to his verse, which does not mean that his verses were bad, but that his prose was the vehicle for what interested him most—critical thought.

His verses are distributed in nine volumes: *Minúsculas* (1901), *Presbiterianas* (1909), *Exóticas* (1911) written between 1869 and 1900. The other volumes are posthumous and include poetry from 1866 to 1918: *Peruvian Ballads* (*Baladas peruanas*), *Graphites* (*Grafitos*), *Ballads* (*Baladas*), *Adoration* (*Adoración*), *Libertarians* (*Libertarias*), and *Fragments of Life* (*Trozos de vida*). In his work we see him changing posture: now González Prada, the thinker, puts his foot forward, now González Prada, the lyricist or the technician of the verse. He believed that poetry should give rhythm to intelligence and images to the communication of knowledge. Part of his poetry was, therefore, intellectual and didactic. *Graphites* are epigrams on man and his activity. *Presbiterianas* is anti-clerical satire. In *Libertarians* the theme is social and political. His own life, sentimental, amorous, intimate, is expressed in *Adoration* and *Fragments of Life*. But just as he renewed ideas in his prose, he renewed forms in his verse. His protestations became lyrical, exalted; his scholarly spirit led him to experiment wth the rhythmic structure of verse. Until the advent of modernism we could find nowhere in the Spanish language such a great variety of verses as in those of González Prada.

In *Ballads* one sees his familiarity with the poetry of all languages (Spanish, French, Italian, German, English, Scandinavian) and the use he made of it in imitations, adaptations, and

translations. *Minúsculas* and *Exóticas* were the books of poems
that put him on the road to modernism. He had lived in Paris. He
had read Parnassians and symbolists. With the refinement of a virtuoso he plays with imaginative and formal novelties. He adapts the
French rondel, triolet, villanelle, pantoum; the English Spenser-
ian; the Italian *laude, ballata, stornello, rispetto;* the Persian quar-
tets. And he invents the polyrhythm without rhyme: "White
Horses" (*"Los caballos blancos"*). In the manner of Baudelaire
he cultivated the "correspondences" between senses, the "synesthesia" so preferred by the impressionists: "In a Strange Country"
(*"En país extraño"*). Although he was aware of the new movement in poetry, he did not proffer any judgment on the modernists.
In fact he wrote little on Hispanic-American poetry. Aside from
his rhythmic experiments, his most original contribution was his
Peruvian Ballads in which the Indian theme appeared viewed from
a different angle; the Indian was no longer idealized for decorative
purposes as the romantics had done, but was presented as a real
Indian, with all of his anguish, understood within history and the
Peruvian land.

We have just seen that, in dealing with the scholarly and critical intellectuals, we have outlined some aspects of their literary creation, even though
this was not where they made their greatest efforts. The less lyrical intellectuals do not lend themselves to such treatment. These are: ALEJANDRO
DÉUSTUA (Peru, 1849–1945), early influenced by Krause and later one of
those who introduced Bergson in America, whose *Esthetics* (*Estética*) was
founded on the metaphysical principle of liberty; and GABRIEL RENÉ-
MORENO (Bolivia, 1836–1908), the greatest glory of Bolivian letters. His
lively, variegated, and playful prose is among the best of his time; but the
work of this great recluse—secluded in his Bolivian theme, and, within
Bolivia, secluded in his intellectual aristocracy—was rather that of an
historian.

C. THEATER

Plays were written by the same authors we studied in other genres.
Therefore, it would be necessary to repeat a few names, that of Daniel
Barros Grez, for example, who was Chile's principal dramatist. Here are
four new names: In Mexico, JOSÉ PEON CONTRERAS (1843–1907) was
highly prolific in his plays in verse, generally on historical themes or on
subjects like honor, passion, religious feeling, and disillusion, all very wel-
come to the romantics who felt a nostalgia for the comedy of the golden

age. *The King's Daughter* (*La hija del rey,* 1876), one of his most successful dramas, is about a bastard daughter of Philip II who lived in Mexico.
JOSÉ ROSAS MORENO (1838–1883) was the author of historical dramas,
comedies on local customs and critical observations of society and plays
for children. His drama *Sor Inéz de la Cruz* is documentary evidence of the
current vogue for putting episodes from the lives of writers on the stage.

Othón had written a play with Cervantes as a character, and ALFREDO
CHAVERO (1841–1906) had written another on *The Loves of Alarcón* (*Los
amores de Alarcón*). DANIEL CALDERA (Chile, 1852–1896), OROSMAN
MORATORIO (Uruguay, 1852–1898) and MARTÍN CORONADO (Argentina,
1850–1919).

X. 1880-1895

Authors born between 1855 and 1870

Historical framework: New economic and social forces. Prosperity, immigration, technical advances, capitalism. Greater political stability. The oligarchies and the democratic opposition.

Cultural tendencies: The cult of European innovations. French Parnassianism. Naturalism. The first generation of "Modernists."

Introduction

The Hispanic-Americans who came into public life around 1880 (that is, when their countries had already passed through the worst of anarchism) still admired, romantically, the heroes of political action; but they had a presentiment that, were the circumstances to change, their role would not be an heroic one. With an air of bitterness, irony, or disillusion, depending on the particular case, they withdrew from the fight and dedicated themselves to literature. And even within literature they withdrew into nostalgic moods, into humanistic studies, into ideals of formal perfection, either clearly seen or half seen in European writers, especially in the French. In this period the writers were varied; but what they had in common seems to be a resentment against the immediate conditions of social life and a boastful air of being the first to cultivate literature for its own sake. The humanists of classical tastes, as well as the romantics, the realists, the Parnassians, and, finally, those who later would be called modernists all felt irritated by society, and this irritation (as in oysters) made them secrete pearls of literature. From Rubén Darío on, modernism will be a movement with an unmistakable direction (therefore, we will study it in the following chapter); but until Rubén Darío, the different directions of those interested exclusively in literature will be confused. In this sense, the list of the "precursors of modernism" must be much longer than is believed. Long before modernism, for example, poets who had not been considered precursors had achieved, nevertheless, extremely varied combinations of new verses. Let us enter this period through its poetry and come out by its prose; and when we deal with the poets, let us leave to the last those who will prevail when modernism triumphs.

A. MAINLY POETRY

1. The Last Academicians, Romantics, and Traditionalists

It has been said already that various poets were sleeping in an academic position, in a neoclassical convalescence. For this reason, when a new poetry emerged during these years, in a certain way equivalent to the renovation realized in Europe by the French Parnassians and the English pre-Raphaelites, it was a reaction, not against romanticism, but against the dying neoclassicism. The fascination for the unknown German and English languages (Heine, Poe), lyricism shimmering in mystery (Bécquer), the art of perfect ornamentation (Gautier), the pure beauty of French Parnassus (the masters Gautier, Leconte de Lisle, Banville, Baudelaire and their disciples Sully-Prudhomme, Heredia, Coppée, and Mendès) made their heads giddy as if they were sailing on a swelling sea; but they were all anxious to reach a port, they did not know which, where "things modern" awaited them. In this sense they are "forerunners." But, of course, forerunners do not know what they are forerunning. The critic then must be overly cautious, or he may fall into confusion. We shall go from (1) those poets who value tradition most to (2) those who value innovation most.

(i) *Central America* / In Honduras, JOSÉ ANTONIO DOMÍNGUEZ (1869–1903) was a melancholic and patriotic romantic, deeply attached to the rules. In El Salvador, VICENTE ACOSTA (1867–1908) versified on vernacular themes. In Costa Rica, JUSTO A. FACIO (1859–1931) and JOSÉ MARÍA ALFARO COOPER (1861–1931) preferred old molds. But the best of the

Costa Rican poets was the regionalist AQUILEO J. ECHEVERRÍA (1866–1909), who versified the customs of rural life in short meters in a language rich in colloquialisms, in descriptions of types, landscapes, events, and in the nature and folklore of his region. He was a romantic in his sentimental keynotes and a realist in his desire to reproduce things as they appeared to the eyes of everyone. "Concho" is the rural inhabitant of Costa Rica; "*concherías*" are his actions and expressions. Echeverría's country folk are not poor nor rich: they are of the comfortable middle class. So authentic are his scenes that one could study in his verses the social reality of the Costa Rica of his day. The lucidity of his observations has given him renown. But his renown is greater than his value as a poet. Echeverría's Costa Rica is not the same today, so that *Concherías* (1905) has acquired another virtue with the passage of time: that of awakening in its readers patriotic nostalgias and emotions. A capable versifier within the poverty of traditional rhythms, Echeverría is not a poet who surprises his readers with new findings. One fears that each verse will be followed by a commonplace, and this is what happens. The *Ballads* (*Romances*, 1903) are romantic in the fashion of Spain and all Hispanic-America—familiar, erotic sentiments, embroidered with cultural images and even with Greek myths.

(ii) *Antilles* / The Puerto Ricans LUIS MUÑOZ RIVERA (1859–1916), JOSÉ DE DIEGO (1868–1918), and FRANCISCO GONZALO MARÍN (1863–1897) were straggling cultivators of a civic and political poetry still romantic in form.

(iii) *Venezuela* / FRANCISCO LAZO MARTÍ (1864–1909) was the first poet in his country to stand out after the figures of Bello and Pérez Bonalde. Although his poetry was somewhat modernistic (*Glimmerings* [*Crepusculares*]) he was partial to the Venezuelan setting and in his collection of Creole poetry (*Silva criolla*, 1901) he wrote verses on native themes, containing occasional descriptions that are rich in lyric power.

(iv) *Colombia* / JULIO FLÓREZ (1867–1923) interpreted, without complications, popular feelings. Instead of stumped and shaded tones, he worked in jets of colors; but this ardent, this passionate, this spontaneous man had a sombre outlook on life. JOSÉ JOAQUÍN CASAS (1865–1951) was a versifier of classical precepts, popular themes, and religious moods. DIEGO URIBE (1867–1921), popular in his inspiration and in his direction, was a sincere elegist. ENRIQUE ALVAREZ HENAO (1861–1914). LUIS MARÍA MORA (1869–1936).

(v) *Ecuador* / REMIGIO CRESPO TORAL (1860–1939) was careful in his form, but without modernity.

(vi) *Chile* / JULIO VICUÑA CIFUENTES (1865–1936), as a poet, was a formal humanist. Something of Rubén Darío made its way into a few of his verses; in general, however, his most lyrical tone is found in his reminiscences of youth: *Autumn Harvest* (*Cosecha de otoño*, 1920). FRANCISCO CONCHA CASTILLO (1855–1927) was a poet of the old school, melancholy and moralizing.

(vii) *Uruguay* / At the time JOSÉ ALONSO Y TRELLES, "Old Pancho" (Spain-Uruguay, 1857–1924), belatedly began as a poet (1899), romanticism *à la* Zorrilla de San Martín was in its death throes and the modernism of Herrera y Reissig was being born. Old Pancho, unattached to either group, wrote poetry within the popular gaucho current. In 1915 he collected his poetry in his only significant book *Wild Weeds* (*Paja brava*)—expressing a sentimentalism that seemed worthwhile precisely because it was not touched by art.

(viii) *Argentina* / Standing in the doorway, looking into the streets of the past is CALIXTO OYUELA (1857–1935), of classical and Hispanic tastes, disciplined in his respect for the academies, a preserver of dry lyrical forms.

We could continue like this in an unending list, but it would be better to describe two grades of this non-modernist poetry: Othón's and Zorrilla de San Martín's.

MANUEL JOSÉ OTHÓN (Mexico, 1858–1906), one of the best describers of nature in our literature, was of the classical tradition. His tradition came from so far away (Horace, Vergil, Garcilaso and Fray Luis de León) that he appeared to be a solitary figure. He had more recent antecedents: in Spain, Núñez de Arce; in Mexico, Monsignor Arcadia Pagaza. But Othón's communication with nature was personal and direct, and in this sense, the sources of his poetry need no explanation. "We should not express anything that we have not seen," was his formula for artistic sincerity. And no one expressed better than he what he saw in the valleys, forests, rivers, mountains, and deserts of Mexico. In describing what he sees, he places his own spiritual vibrations into each thing, in a kind of pan-Othonism or pantheism, since Othón, after all, was a religious man. His constant intervention in rustic landscapes tends to have metaphysical force or the atmosphere of a prayer. He did not confine himself to bucolic themes; but in the context of pastoral life, he gave us the totality of his personal feeling for life. The identification of soul with nature is in itself romantic, but the verses are written with a classical technique. He did not innovate forms; on the contrary, he was content with those of the Golden Age. His musty literary lineage did not allow him to sympathize with the style that would be called modernist. Furthermore, his traditionalism changed to rancor. He thought modernism was the enemy of poetry. The idea of writing *Hymn to the Forests* (*Himno de los bosques*, 1891) came to him while reading a critic who lamented that Gutiérrez Nájera's *"Tristissima Nox"* (1884) did not understand love, or describe the Mexican landscape. This controversial attitude did not detract from the greatness of his poetry, but it enclosed it within the history of styles. Despite the fact that his decisive book *Rustic Poems (Poemas rústicos)* dates from 1902, the significance of his total works is clearer in the period that we are now studying, 1880–1895. He published in this period his first two books of verses: the first in 1880 and the second in 1888. But his echo will be heard among the modernists; and at the height of modernism, his "Savage Idyll" (*"Idilio salvaje"*) will stun us with its powerful voice. This poem is the one that best measures Othón's stature, and in the poetry prior to Darío, his stature is one of the most imposing. An ardent and sudden passion for a young woman inspired his "Savage Idyll." Artemio de Valle-Arizpe in his *Book of Anecdotes on Manuel José Othón (Anecdotario de Manuel José Othón)* relates that the poet, fearing that his wife would find out about his other woman, took on an air of innocence and attributed the love affair to the historian Alfonso Toro, a bachelor to whom he dedicated the first sonnet. In spite of this first introductory sonnet which the reader should forget as unworthy of the poem, "Savage Idyll" is a heart-rending confession. In order to understand it better, one must read others of his compositions of the same year, 1905; for example, "Fervent" (*"Urente"*), in which he describes his beloved mistress, and "From a Poem," in which he questions her with allusions to Canto III of Dante's *Inferno*.

We do not wish to explain "Savage Idyll" with a biographical anecdote: the setting of the poem, the poet's frame of mind, and even his images and words had already been tried much earlier, over and over, in sundry compositions. As in all sincere poets, there is in Othón a certain monotony. The landscape as a space wherein the pulsations of his spirit resound was an image already used by Othón. It is possible, then, that that biographical episode about Othón does not explain anything: what is certain is that Othón felt the necessity to poetize the conflict between religious virtue and carnal ardor in a fierce setting. In "Savage Idyll" one sees, clearly, that when he describes nature it is to integrate it with his spirit. The landscape is interiorized; it folds back upon the broken fragments of love and sin. The mountain and its precipices, the desert, the gray sunset, the eagles, the horizons, and the plains are converted into symbols of his own passion, in his solitude and old age. Descriptive, of course, but examined in the mirror of spiritual remorse: "And in me, what a deep and prodigious cataclysm! / What shadows and fear in my conscience / and what a horrible distaste of my own self!" Othón also wrote short stories and short novels in which the landscape and the sentiments of the country people prevail, and theatrical pieces bearing the telltale mark of Echegaray. It has been said that his best dramatic composition is *The Last Chapter* (*El último capítulo*, 1905) in one act and in prose, a judgment which, if it were true, would condemn the others irredeemably, since this one has no theatrical value. The theme is interesting: Cervantes is writing the last chapter of the second part of *Don Quixote* when he receives a visit from the author of the apocryphal Quixote (Avellaneda). Had he had theatrical talent, Othón would have made of Cervantes what Tamayo y Baus made of Shakespeare: a dramatic character. But the work, in spite of being a single act, has no unity—the episode between Cervantes and Avellaneda loses its power because the reader has been distracted already by other unconnected episodes. The dialog is emphatic, oratorical, wholly inflated with words that are not emitted from a mouth on stage but from the romantic conception that the author had of Cervantes' genius, and of his interpretation of Don Quixote.

JUAN ZORRILLA DE SAN MARTÍN (Uruguay, 1855–1931) began to work out his poem *Tabaré* in 1879; finished it in 1886; corrected it in 1887; published it in 1888; republished it—on each occasion with new variants—in 1892 and 1918; and gave the definitive text in the "edition corrected by its author" in Montevideo in 1923. Certain critics have read it with a rhetorical preoccupation: to what genre does it belong? Versified novel? Epic poem? They have tended to detract from its merits because it does not fit their rhetorical notions. Zorrilla gave no importance to the novelistic theme, which is quite ingenuous; Tabaré, a mestizo born of a

Charrúa chief and a captive Spanish woman, receives, from early childhood, the grace of baptism; as a youth, he sees Blanca, sister of the conquistador Don Gonzalo, and he feels intensely attracted to her because she recalls to his mind the memory of his dead mother; his baptized soul and his warrior inclinations struggle inside him; he saves Blanca from the arms of an Indian, but Don Gonzalo, believing Tabaré to be the rapist, kills him. In considering *Tabaré* an epic poem the author warns us that he gave the word "epic" a personal connotation: the demonstration of the laws of God in human happenings. *Tabaré* is a Catholic poem, and, therefore, it is vulgar to interpret it, as has been done, in the light of naturalist verisimilitude. When Zorrilla describes the Indians he is not proceeding from an ethnographic attitude, but from a metaphysical one. His theme, the destiny of the Charrúa race, is conceived theologically—what supernatural will condemned this race? The poem intuits, poetically, the Charrúa race at a moment when it is about to disappear: it is darkness, meaninglessness. Thanks to Tabaré, the mestizo with the blue eyes, Zorrilla looks out upon the abyss and sees the sparks of the vanished race. Tabaré, then, appears on the dividing line between two creations: the Charrúa race, which is nature, and the Spanish race, which is spirit. The death of Tabaré condemns the Charrúa race to eternal silence; with its physical disappearance, the possibility of its being understood also disappears. In spite of its exterior make-up, legendary, novelistic, epic, *Tabaré* is a lyrical poem.

Zorrilla de San Martín, like many other poets of his day, came out of the Spanish romantic school of José Zorrilla, Núñez de Arce, and Bécquer. But it was Bécquer who taught him how to control his voice. Zorrilla de San Martín "Becquerized" with such delicacy—images suggested by mystery, descriptive impressionism, melancholy contemplation of life and death, vague fluctuations between reality and dream—that he placed himself in the lyrical vanguard. He succeeded with a type of suggestive verse, because his lyricism originated from a vision of life as mystery, and a pictorial verse, because it was the poet's purpose to be lucid and perfect in his descriptive forms. Bécquer was not an accidental source, but a kindred spirit who showed him the road to style.

Other poets remained imprisoned within the romantic enclosure. Not Zorrilla. From romanticism two specialized buds emerged, one of plastic perfection (*Parnasse*), the other of musical suggestion (symbolism). Zorrilla goes from romanticism to symbolism, but independently of French literature. His passage was opened by Bécquer's Nordic vagueness. Zorrilla's poetry is clear and he tried, even more than Bécquer, every possibility of expression: idea, fiction, passion, sound, suggestion, descriptive plasticity. But he trod where Bécquer had already trod: the allusion to states of soul that vacillate between wakefulness and dream; the suspicion of a mystery which at once envelops us and lies within us; the trust in the revealing power of the metaphor and the confided secret. Zorrilla's attitude is similar to that which, later on, the initiates to symbolism would have, except that his poetry, deliberately vague, is rich in visual substance. He is always successful with the visual image, which improves the narration and distinguishes it. His images run the gamut of impressionistic language: animation of nature, empathy, synesthesia, etc. From Bécquer he borrowed, together with his delicacy, the simplicity of the verse. Such simplicity is achieved, however, with a rich variety of musical suggestions: the leitmotiv ("to the river fell the flower . . ."), the sudden shift of accent from the penult to the ultimate syllable, the unfolding of hendecasyllables and heptasyllables. The choice of this versification responded to a vague, persuasive mood, more interested in the fluid and subdued communication of metaphors than a strong and articulated sonority. This tendency in Zorrilla toward a poetry of allusions makes him one of the purest and freshest lyrical poets in America; if we set aside the naive novelistic architecture of *Tabaré*, many of his verses will be modern. His prose works—essays, travelogs, discourses, history—are less renovating.

We have said that a displeased Othón had turned his face away from those who were ushering in a new poetry. Among those who took delight in the new breeze on their brows, making them heralds of the new esthetics that was to take the name modernist, one must include, from Mexico, Agustín F. Cuenca and especially, Justo Sierra, with whom we have already dealt.

2. The First Modernists

Díaz Mirón / Difficult to place in this zigzagging march of poets is SALVADOR DÍAZ MIRÓN (1853–1928). He rests between Justo Sierra, who announces the arrival of modernism, and Gutiérrez Nájera, who opens up the door. Or better, Díaz Mirón is the one who enters through the window. Since 1886, the year in which Díaz Mirón published a notebook of poetry, his voice has been a moving force all over our America; in 1889 Darío payed tribute to his libertarian spirit; and in 1890 he dedicated a "Medallion" to him in his new edition of *Azul.* Later Díaz Mirón deserted his past and recognized only *Stone Chips* (*Lascas,* 1901). The poet himself points to the year 1892, when he was imprisoned for having killed a man, as the beginning of a new "artistic criterion." Prior to 1892 he was a Victor-Hugoesque and Byronian poet, grandiloquent in thought and metaphor. "*Sursum,*" "To Glory" ("*A gloria*"), "Interior Voices" ("*Voces interiores*") illustrate this manner, his most temperamental. The poet means to be a tribune, a prophet, a revolutionary. "To sing to Filis for her sweet name / when the clarion calls: 'awaken, steel!' / that is not a poet, nor a man." He scorns "the muse of tinsel and ermine" and prefers, on the contrary, to sing to "human suffering," "the city with its beehive noises," truth, justice, virtue . . . ("*Sursum*"). However, in spite of his social art, his clamorous hyperboles, and his aphoristic reflections, Díaz Mirón managed to keep unblemished his standing as an artist. He was bombastic but elegant. And the cultural breeze that blew through his verses—citations from mythology and history, the selection of words and effects that ran against the grain—please even the modernists who did not share his disdain for ivory towers. In his second period, that of *Stone Chips,* Díaz Mirón became serene. He who had prophesied political revolutions, carried out the only revolution possible for a poet—a revolution within himself. However, it was not a great revolution. Basically he did not change: just as we had seen modern flashes in his rhymed oratory earlier, now we will also encounter rhetorical declamations in his verses, so beaten and worked over that they fall away like sparkling "stone chips." He

is the same old Díaz Mirón, but in *Stone Chips* he spends his solitude in interplays of accents and rhythms. There is more delicacy.
He feels pleasure in overcoming technical difficulties that he himself creates. One should read "Pepilla," "Vigil or Sleep" (*"Vigilia
y sueño"*), "Exemplar" (*"Ejemplo"*), *"Nox"* and it will be seen
that he sacrificed his volcanic energy for the perfections of a miniaturist—a great sacrifice for him, because of the eruptive force
which he had to contain himself. The Parnassian decorousness of
his strophes often congealed his emotions. Despite all chastise-
ment, his emotions reappear, converted into an heroic will for
technical improvement in the art of verse. With manly restraint,
he refused to fall into the use of easy rhymes and rhythms. His
musical effects were so rigorous that no one has been able to imitate his difficult verses. He Latinized his sentences, suppressed un-
accented grammatical particles, enriched the rhyme, avoided
assonance at key points, brought the five vowels into choral harmony through his accentuation, magnified each detail in the crystal
ball of a metaphor, and fused sensations in synesthetic impressions. In addition to word-sound, he produced a musical effect that
was psychic, penetrating, suggestive. In *Stone Chips* he was a
modernist, though always solitary, rebellious, and menacing in his
modernism. His last period is that from 1902 to 1928: these
poems, in which he sharpened his technical talent, were collected
by Antonio Castro Leal into the volume, *Complete Poems* (*Poesías completas*).

In our literary history, Martí, Gutiérrez Nájera, Casal, and
Silva seem to form part of the first group of modernists. The death
of all of them before 1896 has influenced historians to round out
this group. But we must resist the temptation of embellishing history with geometric schemes. Other schemes have been proposed:
for example, that this modernist group has a meridian in time—
1882, the date of Martí's *Ismaelillo*, or 1888, the date of Darío's
Azul—and a latitude in space—to the north of Ecuador lived the
Colombian Silva, the Mexican Gutiérrez Nájera, the Cubans Martí
and Casal, the Nicaraguan Darío. It is not easy to set boundary
lines for this "first Modernism." González Prada, Zorrilla de San
Martín, Almafuerte, each of whom contributed to the poetic reno-

vation in his own way, were older than those considered modernists; and they lived to the south of Ecuador. If these are withdrawn, then Silva and even Martí should be withdrawn because
they do not fit comfortably within modernism either. Gutiérrez
Nájera himself was a post-romantic who lacked sufficient combative or reformative spirit to be a modernist. Of this group, only
Del Casal, in the end, reflects clearly the models of Parnassus and
symbolism.

On the other hand, the great figure, Rubén Darío, fills not only
the first modernist period, but also the second, which began in the
year 1896; and we prefer to study him in the next chapter when it
is possible to speak of modernism as a well-defined esthetic movement. One must not expect a clear division between romanticism
and modernism. They are not opposite categories. They could not
be because, in spite of their differences, both stand partially on
common ground. It was, after all, those who were unsatisfied with
romanticism who left it, seeking modernities. So-called modernist
literature adds, to the discovery of emotional life made by the
romantics, the almost professional awareness of what literature
and its latest fashions are, a feeling for the more prestigious forms,
the aristocratic effort to reach a high sphere of culture, the industry of combining diverse styles, the conviction that this, in
itself, is a new art, and the pride of belonging to an Hispanic-
American generation which, for the first time, is able to specialize
in art. Let us leave, for the moment, the definition of modernism.
This is not a history of "isms" but of creative personalities, and,
remaining faithful to our chronological approach, we will pause
now before the authors of the period which ends in 1895: Martí,
Gutiérrez Nájera, Casal, and Silva.

José Martí (Cuba, 1853–1895) is the most titanic figure of
all this period. Cubans are right to revere his memory; he lived
and died heroically in the service of Cuba's liberty. But Martí belongs even to those of us who are not Cubans. He is too big for
Cuba; he is too big for America: he is one of those luxuries that
the Spanish language can offer a universal public. He scarcely had
time, however, to devote himself to letters. He left a few organized
works, though these are not among his best. He was an essayist, a

chronicler, a public speaker; that is to say, he was fragmentary, and his fragments often reach poetic heights. With him culminates the romantic effort toward an esthetically elaborated prose. In the history of prose, Martí stands between two other giants: Montalvo and Rubén Darío. He still seems close to Montalvo for the prevalence of syntactical structures that could be found in any author of the Golden Age; and he seems close to Darío for his references to an aristocratic, cosmopolitan, and estheticist culture. His greatest literary heritage was Hispanic—Renaissance and Baroque writers—not French. However slightly Gallicized he may have been, certainly the poetic air of many of his pages becomes clear if we keep in mind that Martí esteemed the French writers who had created a pictorial prose (Gautier, Flaubert) and an impressionist prose (Daudet, the Goncourt brothers). He complained of the linguistic inertia of the Spaniards, and in seeking elegant forms in others' languages, he preferred French literature to English. He was not an esthete. He did not conceive of literature as the activity of a special esthetic organ. Writing for him was a way of serving. He revered letters for their practical virtues: the sincerity with which they unbosomed the generous emotions of man, the usefulness with which they helped to better society, the patriotism with which they shaped a Creole conscience. For this reason, even in his evaluation of artistic prose, there were moral overtones. In this sense, the pages he wrote in 1882 on Oscar Wilde are very significant. He valued "the noble and judicious things" that Wilde had said in propagating his faith in the cult of beauty and art for art's sake; but he corrected them with reflections on "the moral power and transcendental purpose of beauty."

Martí's ideas on art changed in the course of his career, and if some of them were not contradictory, at least they were accentuated contradictorily. It is as if the will to artistic perfection and the will to exemplary conduct were struggling within Martí. He always restrained his taste for pure art—a repudiation which in him was more energetic than in others because he was splendidly gifted for pure artistic expression—but in his later years he pulled on the reins so hard that his artistic momentum was held back also. Roughly around 1887, as his impatience for action grew, Martí began to reject the quintessence of literature and the profit derived from the European modernists, especially the French. There are in his works two periods: one more esthetic and the other more moral. The first crystallized in a novel, the only one he wrote: *Ill-Omened Friendship* (*Amistad funesta*, 1885). The plot, with the story of a tragic love, interweaves romantic threads. But on this romantic canvas Martí embroidered a few garlands that have no equal in the Hispanic-American novel of those years. Martí was the first to contribute to the novelistic genre within the literary renovation we call modernism. He describes a bucolic, Arcadian, pastoral, rococo, "literatized" nature. He also embellishes his characters with a twofold procedure: the first, that of artistic *composition*, wherein the movement of the bodies strikes supreme attitudes in the manner of live pictures, and the second, that of artistic *transposition*, wherein the human figures become more impressive because they are compared with masterpieces in museums. In the use of paintings, sculptures, precious stones, objects of luxury—becoming more frequent in literature from Gautier to the Goncourts—Martí succeeded more than anyone else in the Modernist literature of the Spanish language. As with Gutiérrez Nájera, Rubén Darío, Casal, and all the others who are to come, Paris is the ideal avenue of escape from the immediate reality to more beautiful horizons. *Ill-Omened Friendship* is the first book of artistic atmosphere, of sophistication, of snobbism, of softness and intellectual preciosity in Hispanic-American literature. Other novels of this type will come later, those of José María Rivas Groot, Vargas Vila, Díaz Rodríguez, Angel de Estrada, etc. Within the narrative genre, Martí will continue his estheticism in children's stories for the magazine *La Edad de Oro* (1889). Yet his prose is not as French as that of Darío, who is already writing. Martí was an orator and he used all of the little whiplashes of persuasion of which the Spanish language is capable. As he wrote, excited by the practical needs of the public speaker or shaken by the declamatory urge, he tended to give his prose the structure of the sermon, the discourse, the proclamation, the oration. It is not the classical architecture of our preachers of the Golden Age, nor that of Donoso Cortés, nor that of Castelar. He overloads, complicates, amplifies, subordinates, and disproportions excessively. He looses a storm of ideas, thunderclaps of emotion, and lightning strokes of metaphors that cause his perorations to explode. His sincerity is torrential; it demolishes dikes and cuts new river beds.

But behind his eloquence is a hard-working architect. His prose is not a museum of classical tropes as was Montalvo's during those same years; all told, he still preserves some of the harness in which classical elocution moved. That these schemes of oratorical prose are old in our literature did not deter Martí from fortifying them. In Martí the schemes are used as frames for his impressionistic paintings. His oratorical moments are replete with descriptions, reflections, and lyrical images. No doubt he is an emphatic writer, but frequently his emphasis is not eloquent, but expressive. He is rich in melodic variety, unmeasured phrases, and at the other extreme of the rhythmic scale, concise, elliptical, exclamatory sentences. Martí gave suppleness to his prose in order to better convey his impressionistic experiences. As a poet he was no less excellent. *Ismaelillo* (1882) was, for its time, a strange book: in meters of popular appearance, and with a popular theme—remembrances of home and the faraway son—Martí elaborated a brief, pictorial poetry of unexpected rhymes, of complex syntax, or archaisms and verbal riches, of condensation and detailed art. The language and metrics are regular: the new subtlety lies in the images of a tender, yet virile, sensibility. Martí continues to be preoccupied with his involvement in civil and political fights: in the midst of these things, he becomes as serene as a lake. It is an enchanting, crepuscular lake where all is tenuously veiled and vanishes in a beautiful unreality. With the years, romanticism had become overloaded with much rhetoric; when Martí lay bare his tenderness in *Ismaelillo*, that bareness, although romantic, seemed new, and the modernists considered it to be an inauguration of new forms. They had also considered Bécquer in this light. His posthumous *Free Verses* (*Versos libres*), written about the same date, were quite different. His violence occasionally emits smoke, like the burning of green wood. On other occasions—"Sky Flowers" ("*Flores del cielo*")—it burns in flame, the last great blazing of the romantic Titans: "Pallid with love, standing in the shadows, in my garden,

/ the sky enveloped in gigantic raiments / of astral light, / I'll
make a magnificent bouquet of stars. / My hand will not tremble
at seizing light!" And romantic love, as in "Winged Cup" ("*Copa
con alas*"): "I felt, embracing thee, that all of life embraced me!"
"Thou alone, only thou, knowest the way / to reduce the Universe
to just one kiss!" Since they were published many years after the
death of Martí, the *Free Verses* had no influence on modernism,
and this can also be said of another posthumous collection—
Flowers of Exile (*Flores del destierro*). In *Simple Verses* (*Versos
sencillos*, 1891) Martí was original because he reached more profound depths within himself and he revealed them to us in compact symbols. These verses, "playfully" written, are octosyllables,
some are monorhymes, which was a novelty, and others are written
with a capricious use of rhyme, repeating the same word, or having it reverberate in the interior of a line. But with all this, the
simplicity is apparent. "I love simplicity, and I believe in the necessity of putting sentiment in plain and simple forms," he announced
in the prolog; but it was the simplicity of a sincere and ingenious
man. From this trait derives his power of seduction over the not-
very-simple modernists.

Occasionally one notices the preciosities that enter into the
current definitions of modernism: impressionistic traits, cultured
exquisiteness (for example, compositions X, "The Tremulous and
Lonely Soul"; XVI, "At the Fretted Embrasure"; XXII, "I Am at
the Strange Ball"; XLII, "At the Strange Bazaar"). Even in poem
IX the serious theme of "the child from Guatemala / she who
died of love" is converted gracefully into a plastic and melodic
game: in contrapuntal form Martí harmonizes, in quatrains that
pursue one another, the description of a death in the present (the
cadaver, the burial, the funeral procession) and the evocation of
a love in the past (the leave-taking, the return of the lover with
his new spouse, the suicide in the river of the forgotten one). It is
not a biographical episode; it is an esthetic exercise, with artful
vignettes and musical accompaniment, very much to the modernist
taste. He was a poet of double accent, romantic and modernist, always very personal, quick in his leaps from intuition to intuition,
capable of dressing the most abstract idea in a concrete image:

"and time flew by and an eagle / flew over the sea" is his dynamic
way of counting the minutes.

3. The Other Modernists

MANUEL GUTIÉRREZ NÁJERA (Mexico, 1859–1895) was not
a renovator of metrics: he felt comfortable in the tradition of the
octosyllable and the hendecsyllable. But he was, to be sure, a
renovator of the mood of the poetic image. He overcame the
doubts that tormented him, coincidental with the irreligious crisis
of his time, and sounded, for the first time, the elegant, graceful,
refined, light notes that Rubén Darío would continue to orchestrate. With romantically preferred sentiments—above all, those
preferred by Musset and Bécquer: sadness, impossible love, mystery and death, grief—Gutiérrez Nájera sets himself before his
mirror and dresses elegantly. In this self-contemplation, the poet
takes pleasure, not so much in his own sentiments, but in the
images in which he clothes them. Because of this attitude even
elegiac themes take on a brilliance, a coloring, a pleasant array, as
in his "Elegy" on the death of his friend Alvarez del Castillo,
where death is a beautiful, enamored lady. There was a "before" in
which Gutiérrez Nájera was melancholy, depressed, anguished;
but now, as he looks at himself in the mirror of art, he grooms
himself to go out, and smiles. "Are you suffering? Seek the gentle
lover, / the immobile and immortal beauty," he say in *"Pax
Anima";* and here he gives us an idea on how to convert ethics
into esthetics: "While there are flowers, gather them; / forgive the
rose its thorns. / When anguish overshadows my spirit / I seek
clarity and calm in the heights / and an infinite compassion
whitens / on the frozen crests of my soul!" This is estheticism,
neither frigid nor frivolous, at least not as frigid nor as frivolous as
will be seen in other poets to follow, an estheticism that plays with
life until it gives it a figure of pure beauty: "and make, artist, with
thine anguish, / lofty sepulchral monuments." Life becomes an
artistic monument. There are plastic images, well contoured so
that we can see them; but other images also suggest visions without showing us the concrete things that those visions see, in a kind
of vague musical language. In his verses to "Schubert's Serenade"

he exclaims in envy: "Thus would my soul speak . . . if only it could!" He envies music for its ability to insinuate—a new attitude in our literature. In *"Non omnis moriar"* Gutiérrez Nájera takes the theme of Horace and works it out against the opposing figure of the man-poet, so dear to esthetes. The poet expresses the ineffable in man. Here Hispanic-American romanticism, as was the case earlier in Europe, begins to withdraw from the public and the poet ends up by believing himself to be God's tortured soul. Gutiérrez Nájera—*el Duque Job* (Duke Job) was his most famous pseudonym—does not feel chosen, but he does feel aristocratic; he was more duke than Job.

Justo Sierra, who wrote the prolog of the posthumous edition of his *Poetry* (*Poesía*, 1896) attributed to him, "French thoughts in Spanish verses" (as Valera would attribute to Darío a "mental Gallicism"). Not only did Gutiérrez Nájera read the French writers in French (in poetry, from Lamartine to Baudelaire and especially Musset, who was most like him; in prose, from Chateaubriand to Flaubert and Mendès), but also literature in translation—he had no connections with earlier Mexican writers. Seen from America he was a solitary figure who, along the way, would meet others like himself, and together they would constitute a group: that of the so-called first modernist generation. In Spain there was no poetry of this kind, with such grace, distinction, and refinement, and for this reason Gutiérrez Nájera would amaze the Spaniards (Villaespesa, less of a poet, was to be one of those amazed). His images, disconcerting to the readers of the day, were constructed into a melody of perfect unity: images arranged like a panorama that unfolds towards planes increasingly profound, enriching itself with the discovery of new beauty; images which, in spite of the coherent composition, file by like agile, individual bodies. (Read "To the Corregidor's Wife" ["*A la corregidora*"], a work of admirable rhythmic mastery; the soul of every object in it seems to speak with a voice that is insinuating and onomatopoeic.) The words that Gutiérrez Nájera's ears choose, the harmonious ones, those that are best entwined in rhythms and rhymes, coincide with what his eyes chose, the most luxuriant objects, the prettiest, the most exquisite. He was also able to make out another reality, that of "the dark, / silent currents of my soul" (read "Dead Waves" [*"Ondas muertas"*] and *"Tristissima Nox"*), and this is the dimension we most value. The poetry of Gutiérrez Nájera has lost its power to excite the reader of today—when Mexican youths look for the sources of modern poetry they find them in González Martínez, Tablada, and López Velarde. A few steps more and they would find Gutiérrez Nájera as a pristine source.

Gutiérrez Nájera's prose is excellent and more significant than his poetry, at least in the history of modernism. A tireless journalist—he was editor of the *Revista Azul*—he devoted himself to displaying his French accessories. His chronicles were masterpieces. They alighted capriciously on the most frivolous happenings of the week, and thus created the illusion of an ironic and beautifying veil of fantasy. The impressionistic description, the good humor, the notes on Mexican travels, the ingenious commentary sounded frivolous but they responded to a premeditated theory of prose. There was in him also the literary critic. His fiction has not lost all of its freshness. *Fragile Stones* (*Cuentos frágiles*, 1883) and the posthumous *Smoke-Colored Stories* (*Cuentos color de humo*) gathered together a few of them. Today, thanks to the *Complete Stories* (*Cuentos completos*, 1958 edition), we can appreciate in its total value the transformation of narrative prose in the hands of a poet. Samples of his storytelling art are "History of a Counterfeit Coin" and "The Novel of the Trolley." He was aware of the dangers of poetic prose: one, keeping in the coffer—he used to say—loose pearls, instead of stringing them into a necklace of action; another, the breaking of Spanish grammar because of the intercalation of French forms. The remedy—he noted—is to read Jovellanos, a good administrator of the language.

JOSÉ ASUNCIÓN SILVA (Colombia, 1865–1896) went for a walk in a romantic garden that had already withered; and no sooner do we see him following the footsteps of the prosaic Campoamor and Bartrina (*"Gotas amargas"*) than he moves toward the places preferred by Bécquer (*"Crisálidas"* and *"Notas perdidas"*). On his return from Paris and from London he brought a library of contemporary writers and initiated his friends in the spirit of the new literature. Nevertheless, the affected mannerisms of the "Rubendarians," as he used to call them, annoyed him, and under the signature of Benjamín Bibelot Ramírez, he dedicated a satire called "Strawberry-Colored Symphony with Cream" ("*Sinfonía color de fresa con leche*") to the "decadent humming birds." All his work was done in his youth, this must be kept in mind; and it was achieved as an inspiration, almost as though he had divined his early death. This is without counting the loss in a shipwreck of manuscripts representing five years of poetic work. According to the testimonies of those who had seen those manuscripts, they were his best poetry. Silva neglected his public relations; since the favor of his readers did not interest him, he did not help them by arranging his own work which, because of its confused mixture, produces a false impression of immaturity. His little volume of poetry lacked unity, and the diversity of his patriotic, festive, folkloric, narrative, erotic, and philosophic compositions obscures his merit. Now that we have his *Complete Works* (*Obra completa*, 1956), gathered by Rafael Maya, the critic can turn away from trodden paths and follow Silva when he enters the mysterious, intimate, thrilling, lyrical path which will take him to the poetic renovation that other poets had ventured on.

His literary culture was up to date with the latest French and English quotations. He had read Poe and Baudelaire, and in his prose page "Me, a Poet?" he cites Rossetti, Verlaine and Swinburne. He had spiritual affinity with Poe, above all. The influence of Poe has been pointed out in the rhythms of "All Souls Day" and of the third "Nocturne," two compositions in the new metric technique. There is no doubt of the affinity between the shadows and mysteries of Poe and the nocturnal quality of Silva: cf. "Tell Me," "Ronde," "Nocturne," "Midnight Dreams," "Moon Light," "Serenade," "All Souls Day." The influence of Poe was present in the procedure of changing meters. But Silva followed his own pleasure in displacing rhythms. His versification becomes sweeter as it moves toward free verse. In "A Poem" he gave us his esthetics: "I dreamed, in those days of forging a poem / of rare and nervous art, supreme and audacious work." He was not always faithful to that idea of esthetics. When he was, the moments that count, he left us tremulous poems of morbid sentiments, suggestive of enigmas, with accents of tenderness and melancholy. Silva's pessimism had its roots in his body, in his soul, in the philosophy of the day. His best poems, a good example of which is "Ebbing of Life" (*"Vejeces"*), are those that evoke time gone by, the voice of things outworn, the visions of childhood, the shadows, the noises, and forgotten fragrances, and all this in a poetic language that is vague, evanescent, musical. What is deserving of his fame are his "Nocturnes," especially the third, the one of the "long shadow." With a faltering voice whose silent moments are like tremors, with a kind of poetic stammering as though the poet were bewildered by a supernatural apparition, and in his stupor, could only manage to move his lips or to bite them in order to contain his weeping, this "Nocturne," written, as they say, at the death of his sister Elvira, is one of the loftiest expressions of lyricism of the epoch; it is new in timbre, in tone, in musical structure, in its phantasmal, elegiac theme, in its rhythmic imitation of sobbing. This Silva of the nocturnes is the one closest to us. He is, of all the Colombian poets of the nineteenth century, the only one who speaks to the poetic sensibilities of today. While other modernists were discerning the world, Silva discerned himself. His melancholy lyricism made him disdain romantic grandiloquence and modernist sumptuousness, and it is his poems of obscure mysteries that save him for us. He elaborated sensations, especially rare sensations, in which he took pride as a unique person, free of the instincts common to the species; but he did it with simplicity. It was only in his prose that he was contriving, in the manner of the modernists. His prose was rich in pictorial effects in "Transpositions" (*"Transposiciones"*). His novel *After Dinner* (*De Sobremesa*) analyzes the character's hypersensitive psychology in a Paul Bourget fashion.

JULIÁN DEL CASAL (Cuba, 1863–1893) published two books of poetry, *Leaves to the Wind* (*Hojas al viento*, 1890) and *Snow* (*Nieve*, 1892); and another, posthumously, *Busts and Rhymes* (*Bustos y rimas*, 1893), in prose and verse. Recently collected were his short stories, poems in prose and chronicles: pages of artistic aspirations, interesting as guides for the study of Casal's poetry, not as substitutes for them. His three books of poems have an elegiac intonation. In the first, Casal has not completely disentangled himself from the Spaniards Zorrilla, Bartrina, Bécquer, and Campoamor, although his romanticism twitches spasmodically with expressions in the manner of Heine and Leopardi, and already there are reflections of the French lyrics of Gautier, Heredia, Coppée and Baudelaire. In the second book, the transcendental pessimism, the aristocratic vocabulary, the metric renovation, the search for perfect forms, and the cultivation of the descriptive-pictorial poem are already modernist. Not only does he pay tribute to the Frenchmen Baudelaire, Gautier, Banville, Mendès, Leconte, Heredia, Richepin, Verlaine and Moréas, but also to the Hispanic-Americans Gutiérrez Nájera and Darío. At this point he is a Parnassian, and his greatest god, Gautier. Verlaine himself, no less, commented on *Snow*, and reproached Casal for his Parnassian addiction. "I believe," he said, "that present-day mysticism will reach him and when the terrible Faith has bathed his young soul, poems shall bud from his lips like sacred flowers." He was right: the Parnassian ideal of cold and objective forms impelled Casal to neglect the vibrations of his melancholy. In the third book of poems, he reveals himself to be more somber, personal, audacious and innovating. Now on the altar, next to Gautier, are Verlaine and Baudelaire. The yearning for a supreme form, the flexibility of the verse, the cult of morbid sensations, the artistic transpositions, the taste for Hellenistic, rococo, and Japanese cultures, the mastery in the arrangement of radiant words, symbols and objects, all bring Casal into the orbit of modernism. Seen in its better moments, his poetry is intimate. It is filled to the brim with the brief life of the poet, but it does not spill over. Absent from it are civic chants, descriptions of the homeland, and erotic tales. Or, better said, the few verses on topical themes are insignificant. He did not feel the natural beauty of the Cuban landscape. In an island of sun, greenery, gayety, bustle, he preferred to shut his doors and remain in the darkness, alone, in his sickly confinement. His poetry, then, is utterly directed to his sad soul. The exclamations of sadness were repeated so often in European and American romanticism that at times it is difficult to distinguish between the voice and the echo; but there is no doubt that Casal's verse "Why, O Lord, hast thou made my soul so sad?" was an authentic voice. It may well resemble other romantic voices, but it is so revealing of Casal's being that were a similar verse found in an earlier poet (in Vigny there are two like it) Casal's would still be original.

He was taciturn, not so much because he had a pessimistic concept of life, nor simply because he was poor, timid and ill, but because, besides all that, he was not constitutionally made for participating in the pleasurable enticements of the world. He does not judge this world: his theme is his own sadness that arises from a hidden source. He feels discontented with life, that is all. But he does not complain; he is indifferent to the world, and when he declares that it is mud and morass, he is giving us an impression, not a philosophy. He feels dead in life; and there is in him a joyful expectancy of the finite death which, at least in certain verses that were unnoticed in newspapers, made him think of suicide: "And in the distance, toasting consolation / to my bitterness, only the pistol's mouth / smiles at me." If one reads "Nihilism," it can be seen how sincere was his desire to be dead: "I feel only the urge to consume myself / or to live in my eternal poverty / with my faithful companion, discontentment, / and my pallid lover, sadness." It is a tragic beat that is heard in all his poetry. In "Autobiography" one sees that the poet is not merely doing poetic exercises on the romantic theme of anguish, but is expressing himself sincerely. What is most moving in Casal is, precisely, his not wishing to play with forms, which he could have done since he had a gift for expressing himself in artifices, but he preferred to give simple form to one obsession: that of dying. Art was for him a refuge. He had no illusions about his poetry: he thought it would be dispersed in "the bitter waves of oblivion." But he abandoned himself to his art, as one does to opium, and submerged himself ever deeper into his dreams. His early romanticism had been superficial: his soul drifted on the conventions of his day, his verses floated emptily. But in his best compositions Casal sinks like a deep-sea diver. At times his diver's gear is the plastic, colorful, refined poetry that Casal admired in Gautier and Heredia; at times, it is the crepuscular and insinuating poetry that Casal admired in Baudelaire. The first type of poetry, because it was similar to the poetic language of French Parnassianism, took on a kinship with that of the other Hispanic-Americans who were reading the same authors. There are verses by Casal which bear a notable resemblance to others by Gutiérrez Nájera and Rubén Darío. He would compose live pictures as if he were inspired by paintings: like those of Gustave Moreau. Huysmans, in *A Rebours*, had likewise described paintings by Moreau.

Objects are not embellished by Casal; they were already beautiful in art and the poet carries them like adornments. It is an aristocratic, cosmopolitan, exotic atmosphere, with the luster of Paris and of Tokyo, with swans, eighteenth-century courtesans, precious stones. The titles, "medallions," "chromos," "cameos," "old ivory," "sketches," "Ideal Museum," declare his intent to be an artisan of forms and colors. Turning to the other direction of his poetry, toward the most secret penumbra of his inner life, Casal (dazzled by Baudelaire) expressed his "sanguinary vision of neurosis," his voyage "toward the glacial land of insanity"; his synesthesia "the dormant body perceives / through my magic sopor, / sounds in color, / color in sounds." See "*Post Umbra*," "The Song of Morphine" ("*La canción de la morfina*"), "*Horridum somnium*," "Body and Soul" ("*Cuerpo y alma*").

In every country there were poets, and national pride will take us to task if we omit them.

(i) *Mexico* / FRANCISCO ASÍS DE ICAZA (1863–1925), JOSÉ MARÍA BUSTILLOS (1866–1899) and BALBINO DÁVALOS (1866–1951).

(ii) *Antilles* / There were other Cubans who took the first steps of modernism with Casal, but so timidly that alongside him they seem to be taking another direction. ANICETO VALDIVIA, *Count Kostia* (1859–1927), encouraged the taste for French novelty, but in Castilian he preferred not to innovate. BONIFACIO BYRNE (1861–1936), hailed by Casal as a poet of new accents, did not do his tour of service under modernism. He was, rather, a poet of patriotic emotion. EMILIO BOBADILLA (1862–1920), better known for his mordant criticism under the pseudonym Fray Candil, worked in Spain. Though he attacked modernism, his verses took advantage of the metric reforms of the modernists. The Dominican Republic had given two poets: José Joaquín Pérez and Salomé Ureña de Henríquez. Not unlike them in quality, we may add GASTÓN FERNANDO DELIGNE (1861–1913), author of *Galaripsos*. He excelled in the brief poem, somewhat in the manner of Campoamor. Because of his power of observation and of the depth of his thought, he almost converted the psychological poem into a new genre, in which the intimate life of a person is illumined in a critical instant—"Woes," ("*Angustias*"), "Secrets of Cristina" ("*Confidencias de Cristina*"). He also wrote philosophical poems—"Annihilation" ("*Aniquilamiento*")—and political ones—"*Ololoi*." Deligne derided modernism: he was in truth a realist, and even a naturalist, with lapses into prosaic discourses. He practised metric innovations. It must be said that modernism taught the Dominicans the art of varying versification, but it did not uproot them from the romantic and realist orbit. ENRIQUE HENRÍQUEZ (1859–1940), of the nocturnes, was a romantic. And even FABIO FIALLO (1866–1942), in spite of his participation in modernist literary life, romanticized anguished love, like Heine and Bécquer, as can be seen in *A Life's Song* (*La canción de una vida*, 1926), in which he collected a great deal of his work. We shall not go into the lesser poets: EMILIO PRUDHOMME (1856–1932), CÉSAR NICOLÁS PENSON (1855–1901), PABLO PUMAROL (1857–1889), RAFAEL DELIGNE (1863–1902) and ARTURO BAUTISTA PELLERANO CASTRO (1865–1916), author of the popular *Creoles* (*Criollas*). In Puerto Rico JESÚS MARÍA LAGO (1860–1929) was a modernist in his belated *Sandalwood Coffer* (*Cofre sándalo*, 1927).

(iii) *Venezuela* / Here too modernism arrived late and manifested itself more in prose. One can scarcely mention, as modernist poets, the names of MANUEL PIMENTEL CORONEL (1863–1907), and GABRIEL MUÑÓZ (1864–1908).

(iv) *Colombia* / ISMAEL ENRIQUE ARCINIEGAS (1865–1937), in his early years a follower of Bécquer, later exchanged his spontaneity for Parnassian jewels. JOAQUÍN GONZÁLEZ CAMARGO (1865–1886). A. JOSÉ RIVAS GROOT, who will be found among the prose writers.

(v) *Bolivia* / ROSENDO VILLALOBOS (1860–1939), writer of madrigals (see "Blush of Modesty" ["*Rubor*"]), translator of Parnassians and symbolists. ADELA ZAMUDIO (1860–1926), rebellious and sincere. RICARDO MUJIA (1860).

(vi) *Chile* / NARCISO TONDREAU (1861–1949) is remembered more for his friendship with Rubén Darío than for his few verses. PEDRO ANTONIO GONZÁLEZ (1863–1903) was a strange person; nervous, suffering, bohemian, rebellious, atheistic, pessimistic; his themes were more or less philosophical and he was a romantic in his devotion to the great exponents of emotional eloquence, not decorative like the modernists but, like them, fond of seeking rare forms and being considered original. He became a character in two novels, Marcial Cabrera Guerra's *The White Feather* (*La pluma blanca*) and Luis Enrique Délano's *The Laurel on the Lyre* (*El laurel sobre la lira*), rather than a figure in literary history. His role was that of the poet coming from the past with his head bent down, who all of a sudden stumbles upon the first modernist poets, is amazed at their brilliance and begins immediately to cultivate the superficial and external aspects of the new poetic language. GUSTAVO VALLEDOR SÁNCHEZ (1868–1930) who began by writing Parnassian sonnets, then turned to simple descriptions of things in his country.

(vii) *Argentina* / Here there are various writers who break with tradition and create a movement that in 1893 will recognize Rubén Darío as the greatest poet of the language: we will list the most important one, LEOPOLDO DÍAZ (1862–1947). He was one of the first frequenters of the French *Parnasse*. In his *Sonnets* (*Sonetos*, 1888) there already is a searching for Greek myths, a transferring of figures from the plastic arts to poetry, a relishing of pagan pleasures, a polishing of perfect forms—actions common to all modernists. His Parnassian *Bas Reliefs* (*Bajorrelieves*) are from 1895. Darío was already in Buenos Aires and he eulogized it with brotherly affection. In his later work—*The Shadows of Hellas* (*Las sombras de Hellas*, 1902), *Atlantis Conquered* (*Atlántida conquistada*, 1906), *Amphoras and Urns* (*Las ánforas y las urnas*, 1923)—Díaz continued to gyrate in the center of his Parnassian esthetics, always golden but ever more frigid, with occasional symbolist poems, like "Belphegor," "The Golden Isles" (*Las islas de oro*), "The White Legend" (*"La leyenda blanca"*).

Rubén Darío, because of his birth date, should be studied here. But Rubén Darío was younger than Gutiérrez Nájera and Casal; he published *Profane Prose* (*Prosas profanas*) when they, and Martí, and Silva had already died, and it was with this book of 1896 that estheticism reaches its fulness, becomes conscious of its revolutionary program, is given a name, "modernism," and its influence reaches Spain. Therefore, we will find Rubén Darío in the next chapter.

B. MAINLY PROSE

1. Novel and Short Story

(i) *Mexico* / Among the Mexicans who enriched the realist art of narration, several of whom we mentioned in the preceding chapter and others whom we will mention in the following, two come to the fore during these years: Micrós and Gamboa. ANGEL DE CAMPO, who used the pen name MICRÓS (1868–1908), printed sketches of customs in the newspapers. From his impressions of society came short stories and a short novel, *The Rumba* (*La rumba*), in which he poured heaps and heaps of naturalist detail onto a woeful story. *Things Seen* (*Cosas vistas*) is the title of one of his books, a title that professes an objectivity that Micrós did not possess. When he was not caricaturizing or displaying his irony, he appeared as a sentimentalist. He felt tenderness and pity for all humble, poor, unprotected, and infirm life. In his compassion, he included animals, who he imagined suffered like human beings. From his sympathy for all who suffered grew his moral criticism, which at times became inflamed. FEDERICO GAMBOA (1864–1939) is the Mexican novelist who came the closest to what was then considered the modern novel, that is to say, the experimental novel that seriously studied Mexican society. He documented the customs of the people in the naturalist method, and preferred erotic themes. *Supreme Law* (*Suprema ley*, 1896), the story of a consumptive who is ruined by love, is set against a vast background of Mexican society. In *Santa* (1903) he achieved a greater equilibrium between his naturalism, his eroticism, and his depictions of customs. Is Santa, the prostitute, a literary first cousin to Zola's Nana or to the Goncourts' Elisa? Gamboa recovered his Catholic faith, already effective in *Reconquest* (*Reconquista*) and in *The Wound* (*La llaga*), and became a reactionary. He was an intense dramatist; perhaps his best constructed drama was *Between Brothers* (*Entre hermanos*, 1928).

(ii) *Central America / Honduras:* The first novel, *Angelina,* was by CARLOS F. GUTIÉRREZ (1861–1899).

Nicaragua: SALVADOR CALDERÓN RAMÍREZ (1868–1940) cultivated the fantastic in *Stories for My Carmencita* (*Cuentos a mi Carmencita*).

Costa Rica: The tradition of the sketch of customs lasted longer in America than anywhere else. Many writers, wanting to adhere to reality, scarcely managed to express themselves literarily. They would emerge from the mucky depths, and look about; they were part of the nature they described. It is not worthwhile listing names. In Costa Rica the depiction of customs, an old form in other places, surged forth at the end of the century with a new vigor, as if it were revolutionary. From the land mass of America comes a nation, Costa Rica, but it comes without a literature. For almost four centuries that land did not produce writers, either significant or insignificant—they did not even have a press until 1830. When writers finally appeared they split into two groups, one, the cosmopolitan estheticists, the other, regional realists. It was the realist group that has been rated the better, because it was closer to reality. After PÍO VÍQUEZ (1848–1899), a rich temperament although a poor writer, after MANUEL ARGÜELLO MORA (1845–1902), the first notable narrator, and after JUAN GARITA (1859–1914), depicter of customs, rises the important—important in Costa Rica —figure of MANUEL GONZÁLEZ ZELEDÓN (1864–1936), better known by the pen name MAGÓN. He described the city of San José, a city that was barely a city; he described it inside and out, home life, school life, life of the bureaucracy, of social clubs, and of cafes, of the plains, of the valleys and of the coffee plantations; he described poverty, feast days, love, popular types, everyday things, things he saw and, in the country, things he thought he saw. He did all this with the rapidity of the conversationalist, with dialectic colloquialisms, without worrying about creating situations or drawing characters. He was an observer of details, preferring indelicate subjects since he was a naturalist. Literature of the people, by the people, and for the people: a democratic formula of slight esthetic value but well documented. To be sure, there is no corny sentimentality in Magón. This is a negative value. Nor is there brashness: another negative value. It is not that Magón is forward and natural in manner, but that in his sketches of

customs there is no room for mawkishness nor for brashness because neither
is there room for literature. His mood is one of joyfulness, irony, and mischievousness. His sketches of customs rarely acquire the architecture of the
short story. One built-up story is "Eclipse of the Sun" (*"El clis de sol"*);
and another, "One's Own" (*"La propia"*). The former has antecedents in
"*¿Por qué era rubia?*" by P. A. Alarcón. González Zeledón enumerated, described, but did not construct a story. He is entertaining, like coarse conversation; and he is worthwhile because he has understood a people who,
since they have a place under the sun, deserve to be placed before a literary
mirror so their reflection can be seen. Magón did in prose what his cousin
Aquileo Echeverría used to do in verse. Other writers of customs copied
him, such as MANUEL DE JESÚS JIMÉNEZ (1854–1916), CLAUDIO GON-
ZÁLEZ RUCAVADO (1865–1925), CARLOS CAGINI (1865–1925), RICARDO
FERNÁNDEZ GUARDIA (1867–1950). The latter was a meticulous and
learned writer of prose. The realist novelist of most substance in Costa Rica
in these years was JENARO CARDONA (1863–1930), author of *The Cousin*
(*El primo*, 1905), a novel of the city about middle-class people, and *The
Sphinx of the Path* (*La esfinge del sendero*, 1914), even more removed from
the depiction of customs because of the analysis of the struggle of conscience
in a priest.

(iii) *Antilles* / In the Antilles the narrative genre did not have luster.
    Cuba: RAMÓN MEZA Y SUÁREZ INCLÁN (1861–1911) is an outstanding
figure, the most notable Cuban author to appear after Cirilo Villaverde.
Something of Villaverde's message appears in *Carmela* (1887), except that
Meza is more realistic. His two best novels are *My Uncle, the Civil Servant*
(*Mi tío el empleado*, 1886) and *Aniceto the Shopkeeper* (*Aniceto el ten-
dero*, 1889). *My Uncle, the Civil Servant* is a satirical novel on colonial
Havana. The first part is a satire on bureaucracy. Using the technique of
the author-witness, he has a young boy relate his life and that of his uncle,
Vicente Cuevas, from the time they reach Havana from their Andalusian
village, possessing nothing but a letter of recommendation, and find work
in a government office, until they are taken prisoner and escape from the
island, and the author leaves them on their way to Mexico. In the second
part, seven years later, the satire extends to other high circles of Cuban
society during the time of the colony. This part seems to be told in the third
person and it tells about the life, marriage and fortunes of Count Coveo. It
does not take the reader long to learn that Count Coveo is one and the same
Vicente Cuevas who was "my uncle" in the first part. In fact, in the penulti-
mate chapter it is revealed that the narrator is one and the same nephew,
with the difference that, separated from his uncle, he writes from a distance,
with the technique of the author-observer. This change of narrative focus is
part of the dynamic means Meza uses to leap from one perspective to another. Actually, Meza intrudes himself into the narrative as the omniscient
author. The novel is not a great success, but Meza undoubtedly had an
original personality and a gift for capturing metaphoric detail with poetic
dexterity, for the effective refinement of sensations and for the descriptive
miniature. In the first part of the book his style appears as a hasty and
exaggerated caricature. The events seem to be distorted by a mocking fan-

tasy, and in this grotesque and senseless labyrinth, with touches of picaresque literature and a nightmare atmosphere, we can hear constant peals of laughter. In the second part the narrative moves at a slower pace, although it contains some of his best impressionistic effects. Throughout the book, however, Meza intermittently displays a talent for fugitive impressions and for shaping them into imaginative and symbolic scenes. Although he had the sensitivity and imagination of a modernist, Meza preferred to confine himself to satirical realism.

Santo Domingo: FABIO FIALLO (1866–1942) went from poetry to prose, to the point where some of his poems were actually paraphrased into short stories. We have already placed him as a poet elsewhere. The motif of his *Fragile Stories* (*Cuentos frágiles*, 1908) is the female figure as an object of artistic contemplation. He is also the author of *Mefisto's Apples* (*Las manzanas de Mefisto*, 1934) and of a dramatic work. He remained impervious to vernacular themes. On the other hand, FEDERICO GARCÍA GODOY (1857–1924), essayist and critic, wrote a novelistic trilogy with episodes of national history. The first novel was the best, *Rufinito* (1908), whose protagonist is a political boss. This was followed by *Dominican Soul* (*Alma dominicana*, 1911) and *Guanuma* (1914). Others: CÉSAR NICOLÁS PENSON (1855–1901), who collected in his *Old Things* (*Cosas añejas*), traditions of the end of the eighteenth and of the nineteenth century in the manner of Ricardo Palma. JOSÉ RAMÓN LÓPEZ (1866–1922), whose *Stories of Puerto Plata* (*Cuentos puertoplateños*, 1904), although clumsy and not very original, do have some attraction. PEDRO MARÍA ARCHAMBAULT (1862–1944), in *Pine Groves* (*Pinares adentro*, 1929) gave us an eclogue description of highlands. JAIME COLSON (1862–1952) was a depicter of customs in *General Babieca, Patricio Flaquenco*, and *Corporal Chepe* (*El cabo Chepe*). VIRGINIA ELENA ORTEA (1866–1903), a devoted and cultured narrator, author of a mythological story "The Diamonds," also wrote realist works.

Puerto Rico: MATÍAS GONZÁLEZ GARCÍA (1866–1938) crudely novelized the life of Creole workers in *Things* (*Cosas*, 1893) and *Ernest* (*Ernesto*, 1894). But the most important novelist, within this Creole naturalism, was MANUEL ZENO GANDÍA (1855–1930). He was a physician and with a clinical eye wrote his "chronicles of a sick world," *The Pond* (*La charca*, 1895), *Garduña* (1896), *Business* (*El negocio*, 1922) and the posthumous *Redeemers* (*Redentores*). They are studies of wretchedness, hunger, vice, and the anguish of the Puerto Rican colony. As a good naturalist Zeno Gandía intervened in the make-up of his novels with his doctrines. Thus, his personages remained types rather than characters; furthermore, the environment, which is what the author wanted above all to describe, made the characters flat. He wished to regenerate the physical and spiritual life of the fields, and of the villages and cities, to correct materialist egoism, to dignify man. Although more observant than imaginative, Zeno Gandía managed to imbue human and social conflicts with enough substance to merit a place in the history of the Hispanic-American novel.

(iv) *Venezuela* / MANUEL VICENTE ROMERO GARCÍA (1865–1917) was effective with *Peonage* (*Peonía*, 1890), a "novel of Venezuelan customs." The author (or rather, the style) is dry, unappetizing, cynical, sarcastic. It is not that his admittedly materialist conception of life is to blame for his hardness as a writer, because other positivists of his time were more compassionate and human; and it is his materialism that reveals the best of him as a person, which is the spirit of social reform, his criticism of evil Venezuelan traditions. If Romero García does not draw his readers' sympathy, it is because earlier, in creating his novels, he felt no sympathy for his character creations. Or, said in another way, he lacked novelizing power. Although written under the aegis of Isaacs, *Peonage* has nothing of *María*. Even similar scenes are viewed with different eyes. He tells us in an interesting digression on Venezuelan literature that he esteems romantic poetry, but he is not a romantic, rather, a depicter of customs, a realist, even a naturalist. The novel, in itself, does not have much value: it is the story of a love, cut short by exile and death, in the midst of a degraded Venezuelan family. The moral and political reflections add nothing to the story; on the contrary, they hamper the novel's action. The description of customs remains, though. This is what Romero García believed to be most worthwhile, and he advocated an art derived from nature and society. GONZALO PICÓN-FEBRES (1860–1918) is celebrated for *Sergeant Felipe* (*El sargento Felipe*, 1889). In its historical background—the fratricidal war between Matías Salazar and Guzmán Blanco—this novel describes country life and tells of tragic loves and vengeances. Realism? Not much. At any rate it is a realism softened by many romantic tears; when this realism, softened in this way, does become hardened, it is in phrases, cut like jewels, in a poetic style. Some of the metaphors are more intuitions than ornaments. The mood is sentimental. At times the moral judgments on the cruel and stupid civil wars give the prose a declamatory leavening, and the phrasing swells in wide rhythms. His descriptive pages are the best: beautiful landscapes, beautiful portraits like that of Encarnación (on one occasion it says that the girl "resembles a figure from Mistral, the candid poet of Provence"). But there is not one character that really lives—Sergeant Felipe least of all. Picón-Febres always keeps them in his potter's hands and will not release them so they can live. MIGUEL EDUARDO PARDO (1868–1905) a novelist's apprentice, wrote with an abundance of verbiage and a scarcity of vivid expression. *A Whole People* (*Todo un pueblo*) is a novel without unity. A young lad, Julián, the descendant of a destitute Indian family, but who now comes from a good family, wishes to reform society. Anarchist? Socialist? His mother, a widow, gives herself to a scoundrel, the father of Julián's sweetheart. In the end, Julián kills the scoundrel. Balzac, Flaubert, and Zola are mentioned as models for a possible novel on the defects of the society he is describing, but *A Whole People* does not follow those models. JOSÉ GIL FORTOUL (1852–1943) is preferable as a historian rather than as a novelist, although with his *Julián* (1888) he was one of the forerunners of naturalism in the French style.

(v) *Colombia* / Some of the narrators of this generation— Vargas Vila, J. M. Rivas Groot—because of their connection with modernism, will be shifted to the next chapter. Other narrators—LORENZO MARROQUÍN (1885–1918) and FRANCISCO

DE PAULA RENDÓN (1855–1917)—will be only mentioned here,
so that we may devote all the available space to the great novelist
of these years, TOMÁS CARRASQUILLA (1858–1940). His production came late in life; and because of the contrast between
his realism and the cosmopolitan tastes of the modernists there
were those who believed his novels, written between 1896 and
1935, were outmoded stragglers. Carrasquilla, in fact, complained
of the modernist fashion, and in his "homilies" to Max Grillo
and other young esthetes he recommended a realist program—
"to describe man in his medium"—that would reveal the national
character spontaneously. The realism of Carrasquilla, nevertheless, was closer to the artistic novels of the twentieth century than
to the pedestrian sketches of customs of the nineteenth, although
certain of the narrations were pedestrian. He was an original man.
He had writing talent to spare; and he also dominated a language
rich in Antioquian idioms, pure Spanish, and golden down to
its last roots, lithe and agile in its daring moves. But he did not
take the career of novelist seriously. He would scribble down copy
without thinking of his reader; he did not even intend to publish.
Almost as if he had taken a bet that Antioquia would lend itself as
a setting for a novel, he came to write *Fruits from My Land*
(*Frutos de mi tierra*, 1896), "taken directly from Nature," says
Carrasquilla himself, "without idealizing at all the reality of life."
His having written in a void, without regard for a reading public,
and without aspirations of producing a book, damaged the skeletal
frame of his stories. They are of varied structure, of varied themes
—the novels: *Grandeur* (*Grandeza*, 1910); *The Marquise of
Yolombó* (*La Marquesa de Yolombó*, 1926); *A Long Time
Ago: Memoirs of Eloy Gamboa* (*Hace tiempo. Memorias de
Eloy Gamboa*, 1935–36); novelettes: *Little Luther* (*Luterito*),
later entitled "Father Casafús" ("*El padre Casafús*," 1899);
Salve, Regina, 1903; *Child's Affection* (*Entrañas de niño*, 1906);
Ligia Cruz, 1920; *The Blue-Eyed Fellow* (*El zarco*, 1922); and
folklore, fantastic, psychological, and symbolic short stories:
At the Right Hand of God, the Father (*En la diestra de Dios
Padre*, 1897); *The Lonely Soul* (*El ánima sola*, 1898); *The
Rifle* (*El rifle*, 1915); *Palonegro*, 1919. Carrasquilla's narrative

is characterized as a whole by the numerous characters it presents, all taken from the mines, the fields, the highlands, the villages, the Colombian roads, and intertwined in ordinary circumstances; these characters do not show their inner selves directly ("Father Casafús" is an exceptional example of interest in things psychological), but rather live outgoing lives constantly compelled to create dialog. In his pages there is talking and talking: idle chatter, anecdotes, gossiping, with a genuine malice in the people. But the conversation of these characters is not "put" in their mouths mechanically, as the writers of customs used to do; Carrasquilla first listened to popular conversation, assimilated it, and then created characters who speak with natural and expressive vigor. This means that Carrasquilla identified popular speech with his own style and in this way anticipated the manner of the regionalist novelists of today. Even so, although the setting, the customs, the situations and the characters are taken from the people, Carrasquilla does not rub elbows with the crowd, making believe he sees things at their level, as the realists used to coldly feign, but he sincerely surveys all from his solitary lookout. He looks so intently that his eyes probably hurt. Even his humor hurts, because it discovers human weakness. He is more observant of the movement of the masses than of individual actions. His attitude is one of love for his region and for the humble, but with philosophic aloofness. For this reason, he has created deep and complex characters—women, children—for this reason, personal recollections have such power in his stories. He does not offer theses, he does not protest, he does not preach, he does not moralize, but he does have a philosophy—naturalism—which brings him to compare the human quality with the animal. So that the comparison may be better defended, Carrasquilla shows syphilitics, suicides, and ignoramuses, steeped in the "garbage cans" of nature—cf. "Money Mad" (*"A la plata!"*). Carrasquilla preferred *Salve, Regina* and *The Marquise of Yolombó*. With only a few alterations, the history of the beautiful Regina—consumed by the fever of doubt, by purity, faith, love, scruples—could have gained in tragic power. *The Marquise of Yolombó* could be called the possibility of a great novel. It is a historical novel, since the action takes place from the middle of the eighteenth century to the post-Independence war days. However, the novel is more ethnographic than historical. It tells us the story of the Creole woman, Barbara, who, from age sixteen until she becomes wealthy, wishes to become a miner. However, she obtains the title of Marquise from Charles IV, falls victim to a scoundrel who weds her in order to rob her of her reserves of gold, loses her mind and regains it in her old age, when Hispanic America has become a cocoon of republics. If it is not history, at least it is chronicle. And the best part is not the thin novelistic line, but the large daubs of color with which the mining customs of Yolombó are described—customs of the rich Spanish families and customs of the poor Negro families, with artistic sympathy for both. Folklore and human masses are what one sees on the primary plane. From there, receding into the background, are a few, very few, clearcut episodes: the grotesque idyl between Don Chepe and Silverita, the cruel scene between Martín and the crucified Negro, Orellana's baseness. And, even more blurry, a few, very few, attempts at drawing characters: Barbosa, Don Chepe, Martín, María de la Luz. On the whole *The Marquise of Yolombó* is badly constructed—digressions, anachronistic reflections, lessons in history or in ethnography that rupture the story's integrity.

On the other hand, the prose is spiced with regionalisms and neologisms. Carrasquilla has placed himself within the Antioquian language, and from there speaks freely. The effect is surprising. We cannot place this prose in the history of Spanish realism, with Galdós, for example. Carrasquilla lived isolated from current literary tastes, although in *The Marquise of Yolombó* he cites Balzac and Flaubert. He was not only isolated in his Antioquia, but between him and Antioquia he placed an esthetic glass plate. Through this glass, he deformed regional matters. He described with sharpness and irony. He scrutinized minute detail and captured it with stunning words. It is obvious that for him writing was a solitary game. For this reason he was not, nor could he be, popular. If we call him a realist it is for lack of a better word. He made reality crystallize in an apparently rich and colloquial language, but it was really an artistic language. Reality and language, crystallized in this way, are a new creation, like those systematically deformed creations known as *esperpentos*. In fact, Carrasquilla speaks to us of characters who "enter in the form of *esperpentos*." There are horrible scarecrows that Valle-Inclán will tackle later. Carrasquilla coldly laughs at the material he elaborates. There is an atmosphere of farce, as in chapters II and III where the old man Don Chepe seeks the hand of the young marriageable Silverita. The figures are stretched out or made squat, as in a caricature. The pleasure derived from this distortion is not that of the realist novel of the nineteenth century, but that of the artistic prose of the twentieth. In his best moments Carrasquilla does not document his reality; he subjects it to the refractions of aberrant lenses and mirrors. His reality may be humble—ignorant Spaniards, Creoles lost within the American landscape, Negroes adhering to their African traditions, receding Indian shadows—but his stereoscope is aristocratic. This is so only in his better moments (had Valle-Inclán known them, he would have enjoyed them and even profited from them for his *Tirano Banderas*), because otherwise, judged in its totality, *The Marquise of Yolombó* is a failure. As an example of popular short stories the reader should consult *At the Right Hand of God, the Father* where he can admire the humor and irony with which old folklore themes are dressed in the costumes of Antioquia.

(vi) *Ecuador* / We have the novelist ALFREDO BAQUERIZO MORENO (1859–1950), tidy and cultured in *Sonata in Prose* (*Sonata en prosa*), but capable of picking out characters from the crowd of ordinary people as he does in *El Señor Penco*, 1895. He was also a narrator in *Inland* (*Tierra adentro*) and *Evangelina*. The writer who masterfully opened a series of realist Ecuadorian novels of social content was LUIS A. MARTÍNEZ (1868–1909). *On the Coast* (*A la costa*) is a landmark novel with its almost scientific eagerness for truth. It records changes in the life of Ecuador: its old social customs, its new hopes for transformation. The prose is lively and clearcut, although capable of crudities. It was Martínez who made forward strides in Ecuadorian realism. There were others of less momentum: everything considered, the most important of these were JOSÉ RAFAEL BUSTAMANTE, whose novel *To Kill the Worm* (*Para matar el gusano*, 1912) has to do with a drunkard from the middle class of Quito; and JOSÉ ANTONIO CAMPOS, with his more or less humorous narrations, tending in general toward lessons in liberal politics—*Cathodic Rays* (*Rayos catódicos*). *Will-o'-the-Wisps* (*Fuegos fátuos*), *Things of My Land* (*Cosas de mi tierra*).

(vii) *Peru* / There were women novelists beginning with the first group of romantics, and women also made their contribution to realism. The Peruvian CLORINDA MATTO DE TURNER (1854–1909) is remembered for her boldness in bringing to the novel the formulas of Indian liberation put forth by González Prada. *Birds Without Nests* (*Aves sin nido*, 1889) refers to two lovers, Manuel and Margarita, who turn out to be half-brother and -sister, begotten by two Indian women and the parish priest. The novel affirmed the principle that the Peruvian nation was formed by the multitudes of Indians disseminated on the eastern side of the Andes range and it also denounced the tyranny of the governor, the clergy, and the landowners. In spite of its romantic content, the book created a scandal. There were protests and persecutions. The author had put her finger on the wound—the clerics and oligarchs felt the pain. The novels that followed, *The Nature of Men* (*Índole*), *Heritage* (*Herencia*), do not broaden the place in literary history that *Birds Without Nests* gave the author; but that place is already broad since it belongs to those who awaken the social conscience; and, in fact, after Matto de Turner will come the revolutionary posing of Indian problems. Her *Cuzco Traditions* (*Tradiciones cuzqueñas*, 1884–86) lacks the variety, imagination, and mischievousness of the "Peruvian traditions" of Palma, whom she called "my teacher."

We have already seen that, forty years back, Narciso Aréstegui had anticipated the movement of the vindication of the Indians. This movement was also developed during Matto de Turner's time by JOSÉ T. ITOLARRES, through *The Trinity of the Indian* (*La Trinidad del indio,* 1855) and later by JOAQUÍN CAPELO (1852–1929) with *The Stunted Ones* (*Los menguados,* 1912). EMILIO GUTIÉRREZ DE QUINTANILLA (1858–1935) narrated the lives of rogues, but although the scene is Peruvian, the archaic, Cervantesque language, artificial in the Montalvo manner, robs them of real life.

(viii) *Chile* / After Alberto Blest Gana, the first important narrators to emerge in Chile, in the order of our preference, are Lillo and Orrego Luco, and perhaps we should also mention Gana. These are the ones who blaze a trail for legions to follow. In the next chapter we shall examine the novelists and short story writers who continue to explore Chile's social reality: Prado, D'Halmar, Santiván, Edwards Bello, and others.

BALDOMERO LILLO (1867–1923) stands out, not only for his original talent, but also for the newness of his themes. He worked in a mining town of southern Chile, and from his first-hand observations of the misery and suffering there, his short stories emerged. From first-hand observation, to be sure, although it was from the literature of the French naturalists, especially Zola's *Germinal*, that he learned to relate and denounce at the same time. In the stories of *Sub Terra* (1904) the prose, in spite of an occasional stumbling over the grammar, and an occasional falling into artistic mannerisms, advances effectively with measured steps. With a vigorous realism it shows the hardships of the coal miners. He cries in protest, but his protest does not remain an outcry; it becomes literature. From the same recesses of his soul whence the protest rose, came his understanding for the underdog, the ragged, the Indian: it was this understanding, more than the protest, that made Lillo one of the most effective writers of his time. He seldom wrote stories with humorous intent; his mood is one of pathos. He showed his emotions without any pretense and he sought the sympathy of his readers, as in "Compartment Number 12," "Repayment," "The Screwloose Devil," "Juan Fariña." The stories in *Sub Sole* (1907) were more ambitious, but not thereby better. In his collection, he barely relates scenes at the mines; rather, he writes stories of local color set in the countryside or at the seaside. There is less sentimentalism and, in compensation, much better humor. Above all, he cultivates a type of parable, allegory, and legend related to the poetic prose of the modernists. In his posthumous collections, *Popular Stories* (*Relatos populares*), *The Find and Other Stories of the Sea* (*El hallazgo y otros cuentos del mar*), the variety of moods and themes is more visible.

The Chilean realists devoted themselves almost entirely to country themes; if they dealt with the city it was in relation to the country. Nevertheless, the first novelist of this type, LUIS ORREGO LUCO (1866–1949) excelled in city themes and, within the city, in social themes of the distinguished and privileged class. He was the novelist of Chile's rapid social and economic growth. With some French naturalism, and somewhat more Spanish naturalism, he observed the life of the upper bourgeoisie. He does not record healthy life, but rather moral sicknesses. He intended to paint a vast series of "scenes on the life of Chile." The first was *A New Idyll* (*Un idilio nuevo*, 1900), which took place in the city of Santiago, in the contemporary epoch, in high society; its theme is the importance of love, and of righteousness in the face of the power of money. In *Big House* (*Casa grande*, 1908)—the most famous of his novels—he exposes matrimonial discord in a distinguished house, in a world of business dealings, parties, luxury, neurosis and immoralities that end with the husband's murdering his wife. It is a novel of parlor customs and of gossiping, the first in which the way of thinking, acting, and feeling of the opulent class of Chile is analyzed. *In the Family* (*En familia*, 1912), *Wounded Tree Trunk* (*Tronco herido*, 1929), *Black Beach* (*Playa negra*, 1947) are several more incisions into the flesh of Chilean society. His novels make up a monochord cycle which is stylistically out of tune; but they are valuable as chronicles of Chilean life. At times his chronicle becomes history, as in *Memoirs of a Volunteer of the Old Fatherland* (*Memorias de un voluntario de la Patria Vieja*, 1905) and *Through the Storm* (*Al través de la tempestad*, 1914).

FEDERICO GANA (1868–1926) did not confine himself to the mere description of customs, but enriched them with feeling, psychological acuteness, and even poetry. His stories *Days in the Field* (*Días de campo*, 1916)—the most celebrated is "The Señora"—is a collection of capably done sketches. This author, who goes out hunting, gallops over the countryside conversing with the country folk and making observations on them, is at bottom a timid, languid, saddened man. Gana revealed his melancholy, more than in his stories, in brief poems in prose which he called "daubs of color." Other Chileans: the depicter of customs DANIEL RIQUELME (1857–1912), MANUEL J. ORTIZ (1870–1945), successful with his *Letters From the Village* (*Cartas de la aldea*, 1908) and ALBERTO DEL SOLAR (1860–1921) who, although he left his country, published an Indianist novel, *Huincahual*, in 1888. In 1890 he published a realist one, *Rastaquouère*, on the disillusionments of South Americans in Paris.

(ix) *Uruguay* / Of the Uruguayan generation that yielded its best fruits between 1895 and 1910 (Rodó, Carlos and María Eugenia Vaz Ferreira, Herrera y Reissig, Florencio Sánchez, Horacio Quiroga) we will carry here two realist narrators: Viana and Reyles.

JAVIER DE VIANA (1868–1926) wrote a forgettable novel, *Gaucha*, 1899, whose burden of defects outweighs the virtues of its composition. He was a forceful writer, and so prolific that he conceived four stories in three hours, or so he tells us. The first collections indicate a greater effort at composition: *Countryside* (*Campo*, 1896), *Gurí and Other Stories* (*Gurí y otras novelas*, 1901). Later his narrations develop more rapidly: *Macachines* (1910), *Dry Kindling* (*Leña seca*, 1911), *Yuyos* (1912). At the end of his career, Viana was proceeding mechanically and produced several volumes in which he rarely added anything new. He admits that he had learned to tell a story from Zola, Maupassant, Turgenev and Sacher-Masoch. Nevertheless, his art was spontaneous, so typically conversational that to cite these masters was just coyness. His theme was life in the country, and he destroyed the romantic image of the gaucho by presenting him as an animal. Men and women are products of the soil: this naturalist conception of life of his is so apparent that he brings to light every image, ever adjective. He tends toward the anecdote—a passion, a crime, a deceit, a civil war scene or one of country life. But at times he wraps up the anecdote in literature—generally landscape literature—and it is clear then that in his library, in addition to the romantics and realists, there is no dearth of modernists. That is, he had learned some techniques from them. But he was inclined toward the ordinary: regional language, the sensationalism of violence and sordidness, the complacency in forms of life that the author, as well as the readers, feel are below them. He cultivated the unexpected development, not always by reversing a situation, but sometimes through a psychological change in the characters.

Carlos Reyles (1868–1938) is the best novelist that Uruguay offers in this generation. In the current of ideas that has been called "philosophy of life" Reyles allied himself with the panegyrists of action, force, energy, power, individual egoism. There is something pragmatic about his thought, which is closer to that of Nietzsche than to that of William James. He was a feudal gentleman, irreligious and anti-socialist; he believed that the basis of everything was matter and that man had emerged from it with an irrepressible "will to consciousness," from which his materialism at intervals rose to heights of idealism. Although he was a man of vast culture—art, literature, philosophy, science—his intellectual position is rather that of the esthete; and his esthetic theories and practices belong to the modernist school (with a strong accent on the French exponents), though his prose was disciplined by his reading of old and new Spanish books. His technique is realism, and the reality he novelized with the greatest conviction was that of the Uruguayan countryside. He dealt with other themes: life of the city in Uruguay (*The Race of Cain* [*La raza de Caín*, 1900]) and in Spain (*The Bewitchment of Seville* [*El embrujo de Sevilla*, 1922]). But it was the landowner in Reyles who, definitively, took up the pen to write, if not the best pages from a stylistic point of view, at least the most enduring. This rich landowner had no sympathy for the poor people who worked his lands, but he knew what it was to work in the fields. His *Beba* (1894) at times sounds like a manual on agronomy and cattle breeding, but ably describes peasant types and customs. *The Piece of Land* (*El terruño*, 1916) is a novel centered on rural scenes in an era agitated by civil wars. A thread of continuity runs through these scenes, but each scene conserves its autonomy. The various episodes have different moods: psychological (the decadence of the Primitive, IX and XV); humorous (Papagayo and the burro, XI); and epic (the heroic death of Pantaleón, XIV). The main action that gives unity to all the episodes is more strictly ideological: the conflict in harmony between the utilitarian philosophy of Mamagela and the idealistic philosophy of Tocles. The title "The Piece of Land" does not refer to real land, but to Tocles' mental landscape. Tocles is a caricature of a certain type of intellectual; at times he is a self-caricature, as though Reyles wanted to invest him with the testimony of a personal crisis of conscience. The author, in his omniscience, gives us his version of what is happening instead of presenting us directly with the spectacle of the action itself. The prose is that of a realist schooled in modernism: Reyles' grammar is more polished than his style, and his style is more polished than his composition. *El Gaucho Florido* (1932) is a novel about the Uruguayan ranch with its "uncouth gauchos." In the protagonist Reyles depicts a peon he knew personally on one of his ranches. It has intense episodes, but the novel as a whole tends to extend itself and weaken its virtue. Reyles' novels are also psychological—morbid psychologies, a little in the manner of Huysmans' *The Race of Cain*, and perhaps even taken from Proust, as in the scene where Pepe spies on the erotic games of the two women in *To Love Battles . . . Fields of Feathers* (*A batallas de amor . . . campos de pluma*).

Although inferior to Viana and Reyles, but still within the literature of country themes, we could cite MANUEL BERNÁRDEZ (Spain–Uruguay, 1868), author of *Narrations* (*Narraciones*) wherein the descriptive is passable and the oratory is worthless.

(x) *Argentina* / In Argentina a group of writers appeared who made the novel their profession. The theme, predominantly social, documents the upheavals in a country that saw at least the optimism of the great presidencies of Mitre, Sarmiento, and Avellaneda crumble away. Their procedure was realist and, in some cases, contained abstract theses and problems, in the manner of the naturalists. The group: MANUEL T. PODESTÁ (1853–1920), FRANCISCO A. SICARDI (1856–1927), JOSÉ SEFERINO ÁLVAREZ, *"Fray Mocho"* (1858–1903), MARTÍN GARCÍA MEROU (1862–1905), SEGUNDO I. VILLAFAÑE (1859–1937). CARLOS MARÍA OCANTOS (1860–1949) wrote his novels looking at Buenos Aires from the point of view of a Spanish literary circle. Since it is impossible for us to study them all (many are not listed), we will pick out a few. MARTINIANO LEGUIZAMÓN (1858–1935) lagged behind, with his historical subject matter and with the still romantic tone of his regional novel, *Montaraz*. The action is placed in Entre Ríos, in 1820. We are shown political bossism, gaucho mobs, and a sentimental plot: the heroic conduct of the outlaw Silva who defends two loves, his woman and his land, until he dies in an epic struggle, a victim of the outrages of the invaders, amidst the horrors of conflagration and destruction. The idyl is weak; the description of peasant life, strong.

If Leguizamón walks at an old man's pace, Miró steps forth at a youthful gait. JOSÉ MIRÓ (1867–1896) wrote his only novel, *The Stock Exchange* (*La Bolsa*, 1891), under the pseudonym of "Julián Martel." He was a business reporter for *La Nación* and, although a young man of twenty-four, he knew the world of stock-jobbing and its shady operators. He had before his eyes a tense, excited society: false cosmopolitanism and the subversion of old Creole values as a consequence of the immigrant inundation, the desire for luxury and ostentation, the parasitism of the ambitious, the opportunism of the politicians, the contrast between quickly amassed fortunes and the chronic poverty of the poor, embezzlement, and vice. His descriptions strive to be realist and even naturalist, but the technique is primitive, immature, coarse in construction. Hand in hand with the direct observations of the atmosphere of the Buenos Aires stock exchange (in the novelty of this theme lies the greatest merit, perhaps the only merit, of the novel) there are second-hand observations, like those that inspire in him an anti-Semitism apparently of European origin, since in Argentina this type of "problem" did not exist at that time. The declamations of moral judgments and the political reflections damage the novel. The life of Dr. Glow is the novelistic axis, but the workings of business deals are clearer than human conflicts. He did not emboss either his characters or his prose.

A novelist who is winning more and more respect with the years is ROBERTO J. PAYRÓ (1867–1928). His patient, understanding, honest, tolerant, and hopeful conception of an Argentina in transition is scattered throughout his chronicles, stories, and dramas. After clearing away twenty or so volumes, we are left with *Laucha's Marriage* (*El casamiento de Laucha*, 1906), *Pago Chico* (1908), which could be fused with the posthumous "stories of Pago Chico," and the *Entertaining Adventures of the Grandson of Juan Moreira* (*Divertidas aventuras del nieto de Juan Moreira*, 1910)—three works built on a common theme: the rogue in Argentine life. They have a family air about them; as a matter of fact, they are neighbors who know each other. But the three novels presuppose three different focal points, dissimilar attitudes toward Argentina and, of course, they crystallize in different modes of style. Three books, three outlooks. That of the rogue, of the humorist, and of the sociologist. *Laucha's Marriage* is the history of an infamous, vile, and scoundrelly act. But Payró treats the roguery of Laucha's behavior with the roguery of the art of narrating; in other words, Payró, since he is as roguish in his art as Laucha is in his conduct, achieved a picaresque novel in which the vision of the author is not tinged with scruples. The world that oozes out of the novel is the world as a rogue intuits it; he assumes his role and rambles on, enjoying himself, confident that no other values exist which are more legitimate than his. The author does not even appear in the written word— the story takes on the appearance of a Laucha monolog. Payró masterfully solved this delicate problem: presenting Laucha chatting before a meeting of Creoles in such a way that the monolog might be psychologically truthful and artistically worthwhile. In this and in many other ways, he is an exemplary novelist. The stories in *Pago Chico* evoke once again the same roguish reality as that of *Laucha's Marriage*, but with an important change in perspective: Laucha was relating an episode of his life, in his own words, and passing on his own judgments. In *Pago Chico*, on the other hand, the episodes are being related from the outside by a chronicler whom one supposes to be a jokester, an outsider writing from documents. In *Laucha's Marriage* there was no civic moral; only the voice of a blackguard without feelings of social solidarity was heard. But in *Pago Chico* a model citizen is describing social ills. However, when he began to recall the political banditry of Argentina, the understanding and reformist soul of Payró impregnated his pages with good humor. He gave us the humorous vision of a world of rogues. In *Entertaining Adventures of the Grandson of Juan Moreira*, on the other hand, he created a rogue with an intent that was absolutely serious. It deals with the same social and human reality that we saw in the previous works. But now Payró constructs the outlines of this reality so that we may judge it. He has mounted the material of the novel on the axes of a theory of progress for the Argentine Republic. It is a novel with theoretical supports. A rogue is speaking—the novel is supposed to be the autobiography of Gómez Herrera—but this rogue moves along the lines of force of Argentine politics. And following behind Gómez Herrera, Payró points out those lines of force, because now, what interests him most is the form the country takes, rather than the anecdotes of his character, Gómez Herrera. Payró was less fortunate with his dramas, although because of the seriousness of the problems posed, they dignified the incipient Río de la Plata theater.

2. Essay

Of the thinkers of this epoch the most systematic was ALE-JANDRO KORN (Argentina, 1860–1936). He criticized positivism but with historical understanding. Korn leaned preferentially toward Kant but supplemented him with Schopenhauer, Bergson, and others. In *Creative Liberty* (*La libertad creadora*, 1920) he formulated the philosophy which he developed later. His philosophy discarded metaphysics as a personal, irrational belief, and undertook an inquiry into the subjective world. He offered us a doctrine of values from which his ethics derive: an energetic exploration of conscience in its struggle for liberty. His prose was extraordinary, incisive, clear, ironic, elegant, and expressive.

In a group of essayists having the double vocation of thinkers and artists the following appear: CARLOS ARTURO TORRES (Colombia, 1867–1911) who as a poet was still a romantic (his poem "Eleonora" [written at the age of twenty, although published in 1898] is a fantasy on eternal and impossible love, inspired by Poe, Heine, Shelley and Byron; his importance, however, does not lie in his *Poetic Works* [*Obra poética*], but in *The Idols of the Forum* [*Los ídolos del foro*]); CÉSAR ZUMETA (Venezuela, 1860–1955), who wasted his complex talent in newspaper work and, in spite of being more capable than others, left fewer works; ALBERTO MASFERRER (El Salvador, 1868–1932) was a self-made intellectual who wrote prose poems and interesting sociological essays; MANUEL J. CALLE (Ecuador, 1866–1919), a liberal journalist, was renowned in his own time for his sarcastic, skeptical, pessimistic but festive "chats." There were intellectuals of great influence in their countries who left no literary works, as in the case of the introducer of positivism in Paraguay: CECILIO BÁEZ (1862–1941).

The great journalists of modernism were not always gilders of style, but in their pages, no matter how simple their language may have been, they gathered gold from the best literatures.

BALDOMERO SANÍN CANO (Colombia, 1861–1957) was one of these. His restless humanist soul unfolded like the pages of a great newspaper, where the themes and news of our time are recorded. It contains all of the sections, including the comics and international news, because he traveled in many countries, and brought back information and commentary on the remote Anglo-Saxon, Germanic, and Scandinavian literatures, not to mention his trips through libraries and through the broad mansions of his own spirit. He was friend and mentor to the first modernists, from Silva to Valencia; and not only because he lived long, but because he understood the new things that came across his path, he continued to be the friend and mentor of youth, and in his old age he discerned the face of surrealism, existentialism, and today's communism with a sharp eye. His skepticism consisted in being attentively alert to all points of view. For him, literary criticism was knowing how to listen to what each author was saying. His prose articulates his logical thought with the same controlled energy with which the artists of his generation articulated their own concept of beauty. Therefore, although it may appear otherwise, Sanín Cano's cold and elegant desire for preciseness is modernist. He collected some essays in *Manual Civilization* (*La civilización manual*, 1925), *Inquiries and*

Images (*Indagaciones e imágenes*, 1926), *Criticism and Art* (*Crítica y arte*, 1932), *Essays* (*Ensayos*, 1942). Not even his memoirs *From My Life and Other Lives* (*De mi vida y otras vidas*, 1949) form an organic whole. In *Humanism and the Progress of Man* (*El humanismo y el progreso del hombre*, 1955) he gathered essays from his last twenty-five years—the bulk of them written in his last ten years. His is a prose inhabited, not visited, by the epigram; that is, the epigram moves about spontaneously wherever it pleases and does not confine itself to the living room.

C. THEATER

The most preoccupied and occupied thinkers were poets. The poets were novelists. The novelists were playwrights. In reality, writers cultivate many genres simultaneously; for this reason, it is difficult to classify our history in terms of literary types, unless we dismember the authors and distribute the parts throughout different paragraphs, thereby sacrificing the living unity of each person to the clarity of the design. So in speaking of the theater, we should return to the authors we listed as novelists. In the Río de la Plata region, we have the interesting case of the theater growing out of the novel. The novels of EDUARDO GUTIÉRREZ (Argentina, 1853–1890) were not noteworthy, but they became noteworthy because of the role they played in the formation of the Río Plata theater. Gutiérrez was a truculent serial writer, of ordinary vintage, who scribbled pages with infallible popular success. In ten years he wrote some thirty novels of adventure, intrigue, violence, and murder. At times it seemed that the author would achieve the novel on Argentine low life, but he lacked the vision and even the imagination.

Some of his novels were gauchesque, along the line of *Martín Fierro*, and they fascinated the readers with their barroom brawls and their outlaws living on the wild frontier between barbarism and civilization. The most famous was *Juan Moreira* (1879), the chronicle of a real bushwhacker who in 1870 or thereabouts, put his knife at the service of the local political bosses, but who was converted by Gutiérrez into a hero, the personification of courage and a symbol of protest against the abuses of law enforcers. In 1884 a Buenos Aires circus asked Gutiérrez to adapt his *Juan Moreira* to a pantomime with songs, guitars, dances, gauchos on horseback, and knife and gun duels. Two years later the actor Podestá, the same one who had organized the pantomime, decided to convert it into a spoken drama. With dialogs taken from Gutiérrez, and others of his own invention, Podestá was founding, in 1886 in the circus arena of Chivilcoy, a crude and uncouth theater, but an original one. In rapid succession new adaptations of other Gutiérrez novels followed; new works were written and *Juan Moreira's* offspring multiplied profusely. There had been theatrical antecedents, unrelated to one another, most of which never reached the stage, and which

25

generally were of little significance. But the popular theater, conceived as a tight world of stability and continuity, with plays, staging, actors, public, and critics, began in the Río de la Plata with the gauchesque drama. It is given the general designation of the Río de la Plata theater because Argentinian and Uruguayan writers became intermingled in a single movement, as shall be seen in another chapter.

In Chile, RICARDO FERNÁNDEZ MONTALVA (1866–1899), poet, novelist, achieved success with his realist dramas.

XI. 1895-1910

Authors born between 1870 and 1885

Historical framework: Industrialization. Growth of international capitalism. Porfirio Díaz in Mexico. Liberal oligarchy in Argentina. Spain loses its last possessions in America.

Cultural tendencies: Height of modernism.

Introduction to the Characteristics of Modernism

In the preceding chapter we saw how our own America, which by the end of 1880 had been through the worst phase of anarchy, entered into an era of prosperity—at least in some cities. There was more division of labor, and one of the specializations was literature. The young writers rebelled against the old farrago and set about forging a new poetic language. What had been written in their countries up to that time no longer inspired them. Nor did Spain have anything to say to them. The voices that beckoned them to freedom and beauty came from elsewhere—from England, but above all from France. In contrast to the English Pre-Raphaelites who, repelled by the ugliness of industrial cities, had turned to medieval candor, certain French poets reconciled art and science. So France, who had given us the formulas by which we were able to enter into romanticism, also provided formulas for the way out.

It was with the French Parnassians that Hispanic Americans learned to aspire to perfection in form. While they advanced triumphantly, with Darío leading the way, they learned about the success that symbolism was having in France during those very years, and on their way they added to their Parnassian style, rich in vision, the symbolist style, rich in musicality. In verse as well as in prose they tried out the newest procedures, above all an amazing rhythmic renovation, using the rhythms in the language and, furthermore, those in feelings and thought. They cultivated nervous refinements, synesthesias and morbidities, moral crises, anti-bourgeois philosophies and political paradoxes. They transposed to literature what they had appreciated in other arts, in chamber concerts, in ballet presentations and, above all, in museums with Hellenic halls, in much of the rococo of the eighteenth century, in the art of Japan and China, in impressionistic chromatics and harmonies. They used symbols of the aristocracy, like the neck of the swan and the tail of the peacock, the rose and the fleur-de-lis, miniatures in poetic prose, unusual graphs with non-Latin words and an abuse of capital letters. These Hispanic Americans were in accord with one another, not because they had previously reached an agreement, but because in all of them the common pose was one of keeping their eyes fixed on Europe. So that they might better adapt themselves to the row of lights on the European horizon, they lined up shoulder to shoulder and turned their backs on America. Of course they had behind them a cultural heritage—especially that of the Spanish language, which with its particular internal forms opened up some avenues for them and shut off others; and there was also something in their literary tradition, for example, that of the Spanish baroque of the 17th century, that they elaborated with new preciosities. But in general they were cosmopolitan and exotic. Through romantic, Parnassian and symbolist books they had achieved a mental synthesis, and with that synthesized mentality they chose sensations, motives, objects, words, insinuations and harmonies. Literature became saturated with luxury. Seen from a bird's-eye view, the dark countries of America began to glow with a strange phosphorescence. Like brokers on the stock exchange who know the quotations for each foreign coin, the young people who appeared after 1880 could tell which phenomenon had the mintage with the highest prestige in the international bank. They were convinced that the work of combining styles was in itself a new form of expression. And they were proud to belong to a minority that for the first time could specialize in the arts. They gave to literary forms the adoration due to supreme values. Everything could be put into those forms, the old as well as the new (they were anti-routine, not anti-tradition), but it was the forms themselves that should present a challenge. Their passion for form led them to estheticism, and this is the aspect that critics have studied most. They were enthusiastic about any spiritual effort, as long as it had distinction. To be distinguished meant to be a resplendent craftsman in the expression of minority tastes. Tastes for what was attractive, for what was elegant? Naturally. But there was also another minority taste, for a reality that was ugly and sick.

These were the "modern ones" of Hispanic America. The word "modern" connotes a transitory condition. But in manuals the literature of the transitory "modern ones" of the years 1885 to 1910 is still given the adjective "modernist" or the noun "modernism." In reality modernism does not exist. It is simply a mental concept that helps us to understand certain unrelated phenomena. Like all concepts in literary journalism, this concept called "modernism" lends itself to inflation and deflation. The inflationists define the word by giving it an abstract meaning that takes in a great number of decades, countries, languages; intellectual, religious, and artistic activities, genres, tendencies, leaders. The deflationists, on the contrary, give it a concrete meaning: a few years of literary activity promoted by a very select group of Hispanic Americans. Let us not get involved in the controversy. The modernism that interests us here—and we shall not deny that there are other varieties—is the modernism that was born and died with Rubén Darío. It was a movement that ran throughout all of Hispanic-America, but to follow it step by step is difficult. Where and when was the first modernist lamp lit? Along what national lines was all America illuminated by modernist esthetics? At times a very humble poet initiates a formal mutation, and though he is not worth serious study, one should note what he was able to do with it. It is well known that insignificant teachers tend to be obscured by their own students. In each country modernism had its own peculiar rhythm, and a particular poet is not necessarily an indication of national tastes, either because he is a recluse or because he is a perpetual traveler. Perhaps Argentina and Mexico are the only countries where modernism took hold in compact groups, in a sustained activity in every genre, from the very first hours (about 1880 and thereabouts) until its definite liquidation during the first years of World War I. The other countries participated in modernism unevenly and intermittently.

Lacking a better plan, we shall proceed with this one: first we will study the modernists who were more prominent in verse than in prose, beginning with Rubén Darío, the most outstanding. Each time we illuminate one of the great figures, we will take the occasion, in passing, to glance at the other minor figures who hover around him. In this way we shall see the national groupings. Although we will limit ourselves to enumerating poets without studying them individually, the reader must understand that this is not a simple catalog, but rather an atmosphere: these congeries of clouds belong, after all, to literary meteorology and do contribute to the landscape. Then we shall pass to the modernists who distinguished themselves more in prose than in verse: however, before doing so, we shall have to complete the panorama of the verse by referring to the non-modernist or barely modernist poets. In like manner, when we finish reviewing the prose writers we shall dedicate the last pages of this chapter to the non-modernists. The essay and the theater will bring it to an end.

A. MAINLY POETRY

1. Modernist Poets

Rubén Darío / And now RUBÉN DARÍO (Nicaragua, 1867–1916). In Spanish America, where European literary waves came successively to intermingle, young writers were reading the Parnassians, and later the decadents, without giving up Victor Hugo. Rubén Darío has admitted that his friendship with the Salvadorian Gavidia, beginning in 1882, brought him close to Hugo and to the Parnassians. This is the period of his study of French poetic inventions. He reads and imitates Gautier, Coppée and Mendès. In mid-1886 Rubén Darío arrived in Chile and was dazzled by Valparaíso and Santiago, since they were the first important cities that he had seen which had an air of prosperity and certain European pretensions. The poets of the first and even of the second romantic generation had not had a real, immediate experience of luxury, while Rubén Darío and his contemporaries were to have one. In Chile he continued to be informed of the contributions of French literature. But despite his preference for Parnassian poetry, he wrote *Thistles* (*Abrojos*), *Rhymes* (*Rimas*), and *Epic Song* (*Canto épico*, 1887) in the traditional manner. At the same time he wrote *Azure* (*Azul*, 1888) where he made more innovations in the stories and poetic prose than in the verses. In prose he sprang to a high level; on the other hand, he moved slowly toward those exquisite verses he admired from a distance. And as he moved he looked from side to side, selecting friends. Feeling himself surrounded by an army on the move, he launched a second edition of *Azure* (1890), augmented with verse and prose. A comparison of the two editions will show Darío's advance toward nonconformity. There were now daring advances in his poetry that had earlier only been made in his prose. He had realized that his role was to precede others in the modernization of Spanish verse; and, while he did not abandon his old styles, they no longer distracted him from his role. All he needed now was to get a feeling of the atmosphere in Spain. He went there in 1892, and after a two-month survey of that literary bee-hive he was convinced that reform was necessary.

Upon his arrival in Buenos Aires in 1893, Rubén Darío encountered a restlessness among the Parnassian and decadent literati. More talented than the young initiates in French Parnassianism, Darío became part of a circle of which he soon was proclaimed leader. It was then that he decided to explain himself through theoretical canons—his articles *The Strange Ones* (*Los raros*), the "preliminary words" of his *Profane Prose* (*Prosas profanas*), and "The Colors of the Banner" (*"Los colores del estandarte"*) are dated 1896. Ever since his days in Central America Rubén Darío had observed that new poets were making

themselves heard. Now he suspected that these voices were raised
above the chorus of Spanish poets; and he began to feel the pride
of a young independent American generation: "the young writers
have kindled today's revolution." But that revolution had no
name. Little by little the term "modernism" began to creep in.
One of Rubén Darío's highest merits was that of inciting each
poet to grapple with his own formal problems and to resolve
them artistically. He was not alone. But Rubén Darío surpassed
them all, not only because he was congenitally more gifted, but
also because he suddenly propounded a program for himself. He
sought inventions in the literature of his time; and he even sought
them in old Spanish poetry. He knew his job. The desire for verbal
perfection is what gives permanence to his works. Therefore, in
the final analysis, it is the will to forge a style that defines his
modernism, the melting pot and alloy of all the "isms" of the
epoch. When he published his *Profane Prose* in 1896 he must
have felt personally all the responsibility for the new movement.
Martí, Gutiérrez Nájera, Casal, Silva, all had just died prematurely. Others, older than he, who were headed toward the same
goal by a different road (Díaz Mirón, Leopoldo Díaz), changed
direction in order to join him. But his contemporaries, the younger
ones (Lugones, Nervo), grouped themselves around him and
formed the so-called second modernist generation. Rubén Darío
knew what was expected of him, and he began to alter the poetics
of the Spanish language. *Profane Prose* sounded scandalous from
its very title. With unprecedented musical feeling Darío experi-
mented with every kind of rhythm. Regular versification predom-
inated in his experiments (the torrent of ametrical verses was
loosed in Hispanic-America after 1920). His inventions and
restorations—metric combinations, shifts in accentuation, intermediate pauses in composed verses, internal rhymes, the division
of hemistitches within a word or within weak particles, unexpected clashes and dislocations of sounds, free designs, asymmet-
rical strophes, assonance, consonance and dissonance in rapid
interplay, rhythmic prose, daring ruptures in the sonoro-semantic
unity of the verse, etc.—exquisitely modulated the prosody of our
language.

A considerable amount of all this technical ostentation was inspired by French tendencies toward free verse. Darío himself confessed his indebtedness. But on reading the sources pointed out by him or by his critics, one must admire his autonomy of procedure. *Profane Prose* is not just a collection of poems: it is a book of poetry with a soul, with gestures, with a countenance. It was Paris—an ideal Paris—that provided the aperture through which Darío escaped from America. There he enjoyed a virtual world of "art for art's sake." It was the France of Banville and Verlaine, the rococo France of the eighteenth century, the France of Hellenism and orientalia. Even in his evocation of the Argentine countryside there was a distorting mirror, made in Paris. In Rubén Darío an aristocratic feeling, disdainful of the reality of his time, found its expression in a poetry that was: A. exotic: "Symphony in Grey Major" (*"Sinfonía en gris mayor"*), "Portico," "Sonatina"; B. cosmopolitan: "Of the Country" (*"Del campo"*), "Carnival Song" (*"Canción de carnaval"*), "*Garconniere*"; C. reminiscent of art: "There was a soft breeze" (*"Era un aire suave"*); D. nostalgic for historic eras: "Digression" (*"Divagación"*). Darío's spirit seemed to have its own organs of perception. Just as our bodies, through their various sense organs perceive lights, sounds, odors, etc., Darío's spirit, through organs of another nature, was open to experiences of the mind. And just as the stimuli one receives through the various senses of sight, sound, smell, generally coalesce in one's consciousness into one sensation (literature has always been pervaded by synesthetic phenomena, but Beaudelaire's *"Correspondences"* turned synesthesia into a whole style), so the notes of the cultural world that were grasped by the poet Rubén Darío were harmonized by him into a lyrical unity. Some compositions are more perceptive of the exotic, others of the cosmopolitan, others of the assets already accumulated in musical and plastic arts, others of the prestige of Greece, Rome, the Middle Ages, and eighteenth-century France, but in every composition all of these are heard. And this unity is expressed in different climates of emotion:

(1) The frivolous mood. The elegance, the playfulness, "the smiles and shrugs," and the dances, are manifestations of a cult

of pure art; but the estheticism that considers art superior to life implies a serious, difficult, and almost religious commitment to veracity in expression. Frivolity is converted into an austere poetic ideal.

(2) The hedonist mood. Feasts, wines, strollings, kisses, flirtations, contemplation of beautiful forms and of graceful movements, all indicate that Darío, in a deliberate mental act, established pleasure as a goal of life.

(3) The erotic mood. Of all his pleasurable experiences, the erotic was the most powerful, organic, profound, and permanent.

(4) The reflexive mood. Although the poetry of *Profane Prose* floats in an estheticist culture, the poet tends to look within himself and to ask what life is. This reflexive mood will become more acute with the passing of time. It is a philosophy of life. In 1898 he went to Europe. Secure about his importance in America and in Spain, he looked within himself, and his poetry acquired a new depth. There was something of the virtuoso about him that tried to attract attention by presenting novelty rather than originality. But there was also an intuitive nature capable of infusing his poetry with his inner vision. The virtuosity of his *Profane Prose* has been imitated because it was possible to imitate it. Its themes and processes were sufficiently intellectual to stimulate a school of poetry, and his craft had its disciples. But after *Profane Prose* Darío wrote poems of an emotional timbre that could no longer be worked into rhetorical exercises because they flowered from a unique emotional response to the world. The Rubén Darío who wrote the *Songs of Life and Hope* (*Cantos de vida y esperanza*, 1905) is the same as the one who wrote *Profane Prose*. Both have, above all, the same aristocratic excellence. But in *Songs of Life and Hope* we witness the esthetic crisis of *Profane Prose*. The "precious" light of the lamps that were lit in Paris is lowered and the flames of an inner fire go up. This does not mean that there has been a break with the past—merely a change in the scale of values. It is like early autumn when one can see the green leaves of the past still growing along with the new ones of red and yellow. The aristocratic evasion of reality that we saw in *Prose* is still evident. Another direction taken in *Songs of Life and*

Hope is a return to concern for social problems. The views that Darío held prior to *Azure*—politics, love of Spain, an awareness of Spanish America, suspicion of the United States, and moral norms—all of these reappear, but clothed in the virtues of a superb style. The third direction that the book takes, the most intact, is the one that moves toward a knowledge of life. The poet gazes reflexively on his own existence and asks what is art, what is pleasure, what is love, what is time, what is life, what is death, what is religion.

Art is an adventure into the absolute: it is almost a mystic way to knowledge. And the artist is its hero, a demigod suffering in solitude.

Pleasure has a foretaste of death.

Love is painful because, seen in the light of a philosophy of life, it flees whilst we enjoy the flesh, and in its pursuit we grow old and die.

Time produces a duality in us and we contemplate the image of our own life as if we were waving good-by to it from the departing boat.

Life is a bitter mystery of failure and meaninglessness. He who questions life is lost: to want to know what we are and why we live causes us anguish in vain.

Death perhaps is the only answer to the secret of life: we live in the midst of the road to death.

Religion is the trembling before something terrible that overwhelms us with its power. It gives neither peace, nor consolation, nor security. It is only a light beyond this storm in which we agonize, and which we know not how to reach.

Songs of Life and Hope is Rubén Darío's best book. He was to write better poems later, but, as a book, his other books would not surpass it: *Wandering Song* (*El canto errante*, 1907), *Poem of Autumn and Other Poems* (*Poema del otoño y otros poemas*, 1910), *Song to Argentina and Other Poems* (*Canto a la Argentina y otros poemas*, 1914). Many of the poems that were scattered in newspapers, in the tomes of others, or went unpublished, deserved to have ascended to the Olympus of books arranged by Darío himself. Rubén Darío left poetry in a different state from which he found it: in this respect, he joins Garcilaso, Fray Luis de León, San Juan de la Cruz, Lope, Góngora, and Bécquer. His formal changes were immediately appreciated. Spanish poetry had been reduced for centuries to a few types. Suddenly, with Rubén Darío, it became a symphony orchestra. He gave life to metres and strophes of the past, even to those that had only been cultivated occasionally, giving them at times a new sound through unforeseen changes of accent. In addition, he invented a rhythmic language that, without overstepping the bounds of regular versification, presented an infinite number of surprises. Others may have surpassed him in the command of this or that traditional metrical form. But no one can dispute his mastery over the greatest diversity of metres in our language. He not only got every musical possibility out of a word, but he used the right instrument for every nuance of mood. To read him is to improve one's ear; as it improves it can perceive new registers of sound in the recitation. In his technique with words, Darío is one of the greatest poets of all times; his name divides literary history in the Spanish language into a "before" and an "after." But he was not only a master of rhythm. With incomparable elegance he has made poetry an eloquent expression of the joy of life and the terror of death. The transformations that Rubén Darío brought about in Castilian prose were on a par with those he effected in poetry, but they bear less the stamp of his genius. We have already spoken of the stories and prose poems in *Azure*. Rubén Darío surpassed them with other stories, and with other prose poems, collected in various posthumous books. His fantastic stories, which reflect his preoccupation with theosophy, the occult sciences and esoteric doctrines, help us to understand many of his poems, inspired by a curious religious syncretism. His non-narrative and not deliberately poetic prose—*The Strange Ones* (*Los raros*, 1896), *Peregrinations* (*Peregrinaciones*, 1901), *The Caravan Moves On* (*La caravana pasa*, 1902), *Sunny Lands* (*Tierras solares*, 1904)—although fragmentary and casual, is nevertheless energetically victorious over the commonplace.

(i) *Central America / Nicaragua:* Although Darío came from here, there was no select group in this country that promoted modernist tendencies. SANTIAGO ARGÜELLO (1872–1942) was the only poet worthy of mention: *Eye and Soul* (*Ojo y alma*, 1908). He was pedantic, with a penchant for the esoteric, although at times he poetized his native countryside and wrote civic songs. He wrote some theater and, in prose, left some pages useful for a history of modernism. Keeping apart from the influence of Darío were JUAN DE DIOS VANEGAS (1873) and ANTONIO MEDRANO (1881–1928); and even more so, SALVADOR SACASA S. (1881–1937). In the first group of poets who saw the splendor of Rubén Darío—although they did not participate with him—we shall place JOSÉ ÁNGEL SALGADO (1884–1908), JOSÉ TEODORO OLIVARES (1880–1942) and SOLÓN ARGÜELLO (1880–1920).

El Salvador: In reality there were no modernist groups of any value in the countries of Central America. We have already mentioned FRANCISCO GAVIDIA (1863–1955), who was Darío's teacher: with him the new accentuation of the Alexandrine and the adaptation of the Greek hexameter into Castilian are introduced. From his reading of French literature, from his translations, from his "The Idyll of the Woods" (*"El idilio de la selva,"* 1882) and from his *Verses* (*Versos,* 1884) comes the urge for the reformation of metrics. However, the keynote in his poetry, as well as his verse dramas, was romantic. The book that Gavidia himself considered his best was *Sooter or Land of Jewels* (*Sooter o Tierra de Preseas,* 1949), an epic poem about a hero of the struggles for freedom.

Guatemala: The modernist poetry of MÁXIMO SOTO HALL (1871–1944) is less remembered than his novels.

Costa Rica: We can scarcely name genuine modernists (LISÍMACO CHAVARRÍA, 1878–1913, was not one) except for ROBERTO BRENES MESÉN (1874–1947), the most militant personality of his country because of the restlessness which he communicated to his environment. He began as a positivist and ended as a theosophist. And in a dozen books of verse, beginning with *In the Silence* (*En el silencio,* 1907), he charged his lyricism with ever greater intuitions of a philosophic nature. In addition to novels, literary and philosophic essays, and didactic treatises, he wrote poetic prose.

Honduras: JUAN RAMÓN MOLINA (1875–1908) was one of those born under the poetic sign of Rubén Darío. His themes and even his words were from the modernist repertory. He was a tortured soul (his pessimism drove him to suicide), and he infused his poetry with an unmistakable, personal mood. His lyricism was varied in its tones: rich, in "Fishing For Mermaids" (*"Pesca de sirenas"*), eloquent, in "The Eagle" (*"El águila"*), descriptive, in "Song to the Río Grande" (*"Canto al Río Grande"*), elegiac, in "To a Dead Woman" (*"A una muerta"*), anguished, in "Mother Melancholy" (*"Madre Melancolía"*). Although he stubbornly sought perfection of form, he was not a mere craftsman. He read a good deal in literature, philosophy, even sciences, and his vision of life was complex. He was an egotist, a bitter person wearied of life. When writing prose he made an effort to achieve an elegant style, no matter how sordid the reality he was describing, as can be seen in the short story *"El chele."* Also Honduran are LUIS ANDRÉS ZÚÑIGA (1878), dramatist, fabulist, and a poet of pessimistic vein, JULIÁN LÓPEZ PINEDA (1882–1958), J. J. REINA (1876–1919) and AUGUSTO C. COELLO (1884–1941).

Panama: In this country (united to Colombia from 1823 to 1903, later an independent republic) the presence of Darío in 1892 encouraged a young group of writers: DARÍO HERRERA (1870–1914), whom we shall see below among the prosists, LEÓN A. SOTO (1874–1902), ADOLFO GARCÍA (1872–1900), SIMÓN RIVAS (1868–1915), GUILLERMO ANDREVE (1879–1940), and others.

(ii) *Argentina: Lugones and Carriego* / In his departure from Central America, Rubén Darío, of course, left it a literary desert. On the other hand, on arriving in Buenos Aires, he found himself surrounded by a modernist multitude. Argentina offers a different picture from that of its sister nations. Here there was a generation well-initiated into European modernities prior to Darío's arrival. We saw this in earlier chapters. And when other countries begin to become modernist, it will be from Argentina— center of intense modernism—that the first generation of writers, purified in a new simplicity, will emerge. We shall see this in the next chapter. In Buenos Aires Darío had his great school, and even those who did not belong to it were aware of what was happening there. There were also cases of much older poets who had begun independently of Darío and who admired and emulated him. (Not only in Argentina: we already mentioned the case of the Mexican Díaz Mirón.) One of these cases, as will be remembered, was that of Leopoldo Díaz. Among the Argentine poets of this generation who clustered about Rubén Darío and formed a modernist group were EUGENIO DÍAZ ROMERO (1877–1927), DIEGO FERNÁNDEZ ESPIRO (1870–1912), CARLOS ORTIZ (1870–1910), CARLOS ALBERTO BECU, MANUEL UGARTE (1878–1951), ALBERTO G. GHIRALDO (1874–1946), MIGUEL ESCALADA (1867–1918), MARTÍN GOYCOECHEA MENÉNDEZ (1877–1906), PEDRO J. NAÓN and others who, because they are outstanding in other genres (Enrique Larreta, for example), will be treated further on.

But, of course, the poet whose contributions to poetry in America were no less valuable than those of Rubén Darío was LEOPOLDO LUGONES (1874–1938). Like Darío, he was an extraordinary verbal gymnast. He explored new territories; and his combative energy was such that even his own credos were at war with one another. At first, it was combat between his political credos and his esthetic credos; later, this combative energy brought him to other dilemmas, conflicts, and defections. The man who began as an anarchist, ended as a fascist. Yet even in his versatility, which was considerable, one recognizes the depth of his character. He possessed, to express it in his own words, "the flexible unity of the current / which, as it runs, changes." Lugones gathered together and absorbed all influences. Later, the hand of Argentine poetry would open and the fingers would point out the different directions to succeeding generations. Minor poets would specialize in several of these directions, at times advantageously; however, after Lugones no poet appears who, like him, is able to grasp all of poetry in one fist. He remains the most copious and renovating of poets, and it is difficult to evaluate him because each epoch selects the Lugones which suits it best. His *Gilded Mountains* (*Montañas del oro*) was too difficult for imitators, but *Garden Twilights* (*Los crepúsculos del jardín*), *Sentimental Lunar Poems* (*Lunario sentimental*), and the *Ballads of Río Seco* (*Romances de Río Seco*) were three apprentice shops for three successive generations.

Nevertheless, in Lugones there is something unaccomplished. His zest for life, his richness of perception, the freshness of his poetic intuition—all of an exceptional intensity—yielded to the sporting vanity of displaying himself with words, forms, and techniques. He wanted to be astonishing. He astonished by exaggerating his virtuosity. He who had lived and felt so much preferred to be seen in the pose of the athlete. *Gilded Mountains* (1897), *Garden Twilights* (1905), and *Sentimental Lunar Poems* (1909) were ostentatious gymnastics. With *Secular Odes* (*Odas seculares*, 1910) he seemed to find himself as an Argentine poet; and in fact, all that follows (*The Faithful Book* [*El libro fiel*, 1912], *The Book of Landscapes* [*El libro de los paisajes*, 1917], *The Golden Hours* [*Las horas doradas*, 1922], *Ballads* [*Romances*, 1924], *Manorial Poems* [*Poemas solariegos*, 1927], and *Ballads of Río Seco* [*Romances de Río Seco*, 1938]) depicts the spiral of his talent, one of the greatest in America.

We shall see how that spiral opens, in ascending and descending curves. The Lugones of *Gilded Mountains* stood to the left of modernism. Compared to these sensations, metaphors, and ideas, convoluted in a tempest of syntactical complications, even the Rubén Darío of *Profane Prose* must have seemed very simple at that time. This book had less lyricism than rhetorical spasms. Lugones furiously whipped the anarchic horses of poetry, now tired from so much running, from Hugo to the recent "strange ones." In a pandemonium of beautiful but shocking images, he called for a revolution of styles. Furthermore, he claimed for himself the role of thinker and prophet. What he knew best were the sky and highlands of his province, but a poet sings of what his spiritual eyes select, not of what his physical eyes have seen. Lugones wished to orchestrate what he knew least: the decadent literature of Parnassians, foreign and local. In *Garden Twilights* his stentorian voice becomes honeyed. Lugones here dominates the art of dissociating metaphors delicately. In two or three poems he was bold enough to transfer Parisian free verse into Spanish; but on the whole what dominates are meters of classical control. Masterful verses, but lacking intimate resonance. Frivolous charm, cold exquisiteness, aristocratic ways of painting a landscape and refining a form. But not even the erotic theme is convincing as something really lived. His gallantries remain a decorative imprint. Also in this, he was inferior to Darío. He moved from huge mountains to miniature gardens like one who changes instruments in order to prove how talented he is, and that he can compete with Samain and company. His lyricism was intellectual; his loves were feigned. They are poems that conform to the conventions of the colorist and to the impressionistic programs of modernism. This much they do, and do well—as, for example, in "The Old Bachelor" ("*El solterón*"). His search for artifices carried him to selenography, an entire book dedicated to the moon, "a kind of vengeance that I have dreamed of ever since childhood, whenever I have been assailed by life." Thus came about the *Sentimental Lunar Poems*, a tree-nursery where he had transplanted, from the symbolist grove, treelets of Moréas, Samain, Laforgue, above all Laforgue! and, once they had taken root, all the new poetry of the continent was forested with them. It is the most influential of Lugones' books. His metaphors were reproduced at times verbatim

by poets in America and Spain. He strove for far-fetched originality, acrobatics in concepts and rhythms, humor that, like a
caricature, animates inanimate things with rapid strokes and, as it
would be called after the first World War, a dehumanized art. His
"Hymn to the Moon" (*"Himno a la luna"*) is a natural for anthologies. Never in our literature had such a feast of prodigious imagination been seen. Each metaphor, an eye. The young writers of
the postwar avant-garde who had rejected Lugones' cult of rhyme
followed him in his cult of metaphor. With these caprices, diver-
sions, exploits, unwonted poetizations of the prosaic, subtleties,
absurdities, clownishness with scientific, plebeian and invented
words, the virtuosity cycle of Lugones' poetry is closed—although
the *Sentimental Lunar Poems* remains somewhat apart, as a
unique book.

Those readers who are always asking for a poet's credentials—
autobiographical lyric verses or patriotic epic poems—will insist
that the best Lugones is the one who opens the cycle with *Secular
Odes*. The centennial anniversary of the May revolution for independence was being celebrated, and Lugones wanted to render
homage to Argentina. He forced his muse and ruined much of the
work.

Still, the *Secular Odes* are happy, optimistic, and alive. Lugones
came out of his interior chambers, so well carpeted by the French,
and jovially looked out upon the fields and towns. He abandoned
the pyrotechnics of the *Sentimental Lunar Poems* and retired to
classical traditions from Vergil to Andrés Bello. With arrows of
light he transfixed even the most ordinary objects of Argentine
reality; and he gave his polyphonic song the dynamism of incep-
tive narratives and outlines of action such as that of the deputy
and the immigrant's daughter in "Cattle and Crops" (*"A los ga-
nados y las mieses"*). The emotion of feeling himself a member of
a large family, the remembrance of heroic deeds, his love for each
thing, the expectations, the sowing of creative energy, sharpened
his capacity for observation. Between the *preludium* of the *Secular
Odes* and the *postludium* of the *Ballads of Río Seco*, there are
the interludes of five books. In *The Faithful Book* love and nature
are the dominant themes: in this instance, it is real love. Lugones,

although an erotic man, was not an erotic poet. He sings of matrimony more than of love, of the hearth more than of the flame. He refers to the periphery: the family; the essence would have been the enamored couple. Lugones possessed a certain hardness. He lacked tenderness, passion. Nevertheless, "White Solitude" (*"La blanca soledad"*) and "The Song of Anguish" (*"El canto de la angustia"*) have a personal harmonious lyricism. The nature theme was more obvious in *The Book of Landscapes*. His poetic orthodoxy of traditional rhythms and strophes and of the subjection of poetry to rhyme, makes his monotonous, but his sincere, varying, lyrical emanations gush forth freely. The "Pluvial Psalm" (*"Salmo pluvial"*) would be sufficient to make us respect his imaginative power, and it must be noted that it is not the only one.

The elegance of the Parnassians and symbolists still enchants him; but Lugones, without ceasing to be elegant, begins to look directly at the movement of the natural realms of his land. In *The Golden Hours* lyricism is interweaved with reflection, the lyrical fibers being the most vivid (see "The Infinite"). But even this original lyricism appears less potent than his descriptive and epic talent. His vignettes, among which Japanese and rococo examples are not lacking, correspond to modernist modes of 1900, but the thoughts on happiness, sorrow, morals, anxiety, and anguish are personal. The compositions in *Ballads* are not all ballads, but generally the traditional voice of Spain and Hispanic-America is heard more than that of France. That which is popular, racy, deep and common in man appears. Lugones feels that his song is the echo of the song of other men. This coming out of oneself and addressing the reality of everyone is accentuated in *Manorial Poems*. Here the spiral, which will culminate in the *Ballads of Río Seco*, begins to ascend. Lugones drops the sham, deepens his own nostalgia, returns to the emotions of his adolescence in Córdoba, restricts his field to control better his old impulse of evasion. His austerity, so terrestrial that it is almost dry, renounces all that is not traditional, national, or familiar. In one of his best compositions, "The Song" (*"El canto"*), he defines himself: "For I am no more than an echo / of the native song I bear within me." In the *Ballads of Río Seco* his will to depersonalize himself so that neither voice nor gesture is distinguishable, to fuse into an anonymous people, to despoil himself of all literary festive dress, and to afford himself an outlet for his collective themes of patriotism, faith, love and courage, reaches the farthest extreme. A little more and he would have gone beyond the realm of poetry. Lugones had a foreboding of his artistic exhaustion, of his failure, and there is a note of resentment as he guards himself against possible attacks: "Perhaps someone may scorn / my stories for being Creole. / This is not for outsiders, / city-slickers nor simpletons." These *Ballads of Río Seco* emanate nevertheless from a great interior tension—a tension contrary to that of the *Sentimental Lunar Poems* (his other great book), but no less ambitious.

His prose did not have the quality of his poetry. He was a great technician of prose, not a great prosist. His skill in the use of a language enriched by dint of study and reflection was not accompanied by skill in the use of ideas. For this reason we shall leave to one side, without denying its merits, what is not pure literature: biographical, historical, ethnographical, philosophic, didactic, political, and philological essays. What he did have was sensibility and imagination, effective above all in visual metaphors. That is to say that on reading his prose one has a desire to return to his verses. Even in *The Gaucho War* (*La guerra gaucha*, 1905) we find the pyrotechnics of the poet. This work consists of twenty-two historical stories of the fight for independence, and introduces into Argentine literature the mountainous north. They deal with anonymous masses and not with leaders: Güemes is alluded to only at the end. It may be that his model was *La legende de l'aigle* by Georges d'Esparbès. Lugones, working with a language having some of the baroque energy of Quevedo's, but in a literary workshop of preciosity and naturalism established by modernism, created a brutal, overwrought, dense style that years later Valle-Inclán would call "*esperpéntico*" (grotesque). The descriptive portion mounts on the back of the narrative forcing it to move at a slow pace. Indeed, the descriptions, with great richness of impressionistic effects, have their own movement of sensations. When the episodic action seems to tarry, what goes into action is the sensitiveness and the imagination of the poet who has risen above the narrator. Let no one be mistaken: he was a talented narrator as proved by *Strange Forces* (*Las fuerzas extrañas,* 1906) and *Fatal Stories* (*Cuentos fatales,* 1924). The first is a book of brief stories, some of which are admirable—"Rain of Fire," "The Horses of Abdera," and "Izur." His fantastic stories are inspired by a vague oriental mysticism, by classical myths and by science fiction. In *Fatal Stories* there is also magic, superstition, truculence, metamorphosis. *The Angel of Shadows* (*El Ángel de la Sombra,* 1926), is a novel of an impossible passion, with characters who are moved not by life by by the springs of an anti-novelistic fatality. Up to his tragic end (he committed suicide) he sought new forms of expression.

With *Garden Twilights* in 1905 Lugones had marked the modernist apogee in Argentina. Later, as will be seen in the next chapter, the poets of the generation of Fernández Moreno will be less defiant. But now that Lugones has led us to Argentina, let us surround his name with others that were born between 1870 and 1885. Many were still romantic, preoccupied with social philosophies or given over to the sentimental: RICARDO ROJAS (1882–1957), ERNESTO MARIO BARREDA (1883–1958), MARIO BRAVO (1882–1944), and above all Carriego. One of the Argentine poets who went farthest in the anti-preciosity reaction was EVARISTO CARRIEGO (1883–1912), who drew his inspiration from the tender, sentimental, and trivial memories of his native suburb. After his *Heretic Mass* (*Misas herejes,* 1908) Carriego's muse abandonded pedantries, obscurities, neologisms, decadentisms and cultivated a poetry with a touch of tango lyrics, but with depth. *The Soul of the Suburbs* (*El alma del suburbio,* 1913) was the title of the posthumous book in which his compositions of this period were gathered. The family scenes, of simple, sincere, and penetrating emotion, are those that are most remembered: "The Little Seamstress Who Took That Bad Step," "The Chair That Now Nobody Occupies," "You Have Returned." He was a Creole from those outlying districts where the city loses itself in sparsely populated areas. Because he wrote of life in the city outskirts, of workers, hoodlums, and enamored girls, because he wrote with much sentiment and even with tears, Carriego pleased his readers and has remained in the memory of the people. He also remained in the memory of younger poets, such as Raúl González Tuñón and Nicolás Olivari. One who placed himself completely beyond modernism was MIGUEL A. CAMINO (1877–1949). With his *Chacayaleras* (1921) he initiated a regional poetry (his region was Neuquén, in the southern mountain range) where one hears rustic voices and sees scenes of the life of the people. The theme of his poetry has been well defined by the title he gave to the compendium of his works: *The Landscape, Man and His Song* (*El paisaje, el hombre y su canción,* 1938).

(iii) *Bolivia* / RICARDO JAIMES FREYRE (Bolivia, 1868–1933) was a friend of Rubén Darío and of Leopoldo Lugones and joined them in the condemnation of routine poetry and in the claim-staking of new poetic lodes. His first book, *Primeval Fountain* (*Castalia bárbara*, 1897) was an experimental laboratory for rhythm. Rhythm for rhythm's sake. He combined verses with such liberty that his name became associated with the introduction of "free verse" in the Castilian language. In reality, he introduced only one attempt at free verse, which was timid in comparison with the polymorphism that was to come later. But we must listen with the ears of the end-of-the-century poets. It was like a strange dance to which words had been invited purely for the beauty of their sonorous bodies: they held each other by the waist and whirled and tapped and interrupted each pose in order to begin over, again and again. No ideal music was heard: at least the spirit of the reader was not penetrated by vague and insinuating sensations. Of course, he watched the rhythmic feast, because the rhythms were forms of dancing words. In the midst of such an exaggeration of rhythms, the reader became distracted and lost the meaning of what he was reading. It was the coldness of Parnassian poets who erected their structures with unfeeling perfection. Since the initial themes of *Primeval Fountain* came from Scandinavian mythology, from Nordic and wintry landscapes (Richard Wagner's lyrical dramas had begun the vogue), the rhythmic beats struck everyone as something strangely savage. And, in fact, "The Song of Evil," "Strange Voice," "*Aeternum vale*," "Errant Venus," "The Nights" were astonishing. The adjective "barbaric" was appropriate to this poetry: it had the same geographic and religious exoticism as Leconte de Lisle's *Poèmes barbares*, and graftings of versification as in Giosuè Carducci's *Odi barbare*. In general this first book of Jaimes Freyre had a minimum of immediate impressions perceived directly from life. Although the poet tells us that he is "nostalgic, sad and dreamy unto death," this way of being does not reach us through the fibers of the verse, but comes down like the white light of an idea burning in some cerebral lamp. In his second book of poems, *Dreams*

Are Life (*Los sueños son vida*, 1917), metric liberty is even greater, but the dance has now quieted and we can capture the meaning of the feast. Here is an album of Parnassian poetry in the collective style of modernism. In "Times Gone By" (*"Tiempos idos . . ."*) Jaimes Freyre gives us the key to his artistic transposition: "I have seen you on the enchanting canvases / where mundane feasts are immortalized / perhaps in the *Embarcation for Cythera . . .*" It is the same canvas of Watteau that had inspired in Darío some of the images of "It was a soft breeze" (*"Era un aire suave"*). "Subliminar," which is more intimate ("it is now time for interior orchestras to play"), is one of the best compositions of the book. Other themes concerning the universal suffering of the masses now emerge vigorously ("The Outcry" [*"El clamor"*], for example), and prophecy is not lacking in "Russia" (1906): The blaze that will consume the remains of the past / will come from the heart of the country of snow . . ." However, in the political life of his country, Freyre was a conservative, not a liberal. He produced theatrical works: *Jephthah's Daughter* (*La hija de Jefthé*) on a biblical subject, and the dramatic poem *The Conquistadors* (*Los conquistadores*). His short stories—printed in magazines—are typically modernist ones (soaring to Byzantium, to China) although two of them do take place in the Andes and have Indian characters.

Bolivia produced Jaimes Freyre and that was all. Modernism will only enter this country at the beginning of the twentieth century, when two outstanding figures will be seen: Reynolds and Tamayo. This completes the triangle of the great Bolivian poets of modernism. GREGORIO REYNOLDS (1882–1947) was a sentimentalist, attired in the vestments of modernism. He expressed deep lyricism in *Psyche's Coffer* (*El cofre de Psiquis*), in which his Parnassian sonnet "The Flame" (*"La llama"*) appears, *Turbid Hours* (*Horas turbias*), *Prisms* (*Prismas*), not to mention his epic poem *Redemption* (*Redención*) and his scenic poem *Chimeras* (*Quimeras*). One of his lyric chords was compounded of voluptuousness and religiosity. He was a good craftsman of verse, using varying forms. FRANZ TAMAYO (1880–1956), who in his *Odes* (*Odas*, 1898) was more Victor-Hugoesque than Rubén-Darían, later became a modernist and cultivated rare and very fascinating interplays of sounds. He studied Greco-Latin classicism with devotion, and derived from this source the inspiration for his lyrical tragedies *Prometheid or Oceanides* (*La Prometheida o Las Oceánides*, 1917), *Scopas* (1939) and others. He is also the author of some *Greek Epigrams* (*Epigramas griegos*, 1945). Sometimes he supersaturates his pages with bookish and pedantic elements, with neologisms and cabalisms. Strangely enough, this verbalist of European educational background, when he felt like thinking, thought in European patterns, went into his ivory tower and fabricated a philosophy that was anti-liberal, anti-positivist, authoritarian and irrational, glorifying the Indian. Just as the German racists talked about Aryan superiority during the Nazi years, Tamayo talked about the superiority of the race of the Bolivian Indians, to the point of making a political issue of it. Other modernists: JUAN FRANCISCO BEDREGAL (1883–1944), a romantic with modernist learnings; MANUEL MARÍA PINTO (1871–1942), who was religious in the manner of Verlaine, included native themes in his modern poetry, but because he lived in Argentina he had hardly any influence in Bolivia. EDUARDO DÍEZ DE MEDINA (1881), sentimental and pro-native. His modernism concealed the true nature of Bolivia under decorations of Hellenic or Nordic mythology, or falsified it by treating it as if it were also exotic.

(iv) *Uruguay: Herrera y Reissig* / In Uruguay (another of Argentina's neighbors) modernism manifested itself first in prose rather than verse, but there were notable poets. If we except the more *outré* writers, such as ROBERTO DE LAS CARRERAS (1875), the nucleus of Uruguayan poetry of this period is Vasseur, Frugoni, María Eugenia Vaz Ferreira and Herrera y Reissig. ÁLVARO ARMANDO VASSEUR (1878) and EMILIO FRUGONI (1880) struck the combative, optimistic, and confident note of an approaching social justice. MARÍA EUGENIA VAZ FERREIRA (1875–1924)—*The Island of Canticles* (*La isla de los cánticos*)—was a solitary voice, solemnly religious, although capable of creating sharp images on a high level.

The ten years of poetic production of JULIO HERRERA Y REISSIG (1875–1910) are like a round mirror in which the figure of modernism is reflected from head to foot. He was not a great poet, but he wrote with an imagination so excited by symbolist literature that his language has a rare anthological quality. Here we will find cemeteries, drugs, satanisms, loathings, exoticisms, synesthesias, violet shades, idealizations of the countryside, a good deal of eroticism, and some magic. It it difficult to point out a precise source; yet to read him is to get an indefinable impression of witnessing an epoch. He did not reach the mass of readers; but those who read him in Spain and throughout Hispanic-America were poets, and in this way he influenced the course of lyricism. For many years he was a landmark in Uruguayan poetry. Even today, when poetry is moving along other paths and Herrera y Reissig is no longer a master, his poems are read with pleasure and admiration. The echoes most easily recognized are those from the European continent—Baudelaire, Verlaine, Mallarmé, Laforgue, Samain, and those from the American continent—Poe and Rubén Darío. He breathed poetry, he fed on poetry, he walked in poetry. In this way, his verses gave voice to a poetic style that was the air, substance, and spirit of his life. Like the symbolists, he was disinterested in practical reality and turned his nocturnal eyes toward the most irrational zones of his being. There he sought what, through his readings, he knew other poets had found. His point of departure was a collective style; but his point of arrival was his own body, wherein he discovered a prodigious source of metaphors. There is not, in our poetry, another such example of a metaphoric machine gun. With *The Pentecosts of Time* (*Las pascuas del tiempo*, 1900) he made himself completely at home in modernism; in a short time he had traversed its large hall and in an obscure corner, complicated by a series of mirrors, attracted attention because of his eccentric figure. Even more than Darío, he was daring in his excessive and even grotesque images, with Hermetic mythologies and quasi-expressionistic allegories. For this reason, ten years after his death, when young writers read *The Evening Matins* (*Los maitines de la noche*, 1902), *The Ecstasies of the Mountain* (*Los éxtasis de la montaña*, 1904–07) and the "Moon Gathering" ("*Tertulia lunática*") in *The Tower of the Sphinxes* (*La Torre de las Esfinges*, 1909), they were dazzled by the compact treasure of images and considered him a precursor of the cult of metaphor to which they were giving themselves. Herrera y Reissig was a discontented person, disenchanted by the world in which he was born, who created for himself an imaginary world where he could better live: a mythical, hallucinated world of pure images, which appears real because of its disorder and contradictions. The conflict between health and morbidity, innocence and sin, happiness and suffering gives his style the oscillating movement between plebeian and luxuriant words, between forms of culture and revery. His mood also changes: ironic, misanthropic, sharp, trivial, playful, enraptured. He sought an inner equilibrium by trying to reconcile in a very personal expression what he saw with his poet's eyes, even the ugly, the base, the monotonous.

(v) *Peru: Chocano and others/* In spite of González Prada's early innovations, verses polished in cosmopolitan shops with Parnassian facets, symbolist lights, and polyrhythmic techniques, Peru accepted modernism quite late. But the two names that it offers are important: Chocano and Eguren.

Because his was the eloquence of words recited in the public squares, the wind has carried away almost all the work of José Santos Chocano (Peru, 1875–1934). He was closer to Díaz Mirón than to Rubén Darío; and if he is grouped with Darío and other modernists it is because he was a visualist who had learned to paint what he saw in the language of the Parnassians. What he saw, however, was different from the reality of the modernists. Chocano dedicated himself to poetizing an external view of America: nature, legends and historical episodes, stories about Indians, themes dealing with political activity. He was a minor poet, because the cloth of poetry is not cut to the size of things seen but to that of the soul that sees. He took the lead in the modernist movement of Peru, and he was equipped, for this purpose, with the egotism and torrential verbal power of the politician. Furthermore, his control of new verse techniques was put to the service of easy and popular themes. A poet of the elite, but operating in the street. It was natural that he should be applauded. His most famous books, *Soul of America, Indo-Spanish Poems* (*Alma América, poemas indo-españoles,* 1906) and *Fiat Lux!* (1908) were an expression of the objective, visible, nationalist aspects of the poetry of those years.

Chocano continued to poetize when suddenly there appeared an anti-Chocano poet (anti-epic, anti-declamatory, anti-realist, anti-obvious) who inaugurated a new poetic style—José María Eguren (Peru, 1882–1942). He was a "strange one" in the exquisite sense which the word had assumed ever since Darío's *The Strange Ones;* but his strangeness was that which came later and was no longer that of modernism. His first book of poems was called *Symbolics* (*Simbólicas,* 1911); but the title was foreign to the symbolism that the symbolists had exposed. In *The Song of the Figures* (*La canción de las figuras,* 1916) and in *Shadows*

and Rounds (*Sombras y rondinelas*), both edited in 1929, together with a collection of the early works bearing the title *Poetry*
(*Poesías*), Eguren became even more introspective, as if he had
closed his eyes and was looking within at hallucinating phospho-
rescences. His poetry had the incoherence of dreams and night-
mares. Figures appear and vanish like phantoms in clouds of
opium. The incredible colors, skyblue blood, bluish gold, purple
nights, green beards, glow for an instant and then feather out,
fuse, and end up by dissolving into shadows. There is no action,
at least no action with meaning. Something moves in that unreal
and misshapen atmosphere, but we do not understand it. It is as
if men, walking in their sleep, had walked through certain magic
mirrors and now slide about like beautiful dehumanized silhou-
ettes. Animals, plants, stars, things, landscapes also yield to
marvelous metamorphoses. The poet mixes his sensations in disordered impressions, and seems to respect only two kinds of
order: a very select artistic vocabulary and fixed musical
schemes.

    LEONIDAS N. YEROVI (1881–1917) versified rather than poetized Peru-
vian customs without the fine esthetic conscience of the modernists, to
whom he alluded ironically.

(vi) *Colombia: Valencia and others* / A few years after Silva's
suicide there appeared in Colombia GUILLERMO VALENCIA
(1873–1943) with his only book: *Rites* (*Ritos*, 1898). Only a
few years intervened, yet it seems that poetry had advanced a
good piece. To measure the distance one need only read Silva
and, right after that, the paired Alexandrines that Valencia shaped
in "On Reading Silva" ("*Leyendo a Silva*"). Silva could only
sense an esthetics of exquisite rarities; Valencia was as familiar
with that same esthetics as he was with the palm of his hand.
What had advanced, of course, was the awareness on the part of
the modernist poets of what they intended to do. When Valencia
made the acquaintance of Darío in Paris he had already published
Rites; but in *Rites* there is an indication of his having known Darío
as a poet. Without any vacillation, without painful calculations,
armed from head to foot on his first expedition, Valencia placed

himself in the vanguard of those who were transforming poetry. He was not going to be a vociferous leader—he was an economical poet, scanty, as compressed as a metal, who struck his great blow and then retired forever. Afterwards he turned to translation (his *Cathay* [*Catay*, 1928] is a collection of ancient Chinese poems). With romantic heart, Parnassian eyes, and symbolist ears, Valencia created a poetic world that was different from that of his colleagues. If we had to give him one label it would have to be the Parnassian, even though his social preoccupations and his mental construction are not what we expect from a school given to pure formal perfection. Among his best poems are: "Job," "St. Anthony and the Centaur" (*"San Antonio y el centauro"*), "Palemón the Stylite" (*"Palemón el estilita"*), "The Two Heads" (*"Las dos cabezas"*). He had the gift of lyrical definition; that is, with a minimum of language he succeeded in reducing the image that had formed in his imagination to its very limits. The words are like grains of sand, which in one of his best poems, "The Camels" (*"Los camellos"*), adhere to and clothe the form of an ideal camel. He selected his words with such economy that at times his definition, though intelligent, is not intelligible. Part of his obscurity was a result, then, of his conciseness; other areas of his poetry were obscure because the poet and his symbols slipped into a mysterious thicket. His Catholicism is not sufficient to decipher the mystery. In "White Storks" (*"Cigüeñas blancas"*) the daring of his metaphors, drawn as if sketched in India ink, is striking. Here he insinuates his esthetics which seems to consist of creating difficult problems to solve or, even more, of standing before them in absolute silence.

In spite of the Parnassian perfection of his descriptions, Valencia did not disregard his emotions. In this, he was closer to Leconte de Lisle than to Heredia. He enriches each verse with impressions and he always wants to feel more, as he says in his translation of D'Annunzio's sonnet: "Ah, were I to be given other new senses!" (*"Doleful Animal"*—*"Animal triste"*). Even his spirit of protest against social inequities found a way into his poetry, and in "Anarkos" he opposed bourgeois hypocrisy with the same force with which his spirit of poetic reform opposed the academies. What is curious is that Valencia was called "conservative" in Colombian politics. In a sense he was a conservative: while other modernists were evolving toward vital expressions and were even indulging in youthful pirouettes during the years of the first World War, Valencia preferred to cultivate modernist orthodoxy. Actually, his Parnassianism was a continuation of the cult of the word, so typical of the Colombian tradition. "The study of the classics," Valencia has said, "taught me to love moderation, clarity, synthesis, and even to make an effort to be transparent." His skill in the aristocratic and sober selection of forms was part of a ceremonial ritual. Today he seems too elegant and cold for the young writers, and he is read much less. Nevertheless, of all those who wrote prior to 1900, Valancia and Silva are the most respected of Colombian poets.

Other poets from this same batch should be placed farther down the scale. VÍCTOR MANUEL LONDOÑO (1876–1936) was a Parnassian in the manner of Heredia. Ismael López, better known by his pseudonym CORNELIO HISPANO (1880), was one of the introducers of modernism, with his magazine *Trofeos* (1906–08). His first book participated in the cult of Parnassian conventions, of Greek mythology and medieval history; but the one with the greatest freshness is his *Caucan Elegies* (*Elegías caucanas*, 1912) sincere and direct in its evocation of memories and scenes actually experienced. And still another: MAX GRILLO (1868). (ISAÍAS GAMBOA, 1872–1904, was appreciated especially in Chile, where he spent a few years, for his melancholic poetry and a novel dealing with Chile.) Baldomero Sanin Cano was more decisively influential than Darío in the formation of Colombian modernism, not because of his poetry, but because of the intellectual restlessness he stirred up through new ideas and European readings. Between the classicism of Caro and the popular sentimentality of Julio Flores, Colombian poetry of the nineteenth century had become rigid. Sanin Cano with his mastery of ideology, and Silva, Valencia and Londoño with their poetry, had to struggle, harder than was necessary in other countries, against traditions that resisted forcefully.

(vii) *Mexico: Nervo, Urbina, Tablada, González Martínez* / During these years Mexico became a principal center of modernist production. Poets appeared in the *Revista Azul* (1894–96), founded by Gutiérrez Nájera and Carlos Díaz Dufoo (1861–1941), in the *Revista Moderna*, directed in 1898 by Amado Nervo and Jesús E. Valenzuela (1856–1911) and in the *Ateneo de la Juventud* (1909). We shall list some of them. EFRÉN REBOLLEDO (1877–1929) ran the gamut of all modernist themes (eroticisms, Parnassianisms, Japanese-isms) carving out verses with a careful chisel. RUBÉN M. CAMPOS (1876–1945), a Hellenist in the manner of Leconte and Heredia, was later sidetracked to prose. FRANCISCO MANUEL DE OLAGUÍBEL (1874–

1924), a romantic in feeling, a modernist in form. MARÍA ENRIQUETA
CAMARILLO DE PEREYRA (1875), sentimental, simple, whom we shall refer to
below, among the narrators. The roster can be completed with RAFAEL
LÓPEZ (1873–1943), a technician and Parnassian, graphic and colorful.
ROBERTO ARGÜELLES BRINGAS (1875–1915), LUIS CASTILLO LEDÓN (1879–
1944), EDUARDO COLÍN (1880–1945), MANUEL DE LA PARRA (1878–1930),
RICARDO GÓMEZ ROBELO (1883–1924), ALFONSO CRAVIOTO (1884–1955).
Now that we have glanced at the Modernist panorama, it is time to pull
out the salient poets.

First of all AMADO NERVO (1870–1919). Once upon a time
the extensive work of Amado Nervo (more than thirty volumes
of poetry, novels, short stories, criticism, chronicles, poems in
prose, essays and even a theatrical piece) held the admiration of
the entire Hispanic world. Today the portion still admired has
shrunk to a fine bouquet of poems and half a dozen short stories.
His poetry has ranged from opulence to simplicity, from sensuality
to religion, from playfulness to sobriety. His poetry was born in
an age of precious stones, tinsels, exoticisms, morbid sensation,
exquisiteness, satanical affectations, voluptuousness, mysteries,
and technical fineries. His first books of poetry, *Black Pearls*
(*Perlas negras*, 1898), *Poems* (*Poemas*, 1901), *Interior Gardens* (*Jardines interiores*, 1905), belong to modernism. Later,
in *Whispering* (*En voz baja*, 1909), Nervo begins to denude
his soul; and in *Serenity* (*Serenidad*, 1914) and *Elevation*
(*Elevación*, 1917)—"from today on, let silence be my best poetry"—he denuded himself to such an extent that he seems diminished. "I seek a discreet tone, a medial shade, the coloring
that does not explode," he confesses. Note the voluntary "I seek."
The fact is that in his simplicity there is much striving for effect
and even a certain amount of rhetoric; after all, once the first
period of verbal luxury and artificial themes had passed, modernism responded to a new slogan: to appear candid and sincere.
One system of esthetics was sacrificed with the hope of gaining the
good graces of another. It has been said that it was a moral crisis
rather than an esthetic change. After ten years of loving a woman
(Ana, the "Constant Lover," who died in 1912) Nervo had tormented his eroticism to the point of converting it into spiritism:
he had to believe "that my Anita still lives in some form and that

she loves me and waits for me." He turned, then, toward the immortality of the soul and toward God. Certainly Nervo continued loving women until his own death. A man's life does not necessarily explain a poet's art. What matters, therefore, is the esthetic transition, not his more or less disconsolate seven years as a widower; and in these very years he wrote some of his best poems. Of posthumous publication were *The Constant Lover* (*La amada inmóvil*) and *The Divine Archer* (*El arquero divino*). The best in Nervo is the lyricist who expresses himself with artistic awareness, choosing from his personal experience the most beautiful moments. When he gives the reader sentimental material not esthetically fashioned, his tone which becomes more confiding than lyrical, goes flat. And it goes flatter still when he changes theme and style and abuses the abstract, conceptual language that he believed to be philosophic. The verse, "I know nothing of literature" (*Serenity*) and his program of writing "without literature" (*Elevation*) are from his later years. He then offered himself charitably to consoling, preaching, and even catechizing with his notions of elevation and renunciation. The public was grateful for his good sentiments; the more demanding readers lamented the lyrical impurity of his moral purity.

In prose he traveled the same road toward simplification from "the extensive periods, the pompous turns, the fertile lexicon" (as he described his own procedures) to a more nervous and aphoristic style. Nevertheless, he did not excel as a writer of prose. He worked to good advantage when his conversational narrative (because he was a conversational artist) dictated the movement of his pen, not when he wanted to imitate the artistic prose he admired (*Plenitude* [*Plenitud*, 1918]). He wrote fantastic stories in which he played with imaginary sciences in the fashion of H. G. Wells, whom he read; or stories with metaphysical visions, like those of Nietzsche's "eternal return," or the Pythagorean transmigration of souls, or about strange extrasensory experiences, which he worked out himself or from reading oriental religions, spiritualist and irrational philosophies.

LUIS G. URBINA (1868–1934) navigates his own skiff. A modernist? Yes, in his serenity, elegance, and musical suggestiveness. But the sadness of his chant and the intimate tone are still romantic. Urbina seems to have brought Mexican romanticism to a close; at least he purified it and retained only the tenderness and the sincere confession of his torment. The inner unity of his work is admirable. It is as if he had succeeded with his first book and the others that followed were confirmations of the first, from *Verses* (*Versos*, 1890) to *The Last Birds* (*Los últimos pájaros*, 1924). As a technician of verse he was also admirable, though he hides the technique and it seems that his music develops directly from his melancholy without the help of words.

JOSÉ JUAN TABLADA (1871–1945), was born in modernism, but made restless by the promises that he caught sight of on the poetic horizon, he tried new styles, remodeled himself constantly and even escaped into Japanese forms (he cultivated the *haikai*) and ultraisms. He was, then, changeable, an adventurer who does not allow himself to be surprised by new fashions: he sees them coming from a distance and goes to meet them. Which is his best book? *Li Po and Other Poems* (*Li Po y otros poemas*), *The Pitcher of Flowers* (*El jarro de flores*), *The Market* (*La feria*). It depends on which of the many Tabladas we consider the best. Though not a great poet, his presence gave encouragement to other young poets who wanted to hazard new trails. Tablada tied together the loose ends of poetry, from Gérard de Nerval, Aloysius Bertrand, Baudelaire and Gautier to Apollinaire and Max Jacob, and attaching himself to this long thread of many knots, traversed the labyrinth of twentieth-century literature. His verses were technically irreproachable. Tablada's images had the virtue of surprising the reader because he esteemed the value of surprise in literary language. He was always on the alert for new modes and, consequently, aware of the decline of old fashions which once had captivated him. In this way he detached himself from themes of sadness, Parnassian insensitiveness, estheticizing bohemianism, when he saw them on the way to becoming outmoded. He was a cosmopolitan writer, or at least one who resisted all provincialism. He was an original spirit, or at least one who resisted established tastes.

Because of his age ENRIQUE GONZÁLEZ MARTÍNEZ (1871–

1952) belongs to the group of Mexican poets formed by Nervo, Urbina and Tablada; or, outside of Mexico, to that of Lugones, Valencia, and Jaimes Freyre. In this sense, he deserves to be studied here. Yet, it was after 1910 that González Martínez achieved his best writing and became one of the great gods of literary circles. Like Lugones, he was admired and followed even by the youths who, shortly after 1920, were shattering the lamps of modernism. His first two books (*Preludes* [*Preludios*, 1903] and *Lyricisms* [*Lirismos*, 1909]) were noble, serious, sincere. Although the author, secluded in his provincial corner distrusted the modernist sect that reigned in Mexico (in fact, he belonged to no faction, not even to that of Rubén Darío). His verses, like all others written in his generation, responded to the very modernist desire to punish forms until they submitted to the artistic models that the French Parnassians recommended. But it was in two subsequent books (*Silenter*, 1909, and *The Hidden Paths* [*Los senderos ocultos*, 1911]) that González Martínez astonished everyone, and has never since ceased to astonish them, because of the limpid serenity of his self-interrogations. "Seek in all things a soul and a hidden / meaning; do not embrace vain appearances." His was lyrical, personal poetry; but the poet does not write of the external happenings of his daily life, but of a distilled autobiography, made of pure spirit, with the essence of his emotions and thoughts. With so much contemplation and so much introspection on what he had contemplated, one ends by desiring not music but silence; however, poetry, which is a delicate body of sounds, cannot be silent; so González Martínez turns toward that portion of his poetry which is almost attached to silence: verbal exquisiteness. Not an estheticizing, extroverted, ornamental exquisiteness, but that of interiorization: "may all things affect thee like a mysterious / imprint intensely engraved . . . for I know not if I be diffused in all / or all penetrates me and abides in me." One of the poems in *The Hidden Paths*, the famous sonnet "Twist the neck of the swan" ("*Tuércele el cuello al cisne*"), indicates how, in González Martínez' scale of values, the direction of exquisiteness is reversed—it no longer leads to the swan of deceitful plumage "who sounds his white note at the blue of the fountain; / he only promenades his charm, but does not feel / the soul of things nor the voice of the landscape," but toward the wise owl: "he has not the charm of the swan, but his restless eye / which pierces the shadows interprets / the mysterious book of the nocturnal silence." Some critics observed in this sonnet certain intentions to express an esthetic manifesto; others, seduced by the image in the first verse ("Twist the neck of the swan of deceitful plumage") believed that that neck was in truth Rubén Darío's. Not only had Rubén Darío certainly twisted the necks of swans before González Martínez, but ever since *Songs of Life and Hope* (1905) no one could accuse him of frivolity and superficial estheticism.

In his memoirs, published under the titles, *The Man of the Owl* (*El hombre del buho*, 1944) and *Peaceful Madness* (*La apacible locura*, 1951) González Martínez made it clear, to those who needed clarification, that he was not reacting against Rubén Darío, but against certain "modernist" topics used by Darío's imitators. In his next book, *The Death of the Swan* (*La muerte del cisne*, 1915), the sonnet reappeared with the title "The Symbol" (*"El símbolo"*): another error on the part of those who supposed that González Martínez had liquidated his modernist past and that he now was moving toward another poetic sign. Not at all. In every book that followed, written in his maturity, in the autumn and winter of his life, González Martínez preserved his initial tone of nobility, of austerity, of fidelity to his esthetics. He is not among the poets who indulge in pirouettes when they are old in order to attract young writers to themselves. In his books (the last one: *The New Narcissus* [*El nuevo Narciso*, 1952]) there are no leaps over an abyss from one esthetics to another, but there is an ascension, within his own way of being, toward an art continually becoming more preoccupied with ultimate problems. Hopelessness, sobbing, doubts, smiles, the anguished feeling of life, of death and of time are purified in an admirable calm.

Other Countries / Up to now only those countries have filed past which have given at least one great modernist poet: Darío, Lugones, Jaimes Freyre, Herrera y Reissig, Santos Chocano, Valencia, Nervo. Other countries were not as fortunate but since they also figure in the Hispanic-American modernist process, we shall see what they have to offer.

(viii) *Antilles / Cuba:* Despite Cuba's being the cradle of Julián del Casal, there was no notable modernist movement until the advent of the twentieth century. The sisters JUANA BORRERO (1877–1896), who only left a little tome of *Rhymes* (*Rimas*, 1895), and DULCE MARÍA BORRERO (1883–1945), intimate, personal, but not a modernist. FRANCISCO JAVIER PICHARDO (1873–1941) approached modernism through his admiration for the Parnassians. AUGUSTO DE ARMAS (1869–1893) went to Paris and wound up writing verses in French—he left us only a few compositions written in Castilian. Other names: FERNANDO DE ZAYAS (1876–1932), JUAN GUERRA NÚÑEZ (1883–1943), JOSÉ MARÍA COLLANTES (1877–1943), JOSÉ MANUEL CARBONELL (1880). The brothers CARLOS PÍO ÚHRBACH (1872–1897) and FEDERICO UHRBACH (1873–1931) published a volume of poetry in 1894: *Twins* (*Gemelas*). Only the section "Ice Flowers" ("*Flores de hielo*") belongs to Carlos Pío . Federico continued his poetic production which is marked by rich sensibility and precise control of expression. His best book: *Resurrection* (*Resurrección*, 1916). REGINO E. BOTI (1878–1958) flows beyond modernism (*Mental Arabesques* [*Arabescos mentales*, 1913]) and runs along the free verse river bed but without joining the one that young writers will open after 1920.

Santo Domingo: We still see no modernist poets here. There were, of course, poets who learned from modernism the art of rich, varied, and complex versification, like the erotic APOLINAR PERDOMO (1882–1918). Names are not lacking: BIENVENIDO SALVADOR NOUEL (1874–1934), BARTOLOMÉ OLEGARIO PÉREZ (1873–1900), ANDREJULIO AYBAR (1872). But, we repeat, the modernists shall be reviewed in the next chapter. Nevertheless, because of his age, we must place here a "strange one," a verbose, pompous ultra-modernist, OTILIO VIGIL DÍAZ (1880). He organized "Vedhrinism," a movement of poetic restlessness which, in its desire to renovate, was the immediate antecedent of "posthumism" which we will study in the following chapter. He was the inventor of free and sonorous rhythms upon which surprising images float.

Puerto Rico: Modernism appeared in Puerto Rico after a delay of two or more decades, when it was already disappearing in other countries. And even then (1911, 1914) Puerto Rican modernism tried to renovate verse without renouncing either the sentimental romantic ballast or the regional themes. It was, in truth, a short-lived fashion which produced no central figure. The most interesting was that of LUIS LLORÉNS TORRES (1878–1944), whose relations with modernism were not very intimate. His books, *At the Foot of the Alhambra* (*Al pie de la Alhambra*), *Visions of My Muse* (*Visiones de mi musa*), *Symphonic Sonnets* (*Sonetos sinfónicos*), *Voices of the Great Bell* (*Voces de la campana mayor*), *Heights of America* (*Alturas de América*), reveal him as a conservative, popular poet, proud of his Hispanic traditions, nationalist in the love of his island, with a preference for historic, civil or Creole themes. His most personal tone was the erotic. He aspired to the formulation of new esthetic theories: *pancalism* (all is beauty), *panedism* (all is verse). These esthetic theories came from those of the German Krause. Lloréns Torres was, after Gautier Benítez, the next highest peak on the island. He began a poetic renovation, and in a new way captured the Puerto Rican landscape and its popular essences. On the lips of

José de Jesús Esteves (1881–1918) modernism still speaks romantically in his use of Hispanic and Creole themes.

(ix) *Venezuela* / Modernism arrived here belatedly. Even in those who came later, modernism did not take deep root: Carlos Borges (1875–1932). In general, the Venezuelans watered down modernism with a great deal of romanticism. In the years of their greatest international influence and largest array of cosmopolitan styles, the four poets we are about to speak about remained faithful to their native land. Alfredo Arvelo Larriva (1883–1934), a poet who toyed with forms, full of playful, easygoing and capricious poetic good humor, stylized national subjects. It is true that he was less successful in his ambitious attempt at epic grandeur than in his poems written in a minor key. A fresh Creole breath blew through his flute, subjected to the severity of difficult music. At a time when the esthetic principle of modernism was better represented by prose writers, he did what he could to bring the current also into verse. José Tadeo Arreaza Calatrava (1885) (*Song to Venezuela* [*Canto a Venezuela*], *The Sad Lady* [*La triste*], *Song to the Mining Engineer* [*Canto al ingeniero de minas*]) was an epic poet in his civic themes, sorrowful in his subjective tones, rich in verbal treasure. Juan Santaella (1883–1927) wrote many verses, both romantic and modernist, for the album of this or that young lady; all in all, his *Ballads of Yesterday* (*Romanzas de ayer*) reveal a lyrical disquiet, minor in key but sincere. Sergio Medina (1882–1933) created through his *Poems of Sun and Solitude* (*Poemas del sol y soledad*) and his *Tropical Cicadas* (*Cigarras del trópico*) a poetry strongly rooted in the land, in the countryside and in the emotions inspired by nature.

(x) *Ecuador* / This country was not very hospitable to modernist poetry. Francisco Fálquez Ampuero (1877–1947) followed the road opened by César Borja. He was still a romantic, although his admiration for the Parnassians, especially for the Heredia of *Les Trophées*, inspired him to create sculptured verses and strophes. Alfonso Moscoso (1879–1952), in scenes which are almost Parnassian, seems to approach modernism, but his metrics are still traditional. Luis Cordero Dávila (1876–1932) revered Rubén Darío but was not among his followers; in spite of his elegances and his polished verses there was in him a non-modernist oratorical pomp. Luis F. Veloz (1884), of quick and epigrammatic wit, walked on the fringes of the garden where Silva and Valencia strolled, but he abandoned poetry prematurely. Manuel María Sánchez (1882–1935) at first civic, circumstantial, and declamatory, later turned elegiac and intimate. Another: Emilio Gallegos del Campo (1875?–1914). In reality, only in the following generation do the fruits of modernism appear.

(xi) *Chile* / The Chilean republic, so important in the history of modernism (that is where Darío published *Azure*) produced no great poet. Minor poets, yes: Francisco Contreras (1880–1932), enthusiastic about modernism, tuned his poems to that key: *Coat of Arms* (*Toisón*, 1906). Later he propounded a new program: *The New Worldism* (*Mundonovismo*, 1917), concerned with native countryside scenes, customs, and speech. Manuel Magallanes Moure (1878–1924) was one of the most outstanding lyricists of Chile. His melancholy, elegant, tender, and at times erotic lyricism was always sensitive to nature and it sought expression in simple verse of short meter: *The House by the Sea* (*La casa junto al mar*, 1919) is one of the good collections of poems of this era. CARLOS R. MONDACA (1881–1928) was an intense elegiac poet. ANTONIO BÓRQUEZ SOLAR (1873–1938) strove to be a modernist, but his talent lay in the evocation of the nature and history of his natal archipelago. MIGUEL LUIS ROCUANT (1877–1948) was a poet of forms sculptured in the Parnassian manner. ERNESTO A. GUZMÁN (1877–1960), who had been a modernist, descriptive, erotic rhymester (*Dawns* [*Albores*, 1902]), gave up rhyme (it is said he did so on the advice of Unamuno) and changed his subject-matter, taking on a more reflexive attitude: *Interior Life* (*Vida interna*, 1909). JORGE GONZÁLEZ BASTIAS (1879–1950) dropped his initial preciosity prevalent in *Masses of Spring* (*Misas de primavera*) and wrote simple verses about the loveliness of the countryside. ZOILO ESCOBAR (1875–1950) was a poet more concerned with ideas than with expressing his inner feelings. ALFREDO MAURET CAAMAÑO (1880–1934) shaped his amorous feelings into sonnets. JERÓNIMO LAGOS LISBOA (1885–1958) broke away from an early addiction to modernist ornamentation and acquired a style of expression that was limpid, current, evocative.

(xii) *Paraguay* / It had no modernists because, in reality, it had no literature. Modernism would arrive much later: the only names that can be intercalated here are those of FRANCISCO LUIS BARREIRO (1872–1929) and, above all, ALEJANDRO GUANES (1872–1925) whose posthumous collection is entitled *Passing Through Life* (*De paso por la vida*). Guanes sang of his country, home, and death. They are verses of minor tone, at times of Parnassian fabrication. His most memorable are those of "The Legends" ("*Las leyendas*"). He was a theosophist and his philosophic-religious ideas are reflected in his poems. It was he and Fariña Núñez (whom we shall meet farther on) who progressed toward modernism.

2. Non-Modernist Poets

Before going on to prose let us pay a courtesy call on those who lived beyond the pale of modernism.

Among the non-modernists there were, as we have seen, poets who did not reach the level of the new style and who were backward in respect to their times. But occasionally their opaqueness and their backwardness (negative values from the esthetic point of view) became, through the pull of circumstances, civic values. In Puerto Rico, for example, there were those who feared that after 1898 the Hispanic configuration of Creole culture might be marred by the assault of Anglo-American civilization. The need was felt to reinforce the work of writers grounded in the reality of Puerto Rico, either those who adopted popular words (Alonso, Vassallo) or those who dealt with Creole themes in a cultured language (Tapia). These are poets, then, who patriotically exalted Hispanic and Puerto Rican traditions. VIRGILIO DÁVILA (1869–1943), in cultured verses, gave expression to the "hillbillyism" of the countryside (*Aromas of the Land* [*Aromas del terruño*, 1916]) and of the urban areas (*Town of Yesteryear* [*Pueblito de antes*, 1917]). In Central America, DEMETRIO FÁBREGA (Panama, 1881–1932). In Venezuela, ANDRÉS MATA (1870–1931). In Colombia, when the reader begins to feel annoyed by the declamatory sonority or the sweetish musicality of the poetry of these years, he becomes grateful to LUIS CARLOS LÓPEZ (1883–1950) for his elemental, schematic verses expressing Creole reaction to international pomp. López (*From My Hamlet* [*De mi villorrio*, 1908]; *Mushrooms from Riba* [*Los hongos de la Riba*, 1909]; *By the Short-cut* [*Por el atajo*, 1938]) is at times coarse in his derision of types and customs of provincial life, but capable of keen irony and can even bring lyrical smiles to a sentimentalism that blushes and hides its face. The poetry he wrote was based on concrete reality before this kind of poetry became a mode, and so his name was saved by the taste of later generations. In Chile CARLOS PEZOA VÉLIZ (1879–1908) wrote sketches of local customs in prose, amatory verses, and poems of social protest. For formalist critics there is too much deformity in his sentimentalism and in his realism; the sociologists, on the other hand, are grateful to him because, having the soul of a plebeian, he reflected in his literature the life of the Chilean people, their typical characteristics (abulia, fatalism, humor) and the sufferings of the lower classes: the ragged, the down-and-out, the vagabonds, the rogues, the rebels, the workers. He had tried his hand at artistic images and novelties during his modernist years, but it was a passing exercise. What he has left us is his understanding of the inertia of the man of the masses. Other non-modernist, or only barely modernist, Chilean poets were: DIEGO DUBLÉ URRUTIA (1877), who turned to the telluric, the auchthonous, the people. His solidarity with the Indians and the proletarians, although serious, did not keep him from enjoying life with good humor. VICTOR DOMINGO SILVA (1882–1960) was a literary man of multiple interests (the theater, the novel, action) but it was his lyrical talent that gave him nobility. His lyricism was of the people, for the people, optimistic, humane, rooted in national concerns. SAMUEL A. LILLO (1870–1958) described and wrote about his native land and its people. He wrote as an observer, but his verses were declamatory. In Paraguay, IGNACIO A. PANE (1880–1920).

B. MAINLY PROSE

Although we have seen the authors of this period rotating around an axis of poetry, they were also, in many cases, excellent prose writers. In the same way, the prosists whom we are about to study were also poets. Frequently their prose was written with the same lyrical tension that informed their verse. One can see a whole gamut from poetry to poetic prose, and from this to an artistically elaborated prose. Even the realists and naturalists, even the narrators of regional and folkloric themes were sensitive to the new art of prose. But of course, realism was a dividing line between two proud attitudes: on one side, the pride with which the modernists organized verses and prose in an esthetic and subjective world; on the other side, stories and novels were organized taking pride in objective description. Literature was no less a calling for the realists. Certain tendencies apparently contrary to estheticism, such as naturalism, were also modern attitudes and arose from the awareness of fashions and from the same desire to renew art.

1. Novel and Short Story

We shall take the narrators by national groups, moving from north to south; and within each national group we shall study first the estheticists, then the more realistic narrators. To avoid repeating the distinctions between the estheticist narrators and the realists, we shall qualify both styles here, once and for all.

(*a*) *Estheticizing Narrators* / Modernist prose was in a predicament when it had to novelize, because of the intimate conflict between the attention given to the pretty, bejeweled phrase and the attention given to the true development of the action. The equilibrium is difficult, and to take care of one virtue generally presupposes to neglect the other. The "poem in prose" was one of the most fervid rites of modernist cult. There were those who mutilated themselves in celebrating it, and, when we read them now, we feel pity for them. It was a lyrical miniaturism which, when in the service of a profound view of life, contributed to the dignity of Castilian prose, but when it was reduced to empty verbalism it became a childish epidemic.

For a history of artistic prose, in good and bad taste, these names should be recorded: ALEJANDRO FERNÁNDEZ GARCÍA (Venezuela, 1879–1939), author of *Alchemist Gold* (*Oro de alquimia*) and *Lilacs in Bloom* (*Búcaros en flor*); AMÉRICO LUGO (Dominican Republic, 1870–1952), author of *Heliotrope* (*Heliotropo*). Some of these prose poets also wrote novels and short stories—artistic, of course. Just as the romantics had preferred the novel to the short story, now the modernists preferred the short story to the novel; they were lyrical, fantastic, escaping from the American reality or penetrating it with glances that estheticized all they saw, like Darío, Gutiérrez Nájera, Coll, Lugones, Jaime Freyre, Quiroga, etc.

(*b*) *Realist Narrators* / Naturalism, with its psychiatry, its monstrous flowers of sordidness, and its strange esthetics of ugliness, occasionally made its way into the poetic literature of modernism. But it followed its own course toward an objective description of reality. On their part, modernist writers usually lowered their sights to the customs and landscapes of their region, diverting themselves in a kind of Creolism and Indianism. It would be too schematic to divide narrative prose into a modernist half where what counts is the subject-contemplator, and a realist half where what counts is the object-contemplated.

(i) *Mexico* / There scarcely was a Hispanic-American country that did not do some gardening in the narrative genre. The same gardens that one had become accustomed to seeing in verse now were also seen in prose. The poetess MARÍA ENRIQUETA CAMARILLO DE PEREYRA (Mexico, 1875) wrote stories and novels. *A Strip of the World* (*Jirón de mundo*, 1918) is a rose-tinted, lachrymose novel. It has no local color; rather it has a temporal color, but of the nineteenth century, with touches of the sentimental, romantic, bourgeois, feminine novel of the type of Charlotte Brontë's *Jane Eyre*. Teresa, abandoned at a convent door, grows up to become a governess in a rich home caring for a sickly girl. The father of the girl, Doctor Santiesteban, is a sad widower, also very ill, and a paragon of perfection. He has a good-natured son who falls in love with Teresa, and an ill-natured daughter who hates her. Teresa had been corresponding with an unknown friend who inevitably turns out to be Santiesteban. When they identify each other, the ill-natured daughter, Laura, screeches insults at them. The doctor dies on the spot, from a heart attack, and Teresa takes permanent refuge in a convent. Within its genre, the novel is well written, with a prose that tends to be poetic, and an action that holds interest. Along with other similar novels, it drifts to all parts of the world. ANTONIO MÉDIZ BOLIO (1884–1957), a poet and dramatist, whose best book is *The Land of the Pheasant and the Deer* (*La tierra del faisán y del venado*), in which he elaborates legends of the Mayas.

Many figures squeeze into the picture of the realist novel of Mexico. We would rather analyze one: Azuela. But since his importance rests on being the founder of the novel of the revolution, as a curiosity we would like to mention first HERIBERTO FRÍAS (1870–1925) who, in *Tomóchic* (1894) gave us the chronicle of an Indian rebellion against Porfirio Díaz with sympathy for the rebels.

MARIANO AZUELA (1873–1952). His first stage as a novelist began with *María Luisa* (1907) and ended with *The Underdogs*

(*Los de abajo*, 1916), his sixth novel. Those who judged it
from a political and not a literary viewpoint believed that *The
Underdogs* was an anti-revolutionary work. In truth, at first
glance the novel does not seem to stand by the revolution, but
rather to criticize the brutal episodes from Madero's assassination to the defeat of Pancho Villa's partisans in the battle of
Celaya. The men who surround Demetrio Macías did not take
arms and hurl themselves into the revolution on principle, but
were impelled by personal motives and events. Demetrio Macías
himself, as their leader, does not have a political awareness. When
his wife asks him at the end why he continues fighting, Demetrio
"distractedly picks up a little stone and hurls it down the canyon.
He stands thoughtfully looking down the gorge, and says, 'Look
at that little stone, how it doesn't come to rest.' " Inertia, not
ideals. The brutality that moves them all is fierce in "Whitey"
Margarito. Nor has the minor intellectual, Luis Cervantes, who
wishes to supply Demetrio with an ideology, become a revolutionary through conviction; he is a resentful person, an oppor-
tunist, a charlatan. Solís is the only authentic revolutionary, and
within the novel he reveals the secret of Azuela as a citizen and
as a novelist. Solís is disillusioned, not by the revolution, but by
its failures. This disenchantment leads him to contemplate the
revolution at a distance, as an objective reality; and from this
esthetic distance he envisages it "beautiful even in its barbarism."
Azuela also is a disillusioned revolutionary: the lack of meaning
in the struggle wounds him. But he feels its tragic beauty and,
though he judges it on a moral plane, he describes it artistically.
The revolution as an object of contemplation: from this Azuela's
realism is born. He depicts circumstances more than men. *The
Underdogs* offers a continuous action: when the novelist skips an
episode he will return to recoup in a retrospective evocation.
The action closes in a perfect circumference—although in in-
verse position, Demetrio and his men will die in the last chapters
on the same spot where they began their fighting in the first chapters. However, in this lineal action there is no intention of showing the psychological growth of the characters. The object, we
repeat, is not the psychology of the characters but the reproduc-

tion of one phase of the revolution. The characters and their vicissitudes are fragments of the composition of the pictures. Azuela's objectivity is that of the naturalist: the circumstances are the determining factors; men, without liberty, without goals, are animals. And, with a naturalist technique, Azuela presents men and animals piled together, fused into a single mass.

By 1916, realism and naturalism had triumphed in the novel the world over. It was not necessary, as in the period from Stendhal and Balzac to the Goncourts and Zola, to prove that the literary treatment of sordid reality could reach serious dignity in art. Azuela had no need to wrestle with an enormous mass of details. Therefore, he efficiently used vigorous, novelistic outlines, rapid, flickering and suggestive prose, dialectical dialogs, impressionistic techniques, and contrasts between the iniquities of man and the beauties of the landscape. His impressionism was the visual one of the realists, not the synesthetic one of the modernists. Azuela used to say that he only wrote to give vent to his emotions and that all his themes were real. His strength, certainly, seems to come from events, not from art. Nevertheless, what is artistic in Azuela is that he allows himself to be permeated by events, giving us the illusion of seeing what the author saw. He possessed sobriety, starkness, the capacity for synthesis, the imagination to encompass in one metaphor of powerful, illuminating violence the whole of a social situation or psychological conflict. In his second stage, from 1916 to 1932, Azuela decided to experiment with some of the tricks of the latest literature of the day. "I abandoned my usual manner, which consists of expressing myself with clarity and conciseness," he explained in some autobiographical notes; and he twisted phrases and proffered conundrums in *That Woman Malhora* (*La Malhora*), *Retaliation* (*El desquite*), and *The Firefly* (*La luciérnaga*). These were the postwar years of "stridentism" which we will define in the next chapter: "Dada" images, "futurist" objects, hermeticism of contorted symbols, anti-logical style, expressionism, obscure monologs. Azuela became infected. Just a few blotches on his skin. He recovered his health and returned to his own metier, which was the chronicle and social criticism. The third stage starts with *Pedro Moreno the Insurgent* (*Pedro Moreno el insurgente*, 1933) to *Lost Paths* (*Sendas perdidas*, 1949) a novel on the working class of the city. He also wrote short stories and theater. But his novels remain the most substantial part of his literature. In it there is the Mexico of Porfirio Díaz, the Mexico of the Revolution, the Mexico that emerged after the revolution. But as a novelist he succeeded more in the negative register of errors, crimes, corruption, treachery. He understood less the efforts at national regeneration. In short, he enriched the novel of Hispanic-America with at least two works, *The Underdogs* and *The Firefly*. His posthumous novels, *The Curse* (*La maldición*) and *That Blood* (*Esa sangre*), continued to denounce the social defects that remained in spite of the revolution or that appeared because of the revolution: crude novels, the first satiric, the other bitter, both born of Azuela's moralist background.

(ii) *Central America / Guatemala:* The goldsmiths of prose (and "goldsmiths" is not always a eulogy, since not all had good taste) even gilded the pages of newspapers. The first name to reach this juncture is that of ENRIQUE GÓMEZ CARRILLO (Guatemala, 1873–1927). His tastes were educated in Europe where he went for the first time in 1889. But there were so many literary, artistic, and philosophic tendencies that what was educated more than his tastes, was an extraordinary skill in referring to all of the tendencies. In spite of the humbleness of his trade—commenting on the creations of others—his prose was one of the most agile of his time. His knowledge of all contemporary European literature was fabulous. He was an impressionist whose impressions were more of literary life than of life. We are indebted to him for having left well-written gossipy tales. He was not a critic in the true sense, not even of what he admired. Some of the writers he knew, Loti, for example, encouraged him to pursue his intellectual curiosity. He traveled a good deal, and from his travels he created such books as: *Present-Day Russia* (*La Rusia actual*), *Heroic and Gallant Japan* (*El Japón heroico y galante*), *The Smile of the Sphinx* (*La sonrisa de la Esfinge*), *Eternal Greece* (*La Grecia eterna*), *Jerusalem and the Holy Land* (*Jerusalén y la Tierra santa*), *From Marseille to Tokyo* (*De Marsella a Tokio*), *Views of Europe* (*Vistas de Europa*), *The Charm of Buenos Aires* (*El encanto de Buenos Aires*). These lands were provinces of his Gallicized soul (and naturally, his best chronicles came from his stay in France). He was a chronicler of genius, in part because he perceived that the "chronicle" was a worthy literary genre and he devoted himself to it with the strength of a lyrical vocation. He placed a magnificently orchestrated language at the service of everyday themes. He seems to be frivolous; but in reality it is because he is so comprehensive that he appears to be on the surface of everything. He wrote novels. The one he preferred was *The Gospel of Love* (*El evangelio del amor*, 1922). It is made with the pap of many books, old ones (the Bible, Jacopo da Voragine's *The Golden Legend*) and new ones (France's *Thaïs*, Flaubert's *La tentation de Saint-Antoine*, Louys' *Aphrodite*). It takes place in the first quarter of the fourteenth century, in Byzantium. Teófilo, an ascetic, tortures his flesh to attain religious purity, until he hears that Jesus wants him to love a woman. He finds her, but learns that what Jesus wished was that he love completely and fully; hence, he goes to live with the anchorets, but this time to preach to them "the gospel of love." They stone him to death. It is a modernist novel in the precious style: the theme is common to estheticism. For the same reason that estheticism was hedonist the modernists fancied its opposite: asceticism. Pleasure was derived from the contrast between sensuality and the denial of the flesh, between the faun and the angel, as Darío would say. From the enjoyers of life, even in the most degrading forms, one passed to the torturers of the flesh through the mechanics of opposites. Gómez Carrillo exalts life, sensuality, love; and even dares to dip into theology and to interpret freely the Bible, the lives of saints, and the writings of the fathers of the Church. His novel is interesting as a variation on a theme of the times, but it lacks movement, vital reality, and psychological depth. It is too replete with conventional phrases and bookish passages. Gómez Carrillo touched upon the religious theme in other books. He called himself a Christian, but his novel, naturally, lies beyond any Christian church. One of his most palatable books is *Thirty Years of My Life* (*Treinta años di mi vida*), in three volumes.

Honduras: FROILÁN TURCIOS (1875–1943) began as a modernist poet (see his anthology *Almond Flowers* [*Flores de almendro*]). He excelled nevertheless in his *Cruel Stories* (*Cuentos crueles*). Villiers de l'Isle-Adam had written stories with the same title; and there are resonances of Poe in two of his novels: *Annabel Lee* and *The Vampire* (*El vampiro*). He also wrote narrations in a tropical setting. He had great influence in the literary life of his country.

El Salvador: ARTURO AMBROGI (1875–1936), author of *Bibelots*, also wrote *Book of the Tropics* (*El libro del Trópico*), narrations that are among the first of a regionalist tendency in his country. JOSÉ MARÍA PERALTA LAGOS (1873–1944) was a genial narrator of social customs.

Costa Rica: The Francophiles, ALEJANDRO ALVARADO QUIRÓS (1876–1945) and RAFAEL ANGEL TROYO (1875–1910) added their names to the list of writers on social customs; the latter was a miniaturist of the modernist school and author of artistic prose. MARÍA FERNÁNDEZ DE TINOCO (1877) carried her love of archeology to two novels, *Zulai* and *Yonta*, which re-create imaginatively the origin and the struggles of the American indigenous races.

Estheticism (Alejandro Alvarado Quirós, Rafael Angel Troyo) and realism (Magón, Jenaro Cardona) emerged from nowhere, the first buds of a national expression amidst a people who had lived centuries without literature. We have already spoken of Magón. But the creator of the realist novel was JOAQUÍN GARCÍA MONGE (1881–1958). In *The Landmark* (*El Moto*, 1900), his first novel and furthermore, the first significant novel in Costa Rican letters, he weaved the adverse loves between peasants on a loom of social customs, with the joys and suffering of the people. Also dated 1900 is his novel *The Daughters of the Fields* (*Las hijas del campo*) which looks into the city and its problems. Dated 1917 are his short stories, *The Evil Shadow and Other Events* (*La mala sombra y otros sucesos*), perhaps his best work because of the reproduction, at times naturalistic, of the social customs and language of the peasants.

Panama: Before his exile in 1898 DARÍO HERRERA (1870–1914) had been the initiator of modernism in his country, in verse and prose. He left Parnassian verse to enlist as a short story writer, but remained a Parnassian in his desire for verbal perfection. Although *Distant Hours* (*Horas lejanas*, 1903), are stories in an American setting, they have such a refined and learned spiritual elegance that they do not seem to have been written in America. The obsession with the unique, the precious, the right word, comes rather from Flaubert. Another Panamanian narrator, GUILLERMO ANDREVE (1879–1940), distinguished himself more as a promoter of the works of others. He is the author of a novel about spiritualists, *A Corner of the Veil* (*Una punta del velo*, 1929). SALOMÓN PONCE AGUILERA (1868–1945), situated between Spanish realism and French naturalism, left a collection of sketches of peasant customs: *The Clods* (*De la gleba*, 1914).

(iii) *Antilles* / MANUEL FLORENTINO CESTERO (Dominican Republic, 1879–1926) composed stories of modernist art in prose that crept into the titles: *Stories for Lila* (*Cuentos a Lila*), and a novel, *The Song of the Swan* (*El canto del cisne*). We might mention here a dozen realist narrators in the Antilles. We shall pause only before those who did not exceed their quota of blunders.

Cuba: First of all, JESÚS CASTELLANOS (1879–1912). He published various stories under the title *The Conspiracy* (*La conjura,* 1909). The first proposes a thesis: there is a social "conspiracy" to destroy all superior, idealistic, noble individuals, here symbolized by the physician Augusto Román. The physician lives in Havana with a hospital nurse, a voluptuous girl, of animal sensuality. He would like a university chair in order to devote himself to scientific investigations. Social conventions bring pressure upon him to abandon his mistress. Augusto, out of goodness, refuses to do so. He is not given either the chair, or the position as director of the hospital. He also loses the opportunity to marry a rich girl. When he realizes his mistress is a prostitute, he decides to become a cynic and yield to social conventions. Quite superior to *The Conspiracy* is *The Heroine* (*La heroina*). Here there is no thesis on which to waste the story. With a careful prose, in which good images flash, and with a vivid and continuous narrative rhythm, he has drawn an intimate episode in the life of the well-to-do Cuban bourgeoisie. The ironic tone is the best in the novelette. Of naturalist parentage are Carrión and Loveira, both of them notable. Taking the would-be standpoint of the scientistic psychologist, MIGUEL DE CAR-RIÓN (1875–1929) dissects the personality of a woman in *The Honorable Women* (*Las honradas,* 1918). CARLOS LOVEIRA (1882–1928) anarchical-unionist in his fight for labor, learned in literature what he could from Zola and diagnosed social ills in various novels: *The Immoral Ones* (*Los inmorales,* 1919), *Generals and Doctors* (*Generales y doctores,* 1920), *The Blind* (*Los ciegos,* 1923), *The Last Lesson* (*La última lección,* 1924) and the best, *John Doe* (*Juan Criollo,* 1928). In this way he documented the last years of the colony and the first years of the republic, but his capacity for observation was counteracted by his incapacity to compose well-structured stories with clearly drawn characters. In him the social material overrides the psychological creation. Others are ARTURO MONTORI (1878–1932), with scenes of social customs, and LUIS RODRÍGUEZ EMBIL (1880–1954), who was still writing historical novels.

Dominican Republic: TULIO MANUEL CESTERO (Dominican Republic, 1877–1954) learned to write so well in the modernist school that he could have become a neat miniaturist. And, in effect, his preciosity (influenced by D'Annunzio's) was registered in several books. But fortunately he cultivated the short story and went from psychological analysis (*Blood of Spring* [*Sangre de primavera,* 1908]) to the description of Dominican life (*Romantic City* [*Ciudad romántica,* 1911]). His novel *Blood* (*La sangre,* 1915) is the best he wrote and, undoubtedly, one of the best novels of the period. He subtitled it "a life under tyranny." The life in question is that of a Quixotic teacher and journalist,

388 *Spanish-American Literature: A History*

Antonio Portocarrero; the tyranny, that of Ulises Heureaux, who was assassinated in 1899. The action runs from 1899 to 1905 in the chaotic period that followed Heureaux' assassination. The "life under tyranny" refers, then, to the chapters in which Portocarrero, from his prison cell, evokes the days of his childhood and adolescence. Consequently, there are two temporal dimensions: the inspection of the present and the retrospection of the past. And it is in the examination of the present, from 1899 to 1905, that Portocarrero's characters come out in relief. This deliberate structure of the novel facilitates psychological analysis. In many other Hispanic-American novels this type of intellectual and political hero who fails because he does not know how or does not wish to come to an agreement with reality has been presented. But Cestero, though he sympathizes with his hero, humanizes him, permeates him, and describes him with lights and shadows. He gives us, then, a double exposure: external, the Dominican Republic, and internal, the life of an unadaptable. The prose also shows Cestero's preoccupation with construction: he coins his phrases in classical molds (seventeenth-century classical) and in modern molds (modernism of the beginning of the twentieth century). Naturalism and estheticism travel side by side.

MANUEL DE JESÚS TRONCOSO DE LA CONCHA (1878–1955) was the most fertile and spontaneous collector of the traditions and anecdotes of national life: *Dominican Narrations* (*Narraciones dominicanas*, 1946). RAFAEL DAMIRÓN (1882–1956), poet, playwright, depicter of customs, and novelist in a series of reconstructions of the conflicts in contemporary political history, beginning with *On Caesarism* (*Del cesarismo*, 1911) up to *The Political Boss's Wife* (*La cacica*, 1944). The latter is a psychological study of a strong and evil woman. HAIM LÓPEZ PENHA (1878) wrote *Renaissance* (*Renacimiento*, 1942), a novel on the customs of the contemporary city. ARTURO FREITES ROQUE (1874–1914), satirized political intrigues in *Relentless* (*Lo inexorable*, 1911).

Puerto Rico: Between Matías González García, of whom we have already spoken, and MIGUEL MELÉNDEZ MUÑÓZ (1884), a group of short-story writers and novelists formed, which was alert to the customs of the people and to the social problems of the island. One of them was ANA ROQUÉ DE DUPREY (1883–1933).

(iv) *Venezuela* / In Venezuela, a country of novelists, the artistic direction is indicated by Coll, Domínici, Urbaneja Achelpohl, and Díaz Rodríguez. In 1894 the first three launched their review *Cosmópolis*, a vent for "all the literary schools of all the countries."

PEDRO EMILIO COLL (1872–1947) wrote very little (among his best: *Words* [*Palabras,* 1896]; *The Castle of Elsinor* [*El castillo de Elsinor,* 1901]; *The Hidden Path* [*La escondida senda,* 1927]), but his chronicles and stories make us feel the presence of a "hospitable mind," (as he himself used to say) a keen, skeptical, smiling and pessimistic spirit. Narrative did not interest him. He was rather a contemplative who glossed his own contemplations. He left, nevertheless, several stories that reveal his understanding of the spiritually poor ("The Broken Tooth" [*"El diente roto"*]), his curiosity for Baudelairean sensuality ("Opoponax") and even his exercises in naturalism written with a modernist pen ("Drunken Creole" [*"Borracho criollo"*]). Like César Zumeta, Coll was capable but unproductive.

PEDRO CÉSAR DOMÍNICI (1872–1954) wrote mannerist novels—with the voluptuous and artificial manners of Pierre Louys or of D'Annunzio—which refused to be American even in theme; for example, *Dionysos* (1907) speaks to us of Alexandrian eroticisms. Other novels, *The Triumph of the Ideal* (*El triunfo del ideal*), *Voluptuous Sadness* (*La tristeza voluptuosa*), refuse contact with life (too vulgar!) and prefer contact with the expressions of an inner-chamber literature. In the prolog to *The Condor* (*El cóndor,* 1925) the author tells us that many years after his Greek novel *Dionysos,* he decided to attempt the "American novel," whose action would unfold in our hemisphere. The *Condor* is a novel that is a little Indianist, a little historical, a little poetic—in any case, not much novel. It relates the war deeds of Angol, the archer of one of the remotest tribes of the Inca Empire. It is set in the times of Atahualpa's "quarrel" with Huáscar and of the Spanish conquest of Peru. From the love of Angol for Guacolda are born twin daughters. One of the conquistadors, in turn, will love one of Angol's daughters, and from this love will be born the first mestizo in Peru; with Huáscar and Atahualpa dead, Angol carries on the struggle until he is killed. There is sympathy for the indigenous cause, but the novel is completely false. The excess of literature—"modernist" literature, if we wish to calumniate modernism—spoils the unraveling of the action.

LUIS MANUEL URBANEJA ACHELPOHL (1874–1937) is, of the three, the one who takes the best advantage of the land in which he lives. Like the rest, he is impregnated with modernism, but he gives a Creole, native direction to his verbal art. His modernism, let it be said in passing, contained naturalist styles. He resembles those painters who turned to impressionism in their desire for truth and for faithfulness to a model. Be that as it may, his novels, *In This Country* (*En este país,* 1916), *The House of the Four Cowhides* (*La casa de las cuatro pencas*) and especially his excellent stories, managed to do without the esthetic ballast of their generation and thus gained in loftiness and in stature. He was one of those who knew how to look, artistically and with sincerity, at life and at the landscape of the villages, mountains and Venezuelan plains. He usually interrupts the action to marvel at nature. First the bucolic note, then, through the pretty trails of modernism, he advanced toward a realism *à la* Zola or *à la* Bourget. With stories like *"Ovejón"* it can be said that Urbaneja Achelpohl initiates the history of the Venezuelan short story.

One of the great Venezuelans, and one of the greatest novelists in all Hispanic-America in this period, was MANUEL DÍAZ ROD-RÍGUEZ (1871–1927). His is an exemplary case of a prose style that, with discretion and measured movements, slips past the reefs of a preciosity which does not know how to novelize, and of a naturalism which novelizes without knowing how to write. His first books, *Secrets of Psyche* (*Confidencias de Psiquis*, 1896), *Sensations of Travel* (*Sensaciones de viaje*, 1896), *About My Pilgrimages* (*De mis romerías*, 1898), *Stories in Color* (*Cuentos de color*, 1899), take solace in European civilizations—he had lived in France, in Italy, and his views were those of Barrès, of D'Annunzio. His *Stories in Color* narrated myths and legends ("blue," "green"), allegories and parables on his artistic ideas ("golden," "pale red"), reflections on love ("pale blue," "red"). Significantly, Venezuela appears in the three stories without any color: "white," "gray," and "black." All is shading, sound, perfume, caresses, evocation, and even human suffering is phrased a little to Parnassian and a little to symbolist tastes. There are no heroes in his stories: impressionistic atmospheres are the motivating characters. In his second group of works (*Broken Idols* [*Idolos rotos*, 1901]; *Patrician Blood* [*Sangre patricia*, 1902]), Díaz Rodríguez clashes with Venezuelan reality and repudiates it esthetically. His ideal man was the "distinguished one" of Nietzsche; but his characters do not struggle. They are pessimists, defeatists, unadaptables who go into exile or to suicide. In *Broken Idols* he shows the aristocratic figure of Alberto Soria, the sculptor, in contrast with sordid and barbarous Venezuelan masses. He wanted to regenerate his country by means of his esthetic cult; the rabble harasses and breaks the icons. But Díaz Rodríguez persists in believing that a disinterested art, proud of the elaboration of beautiful forms, can at least save the liberty of intense souls; and he writes another estheticist novel, *Patrician Blood*. His novelist aim is minimal: to present the social weakening of the upper-class Creole. What is valuable is the description of the states of soul; and this description is not that of a psychologist but of a symbolist writer. This is odd, because the theme would have lent itself to a psychological novel; after all, it is the novel of a neurosis. Metaphoric art insists more on esthetic impression than on psychological observations. The atmosphere is also estheticist: paintings by Botticelli, poetry by Swedenborg, music by Schumann and Wagner, discussions on Nietzsche, the affirmation of the supernatural over scientific reality, immersions into the subconscience, drugs, the theme of the submerged cathedral. It is not accidental that the novel begins with the description of the sailing of a transatlantic liner and that the uprooted Tulio Arcos does not reach the shores of Venezuela. Between 1910 and 1927, the second period of his literary career, he wrote less. What he did write was essay prose: *The Way of Perfection* (*Camino de perfección*, 1910); *Lyric Sermons* (*Sermones líricos*, 1918); *Among the Flowering Hills* (*Entre las colinas en flor*, posthumous); and narrative prose: *Pilgrim or the Enchanted Well* (*Peregrina o el pozo encantado;* a novel and several short stories, 1921). In these narratives Díaz Rodríguez attempted the Creole narrative, a form in which his artistic ideals could function, and function well, immersed in the land and its men. It is as if he took refuge from his disillusion in country life, in the direct emotional encounter with nature. Still, however, he continued to manipulate his narrative material to cast it into a coin of spectacular phrases. In other words, it was Díaz Rodríguez' phraseology rather than Venezuela that make these last works of his spectacular. And he manipulated his material so urgently that it was not merely his descriptions that became congealed in metaphors, but the action itself took on incredible dramatic spasms; for example, in "Summer Eclogue" (*"Egloga de verano"*) when Justa decapitates Gaucharaco with a single axe-blow, the head, which was "stretched in its effort to slip into the room, was cut off cleanly, and leaped, grasping the sheet of the cot with its teeth in its last convulsive moment. That is the way they found it, still hanging from the bedsheet . . ."

We must place RUFINO BLANCO-FOMBONA (1874–1944) in the realist current. His first verses were produced at the modernist still; but what attracted him to this style was only the exaltation of violent personalities, for that is what he was, a violent person. He used to say that he felt "closer to the romantics,

even though I never take my eyes off the truth that I see." He
reproached the modernists for their softness, their exoticism, their
ardor for imitation, their blindness to things of America. It is
certain that he was more concerned with America than other
modernists in his work as a political and critical pamphleteer
and as a historian; but his work of pure literary creation did not
turn out as well as his program for an original American art had
promised. His true merit lies in his *American Stories (Cuentos
americanos*, 1904)—augmented in the edition entitled *Minimal
Dramas (Dramas mínimas*, 1920)—and in novels such as *The
Man of Gold (El hombre de oro*, 1915), *Mitre in Hand (La mitra
en la mano*, 1927). Unfortunately, even here he only showed a
knack for writing novels, and not the novels that can be achieved
with this knack. He left caricatures, not characters. His political
passions, his satirical intentions, his pride in being instinctive and
barbaric, his journalistic techniques applied to art ruined his creative vision. If he is called a "realist" it is to contrast him with the
preciosity of other narrators. In reality, Blanco-Fombona unbosomed his feelings too much to be an objective narrator. He
was obsessed by the stupidity, the evilness, and sordidness of
people (even he himself was not a man of exemplary morals) and
when he was not deforming reality with his diatribes, he impoverished it with sex. *The Man of Gold*, for example, is not a
good novel. The title refers to Irurtia, a miserly person and a
usurer, who becomes the Venezuelan minister of the interior. It
contains brisk, sarcastic pages, but the novel, as a whole, is not
brisk. Its worst defect is its inverisimilitude. If it were a farce it
would not matter, since a farce is based on a forced situation. But
this is half a farce. Furthermore, it intends, without achieving it, to
be a novel of psychological analysis of the characters Irurtia,
Rosaura, Olga, Andrés. The reader feels unsatisfied because
neither the farcical tone nor the psychological tone is pure. There
is in Blanco-Fombona a conflict between his psychological view of
man and his moral-sociological judgment of man. He is better
endowed to do the latter because his was a polemical, reforming,
aggressive talent. But he did not succeed in the selection of his
narrative genre. In the prolog to *Minimal Dramas* he confessed

his philosophy (or his ill-humor): "I have discovered always and everywhere the same: an identical well of stupidity, evil and suffering." Unfortunately, his "minimal dramas" don't even express this misanthropy well, because as he was composing them, the material gave way in his hands. He wanted to inform the reader of what he had seen, heard, or lived, rather than surprise him with new situations and unexpected endings. In his later years he tried to renovate his narrative technique. *The Secret of Happiness* (*El secreto de la felicidad*, 1935) is, rather than a novel, the outline of a novel, with political schemes, written in schematic prose. But it does have innovating characteristics in the technical history of the genre. In short, though he did not leave any really powerful book, Blanco-Fombona left, on the whole, a fairly considerable work which interests us because of his human personality. In this sense, we may enjoy the diary of his life, from 1906 to 1914, which he published in 1933 with the title *Road of Imperfection* (*Camino de imperfección*)—a diary which keeps revealing an erotic, political, and literary mass of anecdotes, always vain and at times brilliant. Another novelist: RAFAEL CABRERA MALO (1872–1936).

(v) *Colombia* / Many novels were written for colleagues and not for the ordinary reader. The relative popularity that the novels of JOSÉ MARÍA VARGAS VILA (Colombia, 1860–1933) enjoyed was exceptional, perhaps because his literary niceties—rhythmic prose, orthographic dislocations, artificial vocabulary and syntax, selfworshipping flights of fancy—were at the service of a morbid bad taste. Among the more than twenty novels he wrote are: *Ibis, Afternoon Roses* (*Rosas de la tarde*), *Swamp Flower* (*Flor de fango*), *The Seed* (*La simiente*). JOSÉ MARÍA RIVAS GROOT (1863–1923) did write good, little artistic novels. *Resurrection* (*Resurrección*), for example, will hardly please the general public, but will offer to the scholar the pleasure of recognizing, one by one, the composites of the refined European cultural world "in the aurora of the 20th century," as the author puts it. Several artist-characters are in love with a woman who possesses the beauty of mystery and death. They discuss Parnassianism, symbolism, and Pre-Raphaelism in literature, impressionism in painting, Wagner in music. The positivism of the natural sciences is denied, and, on the other hand, a Catholicism beautified by artistic imagination is exalted. The irrational is cultivated: neurasthenias, rare sensations, dreams, forebodings of the supernatural, and, crowning all of this, the esthetic aspects of the Catholic religion. His brother, EVARISTO RIVAS GROOT, 1864–1923, also wrote modernist, though more realist, stories. The novel of national or regional atmosphere barely received any incentive from modernism. It had been born in the realist school and continued to be realistic. Although EMILIO CUERVO MÁRQUEZ (1873–1937) wrote *Phinées* (1913), a novel of the time of Christ (similar to Sienkiewicz' *Quo Vadis?*), he did leave narratives about Colombia that were more significant: *La Ráfaga, Lilí,* and *The Dark Jungle* (*La selva oscura*).

CLÍMACO SOTO BORDA (1870–1919) described the social milieu of his time with some naturalist touches: *Diana the Huntress* (*Diana Cazadora*). JESÚS DEL CORRAL (1871–1931) wrote *Stories and Chronicles* (*Cuentos y crónicas*) with a witty feeling for local anecdote, as can be seen in "Let the sawer go by" (*"Que pase el aserrador"*). But the narrator with most substance was Francisco Gómez Escobar, who signed his works EFE GÓMEZ (1873–1938). He stood out in the short story and the short novel: *My People* (*Mi gente,* 1936), *Crude Souls* (*Almas rudas,* posthumous) are titles that declare the theme of his literature, which was to depict— better than anyone else in his country had done—the life of farm workers, miners, the poor, and the down-and-out. He was most interested in man, and for his plots he selected situations where man's failures were due to accidents, injustice, madness, and vice. His stories, collected in several volumes, were the first in Colombia to delve into the psychology of the characters. The linguistic naturalism of many of the regionalist writers of this generation was a bad habit; though not always. There is at least one good short story in this genre: "The Machete" by JULIO POSADA (1881–1947), a story told in the first person by a farm laborer who arrives, looking for work, at a farm. He relates (and the spelling in his story is phonetic) how he found work, how he fell in love with Pachita, how he became friends with the Negro, how the Negro was in love with the same girl, and how the Negro and peon fenced, progressively becoming better friends, while Pachita ran away with another man. In order to carry his linguistic naturalism to an extreme, Posada published the story, not in printer's type, but with manuscript plates.

(vi) *Ecuador* / To the antecedents of Ecuadorian realism already mentioned—Luis A. Martínez and Manuel J. Calle, who also wrote a novel, *Carlota*—we should add EDUARDO MERA (1871–1913), not so much for his travel book, *From Distant Lands* (*De lejanas tierras*), but for certain jocular stories.

(vii) *Peru* / There were no Peruvians among the first modernist narrators; the art of modernist narration did not have any influence in Peru until later, and its results were less evident than in other republics. Nevertheless, there was one, CLEMENTE PALMA (1872–1946), who forsook the realism that dominated the narrative in his country to write fantastic, macabre, irreverent tales: *Evil Stories* (*Cuentos malévolos,* 1904); *Wicked Tales* (*Historietas malignas,* 1925). His last novel, *XYZ,* 1934, is science fiction: written in an island setting it tells of the invention of a process for projecting motion picture images on protoplasm, thus creating lives that repeat exactly those of Hollywood actresses.

The model was *The Eve of the Future* by Villiers, in which Edison offers to do something similar for a millionaire friend who is mourning the death of his beloved. Horacio Quiroga had just used this theme (also to be tried by Bioy Cesares) in *"The Vampire"* (*"El Vampiro"*). Clemente Palma thus entered the stream of fantasy—at times disguised as science, at times inspired by parapsychology and demonology or by Utopias and Uchronias, or by esoteric doctrines—a stream in which Leopoldo Lugones, Horacio Quiroga, Rubén Darío, Amado Nervo, Arévalo Martínez, and others, had dabbled. ENRIQUE AUGUSTO CARRILLO (1877–1938) and MANUEL BEINGOLEA (1875–1963) were modernists in the skill with which they described watering places for wealthy or bourgeois people in Peru—the former in *Letters from a Tourist* (*Cartas de una turista*, 1905), and the latter in *Under the Lilacs* (*Bajo las lilas*, 1923).

The most vigorous of the realist narrators was ENRIQUE LÓPEZ ALBÚJAR (1872). His vignettes of pastoral life were more than stories with their penetrating understanding of the soul of the native, and their spirit of protest and reform against injustices: *Stories of the Andes* (*Cuentos andinos*, 1920); *New Stories of the Andes* (*Nuevos cuentos andinos*, 1937). He used harsh language in his unidealistic analysis of the psychological disturbances caused by humiliation, rage, or resignation in Indians that are cruel or cautious, crafty or honest. From his experience as a judge he preferred criminal cases. Thus López Albújar carried on the tradition of native realism we saw originate in Aréstegui and in Matto de Turner and we shall see develop in Ciro Alegría and José María Arguedas. He also wrote novels: *Matalaché* (1928), a novel about the passion between a Mulatto youth and a white girl, set against a background of slavery on a large hacienda in the period immediately before the independence of Peru. *The Charm of Tomayquichua* (*El hechizo de Tomayquichua*) deals with the beautiful Indian women of that region. ANGÉLICA PALMA (1883–1935) wrote eight realist novels critical of the customs of the people. Her criticism was conservative in spirit. We have read her *Romantic Colonial Times* (*Coloniaje romántico;* 1921) to see if she had inherited her father's sense of history. She had not. The daughter lacks her father's gift. JOSÉ FELIX DE LA PUENTE (1862) was a realist in *Evaristo Buendía*, the life of a rogue in Lima's upper bourgeois society.

(viii) *Bolivia* /ALCIDES ARGUEDAS (1879–1946) made his debut with an Indianist novel, *Wata-Wara*, 1904, later recast as *Race of Bronze* (*Raza de bronce*), and with a novel of the city, *Creole Life* (*Vida criolla*, 1905), but he incorporated himself into the roster of great Hispanic-American novelists with just one book: *Race of Bronze* (1919). This novel, divided into two parts, develops in a continuous time sequence. Its action, however, is broken into loose episodes: voyages, adventures, sketches of local customs, scenes of heavy work, struggles with nature, vices, illnesses, deaths, ethnographic notations with pagan and Christian ceremonies, a parade of multiple characters, reflections and discussions. The plot becomes more solid when he relates the loves of

Agustín and Maruja, their suffering, the abuses heaped upon the Indians by the Creole landowners and their mestizo servants; and it is interwoven with threads of fire and blood when the brutal Pantoja kills Maruja, and Agustín and his family avenge the killing. Actually, there is no characterization: the indigenous community is the protagonist. The first part begins at a pastoral gait and with idyllic promises; but suddenly the novel twists toward an abominable reality, and the second part, after several pages of history and sociology, is an angry denunciation of the cruelty with which the "whites"—including the priest—vent their brutality on the Indians. Arguedas narrates from the outside, in the third person. Constantly he intervenes with moralizing and political judgments—at times he puts his thoughts in the mouth of Suárez, a modernist poet and reader of Gorki, who compares the misery of the natives with that of the Russian muzhiks. Less convincing, artistically speaking, is the oratory in the mouths of the Indians. The prose, always carefully wrought, tends to be poetic, above all in the beautiful passages. These poems in prose are not discordant with the somber picture: Arguedas' modernism is sufficiently ample to accept naturalist procedures.

Schooled in positivist philosophy, but taking an attitude that was more moralistic than scientific, Arguedas decided to tell the truth about Bolivia. The result was a denunciation of national evils which, according to him, stemmed from the psychology of the race and from its political corruption and disastrous history: *A Sick People* (*Pueblo enfermo*, 1909) and a series of important works in the *History of Bolivia* (*Historia de Bolivia*). He is not pessimistic, for he believes in the regeneration of the people through education and progress, but he is merciless in his criticism. His memoirs, *The Dance of the Shadows* (*La danza de las sombras*), especially the parts that recall his travels and his literary life, are very interesting, revealing, and useful for the historian of Hispanic letters. JAIME MENDOZA, the Bolivian Gorki, as Rubén Darío called him, made up an album of miscellaneous scenes of the miserable lives of miners: *In the Lands of Potosí* (*En las tierras de Potosí*, 1911). And in *Pages on Barbarism* (*Páginas Bárbaras*, 1917) he wrote about life on rubber plantations. He was also a poet—*Voices of Yesteryear* (*Voces de antaño,* 1938)—but his influence on Bolivia is due to essays like *The Bolivian Land Mass* (*El Macizo Boliviano,* 1935) which proposed a geographic interpretation of the national character. The close interconnections of the chain of the Andes Mountains were for the optimistic Mendoza the nucleus of an expansive culture. He admired the Indians, but he did not want a European civilization grafted on them; he wanted to see them grafted into the land itself, with a program of agrarian justice.

And DEMETRIO CANELAS (1881), in *Stagnant Waters* (*Aguas estancadas,* 1911) made his characters live in well-sounding and well-produced dialogs. In contrast to both, the Bolivian ABEL ALARCÓN (1881) preferred the historical novel of Inca times (*In the Court of Yáhuar-Huácac* [*En la corte de Yáhuar-Huácac,* 1915]), or of colonial times (*Once Upon a Time* [*Era una vez,* 1935]).

(ix) *Chile* / Augusto Geomine Thomson, better known as AUGUSTO D'HALMAR (Chile, 1882–1950), began as a naturalist with *Juana Lucero* (1902), a raw, hard novel about the fall, the downward course, the prostitution, and the death of a woman of easy virtue. Then he changed his style. He turned to motives and modes that were less and less realist and more and more poetic. His short stories and novellas usually pursue, with effort, a prose ideal of beautiful form. They fall short of achieving it. In this pursuit, the novels and stories, in general addicted to personal reminiscences, overlook the requirements of the narration. *Passion and Death of the Priest Deusto* (*Pasión y muerte del cura Deusto,* 1924) is a novel with a plot, although a simple one. It is set in the year 1913, in Seville—a Seville of tourists, a Seville still pagan in its religious holidays. And it tells us of a questionable, risqué, three-year friendship between a Basque priest and an adolescent. The psychological analysis is not as fine as the delineation of a morbid, "decadent," atmosphere of the type that pleased the modernists. The ecclesiastical life is not austere: the priest is surrounded by bullfighters, trapeze artists, painters, songsters, poets. Deusto himself is a musician; his beloved Pedro Miguel, a singer and dancer. There is more estheticism than "psychology," more Oscar Wildeism than Proustianism in the descrip-

tion of a love which, "having reached its extreme," can no longer
be prolonged. Thus D'Halmar wrote narratives which reflect immediate things as easily as the most artificial fantasies. This fluctuation between naturalism and the ideals of the imagists
was part of the era—even Barrios produced *Lost One* (*Un
perdido*), on the one hand, and on the other, *Brother Ass* (*Her-
mano asno*); and Prado, *Rural Judge* (*Un juez rural*) and *Alsino*.
But if we place D'Halmar, author of *Juana Lucero*, in this section of estheticizing prosists it is because his influence over other
writers was due precisely to his aerial prose which invited subtle
lucubrations.

JOAQUÍN DÍAZ GARCÉS (1877–1921), known by his pseudonym "Angel Pino," was a short-story writer with a preference for
the humorous aspect of the customs of peasants, laborers, soldiers,
and bandits: his novel, *The Voice of the Torrent* (*La voz del to-
rrente*), although disordered, has life. JANUARIO ESPINOSA
(1882–1946) was a novelist of the middle class, though his best
work, *Cecilia*, takes place in the country. GUILLERMO LABARCA
HUBERTSON (1883–1954) continues to be read, because of the
stories in *Watching the Ocean* (*Mirando al océano*, 1911). OLE-
GARIO LAZO BAEZA (1878) specialized in *Military Stories*
(*Cuentos militares*) and was more interested in psychology than
in the external situations; he wrote a novel, *The Last Gallop* (*El
postrer galope*). TOMÁS GATICA MARTÍNEZ (1883–1943) novelized the "great world," his intent being one of social criticism.
Others: VÍCTOR DOMINGO SILVA (1882–1960), TANCREDO
PINOCHET (1880).

(x) *Paraguay* / RAFAEL BARRETT (1877–1910) is a writer of
very complex prose, capable of angry pamphlets (*Argentinian
Terror* [*El terror argentino*], *The Truth About Plantations* [*Lo
que son los yerbales*]) and of harmonious stories (*Short Tales*
[*Cuentos breves*], *Dialogs* [*Diálogos*], and *Conversations* [*Con-
versaciones*]). He left Spain in 1902.

(xi) *Uruguay* / With a curious admixture of estheticism and
naturalism, the great narrator of abnormal themes was HORA-

CIO QUIROGA (Uruguay, last day of 1878–1937). Though he occasionally wrote artistic verse and prose (*Coral Reefs* [*Los arrecifes de coral*, 1901]), novels (*History of a Turbulent Love* [*Historia de un amor turbio*, 1908], and *Past Love* [*Pasado amor*, 1929]), a novelette (*The Persecuted* [*Los perseguidos*, 1905]), drama (*The Sacrificed* [*Las sacrificadas*, 1920]), Horacio Quiroga excelled in the short story. He published several collections: *The Other's Crime* (*El crimen del otro*, 1904), *Tales of Love, Madness and Death* (*Cuentos de amor, de locura y de muerte*, 1917), *Jungle Tales* (*Cuentos de la selva*, 1918), *The Savage* (*El salvaje*, 1920), *Anaconda* (1921), *The Desert* (*El desierto*, 1924), *The Beheaded Chicken and Other Tales* (*La gallina degollada y otros cuentos*, 1925), *The Exiled* (*Los desterrados*, 1926) and *The Great Beyond* (*Más allá*, 1935). To these titles may be added stories scattered in newspapers, now collected in several posthumous editions. A chronological study of the stories, one by one, might permit us to group them in a first period of technical apprenticeship, a period of maturity, and a final period when Quiroga retired with ebbing strength from his art. But his books cannot be classified in stages, because, in general, they comprise stories written in very separate years, so that the date of the volume says nothing of the date of composition of the individual stories. Quiroga chose the stories in each book on a thematic and not a chronological criterion. He never achieved a book of perfect unity (the most integral was *The Exiled*) but at least he had intentions of doing so. In addition, Quiroga usually retouched and even recast his stories on transferring them from periodicals to books. Perhaps his best stories appeared between 1907 ("The Feather Pillow" ["*El almohadón de plumas*"]) and 1928 ("The Son" ["*El hijo*"]). It has been observed that in his later years Quiroga seemed to have shifted from the short story to newspaper writing: articles, news items, commentaries. Nevertheless, he wrote short stories up to the last moment, though not as good as those in the series that ends in "The Son." The action of a great portion of his stories takes place amid untamed nature; sometimes his protagonists are animals; and, if men, they are usually undone by the forces of nature. It has been said, consequently, that Quiroga is typical of only one aspect of Hispanic-American literature in which geography and zoology are more significant than history and anthropology. But neither jungles nor vipers write stories: it is a man who uses them in his writings, and it will always be the vision of this man, and not the things, that is significant in literature. This man Quiroga, for whom nature was a literary theme, had nothing primitive about him. He was an author of complex spirituality, refined in his culture, with a morbid nervous system. He had begun as a modernist and always remained true to this initiation. His prose became more and more clumsy, his narrative technique more and more realist. But he remained faithful to his initial esthetics: to express obscure, odd, personal perceptions. He had a theory of what a short story should be (see the "Decalogue for the Perfect Short Story Writer" ["*Decálogo del perfecto cuentista*"], "The Rhetoric of the Short Story" ["*La retórica del cuento*"], "Before the Tribunal" ["*Ante el tribunal*"]). And even if he had not cited his masters one would have recognized their influence. But he did cite them: "Believe in one master—Poe, Maupassant, Kipling, Chekov—as in God Himself," he said; and he could have mentioned others, because he read a good deal. No, he was not a primitive; and even his view of the jungle was that of an exceptionally educated eye.

The moods of his stories are varied; there was even a humorous one here and there. Nevertheless, a good anthology would be inclined to include his cruel stories in which he describes sickness, death, failure, hallucination, fear of the supernatural, alcoholism. We know of no perfect story of his; generally, he wrote too rapidly and committed errors, not only in style, but also in narrative technique. But the sum total of his stories reveals a writer of the first magnitude in our literature. Let us recall the dynamic scheme of emotions in "The Beheaded Chicken," "Adrift," "The Son," "The Desert," "The Dead Man," and a dozen others. At times his stories have an autobiographical content. But in Quiroga autobiography is a complex subject. Art and life merged together for him. He felt that his life was completely distorted by a cruel destiny; and his literature also wore a fateful grimace.

And he, as a man, went back and forth from life to literature, and from literature to life, impelled by a demon that would force him to love and then destroy the beloved, to long for success while his basic desire was to die. He was an eccentric, and one of his eccentricities was to go through life as though reality were a novel and he played the role of one of his characters, or to plunge into literature as though literature were a store of real events. The many anecdotes that describe him as a harsh, "difficult" man correspond rather to a fictional character; and his short stories are full of characters taken from everyday life. There is an incongruity about his dedication to hard manual labor, while at the same time he wrote sensitive literature with calloused hands. He cursed both his hard work and his literature. He was a solitary figure.

(xii) *Argentina* / In the modernist prose of Argentina the names of Estrada and Larreta are retained today.

ÁNGEL DE ESTRADA (1872–1923) was an aristocratic and solitary figure who wandered through worlds of reality, of dreams, of art, and of history. The backgrounds for his novels (the best, *Redemption* [*Redención*, 1905]) outshine his novels. His heroes are phantoms who escape from the author and live only as phantoms, yearning for beauty, enveloped in museums, literature, and histories of art. Perhaps his most poetic pages are his chronicles, such as *Color and Stone* (*El color y la piedra*) and *Forms and Spirits* (*Formas y espíritus*).

ENRIQUE LARRETA (1873–1961) is the best novelist that Argentina has produced within the elegant style of modernism. *The Glory of Don Ramiro* (*La gloria de don Ramiro*, 1908), an historical novel of the epoch of Philip II, with a voyage to America by the protagonist linking the two Hispanic worlds, was a masterful coordination of the effort to evoke the past and the effort to evoke sensory perceptions. His impressionistic style, the conversion of sensations into objects of art, was exceptional in our literature. *Zogoibi* (1926) brought a new value: that of stylizing with preciosity a tragic adventure in the Argentine plains. Everything occurs within a few months, from the beginning of the summer of 1913 to the beginning of the winter of 1914. Federico de Ahumada, who like Boabdil, the last king of Granada, is called "Zogoibi," the little unfortunate one, and the sweet and pure Lucía love each other idyllically. Lucía's aunts oppose this betrothal because Federico is an atheist. Federico then falls into the arms of Zita, a mysterious and sensual foreigner, married to an American industrialist, Mr. Wilburns. Federico struggles between love and lust; one evening in the country when he takes final leave of Zita, he sees someone in the shadows and, believing him to be an enemy, stabs him, but discovers that he has killed Lucía, dressed in gaucho clothing. Federico kills himself and falls beside the body of his beloved. The novel is related in the third person by an author who strings together happenings that occur in different places on the simple thread of his story; in addition, he knows his characters inside out. This author, however, is not a realist but an impressionist who records exquisite artistic intuitions. *Zogoibi* is a well-constructed novel. Its tragic end, for example, is ably brought about by contingencies in the plot, suggestive details, coincidences and forebodings. The prose images, which are rich in sensibility and also in culture because of the frequent allusions to the plastic arts, music, and literature, are not incongruous because Larreta has domiciled refined Argentinians or high-classed foreigners in his "ranches." His characters are "decadents" who have just returned from Paris or have been educated in European culture. There are even an opium eater and a countess. Federico himself feels like the hero of a French novel, and what he actually does is play the roles that he has read in his books. The Europeanism and even the snobbery of the characters in *Zogoibi* do not falsify the novel. These are traits of Creole oligarchy and Larreta was writing from this aristocratic point of view. There is no superimposition of two conflicting social strata: the novel has a unity in its outlook on life. Although the members of the oligarchy imitated Europe, they had their feet planted in these lands and they governed them; for this reason, when Larreta and his characters listen to peons speaking or glance at rural customs and the rebellious actions of the incipient workers' movement, they document a real life that they knew quite well without any effort. The metaphors fuse the double experience of the Buenos Aires oligarchy: literary mannerism and the immediate knowledge of nature. One example: "it was a sad hut but at the same time smiling, all twisted to one side, like the cowhand when he speaks to the boss." *Zogoibi* reveals the mental process of some of the characters and, like every psychological novel, it forces the reader to participate intensely in the course of an inner time; but a different time is also evoked, that of a Creole, patrician life prior to the first World War. The last novels of Larreta are: *Shores of the Ebro* (*Orillas del Ebro*, 1949), and *El Gerardo* (1956).

Stories and novels about abnormal realities, the abnormality being either in the circumstances or in the minds of the characters, had been written during the romantic period. Now, in cultivating this abnormality, the writers did not conceal their pleasure in playing the esthetic role of eccentrics, decadents, and psychopaths.

ATILIO CHIAPPORI (Argentina, 1880) reached that subtle frontier where morbidness is at one and the same time art and horror. *Borderland* (1907) is the title of his first book of stories. It was also the first book of short stories of this type to be produced in Argentina. Chiappori had studied mental disorders scientifically and knew how to describe them in technical language. He did not fall into "experimental and scientistic" naturalism. He utilized, on the contrary, his psychological penetration to create modernist literature. His characters are usually literary men and artists, or, in any case, victims of their rare perceptions, persons with manias for introspection, sick people who feel that mental aberration is aristocratic. Chiappori himself writes in an atmosphere charged with literary phantoms: Poe, D'Annunzio, Barbey d'Aurevilly. The library of the mad protagonist of "An Impossible Book" (*"Un libro imposible"*)—the first narrative in the book—gives the sources of so many occult, psychiatric, and estheticizing fantasies. The stories explain these disturbances as clinical cases or describe them as mysterious adventures into the unknown. We no longer read them with the same pleasure as the "decadents." Not even "The Blue Tie" (*"La corbata azul"*), which is one of the best, redeems them for posterity. But they had the merit of having initiated a rich genre. Later Chiappori published a novel, *Eternal Anguish* (*La eterna angustia*, 1908) and other stories, *The Island of Red Roses* (*La isla de las rosas rojas*, 1925), in which the morbid note is subdued. Basically, Chiappori was a romantic, which accounts for his preference for elegiac, melancholy, languid, twilight moods. His characters are related to the doomed, satanic and neurotic figures in literature—Des Esseints, Dorian Gray—but they are not story-book types. The author wrote about them because he had actually seen them, either in real life or in his own imagination.

Of this group of writers specializing in the abnormal, there was one who trod on the fringes of madness: MACEDONIO FER-

NÁNDEZ (1874–1952), the comet wheeling outside of its orbit. Because of his age he belongs to this chapter. Because he fascinated both the young writers who heard him (the Borges, Girondo, Marechal, González Lanuza generation) and the young writers who were not able to hear him but who read him with mouths agape (the generation of the '40's), Macedonio would belong to the following chapters. And because of his sparse literary achievements—although he did succeed with witty verbalism as an "oral writer"—he does not belong to any chapter of this *History*. But we shall include him because we knew him and, to be sure, the man was a strange person. His preposterous book was *All Is Not Vigil When the Eyes Are Open* (*No toda es Vigilia la de los Ojos Abiertos*, 1928), a philosophy whose point of departure was epistemological idealism. The rest of his books published later were old pages pulled out, against his will, by prankish friends: *A Newcomer's Papers* (*Papeles de Recienvenido*, 1930), *A Novel That Begins* (*Una novela que comienza*, 1941), *Continuation of Nothingness* (*Continuación de la Nada*, 1945), *Poems* (*Poemas*, 1953). The best Macedonio is the one in the letter to Borges—verbal magic, later published in *Proa*. The rest is unreadable digression, unless one is seeking among the ruins of this broken prose (of this broken reasoning), larvae of a surprising, ingenious, and even poetic, solipsism. He gave us a humorous vision of the universe, a universe which, after the operations to which it was subjected by Macedonio's imagination and sophistry, came out absurd together with all of us who inhabit it. Yet, there is in him a serious aspect, that of illustrating with his life, with his writings, with his conversations, the disintegration of contemporary letters. In the first place, the disintegration of literary genres, then, the disintegration of the writer himself who ends up by disappearing into nothingness. Macedonio scarcely wrote and never worried about organizing his thoughts or his pages. For this reason, when we read him we have the sensation of spying into the soul of a man at the moment of penning his thoughts. That is to say, we are only present at the first discomforts of a difficult pregnancy. But it is exactly these discomforts that interest the present-day readers who are accustomed to a literature that may also be spontaneous, disarticulate, elemental, arbitrary, capricious, and confused.

Neither ALBERTO GHIRALDO (1874–1946) nor MANUEL UGARTE (1878–1951) was typical of the Argentinian realists of these years. Both were in literary debt to modernism; and when they approached reality it was more as politicians than as writers. Let us single out the best writer of all in the category of realism:

BENITO LYNCH (1880–1951). He outlines a piece of land, populates it with men and women, invents a plot rich in human and psychological conflicts, and then makes us believe that what he is relating is real. The characters speak as Argentinians do in real life, in the dialect of the Río Plata region; and if they are Europeans, they speak their jargon. The landscape, the characters, and the situation that motivates their lives form a solid unity. At no time is one aspect overcharged at the expense of another. Lynch will not yield to the temptation of amusing himself by indulging in poetics of nature, dense studies of characters, or social theses. His virtues as a landscapist, as a psychologist, or as a connoisseur are manifested with notable conciseness in evocative metaphors, in details that reveal the insides of souls, in rapid allusions to the ills of rural Argentine society. Fleeting touches, in short, that invite the reader to collaborate imaginatively in the progress of the novel. The progress of the novel—that is what concerns Lynch. Even descriptive passages (for example, the admirable description of the fire in *Rachel* [*Raquela*]) are subservient to the story. The inner agitation of the characters furthers the action and creates surprising denouements, as in *Palo verde:* a man kills another; the law protects him; with a single word in court he could save himself; but, confused, he does not utter it and is condemned. Lynch reduces everything to dynamic lines. From here stems his preference for truculent and brutal effects which accelerate the action and leave the reader in suspense. He had a knack with country novels, but when he attempted city novels the outcome was not as happy. His definite appearance in letters dates back to *The Vultures of the Florida Ranch* (*Los caranchos de la Florida*, 1916), a history of violent hatreds and loves. *Rachel* (1918) showed another side of Lynch—the comical. After *The*

Evasion (*La evasión*, 1922) and *The Ill-Muted Woman* (*Las mal calladas,* 1923) Lynch wrote his masterpiece—*The English-man of the Bones* (*El inglés de los güesos*, 1924). It deals with an English anthropologist who arrives on the pampa to excavate Indians' bones; he takes lodgings in the humble ranch of a peon; Balbina, the peon's daughter, falls in love with him and, for a while, it seems that the Englishman will also yield to love; but when his investigations are over, the gentlemanly, kindly, cold, and selfish Mr. Gray says goodby and leaves; the girl hangs herself. The plot, skeletonized in this fashion, gives no idea of the interior complexity of the novel: the local color, the well-delineated customs, the spicy rural language, and the deft weaving of circumstances and events all serve to provide a sensitive observation of the awakening of love. In the two novelettes that followed (*The Mistress' Whim* [*El antojo de la patrona*] and *Palo verde,* 1925) Lynch created characters possessing more inner life and, consequently, was better able to display his talents as a psychologist. Thirteen short stories appeared in 1931 under the title *Buenos Aires Countryside* (*De los campos porteños*). Two years later Lynch brought his work to a close with *The Romance of a Gaucho* (*El romance del gaucho*). In it, an old gaucho is supposed to be relating aloud the misfortunes of a young peasant, Pantalcón Reyes. Spoiled by his mother, weak in character, in love with a married woman, he is driven about by circumstances. On his way home, where his mother and his beloved, reconciled, await him with open arms, he dies of weariness and fright. It is a situation for a short story or, at most, a novelette, but Lynch stretches it out with unnecessary scenes and dialogs, making it impossible for him to achieve convincing characters in depth. Its greatest literary value lies in the literary artifice of assuming the voice of the gaucho for the story.

Another representative realist was MANUEL GÁLVEZ (1882–1962). The great quantity of writing he did with an eye to commercial success lowered his quality as a writer, which was high in his realist novels: *The Normal School Teacher* (*La maestra normal*, 1914), *The Shadow of the Convent* (*La sombra del convento*, 1917), and *Nacha Regules* (1918). We prefer *Metaphysical Anguish* (*El mal Metafísico*, 1916). He surprised the literary world of Buenos Aires at the turn of the century. His portraits are so similar to his models that one recognizes them: they are no other than Almafuerte, Ingenieros, Florencio Sánchez, Ghiraldo, Gerchunoff, David Peña, and many, many others. Novels on bohemian life already existed: Gálvez' innovation was to describe modernist circles with a non-modernist technique. Hence, some dissonance: his protagonist Carlos Riga represents the romantics' and the symbolists' idea of a poet. Riga's vocation is almost religious. He is dreamy, disdainful of the masses, unadaptable, sick, distraught by the social incomprehension of a young and materialistic country. Gálvez, who sympathizes with the "metaphysical anguish" of purely esthetic contemplation, only describes it apathetically. There is dissonance, then, between Riga's aristocratic ideal and Gálvez' ideal of a democratic novel. Between 1914 and 1938, the dates of *The Normal School Teacher* and *Men in Solitude* (*Hombres en soledad*), respectively, he published seventeen novels. After ten years of dallying with history and memoirs, he returned to his career as a novelist with works on the Rosas epoch (a cycle of five novels) and on contemporary life, including the last days of Perón (*Tránsito Guzmán*, 1956). Whoever is interested in the theme of the autonomous characters and in the form of the interior duplication of the story (with illustrious Spanish antecedents: Galdós, Unamuno, etc.) may enjoy perhaps *The Two Lives of Poor Napoleon* (*Las dos vidas del pobre Napoleón,* 1954). A novelist makes use of certain incidents in the life of a man to write a novel; the man recognizes himself on reading the novel, sets out to imitate himself, and goes mad. The more Gálvez insisted on his Catholicism the more watered-down his art became. In his best novels he knew how to overcome his major defect, namely, the weaving of episodes, details, and useless digressions into the story; but his characters do not stand out in bold relief because they lack polish. Others: the regionalist EDUARDO ACEVEDO DÍAZ, JR. (1882), author of *Ramón Hazaña;* and MATEO BOOZ (1881–1943).

2. Essay

Because of positivism, philosophical interest became generalized, and in this respect we have already seen the work of Varona, Hostos, and others. Now we shall study the emergence of the refuters of positivism. Nevertheless, this philosophical movement, imported from Europe but well accommodated to the social needs of Hispanic-American countries, continued its domination everywhere for some time. Spencer and Stuart Mill were the most frequent sources; somewhat less, Comte. Positivism made us respect the sciences, extricated psychology from metaphysics, promoted sociology, gave experimental solidity to investigative studies, systematized observations, applauded clear reasoning, invited progress, affirmed an autonomous ethics, practiced liberalism. Later, when it reached its exhaustion in Europe, positivism became incarnated in one of the most talented thinkers of this generation: JOSÉ INGENIEROS (Argentina, 1877–1925). He is more important in a history of philosophic ideas than in a history of literature, but he has the right to be studied here as well, because of his influence on literary groups and for the occasionally modernist adornment of his prose. He was the staunchest exponent of a philosophy founded on science. His outlook was more scientific than positivist, since he admitted the possibility of a metaphysic, though only as a transitory hypothesis constantly corrected by the progress of empirical knowledge. Despite the fact that for him biology was at the base of psychology, and that upon the latter all cultural disciplines were constituted, José Ingenieros raised an inspiring ethic, the reason being that at the bottom of positivism, even after it had fallen into disuse as a theory, there was an honest desire for investigation, for betterment, for justice, for truth, for faith in the rationality of man.

In Hispanic-America the animators of worthy liberal and socialist movements were positivists. In contrast, many of their adversaries took advantage of anti-positivist polemics in order to deny the achievements of free examination and even the liberal and non-ecclesiastical history of our countries. In the name of a spiritualism which, were it to be lightly scratched, would reveal the old dogmatic color under the varnish, those so-called anti-positivists were preparing the absolutist Catholic reaction which later was to threaten political freedom. Some of the first reactions against positivism in the field of philosophy have already been mentioned: Deústua, Korn. But, outside the field of philosophy, others had reacted earlier. Modernism spiritualized discursive prose, and one can even say that it initiated a spiritualist philosophical movement.

As we have said already, in the second half of the nineteenth century the natural sciences had been imposed as a model for all knowledge, but in the later years determinism gave ground before heavy polemical attacks. Its basis was scientific systematization: epistemology yanked its base away. As the books on European positivism arrived late in America, so did the books on European anti-positivism. What was dominant in Hispanic-America was positivism in action, diffused, evolved from the practical necessities of our social life. The classical positivism that was known was that of Comte and Spencer, with some Stuart Mill and a lot of reading of Renan and Taine.

The attempts at a new positivist epistemology in Europe—Avenarius, Mach, Vaihinger—had no echo here; the ideas of Nietzsche and of William James would arrive later. It is not at all strange, then, that the first sign of the crisis of positivism would appear in Hispanic-American letters before it appeared in university classrooms. The esthetics of modernism implied a repudiation of the mechanical theory of life. Art was a refuge, a faith, a liberation where nothing was repeated, where nothing was explainable with the logic of the physicist. Alejandro Korn, whose idealistic philosophy of a creative freedom has already been alluded to, has related how the reading of Darío's *Azure* led him, from idea to idea, to a new philosophic current that put the accent on the spirit.

José Enrique Rodó / The thinker who best fused the literature of modernism with spiritualism was JOSÉ ENRIQUE RODÓ (Uruguay, 1871–1917). His background as an adolescent and youth was that of a humanist: classical Greeks, Romans, and moderns

(Plato, Marcus Aurelius, Montaigne, Renan). This humanism
made him restless, anxious for spiritual exaltation, so that on
receiving the influence of the positivists of the nineteenth century
he did not carry the naturalism implicit in them to an extreme.
Comte and Spencer as a basis, and later, Taine, Renan, and
Guyau, constituted his positivist readings. But from them he only
borrowed material with which to cement his concept of the spirit:
at the pinnacle of his building he kept a banner that fluttered to
the anti-positivist winds of Main de Biran, Renouvier, Boutroux,
and Bergson. His anti-positivism was not controversial, however.
It was not really anti-positivism, but a positivism so cautious and
subtle it did not appear to be positivism. It was cautious because
it did not fall into the coarseness that had sometimes denied the
unforeseeable quality of the judgments of conscience; and it was
subtle enough to be able to weave into its strands the finer threads
of a psychology of personality that affirms the freedom to choose
ideals. Rodó always respected rational and experimental knowledge of reality, except that he moderated it with an active idealism. Rodó's idealism was neither metaphysical nor epistemological, but axiological. That is, he saw man raising himself from
nature and striving toward certain ideals, toward the values of
good, truth, justice, and beauty. And these ideals and values
derived from the dynamic and creative life. The world was real,
man was real, and human ideals were real. Rodó was, then, a
realist. Since he was not a philosopher who systematically went
to the roots of problems, there are zones of penumbrae in his
thought. Furthermore, he preferred to express himself in imaginative prose, at times becoming eloquent without strictly defining
his terms. In general, he relied on the data of experience; at times
the vibrations of his aspirations toward a knowledge of the absolute give his pages a metaphysical atmosphere. What is actually
metaphysical in his work, however, is rather his taste for lofty
beliefs in the history of culture, his desire to be tolerant toward
every hypothesis and, above all, his esthetic sensitivity. An example of this is his concept of the Child-God (in *Prospero's Watchtower* [*El mirador de Próspero*]), of the immanent God, in the
process of formation, a God weak and imperfect, who develops in

the world and in human conscience toward a better future. As a realist he believed that a man's whole life and all of his cultural creations grow out of nature; the human desire to be liberated from natural necessity he also considered to be of natural origin. He believed in reason, but as a function of life. Non-vital reason, he used to say, falsifies our knowledge of reality: only vital reason reveals the meaning of the world. He was not, then, an irrationalist, although he admitted intuition, especially in artistic creation —intuition which for Rodó was "the occult, constructive power of nature, which operates in the mind without the interference of reflection." His concept of the world harmonized the complex interior unity of man with the complex exterior unity of the universe; and in the depth of that harmony he felt the strength of a powerful love for form.

The universe for him had one purpose, even though Rodó never made clear what it was. The omission of Rodó in the histories and anthologies of ideas, prepared by professors of philosophy, is unjust. Read the essay, "New Directions," in *Próspero's Watchtower* (*El mirador de Próspero*), which he dedicated to Carlos Arturo Torres' *Idola Fori* in 1910, and you will discover one of the earliest and most lucid analyses that has been written in the Spanish language on the crisis of positivism. His first important work was *Ariel* (1900). After the war of 1898 between the United States and Spain, Rodó became apprehensive of American imperialism. Preoccupied over the growth of the United States at the expense of Spanish America but without confining himself to the political theme, Rodó wrote *Ariel*, which won him international prestige and gave him extraordinary influence in the moral formation of the youth of Hispanic America. Unfortunately some readers reduced *Ariel* to a scheme that discredits its purpose: for these readers Ariel versus Calibán symbolizes Hispanic-America versus Anglo-America, spirit versus technology. Reduced to such a scheme the book does not appear to be a call for mental, spiritual, and physical effort, but rather a school for conformists. If our countries, backward, ignorant, underfed, subjected to foreign capital, barren, stunted, traditionalist and anarchical had, in spite of this, a spirituality superior to that of the

United States, we could consider ourselves satisfied. There is nothing of this sort in *Ariel*. From the point of view of the call to work, *Ariel* continues the series of other books favorable to the United States—those of Sarmiento, for example. The United States theme is only an accident, an illustration for a thesis on the spirit. To contrast the two Americas and to launch a political manifesto were so far from Rodó's intention that *Ariel* was not an anti-imperialist work. His allusion is only to moral imperialism, not so much as it is exercised by the United States as it is created by imitation on the part of Spanish America. He was criticized precisely for having neglected the problem of economic imperialism, differing in this from Manuel Ugarte, Blanco-Fombona, Alfredo L. Palacios. But Rodó had no intention of dealing with this problem.

The United States is an example, not a theme of the essay. What he wanted was to contrast spirit and matter. It was a moral, idealistic essay which anticipated his masterpiece, *The Motifs of Proteus* (*Motivos de Proteo*). The genesis of this work had three stages: from 1897 to 1900 Rodó thought of giving it an epistolary form; from 1900 to 1904 his plan was to make it a didactic treatise to be called *Proteus*, whose Chapter V would contain the motives; from 1904 on the book itself began to take shape and progressed through amplifications and digressions toward its publishing date—1909. Here also Rodó planned to describe the soul in its essential unity and to point out the dangers of mutilating it by exclusive specializations. What did conscience and spirit mean to Rodó? Above all, there is a noticeable turning away (actually, a reaction) from associationistic, atomistic, mechanistic, explicative psychology that had been dominant during positivism. Rodó, with or without Bergson's influence, affirmed the temporality of psychic life. We participate, he says, in the universal process; but, in addition, we have our own individual time. From this double temporality of our lives he draws his dynamic "ethics of becoming" ("*ética del devenir*"): "This continuous transformation is imposed upon us as a necessity; but it serves as a frame in which free and rational energy is evident." If we do not take the initiative at each change in ourselves, our personality will vanish into the world of matter. Our personality is programmatic, prospective, teleological. Its meaning is revealed to us in our vocations. And in this excellent fashion Rodó continues to pursue his theme. The outside appearance of the *Motifs* is fragmentary. The variety of forms used—the parable, the poem in prose, the analysis, the theoretical speculation, the anecdote—contributes also to this mosaic appearance. There is in it, nevertheless, a dialectic. The perspective of *The Motifs of Proteus* is so broad, so open, that it gives unity even to the pages that were left scattered and collected afterwards: *The Road to Paros* (*El camino de Paros*, 1918); *New Motifs of Proteus* (*Nuevos motivos de Proteo*, 1927); and *The Last Motifs of Proteus* (*Los últimos motivos de Proteo*, 1932). Moreover, his ideas were coming to completion in his essays on apparently non-philosophic themes, for example, the admirable *Próspero's Watchtower*, 1913. He was a thinker; he was also an artist. His prose made use of both talents. The sentences are juxtaposed, coordinated, and subordinated to a dignified, serene, noble, and highly finished architecture. All is harmonious and beautiful. A cold prose, of course, the coldness of marble—or better, the coldness of Parnassian forms—but perfect. He was very imaginative, though his imagination accepted discipline. No one, during the modernist period, has described the process of creative writing better than he. As an acute literary critic, he did it on behalf of other writers, but he also spoke to us of his own passion for the beauty of style in "The Genesis of Form" (in *Próspero's Watchtower*) and in "A Single Force in the Depths of the Universe" (in *The Last Motifs of Proteus*). In a list of the ten best writers of Hispanic-America the name of Rodó is indispensable.

Other Essayists / Besides Rodó, Uruguay provided another great refuter of the fallacies of positivism, CARLOS VAZ FERREIRA (1873–1958) an established philosopher. He not only refused to allow his thought to be submerged by the schools of thought already familiar in the history of philosophy, but he also refused to give his thought a systematic form. Dissatisfied with the apparent rigidity of the systems, he preferred a fragmentary form of expression, as in his admirable *Book of Ferments* (*Fermentario*, 1938). However, he went through all the fields related to philosophy: metaphysics, epistemology, intuition, psychology, logic, ethics, pedagogy, sociology. And he laid on all his thought the unique personal seal of his desire to fuse theory with life. His initiation as a thinker was positivism—a positivism closer to that of John Stuart Mill than to that of Comte or Spencer—later modified by William James, Bergson and others. In dealing with problems he sought the roots of these problems, deeply buried in reality. In other words, his philosophy was based on experience, a vital empiricism already evident in *Living Logic* (*Lógica viva*, 1910).

Mexican positivism had a solid doctrinaire consistency and was prevalent from 1860 to the beginning of the twentieth century when the *Ateneo de la Juventud* rallied to its standard William James, Boutroux, and Bergson and declared war on it. In this *Ateneo* the voices of José Vasconcelos, Antonio Caso, and Pedro Henríquez Ureña were heard. JOSÉ VASCONCELOS (1881–1959) has written short stories—*The Citation* (*La cita*, 1945)—plays—*Prometheus, the Victor* (*Prometeo vencedor*, 1920); *The Kidnappers* (*Los robachicos*, 1946)—memoirs—*Creole Ulysses* (*Ulises criollo*, 1935); *The Storm* (*La tormenta*, 1936); *The Proconsul* (*El proconsulado*, 1939); *The Disaster* (*El desastre*, 1946); *The Flame* (*La flama*, posthumously). These would suffice to give him fame. He was outstanding, however, as a thinker, in a series of massive volumes. *Study of Everything* (*Todología*, 1952) is the recasting of a philosophic system. The philosophic figures that influenced him most in the point of departure of his philosophy were Schopenhauer and Bergson. His subsequent conversion to Catholicism did not seal off this source, which continued to nourish him. Vasconcelos is an irrationalist. The purpose of human life is action. The world is also a product of an active principle that continues to achieve qualitative changes, from matter to spirit. But man organizes his life along the lines of an ethical conduct. Except that this ethics is transfigured into esthetics, because in acting man creates his own personality emotionally. Vasconcelos wishes to possess the very reality of the world, in its individual and particular beings; and his organ of possession is esthetics and mystics. He was passionate and self-contradictory. He began as a revolutionary, and ended as a counter-revolutionary. His love for America was the motive of his *The Cosmic Race* (*La raza cósmica*), etc.

ANTONIO CASO (1883–1946) took, as a point of departure, human existence in its most singular sense: life, which is basically biological and subject to a selfish economic principle, "maximum income with minimum effort," in man, is capable of enthusiasm and is exalted by an impartial art and a self-denying charity. Charitable sacrifice opens our eyes to a supernatural order: through the path of moral action we arrive at metaphysics and religion. Caso's Christian philosophy of existence is in no way affiliated with the Church. We will refer to Pedro Henríquez Ureña in the following chapter.

RICARDO ROJAS (Argentina, 1882–1951), a poet, short story writer, dramatist, essayist, historian, is one of the personalities of Argentine culture: this means that more importance is shown to his person than to his books. In 1923 he put together his *Poems* (*Poesías*), generally Romantic and belatedly visited by modernism. His stories in *The Country of Jungles* (*El país de la selva*) describe myths and customs. In the theater he has presented a series of historical evocations: *Ollantay* (Inca times), *Elelín* (the conquest), *The Salamander* (*La salamandra*, colonization), and *The Colonial House* (*La casa colonial*, independence). His most monumental labors, however, are in the fields of the essay, criticism, and literary history.

Other essayists / SANTIAGO KEY AYALA (1874–1959) was an outstanding essayist in his country. Schooled in the ideals of modernism, he was always distinguished for the excellence of his prose even though, in contrast to cosmopolitan modernists, his favorite themes were those of the city where he was born. Another Venezuelan: EDUARDO CARREÑO (1880–1956). In Bolivia, with the predominance of liberalism in the first two decades of the twentieth century, there appeared essayists who sought their bearings in positivism and idealistic ideas. The most representative figure was DANIEL SÁNCHEZ BUSTAMENTE (1871) who, in a prose influenced by that of Rodo, wrote sociological essays to create a national conscience; he also promoted educational reform in a secular and progressive spirit, mindful of the psychology of the child and the Indian. The national examination of conscience was at times merciless, as in Alcides Arguedas, or it absurdly placed its hopes in all that was Indian, as in Tamayo, but we studied these two for their narrative or poetic works.

The literary history of Paraguay begins with this generation. We might mention among the prosists MANUEL GONDRA (1871–1927), BLAS GARAY (1873–1899) and, above all, MANUEL DOMÍNGUEZ (1869–1935). And we end with FERNANDO ORTIZ (Cuba, 1881), NEMESIO R. CANALES (Puerto Rico, 1878–1923), author of *Small Talk* (*Los Paliques,* 1913), and FRANCISCO GARCÍA CALDERÓN (Peru, 1880–1953).

C. THEATER

Now let us step into the theater. First of all, the Río de la Plata theater. The rustic drama, which, as we have seen, rose in a single bound from the circus ring to the theater stage with Gutiérrez-Podestá's *Juan Moreira*, attracted new authors, and before long the initial theme—gaucho versus legal authority—was joined by others to form a Creole braided lasso. Buenos Aires is now an active theatrical center. Spanish, French, and Italian companies bring in an international repertory. And thus the Río de la Plata theater begins to embellish itself with artistic intent. The gauchesque trend continues (ELÍAS REGULES, OROSMÁN MORATORIO, VÍCTOR PÉREZ PETIT) and acquires a certain literary value with *Calandria* (1896) by MARTINIANO LEGUIZAMÓN and *Jesús Nazareno* (1902) by ENRIQUE GARCÍA VELLOSO (1881–1938). Neither *Calandria* nor *Jesús Nazareno* retraces the model of the sanguinary gaucho—the first character redeems himself through his work, the second one is a hero with a "message" in the manner of Echegaray's heavy dramas. Another deviation from the initial theme was that which went from the gauchesque drama of the open plains, barbaric and violent, to the domestic drama of the peasants. MARTÍN CORONADO (1850–1919) effected it in verse with *The Stone of Scandal* (*La piedra del escándalo,* 1902) and the second part of *Don Lorenzo's Farm* (*La chacra de don Lorenzo,* 1918). NICOLÁS GRANADA (1840–1915), in prose, gave a new twist to the rural theme: in *To the Fields!* (*¡Al campo!,* 1902) he showed a married couple (of farmers) living in Buenos Aires, and not until the third act did the pampa appear. Granada also cultivated the historical drama (*Atahualpa,* 1897), a genre in which DAVID PEÑA (1865–1928) excelled with *Facundo* (1906) and many others. The farce, which later would be the unending preference of the Río de la Plata theater public, found good fortune in the efforts of CARLOS MAURICIO PACHECO (d. 1924) and ALBERTO NOVIÓN (1881–1937). The plays of the middle class arose in almost perfect form from the hands of GREGORIO DE LAFERRÈRE (1867–1913), with a vivid comic sense and sureness in the characterization of popular, saloon types. His first piece, *Jinx* (*Jettatore . . . !,* 1940), was elementary—he wanted to produce laughter through the exhibition of a mania. *The Crackpots* (*Locos de verano,* 1905) was more complex. Not one mania, but many, one for each character—and each character, introspective, comically hermetic, isolated from the others. The theme of *In Their Clutches* (*Bajo la garra,* 1906) was the ravages of calumny. Unfortunately Laferrère went suddenly from the satiric acts to the dramatically intense final act. His best work was *The Women of Barranco* (*Las de Barranco,* 1908), a play about shameful poverty, well constructed, well conceived, well described, with two literary creations, Doña María and Carmen, together with other vivid characters. With the example of serious theater offered to the Buenos Aires public by foreign companies, there were those who became oriented toward a theater of conflicts, problems, and theses—EMILIO BERISSO (1878–1922). We spoke of Payró elsewhere because he was essentially a narrator, not a dramatist, despite the fact that his *Tragic Song* (*Canción trágica*, 1902) was, along with the plays of Sánchez and Laferrère, one of the cornerstones of the Río de la Plata theater. We must spend some time on Sánchez, the greatest Hispanic-American theatrical author of this generation.

FLORENCIO SÁNCHEZ (Uruguay, 1875–1910) had seen the best theater of his time: above all the Italian companies—Novelli, Zacconi, Eleonora Duse—who brought to the Río de la Plata the dramatic repertory of Ibsen, Björnson, Sudermann, Bracco, Giacosa, Hauptmann, Tolstoi. Though not a scholar, he read authors with "advanced ideas," generally anarchists and socialists who influenced his concept of social life. His literary preference was the realism of the Russian novelists. His milieu was the bohemian life of journalists, of humble trades, and poor neighborhoods. His first play, *My Son the Doctor* (*M'hijo el dotor*, 1903), was an unripened fruit, but it came from a vigorous tree. It dealt with a rural reality like that of so many of the theatrical pieces of the day, except that it was more colorful, fresh and lively, with a living character—the old Creole Don Olegario—and that it had a serious purpose: to present to us in intense dialogs a conflict of souls, a set of values, a concept of life, of generations, of city and rural customs, all of which end in a crisis when Julio, the "doctor" son, seduces Jesusa and must answer for his action to Don Olegario. His next rural work, which was more ambitious and more successful, was *The Immigrant's Daughter* (*La Gringa*, 1904). A dialog of great realist strength evokes the Creole ranch, the general store, the immigrant's farm, the customs of the pampa; but this dialog is at the service of an allegory: the Italian immigrants invading the land of the gaucho and the birth of a promising Italo-Creole race. The gaucho Cantalicio and son Próspero on one side, the Italian Nicola and his daughter Victoria, on the other. But the children, Próspero and Victoria, resolve the conflict with love and with the mingling of their blood in a new racial offspring. In this abstract scheme there are minor symbols, the *ombú* tree, for example, representing the strength of the pure Creole. Situations already dealt with in the theater of the day are repeated: the nationalistic resentment of the Creoles against the *gringos* or European immigrants. But the whole drama is directed toward the exaltation of the new Argentinian race.

Florencio Sánchez has respected the Creole and *gringo* points of view as equally legitimate. Cantalicio—gambler, loafer, drunkard, cantankerous, carefree, unreliable—and Nicola—stingy, distrustful—are saved through the son that Próspero has had with Victoria. Just as Próspero and Victoria unite the Creole and *gringo* worlds through instinct, Horacio unites them intellectually, through his university culture. Horacio is the progressivist, the exemplary man, understanding, good, superior and dramatically empty, as were all "reasoners" of the nineteenth-century drama. Perhaps his mockery of Victoria's romanticism and his view of the Creole as ugly are the most personal aspects of his character. The construction of *The Immigrant's Daughter* is loose. The drama takes place before our eyes: the spectator sees how Próspero's and Victoria's love begins and how Cantalicio's difficulties develop; but the presentation does not stir the spectator because the scheme is as foreseeable as a geometric theorem.

Florencio Sánchez closed his rural trilogy with *Down Hill* (*Barranca abajo*, 1905), the most somber tragedy of our theater. It does not offer a thesis: at most, it offers a problem, that of the divestiture of the lands of the old Creoles by an oligarchy armed with all the technicalities of the law and police authority. But here, Sánchez has wanted to dramatize not a social theme but the failure of an individual man. The family of Don Zoilo collapses beneath the blows of ill fortune, sickness, sordidness, the deceit of the petty lawyers, and the decadence of base passions. It is a masterpiece that gains validity on stage because it is theater and not literature. Although realist in its dialog, truthful in its rural images and in its details of customs, it is artistically composed, in a crescendo of three acts beginning and ending with deliberate effect. Here, as never before, Sánchez was in command of his scenic art. In the first scene are the four women: the wife, the sister, and Don Zoilo's two daughters. The dialog is interrupted by the apparition of Don Zoilo, who crosses the stage in silence like a phantom, and then, after Robustiana, the good daughter, has left the stage, the three women who will precipitate his downfall speak. Suddenly, Martiniana, a literary descendant of the *Celestina*, another of the Fates, adds her voice to the chorus. Like a tragic chorus, the initial conversation of the women explains the past tragedy (Ibsen's retrospective method) and the crisis which, ominously, we are going to witness. The symbols are well chosen: when Zoilo is about to hang himself, the noose becomes entwined in the nest of an *hornero* bird. He struggles in vain to loosen it and exclaims: "God's doings . . . A man's nest is more easily torn apart than a bird's nest!"

The intense pauses in the dialog are more deeply piercing than the words themselves. This dramatist who had listened to the speech of the humble people so much and so well knew the value of silence. With admirable verbal economy he contrasts the animal desire of the landowner Juan Luis for Prudencia ("Come! Woman.") with the charitableness of Aniceto who proposes marriage to the tubercular Robustiana. Occasionally a few simple words release emotions, as when Don Zoilo, in scene 5 of Act III, says to Aniceto: "Did the cross stand up all right?"—the only allusion to the death of his daughter who has just been buried. The daughter's death is announced with equally simple scenic detail: as the curtain rises in the third act, next to the door of the hut, the iron bedstead in which the tubercular has died is seen. They have taken it outdoors so that it might be cleansed by the sun. The prelude to Don Zoilo's suicide has a quiet and unequivocal effectiveness from the moment the curtain is raised on that act. Against a background of misery, in front of the dead girl's bed, Don Zoilo is waxing the rope and whistling slowly. He is whistling the melody of death: he will whistle till the final moment. Don Zoilo is a complete character, with something of old King Lear about him. A breath of solemn and universal poetry envelops *Down Hill*. The theme of the fall of the house of Zoilo is extended from the country to the city in two of Sánchez' best dramas: *The Family* (*En familia*) and *The Dead* (*Los muertos*), both of 1905. In the score of theatrical pieces he produced there are also farces, plays of suburban environment, and thesis plays *The Rights of the Healthy* (*Los derechos de la salud*, 1907), *Our Children* (*Nuestros hijos*, 1907). Realism triumphed with Sánchez; and

he tasted triumph after triumph, which did not save him from
the depths of poverty but gave him the intoxication of literary
glory.

Other Río de la Plata playwrights and dramatists: PEDRO E. PICO
(1882–1945), CÉSAR IGLESIAS PAZ (1881–1922), JOSÉ LEÓN PAGANO
(1875), JULIO SÁNCHEZ GARDEL (1879–1937).

Nowhere in Hispanic-America was there another playwright like
Florencio Sánchez. Nonetheless, Mexico offers interesting figures. MAR-
CELINO DÁVALOS (1871–1923) is the author of dramas with naturalist
themes, such as the hereditary transmission of alcoholism—*Guadalupe*,
1903—or on social matters—*And So They Pass . . . (Así pasan . . . ,*
1908). And, more cultured and more of a writer, JOSÉ JOAQUÍN GAMBOA
(1878–1931) who, after penning several plays, from *Solitude (Soledad,*
1899) to *The Day of Judgment (El día del juicio)*, retired from the theater, only to return to it many years later with even more robust works: a
social drama, *The Devil Is Cold (El diablo tiene frío)*; a high society
drama, *The Revillagigedo;* a comedy, *If Youth Knew (Si la juventud
supiera)*; and what appears to be his masterpiece: *The Gentleman,
Death and the Devil (El caballero, la muerte, y el diablo,* 1931). In
The Same Case (El mismo caso, 1929) Gamboa tried ingenious novelties.
He divided the stage in three parts—"comedy," "drama," "farce"—and in
each one he presented the same theme with different denouements.

Other playwrights were EDUARDO CALSAMIGLIA (1880–1918), and
JOSÉ FABIO GARNIER (1884), the most productive in Costa Rica. In
Chile, VÍCTOR DOMINGO SILVA (1882–1960).

Confronted with such an abundance of dramatic production, perhaps
it would be worth while to take cognizance of two esthetic currents that
we have seen functioning since the beginning of our history. The cultural current, based on European models enjoyed by minorities: the
scholarly theater of the middle of the sixteenth century; prologs and
comedies of the seventeenth and eighteenth centuries; neoclassic tragedies
of the early part of the nineteenth century; and dramas based on history
and legend by the romantics who came later. And the current which
draws its themes from the American scene: interludes during colonial
times, farces on social customs (now neo-classical, now romantic, now realist) in the nineteenth century; plays about local people with local situations, and casts and dialog in the vernacular, as in the case of presentations
having gaucho themes, conflicts of conscience or social interest in the
growing cities.

BIBLIOGRAPHY

WE OFFER to those who commence their study of Spanish-American literature this elementary bibliography.

I. General Histories

We recommend, first of all, PEDRO HENRÍQUEZ UREÑA, *Literary Currents in Hispanic America,* Harvard University Press, 1945. Very useful are the histories by LUIS ALBERTO SÁNCHEZ, *Nueva historia de la literatura americana,* Buenos Aires, Editorial Guarania, 1950, fifth edition; and by ARTURO TORRES-RIOSECO, *The Epic of Latin-American Literature,* University of California Press, 1959. J. A. LEGUIZAMÓN has now published separately the *Bibliografía general de la literatura hispanoamericana,* Buenos Aires, 1954, which was what made his two-volume *Historia de la literatura hispanoamericana,* Buenos Aires, 1945, useful before. ALBERTO ZUM FELDE has divided his history according to genre. Until now: *Indice crítico de la literatura hispanoamericana,* Volume I: *Los ensayistas,* Mexico, Editorial Guarania, 1954; Volume II, *La narrativa, ibidem,* 1959. Two recent additions: CARLOS HAMILTON, *Historia de la literatura hispanoamericana,* 2 vols., New York, 1961; ANGEL VALBUENA BRIONES, *Literatura hispanoamericana,* Madrid, 1962. JOSÉ JUAN ARROM, *Esquema generacional de las letras hispanoamericanas,* Bogotá, 1963.

There have recently appeared histories written in other languages: ROBERT BAZIN, *Histoire de la littérature américaine de langue espagnole,* Paris, 1953; CHARLES V. AUBRUN, *Histoire des lettres hispanoaméricaines,* Paris, 1954; JOAO-FRANCISCO FERREIRA, *Capítulos de literatura Hispano-Americana,* Porto-Alegre, Brazil, 1959; UGO GALLO-GIUSEPPE BELLINI, *Storia della letteratura ispanoamericana,* Milano, 1958; MATEO PASTOR-LÓPEZ, *Modern Spansk Litteratur. Spanien och Latinoamerika,* Stockholm, 1960. *An Outline History of Spanish American Literature,* ed. by J. E. ENGLEKIRK, I. A. LEONARD, J. T. REID and A. CROW, 3d edition, New York, 1965.

In the Spanish translation of GIACOMO PRAMPOLINI's *Historia universal de la literatura,* Buenos Aires, Uthea Argentina, 1941–42, in Volumes XI and XII, there are a few "amplifications" of the national panoramas of our literature made by critics like Roberto F. Giusti, José María Chacón y Calvo, Alfonso Reyes, Pedro Henríquez Ureña, Isaac Barrera, and others. A similar project is the *Panorama das literaturas das Americas* edited by JOAQUIM DE MONTEZUMA DE CARVALHO. Until now four volumes have been published (Edição do Município de Nova Lisboa, Angola, 1958–65). It is a collection of monographs contributed by different historians on national literatures. The Pan American Union has initiated a *Diccionario de la*

422 *Spanish-American Literature: A History*

literatura latinoamericana: already the volumes corresponding to *Chile, Bolivia, Colombia,* and *Argentina* have been printed (Washington, D.C., 1958–61).

General histories that are limited to certain periods, tendencies, genres, or themes are numerous. We need name only a few.

Periods and tendencies: MARIANO PICÓN-SALAS, *De la Conquista a la Independencia: tres siglos de historia cultural,* México, Fondo de Cultural Económica, 1965; IRVING A. LEONARD, *Books of the Brave,* Cambridge, Harvard University Press, 1949, and *Baroque Times in Old Mexico,* Ann Arbor, The University of Michigan Press, 1959; EMILIO CARILLA, *El gongorismo en América,* Buenos Aires, 1946, and *El Romanticismo en la América Hispánica,* Madrid, Gredos, 1958; MAX HENRÍQUEZ UREÑA, *Breve historia del Modernismo,* México, Fondo de Cultura Económica, 1954; OCTAVIO CORVALÁN, *El posmodernismo,* New York, 1961; A. BERENGUER CARISOMO and JORGE BOGLIANO, *Medio siglo de literatura americana,* Madrid, 1952.

Genres: FEDERICO DE ONÍS, "La poesía iberoamericana" (in *España en América,* Universidad de Puerto Rico, 1955). ARTURO TORRES-RIOSECO, *La novela en la América hispana,* Berkeley, 1939, and *Grandes novelistas de la América hispana,* Berkeley, 1949, 2nd ed.; FERNANDO ALEGRÍA, *Breve historia de la novela hispanoamericana,* México, Ediciones De Andrea, 1959; LUIS ALBERTO SÁNCHEZ, *Proceso y contenido de la novela hispanoamericana,* Madrid, Gredos, 1953; H. D. BARBAGELATA, *La novela y el cuento en Hispanoamérica,* Montevideo, 1947; ARTURO USLAR PIETRI, *Breve historia de la novela hispanoamericana,* Caracas, 1957. JOSÉ JUAN ARROM, *El teatro de Hispanoamérica en la época colonial,* La Habana, 1956; WILLIS KNAPP JONES, *Breve historia del teatro latinoamericano,* México, Ediciones De Andrea, 1956; CARLOS SOLÓRZANO, *El teatro latinoamericano en el siglo XX,* Mexico, 1964, ROBERT G. MEAD JR., *Breve historia del ensayo hispanoamericano,* México, Ediciones De Andrea, 1956; FRANCISCO ROMERO, *Sobre la filosofía en América,* Buenos Aires, Editorial Raigal, 1952; MEDARDO VITIER, *Del ensayo americano,* México, Fondo de Cultura Económica, 1945.

II. National Histories

(a) *Argentina:* ARTURO GIMÉNEZ PASTOR, *Historia de la literatura argentina* (2 vols.), Buenos Aires, Editorial Labor, 1948. *Historia de la literatura argentina,* directed by Rafael Alberto Arrieta (6 vols.), Buenos Aires, Ediciones Peuser, 1958–59.

(b) *Bolivia:* FERNANDO DÍEZ DE MEDINA, *Literatura boliviana,* Madrid, 1959. ENRIQUE FINOT, *Historia de la literatura boliviana,* La Paz, 1953.

(c) *Colombia:* ANTONIO GÓMEZ RESTREPO, *Historia de la literatura colombiana* (4 vols.), 2nd ed., Bogotá, 1945. BALDOMERO SANÍN CANO, *Letras colombianas,* México, Fondo de Cultura Económica, 1944.

(d) *Costa Rica:* ABELARDO BONILLA, *Historia y antología de la literatura costarricense,* San José, 1957. Vol. 1, *Historia.*

(e) *Cuba:* JUAN N. JOSÉ REMOS Y RUBIO, *Historia de la literatura cubana* (3 vols.), Havana, 1945. MAX ENRÍQUEZ UREÑA, *Panorama histórico de la literatura cubana*, 2 vols., Mexico, 1963.

(f) *Chile:* ARTURO TORRES-RIOSECO, *Breve historia de la literatura chilena*, México, Ediciones De Andrea, 1956. RAÚL SILVA CASTRO, *Panorama literario de Chile*, Santiago de Chile, 1961. LUIS MERINO REYES, *Panorama de la literatura chilena*, Washington, D.C., Panamerican Union, 1959.

(g) *Ecuador:* AUGUSTO ARIAS, *Panorama de la literatura ecuatoriana*, 2nd ed., Quito, 1948. ISAAC J. BARRERA, *Historia de la literatura ecuatoriana*, 4 vols., Quito, Casa de la Cultura Ecuatoriana, 1955.

(h) *El Salvador:* LUIS GALLEGOS VALDÉS, *Panorama de la literatura salvadoreña*, San Salvador, 1962.

(i) *Guatemala:* DAVID VELA, *La literatura guatemalteca* (2 vols.), Guatemala, 1944–1945. OTTO-RAÚL GONZÁLEZ, "Panorama de la literatura guatemalteca" (in *Panorama das literaturas das Américas*, vol. III, 1959).

(j) *Honduras:* HUMBERTO RIVERA MORILLO, "La literatura hondureña en el siglo xx" and JORGE FIDEL DURÓN, "La prosa en Honduras" (in *Panorama das literaturas das Américas*, vol. II, 1958). LUIS MARIÑAS OTERO, "Formación de la literatura hondureña" (in *Universidad de Honduras, Tegucigalpa*, septiembre de 1959, número 14).

(k) *México:* CARLOS GONZÁLEZ PEÑA, *Historia de la literatura mexicana,* 7th ed., México, 1960. ALFONSO REYES, *Letras de la Nueva España*, México, Fondo de Cultura Económica, 1948, and *Resumen de la literatura mexicana (siglos xvi-xix)*, México, 1957. JULIO JIMÉNEZ RUEDA, *Letras mexicanas en el siglo xix*, México, Fondo de Cultura Económica, 1944. JOSÉ LUIS MARTÍNEZ, *Literatura mexicana. Siglo xx* (2 vols.), Mexico, 1949. AURORA MAURA OCAMPO DE GÓMEZ, *Literatura mexicana contemporánea. Bibliografía crítica*, Mexico, 1965.

(l) *Nicaragua:* JUAN FELIPE TORUÑO, "Sucinta reseña de las letras nicaragüenses en 50 años: 1900–1959" (en *Panorama das literaturas das Américas*, vol. III, 1959).

(m) *Panamá:* LEONARDO MONTALBÁN, *Historia de la literatura de la América Central* (2 vols.), San Salvador, 1929–31. RODRIGO MIRÓ, "La literatura panameña de la República" (en *Panorama das literaturas das Américas*, vol. III, 1959).

(n) *Paraguay:* CARLOS R. CENTURIÓN, *Historia de las letras paraguayas* (3 vols.), Asunción, 1961. RUBÉN BAREIRO SAGUIER, "Panorama de la literatura paraguaya: 1900–1959" (en *Panorama das literaturas das Américas*, vol. III, 1959).

(o) *Perú:* LUIS ALBERTO SÁNCHEZ, *La literatura peruana* (6 vol.), Buenos Aires, 1951.

(p) *Puerto Rico:* JOSEFINA RIVERA DE ÁLVAREZ. *Diccionario de literatura puertorriqueña*, Universidad de Puerto Rico, 1955 ("Panorama histórico de la literatura puertorriqueña," pp. 3–153). MARÍA TERESA BABIN, *Panorama de la cultura puertorriqueña*, San Juan de Puerto Rico, 1958. FRANCISCO CABRERA MANRIQUE, *Historia de la literatura puertorriqueña*, San Juan, 1956.

(q) *República Dominicana:* MAX HENRÍQUEZ UREÑA, *Panorama his-*

tórico de la literatura dominicana, Río de Janeiro, 1945. JOAQUÍN BALAGUER, *Historia de la literatura dominicana,* 2nd ed., Ciudad Trujillo, 1958.

(r) *Uruguay:* ALBERTO ZUM FELDE, *Proceso intelectual del Uruguay y crítica de su literatura,* Buenos Aires, 1941.

(s) *Venezuela:* JUAN LISCANO, "Ciento cincuenta años de cultura venezolana" (in *Venezuela Independiente* 1810–1960, Caracas, Fundación E. Mendoza, 1962).

III. Genres and Periods

Besides the bibliographical sources already mentioned, the following national histories of genres and particular periods have been most useful:

Poetry: JUAN CARLOS GHIANO, *Poesía Argentina del siglo xx,* México, Fondo de Cultura Económica, 1957. ROBERTO FERNÁNDEZ RETAMAR, *La poesía contemporánea en Cuba,* La Habana, 1954. CINTIO VITIER, *Lo cubano en la poesía,* La Habana, 1958. FERNANDO ALEGRÍA, *La poesía chilena,* México, F.C.E., 1954. RAÚL LEIVA, *Imagen de la poesía mexicana contemporánea,* México, 1959. LUIS MONGUÍO, *La poesía postmodernista peruana,* México, F.C.E., 1954. CESÁREO ROSA-NIEVES, *La poesía en Puerto Rico,* 2nd ed., San Juan, 1958. JOSÉ RAMÓN MEDINA, *Examen de la poesía venezolana contemporánea,* Caracas, 1956. JUAN PINTO, *Breviario de literatura argentina contemporánea,* Buenos Aires, 1958.

Narrative: ANTONIO CURCIO ALTAMAR, *Evolución de la novela en Colombia,* Bogotá, 1957. RAÚL SILVA CASTRO, *Panorama de la novela chilena,* México, Fondo de Cultura Económica, 1955. ÁNGEL F. ROJAS, *La novela ecuatoriana,* México, Fondo de Cultura Económica, 1948. JOAQUINA NAVARRO, *La novela realista mexicana,* México, 1955. JOSÉ FABBIANI RUIZ, *Cuentos y cuentistas,* Caracas, 1951. PASCUAL VENEGAS FILARDO, *Novelas y novelistas de Venezuela,* Caracas, 1955. MARIO CASTRO ARENAS, *La novela peruana y la evolución social,* Lima, 1964?. SEYMOUR MENTON, *Historia crítica de la novela guatemalteca,* Guatemala, 1960.

Theater: ERNESTO MORALES, *Historia del teatro argentino,* Buenos Aires, 1941. JOSÉ JUAN ARROM, *Historia de la literatura dramática cubana,* New Haven, 1944. ENRIQUE OLAVARRÍA Y FERRARI, *Reseña histórica del teatro en México,* 5 vols., Mexico, 1961.

IV. Anthologies

Due to lack of space, we shall only indicate general anthologies that comprehend all the Spanish-American countries. The best and most useful are, however, those which are limited to one country, or to one period in that country.

Literatura hispanoamericana. Antología e introducción histórica by ENRIQUE ANDERSON IMBERT and EUGENIO FLORIT (New York, Holt, Rinehart and Winston, 1960) comprehends various genres (excepting the novel and theater).

(a) *Verse:* Ginés de Albareda and Francisco Garfias, *Antología de la poesía hispanoamericana,* 9 vols., Madrid, 1957–61. Raúl Silva Castro, *Antología crítica del Modernismo hispanoamericana,* New York, 1963. Federico de Onís, *Antología de la poesía española e hispanoamericana (1882–1932),* 2nd edition, New York, 1961. Julio Caillet-Bois, *Antología de la poesía hispanoamericana,* Madrid, 1958.

(b) *Short Story:* See Bernice D. Matlowsky, *Antología del cuento americano. Guía bibliográfica,* Washington, D.C., Unión Panamericana, 1950. Some examples: Ventura García Calderón, *Los mejores cuentos americanos,* Barcelona, s.f. Antonio R. Manzor, *Antología del cuento hispanoamericano,* Santiago de Chile, 1939. Enrique Anderson Imbert and Lawrence B. Kiddle, *Veinte cuentos hispanoamericanos del siglo xx,* New York, 1956. Ricardo Latcham, *Antología del cuento hispanoamericano,* Santiago, 1962.

(c) *Novel:* Angel Flores, *Historia y antología del cuento y la novela en Hispanoamérica,* New York, 1959. Fernando Alegría, *Novelistas contemporáneos hispanoamericanos,* Boston, 1964.

(d) *Essays:* Aníbal Sánchez Reulet, *La filosofía latinoamericana contemporánea,* Washington, D.C., Unión Panamericana, 1949. José Gaos, *Antología del pensamiento hispanoamericano,* México, 1935.

(e) *Theater:* Carlos Solórzano, *El teatro hispanoamericano contemporáneo,* 2 vols., Mexico, Fondo de Cultura Económica, 1964.

V. Bibliographic Indexes

Those who wish further information may turn to: *Handbook of Latin American Studies* prepared annually since 1936 in The Hispanic Foundation in the Library of Congress, Washington, D.C. See also the systematic bibliographies published by the *Revista Hispánica Moderna,* New York, Columbia University, and other specialized publications.

Besides these bibliographies, which include all Hispanic-American countries, in each country bibliographies are published on the national production.

INDEX OF AUTHORS

DATE DUE

GAYLORD   TED IN U.S.A.